FLIRTATION
SEDUCTION
BETRAYAL

FLIRTATION
SEDUCTION
BETRAYAL

Interviews with heroes and villains

NIGEL FARNDALE

CONSTABLE • LONDON

Constable & Robinson Ltd
3 The Lanchesters
162 Fulham Palace Road
London W6 9ER
www.constablerobinson.com

First published in the UK by Constable
an imprint of Constable & Robinson Ltd 2002

A copy of the British Library Cataloguing in
Publication Data is available from the British Library

ISBN 1-84119-644-4

Printed and bound in the EU

Contents

CONTENTS

Acknowledgements

Thanks to the various editors I've worked with at *The Sunday Telegraph*, especially Dominic Lawson, Lucy Tuck, Rebecca Tyrrel, David Jenkins, Melissa Denes and Aurea Carpenter.

Introduction

The first person I interviewed was Harold Wilson and I could tell straight away that he was struck by my dignity, poise and professionalism – I'd taken two friends along with me for support.

It was in 1986, I had just turned twenty-one and was writing for a (now defunct) magazine called *Debate*, which was given away free and didn't pay its contributors. The friends sat either side of me in the empty hotel dining-room, staring slack-jawed at the former PM, while I galloped breathlessly through my list of prepared questions (including one about Wilson's paranoid belief that MI5 had bugged him during his time at Number 10).

The interview done, I demonstrated my nonchalance by asking for his autograph. Even cooler, I asked if I could have my photograph taken standing next to him. I then said 'Goodbye' several times, tried to leave through a door to a cupboard full of cleaning equipment, and added 'Just checking for bugs!' (I didn't add that, actually, but I wish I had. Instead I said goodbye once more and left by the proper door, followed by my two eerily silent companions.)

Soon afterwards, I was offered a job as an interviewer on *The Sunday Telegraph Magazine*. That's 'soon' as in 'a decade later'. In the interim I worked on a sheep and dairy farm in the Yorkshire Dales for three years; read philosophy as a postgraduate at Durham; and was paid my first fee as a writer, £25, for a book review published by Auberon Waugh – my hero – in the *Literary Review*. Also, for the first half of the 1990s, I wrote features about badgers, dukes and organic vegetables as a staff writer on *Country Life*.

While there I was telephoned by Alexander Chancellor who told me *The Sunday Telegraph* was launching a supplement that would be about Britishness and the countryside and he was to

1

be its editor. Its motto would be 'dare to be dull'. I was hired and given the title 'environment editor'. Six weeks after the launch, as Alexander was clearing his desk, he reflected wistfully that perhaps his magazine had been just a little too daring in its dullness. Rebecca Tyrrel, the deputy editor of *Tatler*, had been hired to replace him. Instead of 'letting me go', as everyone advised her she should, she gave me a chance to prove I could write a feature without mentioning the words 'plashy fen' or 'questing vole' once. She sent me to Rome to interview the fashion designer Valentino.

I once asked Michael Parkinson what attracted him to the idea of becoming an interviewer. 'It's the best job in the world,' he said. 'You get paid to meet your heroes.' There's something in that. But in print journalism you also get paid to betray them, in a sense. Indeed Michael Parkinson wrote to Dominic Lawson, the editor of *The Sunday Telegraph,* after I interviewed him, to say how betrayed he felt, or more colourful words to that effect. So did Andrew Neil, Nigel Dempster, Des Lynam and Sir Tim Rice. In fact, mild-mannered Sir Tim threatened to punch me when we next met. He didn't carry out his threat, as it turned out, perhaps because it was a year later and we were both standing in the queue to go through passport control at Nice airport, trying to avoid eye contact with each other. As it happened, I was on my way to interview his friend Elton John, who also later wrote to the editor, via his publicist, to denounce my betrayal.

I don't relate these stories with pride – on the contrary, there's little worse than the feeling that you might have betrayed someone's trust – but as an illustration of the artificial and temporary concord that exists between interviewee and interviewer. When you agree to be interviewed, you agree to sit smiling, sometimes in your own home, with a microphone pointing at you, answering quite intimate questions put to you by a similarly smiling stranger. With the exception of Geoffrey Boycott, you usually want to be liked, for the very good but cynical reason that you have something to promote: the book, the film, the new series. The celebrity, it has been said, faces the choice between starving and being eaten.

Interviewers are also playing a role. They want to be liked for the equally cynical reason that they hope the interviewees will take them into their confidence, forget about the tape recorder and reveal more than they meant to. According to Truman Capote the secret is to let the other person think he's interviewing you. 'You tell him about yourself, and slowly spin your web so that he tells you everything. That's how I trapped Marlon.' (Brando later said: 'The little bastard spent half the night telling me all his problems. I figured the least I could do was tell him a few of mine.') But Capote's approach only works if you have been allocated plenty of time to do the interview – and usually you only have an hour or two.

It's never my intention to betray the person I'm writing about – indeed any 'betrayal' is perceived rather than actual. It's just that interviewer and interviewee have different expectations of what the finished article will be like – which is why it is important never to give the pre-publication copy approval stars sometimes ask for. How you see yourself is rarely the same as others see you. The famous usually dislike what you write about them, even when you think you have been flattering. Capote explained this sense of misrepresentation thus: 'No one likes to see himself as he is or cares to see exactly set down what he said or did. I don't like to myself when I am the sitter and not the painter. And the more accurate the strokes, the greater the resentment.'

Andrew Billen, who writes interviews for *The Times*, compares the exercise to a mutual seduction. 'The three stages of a successful interview,' he believes, 'are flirtation, seduction and betrayal. The fundamental problem is the elapse of time between encounter and composition. Just as you don't know your subject until you teach it, as an interviewer you do not know your subject until you recreate him in print.' I go along with that. The writer needs distance from his alter ego, the sympathetic listener; time for the fairy dust to float away.

Janet Malcolm takes this metaphor a stage further. In her book *The Journalist and the Murderer* she describes a mutual love affair between journalist and subject, with each party being ingratiating to the other. 'Every journalist who is not too stupid or too full of himself to notice what is going on knows that what he does is morally indefensible,' she writes. 'He is a kind of confidence man, preying on people's vanity, ignorance, or loneliness, gaining their trust and betraying them without remorse.' On reading the article, she adds, the interviewee 'has to face the fact that the journalist – who seemed friendly and sympathetic, so keen to understand him fully, so remarkably attuned to his vision of things – never had the slightest intention of collaborating with him on his story but always intended to write a story of his own.'

I don't think interviewers are quite that well organized. Most of the time we stumble about clumsily, hoping not to be found out. We may have done our research, but few of us go into interviews with preconceived ideas. We go in with a willingness to see what will happen. (And, as Lynn Barber has noted, we *do* hope something will happen: a disruption, an unexpected visitor, something to give us colour and show the subject in a different light.) Also, I don't think most subjects, celebrities at least, are as naive as Janet Malcolm suggests they are. They can be just as manipulative as the person interviewing them. They know the score and if they kick up a fuss afterwards, as Sir Elton is wont to do, it's often only because they feel that that is what is expected of them.

The invention of the form has been traced to 1859 when Horace Greenly, editor of the *New York Tribune,* interviewed Brigham Young, the leader of the Mormon Church, in Salt Lake City. It became a routine part of a reporter's job after that. But in the first half of the twentieth century the technique of the interview evolved in two directions: there were either puffing pieces presented in the form of Q&As (questions and answers) that indulged the vanity of celebrities and promoted them on their own terms, or there was interpretative, opinionated prose which came to reflect the model of psychoanalysis, based on an interview in which the analyst had coaxed his patient into self-revelation. *The New Yorker* pioneered the wry, non-sycophantic interview with psychological bite and, in this country, Lynn Barber and Martyn Harris became its best, and best-known, exponents.

The journalist Geoffrey Wheatcroft has suggested that the celebrity's desire to submit himself to the interviewer is the result of a deep-seated human need to confess. 'Most of us are both vain and silly enough to think that by exposing ourselves we will make ourselves more attractive and plausible, though not many moments' thought suggests that this isn't likely to be so.' In a similar vein, the actor William Hurt told me he believes that the media 'take famous people hostage in their own space'. Actually, when I interviewed him it was more the other way round: a few days after we met he began bombarding me with long e-mails which, he explained, were meant to 'clarify' his thoughts. They made them even more opaque. They also lent weight to my conclusion that the man was, if not completely ga-ga, then at least ga.

Despite finding him ga, I generally try to be an empathetic interviewer, especially with men. In contradistinction to 'jugular journalists', I prefer to like the people I am writing about, even if they don't necessarily like what is being written about them. The Wilson Interview, as it became known to my proud parents, was a case in point. It may not have been my finest hour – it was printed as an *Hello!*-style Q&A – but it did make me appreciate that I have an over-active empathy gland. Leave me alone in a room with an old man for a couple of hours and he becomes my grandfather. Harold Wilson seemed vulnerable – his mind kept wandering, he repeated himself, his speech was slightly slurred – and I felt oddly protective towards him. (In retrospect it is obvious that the Alzheimer's disease from which he was to die in 1995 was even then taking hold.)

It sounds trite to say so but we are all someone's son or daughter, we are all born astride the grave and just because a film star might travel everywhere by private jet it doesn't mean we who fly economy can't relate to them. I try to imagine what the world is like from the famous person's perspective, try and identify with their problems and disappointments, put myself in their tasselled Gucci loafers. I ask them to look at themselves and question their lives, their motives, their moods. I often find myself asking the men I interview about their relationships with their fathers – how they measure up, what values they have in common, whether they were close – because however successful a man becomes he still often craves paternal approval. As Tony Parsons said when I interviewed him: 'Every father is a hero to his son. At least when they are too small to know better.' Another Parsons, Nicholas, broke down crying when he was telling me about his father's death. His father, it transpired, had watched an episode of *Sale of the Century* for the first time while on his deathbed – and, huge relief, he had said he enjoyed it.

While I've been writing an interview, I have sometimes heard via a colleague or a publicist that a subject has said they enjoyed it; thought it had gone well; liked me. And during the interview itself stars have sometimes flattered me into thinking that I might be just the sort of person they would invite back to their summer house in the Hamptons. (I have struck up a couple of lasting friendships with people I have interviewed but they are very much the exceptions – and neither, alas, has a summer house in the Hamptons.) In reality, however much they might flatter, I'm sure most stars regard journalists as a necessary evil. They might even feel contempt and pity for us because as a writer in the *Guardian* put it: 'Interviewers are briefly ushered in to the world of limos and high cheekbones, then flung out, howling, like Satan into the pit.'

Either way, you write for the benefit of the reader who has paid for the newspaper, not for the celebrity you are writing about. If the subject chooses to take the profile personally, as though it were a letter addressed to him, that is his problem. About a third of all interviewees let it be known, one way or another, that they liked the interview; a third that they disliked it; a third do not react at all (much the best policy). A year after I interviewed the studiously woolly A.N. Wilson, a friend bumped into him and said how much he had enjoyed what I had written: Wilson had no recollection at all that the interview had ever taken place.

I have included postscripts, where relevant, to *The Sunday Telegraph* profiles reproduced here. These are updates; what has happened to the famous person since the profile was published. Sometimes, though, it would be useful to write a postscript to an interview a week after publication. The Sunday after the paper ran a profile I'd written of David Sullivan, the porn baron, I was the subject of a feature in the *Sunday Sport*, a tabloid which he owns. Under the headline, WE'VE NO DUTY TO LORD SNOOTY was a picture of me wearing tails on my way to a wedding. It had been taken with a telephoto lens outside my house on the Saturday. (Sullivan had ordered that my house be staked out as revenge for what he considered to be my unflattering profile of him. If only he had known how flattered I would feel by all his effortful attention.)

David Starkey took the post-interview footnote to its post-modern conclusion and wrote a diary in *The Spectator* about what it was like to be interviewed. 'If journalism is the first draft of history, then I suppose the newspaper profile must be the first sketch of a biography,' he wrote. 'The interviewer arrives. Each eyes the other up, rather warily. Impressions are formed and the conversation takes off or sags accordingly. To an extent you are in charge. You say as much or as little about yourself as you wish. From the moment Nigel Farndale walked through the door, I decided I liked him. Well-spoken and mildly scruffy, he turned the interview into a kind of tutorial. He'd been a good student; done his reading and come up with an original thesis: I was the new Dr Johnson. At the time, I giggled rather helplessly at the inflated nature of the comparison. But of course I was secretly flattered.'

And so was I when I read *The Spectator*. I'm sometimes asked what I really think of the person I have just written a profile of – 'So what's he *really* like?' – as if a journalist must always hold back certain views because he has been compromised by his editor or, worse, because a deal has been struck with the publicist in order to gain access to the star. There is the occasional awkwardness of an interview subject being an FoD (Friend of Dominic) or an FoC (Friend of Conrad) but neither the editor not the owner of *The Sunday Telegraph* has ever censored me on the grounds that I was writing about one of their friends or acquaintances (though I suppose I may have censored myself a little, consciously or otherwise). No journalist would throw away a half decent insight on the grounds of good taste, or to avoid causing offence.

Equally demoralizing is the question (asked after someone has just read a profile I've written), 'Did you like him?' '*Can't you tell?*' I feel like gibbering. The first few times I was asked this, though, I had another response: I couldn't understand why anyone would care what I thought, one way or the other. My job, I believed, was to be a camera – the readers could draw their own conclusions from my observations. I now see that this was disingenuous. As an interviewer you're in the privileged position of spending a couple of hours, sometimes more, with someone famous. You have had the magic of direct contact. Of course your friends and colleagues want to know whether a celebrity, whose public persona is known well, is likeable in private. It is a legitimate and fundamental question to ask. Rarely, though, does the interviewer get to meet the private person. More likely you are given a performance: the polished anecdotes, the easy manner, the flirtation. Ruby Wax – an FoD I once interviewed – has a good take on this: 'People keep asking me if I liked Fergie. I suppose for that afternoon I liked her, but I don't know her well enough. She was charming to me and she let me into her house and she played the game.'

Carl Gustav Jung believed that we all adopt personas, outward faces we present to the world. This must be especially true of people who live part of their lives under a spotlight, which is why I often ask the celebrities I interview what they think the difference is between their public and private personas. A revealing variation on this question is to ask them how they have changed since they were in their teens, in other words before they were famous – most people have undergone some form of self-invention. It is also useful sometimes to ask someone how they would describe themselves – physically and psychologically – as self image seems closely aligned to self knowledge (or lack of it) and self esteem. Andrew Neil had a pithy come back to this question: 'That's your job.'

I always manage to ask at least one moronic question per interview and, for some reason, it never seems to make it into the final draft of the profile. Example: 'Your brain,' I said to Stephen Fry, the celebrated cleverpants, 'has always been a great asset to you, has it not?' 'Well,' he replied politely. 'Brains are a great asset to everyone.'

Sometimes it isn't so much a question as an icebreaking comment. I began an interview with Norman Cook, better known as Fat Boy Slim, by mentioning we had an old friend in common, someone he had been at Reigate Grammar School with, and who had been the drummer in his band the Stomping Pond Frogs, which later became The Housemartins. I told him I had spoken to our friend only that morning. The temperature in the room dropped, Cook turned my tape recorder off and said simply: 'Did he happen to mention that he slept with my wife?' (His first wife; not Zoe Ball.) No, I said. He, er, didn't.

Occasionally it is the person you are interviewing, or his press officer, who attempts to lighten the mood when you first meet.

At the Ferrari test track near Bologne, I sat down on a comfy black sofa for an interview with Michael Schumacher. His press officer, Sabine, sat with us, noticed my Schumacher cuttings file and asked if she could have a flick through it to see if there was anything she had missed. The top article carried a large photograph of Germany's finest racing driver on which, in an idle moment on the plane, I had drawn a Hitler moustache and side-parting.

From start to finish an interview takes about seven days, which may not all occur in the same week. First comes the ideas meeting – or no-ideas meeting – at which half a dozen editors and writers discuss whom to approach. This is often a triumph of wild optimism over experience: 'So that's agreed then, we'll interview Hillary Clinton for the issue of the 12th.' 'But don't we need someone British for the mix in that one? How about doing Camilla Parker Bowles "at home" instead?' I quite often interview women – and men younger than forty – but I find older men make the best subjects, especially if they are extroverts, egotists or awkward types with emotional texture. In theory it should be more interesting for the interviewer to write about someone who hasn't been written about much before. In practice, few people want to read about someone they have never heard of. The *Observer* magazine once tried a policy of interviewing those whom Lord Falconer would call 'ordinary people' and soon gave up. You need the 'recognition factor', especially if you want to put someone's face on the cover.

Even so, fame is subjective. I always find it sobering how often my parents haven't heard of the 'famous' people I interview. My father, a retired farmer whose favourite paper is the *Yorkshire Post*, will say to me: 'That was a queer beggar [strange person] you interviewed on Sunday.' But it was ever this way: as G.K. Chesterton said, journalism consists largely in saying Lord Jones is dead to people who never knew that Lord Jones was alive. So, what *does* constitute a celebrity? Barry Humphries says it is a non-entity who got lucky. But I prefer Steve Martin's definition: any well known TV or movie star who looks like he spends more than two hours working on his hair.

The call that makes the heart sink a notch is the one from the editor asking if you will interview an actor in an hotel room.

People tend to confuse actors with the exciting and thoughtful characters they play. But, without someone else's lines to mouth, they often turn out to be rather 'ordinary people', after all. As an interview subject, I would take a paranoid professor, depraved novelist or vainglorious politician over a Hollywood actor any day.

If you agree to interview the actor all the same (and you will if you want to keep your job) you will often find yourself on a conveyor belt outside a hotel room, waiting for your hour with the star, while a publicist sits outside (and sometimes, God forbid, alongside you) with a stopwatch. Junkets are soul destroying, for interviewer and interviewee alike. Come to think of it, because junkets mean the promiscuous star is 'all over the place like a madwoman's sick' (Humphries again), the readers must find them pretty disheartening, too. Appeals to find an alternative to the junket usually fall on blocked ears. One journalist on being told that he could have half an hour with Arnold Schwarzenegger said: 'But if I'm going to do the profile properly I'd want to hang around over a few days.' 'Oh God,' Arnie's publicist replied witheringly. 'This wouldn't be one of those profiles where you *try to figure him out*, would it?'

The choice of subject being agreed at the no-ideas meeting, the process of trying to fix up the interview begins: letters and phone calls that can take weeks of chasing. Then I do as much research as I can – talk to people who know the star, friends and enemies alike, read books, watch films, trawl through cuttings. The cuttings file, incidentally, is the perfect cure for any nerves you might feel as an interviewer about meeting someone you might ordinarily be star-struck by. When you realize how many times the star has already answered the questions which you had hoped might be original, you are more likely to feel contempt for yourself, and them – media-whores both, meeting furtively in hotel rooms. That's not to say I haven't suffered impostor syndrome just before going into an interview – I'm sure I must have done when I met the Dalai Lama, Stephen Hawking, Henry Kissinger, Woody Allen, Paul McCartney and the Prince of Wales. But once an interview starts you don't feel intimidated or overawed, partly because, *pace* Dr Starkey, as interviewer you are in charge, sort of. You are the one asking the questions.

Before an interview I make a list of about thirty key words – areas I would like to cover – but I rarely refer to it as it is much easier to have a free-flowing conversation. At the end of the interview I find nearly all the questions will have been touched upon anyway. It is often as well to resist rushing to fill an awkward silence with another question; and the most revealing answers can come when you ask someone to clarify a point – why?

Eventually comes the writing. With all the stopping and starting involved, transcribing the tape of a two or three hour interview can take a couple of days, but it is as well to do it yourself – rather than inflict it upon a work experience person in the office – because it helps you get back into the mood of the interview and you can edit as you go along. I then read through the transcript several times looking for a theme, a shape and an opening.

Novelistic devices can be useful: with the interviewer sometimes featuring as a character in the story of the interview, revealing his thoughts during and after the encounter. And I find it helps bring the subject to life on the page if you leave in some of the ragged grammatical edges, repetitions and nuances of their speech. Interviews can be like novels in other respects: they are not concerned with news so much as conveying character, atmosphere and certain psychological truths. But all you are doing really is whisking up a readable journalistic soufflé out of what are sometimes meagre ingredients. You concoct something out of an hour or two in someone's life and give it a meaning that might not have existed had you not been there. It's a harmless conceit, I think. It's artifice. It's entertainment. Interviews should aspire to the condition of the obituary – in both you have the last word – but they don't really matter much. They are just a chance for the interviewer to spend a little time with Arnie and, yes, *try to figure him out.*

James Hewitt

In the outer morning room of a gentleman's club in Pall Mall, a tall, languid figure stoops over a table. The day's papers are fanned out in front of him. As he browses, he purses his lips and nods to himself.

I can't believe it, I say as I walk over and join him. He hasn't made it on to a single front page.

'I know,' he says with a soft, joyless laugh. 'It's been three whole days now. It's like being in cold turkey.'

Ah yes, that headline in last Sunday's *News of the World*: RAT HEWITT 3-IN-A-BED AND A RABBIT FUR GLOVE. And all the headlines over the past four weeks excoriating him for writing his memoirs about his affair with Diana, Princess of Wales. It must be interesting being James Hewitt. I indicate a couple of armchairs in the corner, under a portrait of a glowering First World War general. The 41-year-old former Life Guards officer tucks his furled umbrella under one arm and saunters towards them. 'So,' he says. 'You planning a hatchet job?'

Well, it is traditional isn't it?

'Yes, I suppose it is,' he sighs. 'People are frightened of going off on another tack. It's easier just to repeat the usual crap. And I suppose papers that have written badly of me in the past can't suddenly turn round and write nice things.'

As you would expect, he pronounces yes 'yah', off 'orf', room 'rum' – and he peppers his speech with words like golly, chap and ghastly. He has an occasional stammer and his delivery is gentle, slow and ponderous, in the manner of one suffering shell-shock. It soon becomes apparent, though, that this tone is not that of the bewildered or traumatized but of the blithely complacent.

James Hewitt sinks low into his chair. He is wearing a dark double-breasted suit and as he unbuttons it – revealing felt braces – he grimaces jokily and mouths the words 'Got a bit of a hangover.' He bumped into Marco Pierre White for the first time last night and the chef had insisted on buying him drinks. Such is Hewitt's insouciant charm. But strangers also seek his company because they find him creepily mesmerising. After all, it's not every day you meet The Most Hated Man in Britain. This is what the tabloids dubbed James Hewitt. The *Daily Mirror* even invited its readers to attempt a citizen's arrest under the Treason Act, should they ever encounter him. A few weeks ago someone did accost him in the street with the words 'Oy James!' As he turned around to see who was shouting at him the shouter added: 'You're an arsehole!' He must get that quite a lot. 'You know,' Hewitt says, 'I'm not hated or thrown out of restaurants or treated differently from anyone else. On the contrary, sometimes people give me the better table in a restaurant or upgrade me on an airline. I mean, these are stupid little examples but if you believe what you read in the papers then I am shunned by the whole of society.'

He checks his slicked back, strawberry blond hair with a hand. 'It's true,' he continues. 'I do get recognized in the street. Great deal of nudging with elbows after I've gone past. You know, "Did you see who that was?" But I've never been spat at or abused or shouted at.' Pause. 'Once, actually, in Ebury Street, but they were drunk and they would have shouted at anyone. Nevertheless, it still affects you. It would be insensitive to say it's water off a duck's back. But I think it affects my family and friends more.'

He still has friends, then?

'Well, you see, there you are being affected by what you read in the tabloids. Yes, I do. I have a very strong intimate circle of friends. Real friends who stick with you through thick and thin.'

Can he give me their names and phone numbers for character references?

'You want to contact them? Yes. They will probably be cagey unless I tell them you are calling. Rupert Mackenzie-Hill, who was in the Gulf War with me. Great friend. Um. Francis

Showering. Mark Macauley. Um. Um. Paulie Andrews. Simon Nunes. I think, for a lot of people, friendship goes untested. There have been a few friends who I thought were friends who haven't spoken to me for a long time. Army. I suppose they see themselves as being caught between two loyalties and they see their career as more important, which is fine. I can think of one who still asks after my health when he sees my mother. So I haven't really made any enemies or at least none who are man enough to come forward and tell me they are. Apart from Piers Morgan [editor of the *Mirror*]. But I shouldn't think he's got the balls to come up to me face to face.'

Hewitt smoothes his silk tie and draws his leg up defensively, so that his right ankle is resting on his left knee. His black brogues glint with fresh polish. He seems composed today but I have heard about his bouts of depression and heavy drinking: has he ever feared for his mental health?

'Some people would suggest I have completely broken down. It's difficult. I do try and keep a balanced view and a sense of humour. You would think from reading the tabloids that I would have been shot by now on the streets of London. The mob would have come and taken me away. The reality is very different. I've never been refused anything by anybody. Never been ostracized.'

Is it a myth, then, that his local hunt returned his membership cheque?

'No. That's not a myth. That is true.'

So there is an example of his getting the cold shoulder.

'All right, yes. And I am no longer a member of the Life Guards Officers Club, the Life Guards Association, the Cavalry and Guards Club or the Special Forces Club. In fact, I don't have a club any more. There is an arsehole called Christopher Doyley who became a lieutenant-colonel in the Life Guards – I don't think I'd have him as my corporal. He's the sort of person who wears nylon breeches, you know. He caused my cheque to be returned from the South Devon hunt, which used to be quite a good pack. But the Eggesford, the Mid-Devon, the Taunton Vale and one or two other packs wrote to me and said you are welcome to hunt with us. So I sort of lost one and gained five. Actually, I don't hunt much now. Had to sell my horse.'

James Hewitt is an amiable fellow with an unexpectedly dry sense of humour, but he is also pathetic. He bemoans his notoriety yet seeks to make a living from it. And his motto seems to be once bitten, twice . . . bitten. The recent spate of hostile press coverage about him has been prompted by the news that he plans to publish his memoirs, *Love and War*, this week, shortly after the second anniversary of the death of Diana, Princess of Wales. Yet he refers to his decision to collaborate on an earlier book, *Princess in Love*, written by Anna Pasternak five years ago, as the biggest mistake of his life.

It presented the story of his affair with the princess as a Mills & Boon romance. He was paid an advance for it, something which he repeatedly denied at the time, but now admits. The initial print run of 75,000 copies sold out in a day and the front page of the *Guardian* carried the headline ROYALS MADE LAUGHING STOCK. Hewitt went into hiding in France with his mother. Over the next few days he went for lone walks in the woods, always feeling sick. He contemplated suicide. And, as his shotgun was back in England, he decided to buy a hose pipe and gas himself using the exhaust of his car. But when the time came he couldn't go through with it – because he couldn't stand the thought of hurting his mother.

What on earth has possessed Hewitt to put himself through it all again? Can he really be so naive as to imagine his second book will be better received than his first? 'I didn't really want to write it,' he tells me. 'And by choice I wouldn't have because I'm too lazy. But I decided to do it when my letters were stolen from my house by Piers Morgan. I decided to say something rather than say nothing. Put the record straight. Because I tried to say nothing and they wrote about me anyway. Mostly untruths.'

In March last year James Hewitt's then fiancée, Anna Ferretti, broke into his safe in his house in Devon and stole sixty-two love letters written by Diana, Princess of Wales, to Hewitt. She tried to sell them to the *Mirror* – which has admitted it egged her on – but they handed them over to Kensington Palace and Ferretti was subsequently arrested but not charged. The *Mirror* claimed that Hewitt was planning to sell the letters. Hewitt denied this, though acknowledged that he had been offered millions of dollars for them in the past. Kensington Palace officials tried to keep the letters but Hewitt threatened to take them to court and, after months of legal negotiations, he was finally given his property back.

There has been speculation that *Love and War* includes extracts from the Princess of Wales's love letters. It doesn't – although they are paraphrased on occasion. It is a self-justifying book, full of bitterness and paranoid theories that the Army, the press, the police and the Palace were all conspiring against Hewitt. It is not, contrary to rumour, a particularly vulgar book, though there are odd details about the time the major and the princess spent together at Highgrove, Kensington Palace and Hewitt's mother's house in Devon that will raise eyebrows – if only because they reveal that the couple were able to conduct a fairly open and normal relationship, in spite of the princess's high public profile. He would buy her chocolates and cuddly toys. They would regularly watch *EastEnders* together.

Large sections of the book are devoted to Hewitt's memories of the Gulf War. He was mentioned in dispatches, got so close to the enemy he was able to lob grenades into their trenches. The squadron of 14 tanks he commanded advanced 300 kilometres, attacked 10 positions, killed or wounded 1,000 Iraqis and destroyed more that 40 tanks and armoured vehicles. He had a good war, didn't he?

'Yes, I did have a good war. Did well. Not me personally but my squadron.'

Diana, Princess of Wales, wrote more than 120 letters to Hewitt during the build-up to the Gulf War, sometimes as many as three a day. Hewitt sent many of them home to his mother, but he burnt others, with the rest of his identifying documents, on the eve of the attack. He feared then that he might be killed in action. Now he sometimes wishes he had been. 'There is something noble and romantic about dying in war, serving your country. It's an easy way out. I was prepared to die. Many of us out there were expecting to. I think sometimes you acquit yourself better if you are not worried about being killed.'

This is an officer and a gentleman speaking. But because Hewitt tries too hard in presenting himself as such, wearing cravats that look absurdly out of place in the modern age, he has become a parody of one – and journalists have cast him as that most old-fashioned of scoundrels, the cad. He is, is he not, a cad?

'Or a love rat.'

Or, indeed, a love rat. It's good joke, but then cad as a term of abuse is a bit playful, isn't it?

'True, I don't think the word cad is particularly vicious. I've got to learn to live with it. I think I can.' Is he familiar with the dictionary definition?

'Cad? I haven't really analysed it. Actually. Strange that, isn't it? Cad? Cad? I think it is a bit of a derogatory term – more than just a joke.'

A cad is someone who behaves dishonourably.

'Is it? I don't think I'm dishonourable. At all.'

Has he ever felt shame?

'Yes. About my life and the heartache I've brought on my family. But it's not a lasting shame. Yes, when I analyse the whole situation, I suppose it is a bit shameful. It's not what I would have wished.'

Wouldn't his problems have been alleviated and his public image improved if he had just thrown up his hands and said, 'Mea culpa. I'm a sinner. I ask for forgiveness?'

'I think that's what I've done.' Pause. 'I'm not saying I am without sin, for heaven's sake. But there are more important things in life than writing about me. I've made mistakes but I am not in any way mean or vindictive or horrid at all. I think quite the contrary, actually. Take this book, I don't think it can be described as salacious or tittle-tattle.'

But he must have known that whatever he wrote he was going to be criticized?

'Yes, I could have written about Andy Pandy and the rubbish the tabloids came out with would have been the same. I mean, the *Sunday Express* had "Cruel Hewitt claimed to be father figure of the boys." I don't think I've suggested that ever. And it was going on and on about the ghastliness of writing about the book and yet there they were reporting it. And if I say nothing they write more. So I am in a no-win situation here.'

Presumably the father-figure story arises because in the book he describes reading bedtime stories to the two princes, as well as having pillow fights with them. 'Yes, perhaps. But it depends how you put things. I never claimed to be a father figure. I played with them, swam with them, taught them to ride.'

So what does he think is behind this idea that he is the most hated man in Britain? 'I think, OK. Um. Let me get my mind behind that. I've become a hate figure and I haven't been able to defend myself so it has just gone on and on and they are not going to stop. Um. So it isn't exactly a risky business for an editor. It was, for instance, risky for them to attack Diana. There is a need for people out there to have someone to throw darts at. And, well, holding out over this last barrage has been quite difficult, really. I would prefer to be in Iraq, I have to say.'

Why does he face it? Why not disappear to South America, grow a beard, change his name by deed-poll? 'Because I don't want to run away. I want to fight and succeed here. And then it's my own choice to disappear if I want to . . . It would be quite nice to find a country that isn't attacking and jealous and hypocritical. But I am not going to run away. I have done *nothing wrong*. That is the whole point. You would think I had done something worse than a child-killer. I'm sure if I was part of an ethnic minority they wouldn't be allowed to do what they are doing. But instead it's open season on me and has been for a long time. I don't mean to sound whingey. But I think I've been in the dock without my defence counsel having spoken and so I'm doing that now – that is one reason why I have done the book.'

Another reason is that he is going to profit from it.

'I think people understand that if an author writes a book he gets paid for doing so. I mean, *why not*? People say it's despicable that he is profiting from his book but if they stand back and think about it they should think, "Well, why shouldn't he?"'

One reason is that Diana, Princess of Wales, probably wouldn't have wanted him to write this book. And another is that she is no longer around to defend herself against the suggestions he makes in it.

'I'm sure she would be absolutely thrilled with it,' Hewitt counters. 'Absolutely thrilled. To put across a more accurate, *the* accurate version. I don't think my book says one nasty word about her. I think it's honest, it doesn't make her out to be a saint. But I believe she was a good person inside and I think that comes across. And I don't think it will hurt her boys in any way at all.'

But if he was going to write it, wouldn't it have been better to wait ten or twenty years – give it historical distance?

'Yes, I did think about that but I thought. Um.' Pause. 'Everyone would have forgotten about me then, hopefully, and so it would be stupid then to rake up trouble for myself all over again. But then, balanced against that, I didn't want to go to my grave with tabloid headlines engraved on my headstone, you know?'

James Hewitt believes that, right from the start of his affair with Diana, there was an understanding in Palace circles that Charles had Camilla therefore it was all right for Diana to have him. Doesn't he wish now that he had been more like Camilla in other ways, that he had remained silent and enigmatic?

'Yes, um, yes . . . I think Camilla is brilliant. She has had a very bad press, like me. She's very nice. I don't think she's an evil woman at all. I think she's wonderful for him and they should get married – don't see why they shouldn't – it's a load of bloody poppycock, really. She has been supported hugely by Charles, which makes a difference. I mean, had Diana not asked me to speak to the press, you know, I would still have been kicked out of the Army – probably – but at least I would be in another job now. I have to work.' He shoots his cuffs and looks away. 'I never wanted to speak to the press at all. In fact I hate being in a situation where I am a public figure. I never wanted that. I would have become an actor or an MP or singer if I had wanted that. I never wanted anything other than to be a soldier and to serve my country.' He knits his freckled brow. 'I was really asked to talk to the press by Diana. That was where it all started. The downward turn. In 1993.'

She wanted him to clear the air?

'No, she wanted me to lie about the depth of our relationship. Which I did. But it *didn't work*.'

He means by saying that it wasn't physical?

'Yes. But people tapped telephones and were aware. It was fatuous to do what I did because people wouldn't believe it. It would have been far better to say nothing. But Diana was about

20

to be divorced and I suppose it would have been unhelpful for her to be seen to be having an extramarital affair. So I did it and it was the cause of my downfall. But the story had first appeared in the *News of the World* when I was in the Gulf. So to suggest that I kissed and told was wholly inaccurate. It was more a damage limitation exercise that turned badly wrong . . . Anyway, I think it must be borne in mind that both Diana and Charles spoke to people before I did.'

So what about Anna Pasternak? He gave an interview to her for the *Daily Express* and then she came back with an idea for a book? Or was it his idea?

'No, she approached me. She said I approached her and begged her to do it which is wholly inaccurate and very naughty of her. Um. In fact I tried to stop her from doing it in the end, when I saw the way it was going . . . I didn't really have anything to do with it. I've never read the book.'

Come off it, I say. He must have. It would be inhuman to be so lacking in curiosity.

'Well, it's partly so I can say I have never read it. Stand back from it. I'm not curious at all. I know the true story is in my book. Anyway, I hear the Pasternak book is not very well written. Have you read it?'

I, er, dipped into it yesterday actually.

Hewitt laughs. 'You can admit to reading it, you know!'

Well, I found it pretty hard to get beyond the first few pages, to be honest – her arms ached for him, their eyes met etc.

'Yes. Ridiculous.'

When Diana, Princess of Wales, did her *Panorama* interview in 1995 and said of Hewitt, 'Yes, I adored him. Yes, I was in love with him. But I was very let down,' she was obviously referring to the Pasternak book. Yet Hewitt maintains that she was referring to his decision in 1989 to accept a posting to Germany, rather than stay at the Knightsbridge barracks where he could be near to her. 'I don't think she was bothered by the book, to be honest,' Hewitt tells me. 'I think she was more bothered by the effect that it had. Really. She was quite clever in the way that she used people and I do think she used me. Um. That interview was well-rehearsed and well-orchestrated and worked rather well. I mean she wasn't asked about any of the other chaps in her life. She was able to say I let her down and she didn't expand on it. And the interviewer didn't ask her to. It just served its purpose. She admitted that she had been unfaithful to her husband and then she immediately turned the sympathy back on herself by suggesting I let her down.'

So when the princess said those actual words, well, the rest of us were on the edges of our seats, what must it have been like for him? How did he feel? Flattered or devastated?

'Both really. Flattered that she admitted she loved me. I mean I'd have preferred not to have been mentioned at all. I mean, why not Will Carling or whoever else? Um. The interviewer had agreed not to ask about him, of course. Just about someone who could be used . . . It was a heart-racing moment. I was in Devon and the whole place lit up. Blinding white light. Five minutes after the programme finished. They were waiting on the hillside outside my house. There was a fucking great light the size of that mirror.' He nods at an 8ft by 12ft mirror above the fireplace in the room. 'An enormous searchlight of the kind anti-aircraft gunners used in the Second World War. A dozen television cameras were trained on the house like snipers – I was under siege in my own house and it was more than a week before I went out.'

Unorthodox though it is to say it, I don't think James Hewitt qualifies as a proper cad. Whether it is because he is just amoral or too thick I can't say, but he simply doesn't appear to understand why he has been vilified. And a true cad would. A true cad would instinctively know that a gentleman doesn't talk about a woman with whom he has been intimate – but would callously do it anyway.

I don't think Hewitt knows why he shouldn't do it. In Hewitt's world he thinks Diana, Princess of Wales, used him and then failed to support him when he needed help. When their relationship began she was feeling trapped in a loveless marriage. She was suffering from bulimia and low self-esteem. According to Hewitt, she believed that British Intelligence officers had arranged the motorcycle accident that killed her bodyguard Barry Mannakee. And Hewitt rebuilt her confidence, gave her the approval she craved and then, when she felt she was back in control of her life, she dropped him.

And he thinks the main reason men hate him is that they envy him for having slept with the Princess of Wales. Also, he may go through the motions of saying he feels guilty and depressed about what he has done – because he thinks that is what people want to hear – but I don't think he understands why it is bad form to profit from revealing secrets about your lover. His view seems to be that others have made money from their memories of the princess, so why shouldn't he? Is that about the strength of it?

'No,' he says. 'I'm not prepared to pass the buck and say because they've done it, why can't I? I mean, it would be a bit like saying, they have murdered so why shouldn't I? I haven't kissed and told. I've never gone out deliberately to make money. I've gone out to try and redress the balance and in doing so have been paid. Now I'm hardly likely to say, "No, that's all right, you keep the money." You know, to say I don't want the money. I mean, I have to live.'

What sort of money are we talking about?

'I think I've lost a lot more than I have been paid. In almost every respect, actually.'

He means emotionally, I mean in terms of his bank balance.

'I don't know how much I've been paid. And I don't think necessarily that that is important.'

One million pounds. Does that sound about right?

'Absolutely not. Absolutely not. Absolutely not. Not at all.'

A recent investigation revealed that he had been paid £150,000 for tabloid interviews; £100,000 for the *Daily Express* serialization . . .

'Nope. Nope.'

The Pasternak book, £100,000 plus . . .

'Nope.'

£600,000 for the serialization of his memoirs . . .

'Well I haven't been paid that, so you can scrub that right off. And also you have to deduct the £70,000 it has cost me in legal terms. To be advised on libel cases. And also to get my property back, the letters stolen by Piers Morgan and handed to Kensington Palace – eventually – after he had copied them and made use of them. Ask him how much he has made from Diana . . .'

But I suppose . . .

'That's his job, is it?'

No, but he was never the lover of Diana, Princess of Wales. He was never in love with her, nor ever had that love reciprocated.

'Um. I don't know. There seems to be some kind of hang-up about that. I have no easy answer. I have explained my actions . . . You know I'm not a man of huge means. I haven't got a job. I've tried to get one. Tried to do it but haven't been allowed to. I've tried to shut up and disappear. But it doesn't work and I'm not prepared to be slandered any more. I'm prepared to fight, right or wrong, live or die. I don't mind if I am told to go and shoot myself in a library after this book has been read, at least I'll have had my say.'

Hmm. The smoke-filled room, the revolver, the bottle of Scotch. We are in the realm of the *Boy's Own* comic again. Hewitt says that when he began his affair with the Princess of Wales, he looked up the definition of treason in an encyclopaedia. It said that to violate the consort of the monarch's eldest son and heir was an act of treason. What did it feel like for Hewitt, a cavalry officer, to know he was a traitor? 'At the time it just seemed like any man and any woman in a relationship that's gone wrong. I thought of it like that really. I mean, Charles and Diana were just individuals, fellow human beings. One was so involved. But when you stand back from it, and look from a distance – and one should probably do that more often than one does – um, it's only in that sense that it had far-reaching effects. No other personal thoughts. I like the chap actually [Prince Charles]. I think he's all right. I think he's been much maligned as well.'

James Hewitt has met Prince Charles on numerous occasions, at social gatherings and on the polo field, before, during and after his affair with the princess. He says the prince has always been civil and friendly to him. 'Quite clearly he [Prince Charles] knew about our affair while it was happening. Although at the time one didn't necessarily think about that, or rationalize to what extent people would know. Again, foolishly, I suppose. Of course the Establishment knew . . . The bottom line is that, yes, I have been ill-advised and naive and sometimes very foolish in the past but I haven't been treacherous or evil . . . I wonder what he [Prince Charles] felt when he was seeing Camilla, knowing she was a brother officer's wife? I think it [treason and adultery] does matter. I think it mattered terribly to me. But then there was a young lady who needed help and I thought that was more important.'

One of the reasons we all found it so hard to believe that both the Prince and Princess of Wales were having extramarital affairs so soon after their marriage was that theirs seemed to be a fairy-tale wedding, the most dramatic in history, and we all witnessed it on television. Could they really have been that cynical? James Hewitt now says that the princess once told him she was having doubts even as she walked up the aisle. 'I couldn't believe it,' he says. 'I never wanted them to break up. I thought they made an ideal couple, whatever that means. I don't think it was calculated on his [Princes Charles's] part. I think he might have wanted to give it a try. I think, actually, he is quite a good man. And clearly he knew about me but he just didn't react. What was he meant to say? You bounder! You cad! Meet me at dawn with pistols. He was perfectly civil. Very well mannered. Someone suggested I shouldn't play against him in that post-Gulf War polo match but Charles said I should. Probably wanted to hit me on the field or something. But why should he? He was having an affair. He wasn't in love with his wife. His wife was being made happy by me, what's wrong with that? Actually, what *is* wrong with that?'

And Hewitt was being made happy by Diana. But is he happy now?

'No, I am not happy. No. No. Not yet. But I'm ever the optimist . . . I suppose winning the case over the letters made me feel . . . Well, actually, why should I have felt vindicated and happy just about getting my property back?'

We're back on to the letters. One of them said, 'Please can you burn my letters after reading them now, in case they get into the wrong hands.' Hewitt thinks the significant word is 'now', as in 'from now on' and not including all the correspondence of the past five years. Yet according to the journalist Richard Kay, who was something of a confidant – and propagandist – to the Princess of Wales, Hewitt once assured Diana that his mother had burnt all the letters. Not believing him, she set off to drive down to Devon to try to persuade Hewitt to destroy the letters – then changed her mind. According to Simone Simmonds, the princess's spiritual advisor, she was even prepared to buy the letters from Hewitt. Whatever actually happened it remains a mystery why Hewitt doesn't just spare himself a lot of humiliation and burn them now. 'I might have burnt them,' he says when I put this to him.

Well has he?

'It was a matter of principle that I should get them back. No one came to me from the Palace or from the Spencer family and spoke to me sensibly, man to man, about them. And no one has about this book. They have probably read it now anyway. I should think they have sent a spy in to the printers. They really behaved disgracefully over the theft of the letters.'

Before they would hand the letters back to him, Kensington Palace officials wanted Hewitt to sign a form saying that they should be destroyed after his death. Correct? 'I wanted my property back. I don't know why people can't understand that. Then I would make a choice whether to burn them or paper my loo with them or wear them as a hat or keep them locked in a bank vault.'

So are they in bank vault at the moment? 'I don't know where they are. My solicitor has taken care of them. I have not had them alone since they were returned to me. Because when Piers Morgan sells his copies of them, he won't be able to blame them on me.'

Again, wouldn't it be a good idea for Hewitt to just burn them now and make a press statement to that effect? 'What? For the sake of it being a good idea? I think it would be irresponsible of me to burn them. I would probably like to, but in seventy years' time they will be important historical documents. They are wonderful letters. There is nothing horrible in any of them. You know, there's nothing like "Wasn't it fantastic when you bent me over the sofa," there's nothing like that in it.' He chuckles at his own coarseness. 'Not that I ever did that!'

But Diana wanted you to burn them?

'I did burn many, in the war.'

Because she was afraid they would fall into enemy hands rather than because she thought you would try to sell them?

'Has she said any different?'

Does he think that the princess's romantic nature was fired by the notion that her lover was at war and might not return and that she had to declare her love for him in letters before he died?

'Probably. We were deeply in love at one stage.'

Was the love equal on both sides?

'Yes, but probably not at the same time. Occasionally, yes. It was very difficult. It was always tense. It was a very difficult situation. But, yes, it was mutual.'

Did he ever fall out of love? Long pause. Only the ticking of a clock on the mantelpiece disturbs the silence.

'No, I don't think so.'

James Hewitt was introduced to the Princess of Wales in 1986. He was twenty-eight, she twenty-five. She said she felt nervous about riding horses after falling off one as a child. He offered to give her lessons to rebuild her confidence. She accepted. This meeting occurred at a drinks party given by Hazel West, wife of Lt-Colonel George West, the Assistant-Comptroller in the Lord Chamberlain's Office. At the time, Hewitt thought it odd that he, an ordinary soldier, should be invited to drink with senior courtiers. He now believes that the introduction had been planned because he, a single handsome Guards officer, would be the ideal person to keep the princess quiet. Does he now wish he had never gone to that party?

'My life probably would have been easier. And I probably would still be in the Army. But it did happen, you know. And I did all that I did for the right reasons. Regret is a funny word and I think that, you know, the ride was worth the fall.'

So he still regards Diana as the love of his life?

'Yes. Yes. Yah. We had a very special relationship and they can't take that away. Um.'

His mobile phone rings. 'Is that mine?' he asks, patting his jacket. 'Hello,' he says. 'Are you? It was in my pocket. No, Victoria . . . It's in Pall Mall . . . No, that piece about the glove puppet, you mean? . . . Anyway. I'll call you later.'

I ask Hewitt if anyone has ever told him he sounds just like Prince Charles? 'I can't help that,' he says with a gentle laugh. 'It's not meant. I have been told that. My publisher says I should go on television without a tie and jacket. But I can't bring myself to. It's not what I do.'

Does he ever actually wear cravats or is that just an ugly rumour? 'I don't think I've ever worn a cravat in the proper sense – things that come out like this.' He holds his hand several inches in front of his neck. 'I saw someone wearing one in Zermatt and the poor chap looked like a complete idiot. I do wear a handkerchief around my neck when I am skiing.'

James Hewitt was in Spain on business when he heard the news that Diana, Princess of Wales, had been killed in a car crash. Did he go into shock? 'No, not immediately, I don't think. I went into a state of suspended animation for four or five days once I got home. Bit numbed. Bit glued to the television, really.'

Did he cry?

'No, not a lot. I cried. But I don't really cry a lot.'

He bottles things up?

'Yes. Totally unhealthy. I should see a shrink.'

Has he ever?

'No, why should I burden anyone else with my problems? I look on it as, well, I wouldn't have been much of an officer if every time there had been a problem I had run off to a shrink. One copes and moves on.'

What did he make of the public reaction to the death of Diana, Princess of Wales?

'Mob rule, really. Cringe-making. I think it wasn't a particularly dignified spectacle. A lot of people trying to blame other people. A lot of back-pedalling by the tabloids who had the previous week vilified her. So hypocritical. A few days later calling her a saint. Ridiculous. Swung the other way far too much. Like Kipling's line: "If you can treat these two impostors the same." I try and do that. There was a piece in the *Evening Standard* two days ago by a chap called Wilson which compared me to Rupert Brooke – I love Brooke, I love that line "In the corner of a foreign field there is a part of England" [sic] – and at the end of the article it said, "Hewitt can be called many unkind names, but he is surely not a predator. Like Rupert Brooke, he is a beautiful man whom women adore." I mean, that's as fatuous and extreme as calling me a cad rat bastard. You are very good or bloody awful. It means nothing. Two impostors.'

So really we must conclude from that that he has been cursed with good looks.

'How sweet of you!'

But it's been his downfall?

'I don't think I'm good-looking. I really don't. I don't see that at all.'

I have been told by someone who knows Hewitt socially that when he is in a bar beautiful women he has never met before come up to him and give him their phone numbers. He must be aware of the affect he has on women?

He laughs. 'Hmm. Yes. Perhaps. I just like to joke about it. If they do find me attractive, I think it is wonderful because I love women.'

Is there a current girlfriend?

'I have a friend with whom I am particularly friendly and close – but I don't have a proper girlfriend because I don't want to have to put whoever I am going out with through all that I am going through at the moment. When I am in a relationship I give quite a lot and feel guilty if I don't give – and I'm not in a position to give at the moment, emotionally.'

How many times has he been in love?

Another chuckle. 'Every time I see a pretty girl! Um. Probably, deeply in love, two or three times. I have had a lot of girlfriends and I do like women, I have to say.'

Has he kept count?

'Um. No. Um. And if I had, I wouldn't tell you because you would ask me how many. I don't see it as a tally, marking a swastika on the side of your Spitfire. It's just part of the passage of life; having quick flings or longer affairs. I've never lived with anybody.' He checks his watch. Lunchtime. 'Do they do a good Bloody Mary here? Should we have one? I'm a wee bit hungover from last night.'

We order and, as we wait for the drinks to arrive, Hewitt tells me that he is 'paranoid' now that whenever he goes out with a woman she will kiss and tell afterwards – 'the anxiety normally comes on a Saturday night when I don't sleep at all, wondering whether another girl has spoken.'

Does he find that women want to sleep with him because they know he slept with Diana, Princess of Wales? 'I suppose so.

Curiosity. I hope not. But I can't really flatter myself that it's for any other reason. Probably. But not knowingly.'

James Hewitt was given £40,000 in redundancy money when he left the Life Guards and he still receives a pension from the Army of £500 a month. He had been in the Army for seventeen years before being made redundant in 1993. He reached the rank of acting major but was never made full major because he failed his promotion exams, twice, by one per cent – something which he considers to be part of the Establishment conspiracy against him. He has made two attempts to set up his own business since leaving the Army – establishing a riding school and a golf course – and both have failed. No one will employ him. Not least, he says, because he is only good at two things, horses and sex. What would be his dream job?

Long pause. Wide grin. 'A journalist.'

Wherever James Hewitt ends up living, it is safe to assume that his mother, Shirley, won't be far away. He is the archetypal mummy's boy. They do everything together and she, clearly, adores him. He, equally clearly, can't understand why the rest of the world doesn't share his mother's adoration. He was twenty-five when his mother divorced his father, John (a captain in the Royal Marines who used to punch the young James in the stomach when he got maths homework answers wrong). How did that affect him?

'Didn't really. Saw it coming. There were huge tensions for years. But even inevitable situations surprise you. But it didn't affect me. Had no one to blame for my shortcomings but myself.'

It may be one of the reasons he has never married, though. He claims, and again we only have his word for it, that he and the Princess of Wales planned to get married. How far did the plans go?

'Not far. If the timing had been different . . .'

According to Hewitt the couple selected a thatched Devon longhouse to live in, from the property pages of *Country Life* – and the princess said she would buy it anonymously. But they wouldn't have been able to live a normal life together, would they?

'What? And I have now? No, I could quite easily have seen that scenario work out . . . But she was a royalist and wanted her son to succeed to the throne. I suppose she could see the alternative which was less attractive. But, you see, when we were having an affair the mere idea of divorce was not something you could contemplate. There was no way out, other than Charles being killed in an accident – something which, incidentally, Diana had predicted for her by a Tarot reader. It nearly came true with the skiing accident. Instead it was poor old Hugh Lindsay.'

I ask Hewitt about the cartoon the Princess of Wales kept on her lavatory wall of a pile of manure swarming with flies. The caption read: 'What's that smell? Must be James Hewitt.' How does that square with his view that she didn't really mind his being behind the Pasternak book? Does he think she came to . . .

'Hate me? No, I don't think so. Hadn't really thought of that, actually. I would hope that she didn't. I don't think it rubs with the Diana I knew. No, I don't think she was capable of hate. She had a wicked sense of humour. We would speak on the phone as recently as a few months before her death and I asked her how her love life was and she said she was going to shock the world and run off with a big fat black man. It was nearly true!'

Does Hewitt think the princess went out with Dodi as revenge against the Royal Family?

'Well, it was very in your face. I suppose if they had wanted to conduct a private affair she could have done it with him – because his money would have allowed them to. But I think she had become much more in control of herself, she said, "Take it or leave it." Whether they would have got married I don't know, difficult one that. I don't think so. Apparently Dodi was a very nice chap. Apart from being a cokehead.'

Does James Hewitt ever fantasize about what might have been with the princess?

'No. I don't really dream much. I just want to face up to things. Get this book out and draw a line under the whole thing. Forget the last ten years of my life. I like the idea of doing what that man did in that wonderful film. You know, white suit, he goes away, comes back as one of the wealthiest men, and gets the girl. What's it called?'

The Great Gatsby?

'*The Great Gatsby*. Go away and build a rubber plantation somewhere and then come back. My favourite film.'

I thought that would be *The Four Feathers*.

'Yes, another great film, *The Four Feathers*. I hope I can get a few of mine taken back.'

We part company with this guileless comment still hanging in the air. As I walk out on to Pall Mall I find I can't shake off a melancholic image of James Hewitt twenty years from now – still wearing his cravats that aren't cravats; still roaming around the bars of Knightsbridge and Kensington telling the story of his affair to anyone who will buy him a drink; still playing the cad and making self-deprecating jokes about having his name on the gate, about being horsewhipped, about being blackballed from all the gentleman's clubs. But all the while still hoping that, one day, his good name will be cleared and he will be able to give his white feathers back.

A year later, in the company of a couple of prostitutes, and while suffering from depression, James Hewitt got drunk and drove at high speed along the route in Paris taken by Princess Diana's car just before it crashed. He was conducting an experiment, he said, to prove the crash wasn't an accident.

Geoffrey Boycott

MAY 1999

There are many reasons to feel queasy at the prospect of interviewing Geoffrey Boycott – but the most obvious are that he's
rude, obnoxious and, when he's in a good mood, charmless. Such
a pity he has to be morbidly fascinating as well. Or at least that's
what I tell myself as I approach Wakefield station. The clouds
over the taxi rank are inky black. Boycott has insisted on being
interviewed by a man. I'm a Yorkshireman as well, but this
doesn't necessarily mean I'm obsessed with cricket or proud that
Boycott is the county mascot. As it happens, I do recall queuing
for half an hour to get Geoffrey Boycott's autograph (and Chris
Old's) when I was twelve. And I did get goosebumps watching
him score his hundredth first-class century against Australia at
Headingley in 1977. But that doesn't mean anything. Call it
denial if you like but I do not believe, as many people seem to,
that this boorish, pantomime northerner is the archetypal Yorkshireman.

The conference hotel where we are to meet is a few miles from
Boycott's house. According to one chambermaid, this is where
Boycott 'brings his womenfolk' (but she may have been pulling
my leg). The demagogue himself arrives late – dressed in a pastel-
blue jacket, fawn slacks and pale slip-on shoes which may well
be snakeskin. He applies some Lipsyl and is soon telling the
photographer to stop 'arsing about' and get on with it.

I cross myself and prepare for the interview that is to follow.
At least I've got a panic button I can press if things get too ghastly.
I can mention Margaret Moore, Boycott's former girlfriend. If I
do this, Boycott will walk out – or so I've been warned in a fax

from his publicist. The 58-year-old former England batsman allegedly beat Moore up in an Antibes hotel room in 1996. In January last year a French court found him guilty of the charge, fined him £5,300 and gave him a three-month suspended sentence. He didn't turn up for the trial, though he did deny the charge, adamantly. Indeed, he launched a bizarre charm offensive intended to show he wasn't an aggressive man – then rather undermined the thing by losing his temper and saying to one reporter: '*Shut oop*, this is my press conference, not yours.' Boycott appealed, attended the second trial last October, complained it was 'all in bloody French', and lost again.

I sit down on a low sofa. Boycott orders tea with honey and sits opposite me in a high, upright chair – barrel-chested, stiff-backed with his jacket buttons done up, looking down his nose. He has a mobile face: eyebrows that arch and dip; a recurring blink; a mouth so lopsided it's as if he's chewing his left cheek. He has mad, starey eyes, the sort you imagine Rasputin must have had. They are a cold, cobalt blue (but this is not, contrary to folklore, because he wears coloured contact lenses). There are no awkward silences when Boycott is on the subject of cricket. He rarely draws breath and when he runs out of things to say he just repeats himself. Loudly. Flat-vowelledly. With a frankness that is exciting and dangerous. I find myself wondering if there is an element of self-parody to his manner. Mistake. 'I don't know what that *means*. Self-parody. I don't have your words.' I explain. '*What are you going on about?* I'm just being *myself*. I haven't changed for anyone. I only know about *creakit*. I love it. Self-parody.'

Actually, he's not as intimidating as you expect him to be. Over the next two and a half hours he reveals himself to be an animated storyteller and we have, to my surprise, a few laughs. But for Boycott there is little difference between a conversation and a contretemps. And so we also have – again to my surprise – two full-blown arguments. These help me appreciate Boycott's genius for making enemies. His worst feuds have been with his fellow Yorkshiremen, notably Fred Trueman, Brian Close and Ray Illingworth. 'I suppose it's because Yorkshiremen are strong-minded and individualistic,' Boycott says when I ask why this is.

Boycott is a private man, self-contained to the point of intro-version. Before he appeared on *In the Psychiatrist's Chair* in 1987 he told Dr Anthony Clare, 'You'll get nowt from me, Mister.' After the programme, a gibbering Dr Clare said he had had to revize his opinion that no man is an island. I suspect, for all his protestations to the contrary, Boycott simply doesn't care if he rubs people up the wrong way. He doesn't crave approval. And surely even he would be able to curb his pathological rudeness if he did. It is clear, too, that he hates having to woo the media. And that he only attempts to because he loves making money. His main motive for trying so hard to clear his name last year was, I bet, that he wanted the BBC to renew his lucrative contract as a commentator. It didn't. (And Channel 4, which is taking over Test coverage this summer, has boycotted him too.)

This week, Boycott is trying to charm the media again because he has something to sell, a book on cricket called . . . *Geoffrey Boycott on Cricket*. In it he gives his version of the various spats he has been involved in over the years. With a characteristic lack of pretension, he tells me about his writing process: he records his thoughts on to tapes which he gives to his ghost writer, John Callaghan, 'to be tarted up'. *Geoffrey Boycott on Cricket* is a self-serving book, of course, and could be subtitled 'Everyone Else Is To Blame'. But it is also entertaining, especially in his account of the internecine warfare that followed his sacking from Yorkshire County Cricket Club in 1983. Does it occur to him that his own bloody-mindedness is the common denominator in all the feuds he writes about?

'Of course it is me. It's my character. But it's their character, too. Take Fred Trueman. He started it. He was a hero of mine. As a cricketer he still is today. But as a person he went down in my estimation because when the club decided to dispense with my services he slagged me off. He couldn't even bring himself to say I were a good player. He said, "If I get back on the committee I still won't give Boycott a contract." Well that was tantamount to saying, "Fuck you, then." I've never spoken ill of Fred. He caused his own downfall, not me. He had to belittle me. I was hurt. He didn't have to say I couldn't bat. It was dirty tactics, that. But he didn't convince the Yorkshire members. You can't patronize them. They can think for themselves.'

Throughout his Test and county career Boycott has been criticized for being a slow, blocking and, because of all the people he's run out, selfish batsman. Can't he see there was some truth in this caricature? 'Was Trueman trying to say that all those hundreds I got were just for me? Me, slow? Look in the record books. Some innings I was slow but others . . .' He leans forward and fixes me with his beady blue eyes. 'Who got the fastest ever Gillette Cup innings? Eh? In't final. Me. 1963. Still the biggest today. On an uncovered pitch. Wet. I could go through it . . .' He does, his batting averages over his twenty-five-year county and Test career, chapter and verse from *Wisden*. My hand hovers over the Margaret Moore button.

He's a great one for facts and figures, our Geoffrey. He usually carries a bag around with him full of 'papers' – phone records, dates, lawyers' letters – ammunition with which to settle arguments. A recurring theme of his book is that nearly everyone who has attacked him over the years has been motivated by financial greed. 'We all knew Botham's hand was on his wallet rather than his heart,' he writes about Ian Botham's decision to pull out of Boycott's ill-fated 'rebel tour' of South Africa at the height of apartheid in 1982. 'All he could see were the pound signs,' Boycott writes in reference to Trueman's offer a couple of years ago to end their feud and host a series of cricket lunches together. 'Now with his eyes on the pound-note signs with regard to his book sales and newspaper serialization . . .' he writes of Henry Blofeld, the commentator who refused to sign a testimony last year to the effect that his former colleague, Boycott, did not have a violent nature. (Boycott believes Blofeld only refused because he wanted a controversial story to put in his autobiography.) Given that Boycott, a millionaire several times over, is notoriously stingy – former umpire Dickie Bird has a number of anecdotes on the subject – it seems reasonable to assume that he is judging everyone else by his own standards.

'Assume? But I didn't have a row with Botham about the South Africa tour. He decided to pull out because he got two [other] contracts for money. I don't *assume*. It was a *fact*. Botham said that at the meeting. I have recorded everything that went on. How can I assume with Trueman when it's a fact? I've got the papers. It's *you* that's wrong. Why do you assume? The lawyer has seen the papers. You can ring him up.' He spells out the lawyer's name for me before resuming his Pinteresque monologue. 'Fred Trueman only wanted to work with me for the money. *Fact*. With Blofeld it was a fact that the *Daily Mail* only ran the extract about me. Nothing else in his book was interesting enough for them to pay for. I have the papers. I have it in black and white. "Fred's going to contact you." I haven't fucking spoken to him in ten years and he's been slagging me off and now he wants the money. Fifty grand. I don't know why you *assume*. I have the papers. *I have the papers*. Believe me, I have the papers.'

It is telling that, when Boycott describes his old feuds, he slips into the present tense. He does it when he talks about his batting, too, even though he retired thirteen years ago. I have a horrible feeling that I may have started a fresh feud by quoting Dickie Bird to him.

'I am a wealthy man,' Boycott says. 'I think I'm far wealthier than any of those you mention. Very few people know me. Dickie doesn't know me. He lives two miles away but he's been to my house once. *Once*. I'm not that close to him. I'm a very private person. Things become folklore, legend, myth.'

So let's set the record straight, then. He'd describe himself as a generous man, would he? 'I don't describe myself at all.' I suppose that's why he's so fascinating to psychiatrists. 'I don't know why. I'm not so bothered about myself. Not fussed. Not interested. I get on with my life. Good times you enjoy. Bad times you can either crawl away and die or pick yourself up and get on with it.' Bad times being when exactly? 'I used to get really down when I got a nought. But you can't mope about. You have to show character.'

According to folklore, legend, myth, Boycott used to put a towel over his head and cry whenever he got a duck. He cried inconsolably when he had to give up football because he needed glasses – he played for Leeds United under-18s. Does he think he's attuned to his finer feelings, then? Does he find it easy to cry? 'No, not easy. But if I did I wouldn't show it. And I wouldn't tell you. It's a bit like a bowler. If he got me worried, I wouldn't show it. If I felt depressed, I wouldn't ignore it, I'd try and solve it. Christ, I get cross with people like anyone else. People who won't pay up. People who do you a bad turn. Say one thing and do the bloody opposite. I don't sit in a corner and weep and moan. I think there is a weakness in people who aren't straight and fair. You need to get everything in writing because for every eight people who are good there are two buggers out there who are bad. I expect people to be straighter than they are.' So he sees himself as a man of honour? 'No, I'm not bloody perfect. But I like to think I'm pretty straight. I've never done bad things to people. Haven't stolen money or kicked anyone in the balls. I've just made judgements. Nothing I'm ashamed of.'

For all his lack of humility, there is an endearing naivety and vulnerability to Boycott. He seems genuinely baffled by his un-popularity. Does he have a persecution complex? 'I don't have your words but there is a saying in Yorkshire that you can't do right for doing wrong. But I don't have a complex. I don't think I'm always right – even in my creakit commentary. Most times I keep my mouth shut – but you get to the stage where you're sick of being pilloried. Blofeld did his book in the *Mail* and the only bit they ran were about me. Me!'

Boycott seems such a joyless man. Humourless. A real misery. Does he ever have fun? Is he happy? The cricketer exhales and shakes his head. 'What's contentment? What's happiness? I'm living my life. I'm getting on. I'm picking myself up. I'm working in a game I love. Creakit.' Life for Boycott is analogous to cricket in every particular. In a shift from Pinter pastiche to Becket he tells me: 'Creakit mirrors life, if you think about it. Life, death and change in the middle.' Certainly, no game is richer in symbolism than cricket. When a man is honest he is said to play with a straight bat, when dishonest his actions are just not cricket. For Boycott there is only one virtue worth having and that is being straight – it is far more important than being tactful. It's the reason, I imagine, why so many of the newspaper reports about his court case last year took his side. He's so eccentric and guileless, the logic goes, if he really had battered Margaret Moore he would admit it. *He's that perverse.*

As it was, he seemed genuinely outraged at the suggestion. And, as he pointed out, indignantly, to anyone who would listen, there were other factors in his mitigation. He has no history of violence against women, indeed, if his monk-like batting style is anything to go by, he has preternatural self-control. Moore was £800,000 in debt. And before she took Boycott to court she had approached Max Clifford to see if he could get £2 million for her story. When Clifford declined to take her on as a client, she approached Boycott and offered to settle out of court for £1 million. (Fact. Boycott has the papers. Et cetera.)

I realize that I have inadvertently pressed the Moore button. How did he feel last year when nearly all his former friends and colleagues in the world of cricket declined to stand by him? 'I felt sad that Blofeld let me down. I stuck by him when he were down on his luck. And I'm sick of Trueman attacking me. If he walked through the door now I'd say, "What have I ever done to you?" But he'd ignore me. The press was very fair to me, though. There are warts and all when people write about me and I don't mind that. The only people who really let me down were the *Sun*.' (The paper had promised to keep Boycott on as a columnist no matter what the verdict in the Moore trial. They reneged and Boycott is now suing them for breach of contract.)

Geoffrey Boycott's bachelordom is complicated, to say the least. He lived with his mother until she died twenty-two years ago. He has had a relationship with Ann Wyatt for the past forty years (they met when he was a clerk and she was a supervisor at the Ministry of Pensions in Barnsley). She now spends most of her time in their second home in Dorset. He has also had a long-term relationship with Rachel Swinglehurst, the mother of his ten-year-old daughter, Emma. She lives a couple of miles away from him in Wakefield. He has had other long-standing relation-ships and, in his touring days, plenty of one-night stands. As became apparent in the French court last year, he inspires great loyalty in his 'womenfolk'. Several turned up to speak in his defence. When I ask if he thinks this helped, he stares into the middle distance. 'Aye, it showed that things didn't square oop.'

Boycott's cricketing nickname was Fiery because he was so remote and cold. Ann Wyatt's nick-name was Fiery's Mum because she is twelve years his senior. Is he attracted to mother figures? 'No. My mother was my mother. I find I get on better with women than men though. In general. They are more decent. Men can let you down.' Which of his women will he leave his millions to? 'The people closest to me. Ann Wyatt. My daughter.

People closest, Ann Wyatt. My daughter and her mother. People closest.'

Boycott himself was born into poverty. He and his two younger brothers grew up in a two up, two down in the Yorkshire colliery village of Fitzwilliam. Geoffrey went to Hemsworth Grammar and wishes he could have gone on to university. 'But we couldn't bloody afford it.'

His father, Thomas Wilfred Boycott, had a mining accident when Geoffrey was ten – and died seventeen years later. He was in the middle of a match at the Oval on the day his father died, and to 'show character' Geoffrey went out to bat – scoring seventy-odd – before going home for the funeral. 'My father was 6ft 1in but walked with a stoop and a limp because his knees were crushed and his back was broken and his insides were mangled up. He was a ruined man.'

Growing up, Geoffrey Boycott didn't see much of his father. He believes his values come from his mother. 'She was quiet, strong and determined. We were brought up properly. Clout round the earhole if you did owt wrong. But plenty of affection. She got arthritis 1968. Six months after my father died. It was the shock that did it. She got cancer in 1977, at the same time I got my hundredth hundred. She was dead in a year. I saw her suffer. There was a hell of a vacuum when she died. But you deal with it. Just because you don't sit in a corner crying doesn't mean you don't feel pain and hurt.'

In times of adversity Boycott takes no comfort from religion – although he does believe in Chinese horoscopes and spiritualism. 'When you're drowning you turn to anything. When Yorkshire sacked me I didn't know what to do with myself. The medium said I would play for Yorkshire again. I thought she were crackers but she were right.'

Boycott is wanted on the phone in reception. There is a crooked Popeye grin playing across his face when he walks back across the foyer. He has just been told by Talk Radio that he has won the contract to commentate on the Cricket World Cup. I congratulate him and ask if he thinks his second career as a commentator has filled the void in his life left by cricket. 'I felt a sadness when I stopped playing. Something had come to an end. Something wonderful. I just thought, "This is it then." It was

12 September 1986. I walked off the pitch and waited for the ground to clear. Then I wandered around on my own among all the newspapers and food wrappers and tin cans. It didn't feel like a death exactly but I did think a part of my life was finished.' But he has never picked up a bat since. 'I wouldn't even do it for the Queen of England. Not even the Queen of England.'

What about for a million pounds?

'No. I'd just make a fool of myself. I have no intention of doing that. I have too much respect for the game. That would be taking the money for the fucking hell of it. I couldn't live with myself. It would just be shit.'

He says goodbye and runs off across the car park, his shoulders hunched against the rain. As I watch him get into his silver BMW a child's voice in my head whispers, 'I've just met Boycott. *The* Geoffrey Boycott. Folklore, legend, myth.'

Woody Allen

To meet Woody Allen in London is to meet a man violently out of context. Imagine stubbing your toe on the Statue of Liberty while out walking the dog on Tooting Common and you grasp the scale of the incongruity. He belongs in New York, he's synonymous with the place; as he says at the beginning of *Manhattan* (1979), it's his town.

I once saw him there, wearing a baseball cap and a lumberjack shirt, marching towards me across a bridge in Central Park. It was six in the morning – I couldn't sleep – there was no one else around and I was nonchalant about the encounter until the moment he had passed, at which point I began stalking him. A film crew appeared on the opposite side of the lake, he joined them, and so, surreptitiously, did I – and spent the next few hours staring at him, slack-jawed, as he set up shots, played chess with his sound engineer and ate corn muffins. How could I not? For the past three decades he has made a film a year and I, anorak that I am, have them all on video, *in chronological order*. I even have that series of wilfully beige and morose films he did in homage to Bergman – *September, Alice, Another Woman, Interiors* – the ones which nobody likes, including me.

In Central Park he was focused and energetic, but cold in the way he directed his actors. In London, by contrast, sitting on the edge of a large sofa in the Dorchester, his 5ft 7in frame seems almost out of focus: slight, spavined, his edges blurred despite the neatly pressed creases in his cream trousers, blue shirt and white vest. It is to do with the paleness of his eyelashes, his freckled skin, his thinning wires of hair and his right eye which,

43

behind black-rimmed glasses, looks lazy and sore. It's also to do with the way he holds himself. When I ask a question, he cocks his head to one side and leans forward so far he almost slides off the cushion. 'I-I-I'm sorry,' he says softly, with that cracked, reedy, much-impersonated Brooklyn-accented stutter. 'My hearing is dropping a little in my left ear. This is hereditary. I listen keenly and I read lips. If people's lips are covered, or I take my glasses off, I don't hear as well.'

I'd been asking him about the ills the flesh is heir to. He is sixty-six, a good age, presumably, for a hypochondriac? 'Yes, everything falls apart. You, er, you lose your hair and your faculties, and you eventually get a disease from which you do not recover.' He folds his arms defensively. 'I've always thought [pronounced *to-wart*] I was falling apart anyway, but as I get older it becomes a more realistic fear.'

Fear: it's been said that since 11 September we've all become Woody Allens. He and Soon-Yi, his wife, live with their two adopted children in a $17 million, five-storey Georgian town house on the Upper East Side of Manhattan. He was in his kitchen when the planes crashed into the towers. As he has always rhapsodized about the New York skyline in his films, did the attack feel almost personal? 'It was a shock,' he says with a wheezy, nervous laugh. 'Such random slaughter. But not a surprise. We always thought that terrorism would show up in one of our cities. But the government was caught napping when it did.'

Before he began shooting his latest film, *The Curse of the Jade Scorpion*, he sued Jean Doumanian, his producer and one of his oldest and closest friends. Allen claimed Doumanian cheated him out of profits – thought to be about $15 million – from his last eight movies. In July she counter-sued, claiming that a 'self indulgent' Allen squandered her company's money by demanding a large salary, chauffeur-driven cars, rooms at five-star hotels, private jets and a fifty per cent slice of his films' profits. Hasn't he been put off going to court after his ordeals in the early 1990s (when he and Mia Farrow were involved in a bitter, bitter custody case)? 'Er, no. No, I'm a normal citizen and if there are matters that have to be solved in court I go to court. No.'

When Mia Farrow, his leading actress in several films and his long-time companion, came across pornographic Polaroids he had taken of her (not his) 21-year-old adopted daughter Soon-Yi, she went berserk. According to Allen, Farrow had threatened to kill him and commit suicide – she had also sent him a Valentine's card pierced with knives and skewers. Vindictively, it seemed (or protectively, depending on your sympathies), Farrow brought a child abuse charge against Allen (relating to another adopted daughter, Dylan). The police were compelled to investigate, they put together a 200-page report, and Allen took a lie detector test. He counter-sued, ran up legal fees of $7 million and eventually won and lost: all allegations of abuse were dismissed, he married Soon-Yi in 1997, but was banned from seeing Dylan and his natural son Satchel. The judge said Allen was 'the most opaque of narcissists', and added that 'you don't have a clue about the needs of your children.' Since the separation, Farrow has adopted four more children – she already had eleven – and has damned Allen in her autobiography (recording that his neurotic solipsism was such that he needed weeks with his analyst before agreeing to change the bedsheets from polyester satin to cotton).

Does he now regret the scorched earth policy he adopted with Mia Farrow in the courts? 'I, I, I wouldn't know what you meant by scorched earth policy.' I elaborate. 'Ah, OK. It was big and messy and it could have been handled better and had better consequences. But I didn't have any choice. I was put in that position and I had to respond. Normally I like to handle everything quietly and discreetly and I'm a, you know, a friendly and forgiving private type. But I will always . . . There are certain situations where you are forced to act.' He shakes his head. 'It was a terrible, terrible, terrible situation. My not having access to the children is completely cruel and unfair. Not in their best interests. But these dreadful things happen in life. To balance that I had parents with good longevity [his father lived to a hundred, his mother ninety-five]. I've been healthy. I've been blessed with a talent.'

What effect did the scandal have in terms of his commercial success? 'None! I've never had any success commercially! Never.' Now, now. It's not quite true. He had box office successes with his two Oscar-winning films *Annie Hall* (1977) and *Hannah and Her Sisters* (1986). 'No. *Annie Hall* was the smallest earning

Oscar-winning film in the history of the movies. People always ask me, "Why don't you do any more of those early funny films?" Well, my first, *Take the Money and Run* (1969), I made for $1 million and it got great reviews and ten years later it still had not broken even.'

Woody Allen's films may go unnoticed in America, but in Italy, France and Britain they have a devoted following. 'In Europe I'm idolized, it's true. I walk down the street and they shake my hand and throw flowers and kiss me. In the United States I'm a bum. It mystifies me.' He rubs his hands together; hunches his shoulders; gulps. 'I've had this conversation a million times with my producers. They sit me down and say, "What is it? Is it that you are in these films?" Then I would make *The Purple Rose of Cairo* (1985) and not be in it and it would still not do any real business. And they would say, "Maybe it is that they only want to see you as this neurotic New York intellectual type." So I would make a film like *Crimes and Misdemeanors* (1989) and it would not do great business, and then they would say, "Maybe they want to see you in something different, your films are too alike." So I would make *Manhattan Murder Mystery* (1993) and I still don't get a decent sized audience.' He blinks repeatedly and nods to himself. 'Maybe the problem is that my films are like Chinese food. There is no real similarity between an egg roll and spare ribs but in the end it is all Chinese food.'

In 1998 Allen said to *Newsweek*: 'If my films don't make a profit I know I'm doing something right.' Doesn't he take a perverse delight in the fact that they aren't commercial? 'No, I don't delight in it. It would make my life a lot easier if they made money. But I do feel that if you are succeeding all the time you are doing something wrong.'

He claims that failure has dogged his career. But after dropping out of New York University, where he studied film, he found early success as a gag writer for Sid Caesar. He then became a successful cabaret comedian, one of his jokes being that he was kicked out of NYU for cheating in a metaphysics exam. He had looked within the soul of the boy sitting next to him. 'When I was a nightclub comic I used to get these great reviews and club owners would pay me a very substantial salary,' he says. 'But then they would see that half the house was empty. They would have to move these big, potted palm-trees around so that the room looked fuller.'

Dr Johnson believed that all censure of a man's self is oblique praise and this seems to apply to Woody Allen. He talks himself down but only as a strategy, because he so clearly has confidence in his own abilities. And though he has often cast himself as a self-doubting loser in his films, it has always been as an endearing one. He claims his films aren't autobiographical, of course. Yet the characters he plays invariably share his neuroses and phobias – most of which are genuine, apparently. He prefers darkness and rain to sunshine. He is so claustrophobic he has on occasion taken a hundred-mile diversion rather than cross a bridge or go through a tunnel. He has a morbid fear of dogs and deer and a thing about bright colours – which is why he, and the characters he plays, nearly always dress blandly, in green and brown corduroy. And there are enough examples of his own life overlapping with his characters' to make his claim seem disingenuous. In 1973, for instance, he became convinced he had a brain tumour, as his character does in *Hannah and Her Sisters*. Or consider the grimly ironic *Husbands and Wives* (1992) in which his character leaves Mia Farrow's character for a 21-year-old. Tellingly, he slips into the first person when talking about the characters he plays: 'I never went back to Hannah.' Or: 'Julia left me in that movie.'

Can he understand why people assume his films are autobiographical? He coughs into his hand and grins crookedly. 'Right, right. I think what it is, is that the sensibility is me. The character I am playing has hypochondria and he obsesses about his life and his mortality and he fails in his relations and, in that respect, it is me, because that is what I do in my off-screen hours. But the details of the movies are, ninety-nine per cent of the time, made up. Once in a while there will be something that comes up, like the concept of the brain tumour you mentioned, but that is so exaggerated compared to my real life that it may as well be made up. In real life I'm productive. I'm not totally incompetent. I get up in the morning. I'm not a little weakling – I was a good athlete when I was younger. I work at the typewriter. I practise my clarinet [he still plays with his New Orleans Jazz Band every Monday night at The Carlyle Hotel in New

York]. I'm able to make films and run my film company.' He smiles wanly. 'You know, I-I-I I'm not the character in *Deconstructing Harry* (1997). This guy had a writer's block, I've never had a writer's block in my life. I wouldn't know what it meant. This guy was seeing whores, he can't stop his alcohol, he kidnapped his child. These are things I couldn't and wouldn't do, but people think, "So that is how he lives".'

What about when his character contemplates suicide in *Hannah and Her Sisters*? Was that based on experience? 'Not really, no. I would be too afraid to kill myself. I would never contemplate suicide.' He touches his glasses. 'No, that's not quite true. I have contemplated it in the sense that the thought has occurred to me, but that would never have translated into action. I would be too frightened – that is the only reason – to buy a gun and shoot myself.'

I only ask because he is a notorious pessimist and depressive who has been visiting psychiatrists for most of his adult life. 'I have stopped seeing a psychiatrist now,' he says nasally. 'It's very hard to have a good relationship, and I didn't for most of my life. Now, though, I am very, very happily married and that has been a wonderful thing for me and I've got great kids. But, for me, when you get happy then you start to get these awful existential thoughts. When a guy is lonely or miserable he just thinks, "What will I do to meet a girl tonight?" But when you find you are happy with a lovely wife only then do you realize what is in store for you – it is going to end somehow. You are going to die.'

So the trick is to keep yourself as miserable as possible? 'No, my antidote is always to rush to work and blot out these thoughts by distracting myself. Film-making for me is like therapy, like basket-weaving or finger-painting in a mental institution. When I'm not doing that I make sure I watch baseball or basketball or I play my clarinet. If I don't distract myself I know I will get depressed and anxious and give in to morbid introspection.'

He is terrified of being left alone with his thoughts? 'Yes. There have been times when I would buy a newspaper or a magazine prior to a five-flight elevator ride because I didn't want to be alone with my thoughts in the elevator for thirty seconds.'

Must be exhausting being him. 'Let me tell you, when I go for a walk in Central Park on a beautiful day I have to set myself mental tasks, prepare a speech, think about casting. Otherwise I know I will want to run up to people and shake them and say, "Why are you bothering to sunbathe? What is the point of your pregnant belly? Why are you walking your dog? Toward what end? We're all going to die one day. Am I the only one who sees it? Am I the only person in the concentration camp who knows what is going on behind that big hedge?"' He spreads his arms, fingers splayed. 'I will look around the park and think, "We can cut to this scene a hundred years from now and all these people will be dead." Every hundred years a big toilet will have flushed and a new group of people will be in their place. The Islamic fundamentalists, the baseball players, the beautiful models, everybody who is here now will be gone. All gone. You and me. It is hard to combat this thought. It's constantly nagging at me. Our seemingly busy, busy lives ultimately mean nothing in this cruel and hostile universe.'

Poor Woody Allen: he sounds sincere but, because he has had so much comic mileage from his angst over the years – bleak despair combined with Jewish wisecracking – it is hard to take him seriously on the subject. Does he find this reaction frustrating? 'Look, I, I, er, I don't make jokes about these things deliberately. I just saw one day that that was my response to them. I don't think, "If I make people laugh or make myself laugh that will alleviate the problem." I can make jokes, that's all. I've always been able to. It is an awful gift.'

One of my favourite Woody Allen lines is: 'If only God would give me a clear sign. Like making a large deposit in my name at a Swiss bank.' I ask him why he can't take Thomas Carlyle's advice and just 'accept the universe'? 'If I tell you that someone at some point is going to come and shoot you and your wife it's hard to live with it. It's a very disquieting feeling. It's unnerving. You can't breathe easily and relax. I find it impossible to do.'

We're all born astride the grave but surely he has a form of immortality through his films. 'Yes, but as I have said before, it would be nice to live on in the hearts and minds of my audience but I'd rather live on in my apartment.'

I tell him I find his gloomy disposition in real life at odds with the tone of his films, which is often funny, romantic and charming. He presents his audience with these dark existential dilemmas then offers a diversion from them, a consolation: love, he often seems to be saying, is the answer to the question, 'What meaning can there be to life when death is the end of it?' 'Yes, that is the best you can do. I agree with you. To say, "I love you" is the nicest thing, the most meaningful thing you can do in life. That is why my priorities in life are my children and my wife, not my movies. But this is cold comfort. When I'm with my wife and children I think, "This is so impermanent. There will come a point where we have to say goodbye. Love is the best you can do *but it's just not good enough*! It's too little too late. People should be angry instead. Angry at the whole deal."' He pats my arm and grins lopsidedly: 'I hope I'm not depressing you.'

Even as a child, Woody Allen – born Allan Konigsberg – was visited by what he called the bluebird of unhappiness. 'Even as a young child, yes. There was a dark cloud over my head in the cradle.' He was a lonely boy – his sister Letty was born when he was eight – who usually ate alone. His earliest memories are of Nettie and Martin, his volatile parents, arguing. 'They stayed together out of spite. Did everything short of exchange gunfire.' Their arguments were usually about money. Martin, who worked in a poolroom, was a spendthrift, Nettie was frugal. The young Woody would escape the tension by sitting in his room teaching himself conjuring tricks (he became an accomplished amateur magician and at one point considered making a living as a card sharp).

He got married for the first time when he was twenty – to Harlene Rosen, who was three years younger. After six years, the marriage ended in acrimony. Allen had taken to joking about Harlene in public: 'It was my wife's birthday, so I bought her an electric chair. Told her it was a hair dryer.' His second marriage, to actress Louise Lasser, lasted three years, ending in 1969. His longest friendship/relationship has been with Diane Keaton, the Californian actress who monopolized the female leads in his early films. She was his live-in companion for three years in the 1970s and when they split up they remained close friends. They still speak on the phone nearly every day and she is, he says, the only person whose critical opinion he really cares about.

He once joked that he never trusts a woman until she rejects him, yet he has always been successful with women, beautiful women at that. Why does he think this is? 'I never have been.' Do I have to list them? 'OK, but very few. I had a wonderful wife in Louise Lasser and I'm friendly with her to this day. And Diane and I remain very close. Mia I had a bad time with but I had some very nice times with her, too.' Does he speak to her now? 'No, I don't, because it ended too sourly. But I thought she was beautiful and a good actress and in many ways a good person, too. In other ways I had bitter disagreements with her. So, yes, I have had some good relationships in my life but I always thought that when I finally became what I always wanted to be, which is attractive to women, it was too late.' He laughs a laugh that turns into a cough. 'It was only after I was married, happily married and devoted to Soon-Yi, and older, in my sixties, only then did I sense that when I met beautiful women I could, you know, think, "Gee, I could really have a chance with this woman. I could really have an affair with her or go to bed with her." And I never had that feeling before. It's when you're off the market, I guess.'

I'm sure it is, but could it also possibly be because he is a powerful figure in the film world? As Henry Kissinger said, power is the great aphrodisiac. 'Yes, it's possible that all that melds together. I'm a film director and there might be a reason to cultivate a relationship with me because they will get something out of it. But really, you know, I have had a below average record with women.'

A sense of humour, of course, is also a great aphrodisiac. Is there anyone he hasn't been able to win over, eventually, with his relentless joking and banter? 'Yes, the American people.' And on a one-to-one basis? 'I think when people meet me and talk to me they find me a reasonable person. Not a nasty egomaniac. Interesting on arts and sports and on the good side politically – liberal, you know. I don't think I put people off one-to-one, just on a mass scale.'

Some who have worked with Woody Allen might disagree with his analysis. 'Manipulative' and 'self-centred' are two descriptions that have cropped up when his former colleagues have been asked to describe him. 'The last person to accept blame' is another. And, though he has seemed cheerful and engaged enough in this interview, the words which are most often used about him are: reclusive, melancholy and detached. For his part, he considers himself to be drab and once said he felt sorry for his analyst because, 'Whenever I am on the couch, I bore on like an accountant.' Self-loathing, of course, is not incompatible with self-belief and tellingly, in the biographical documentary *Wild Man Blues* (1997), he talked of a chronic sense of dissatisfaction with himself: 'I don't want to be where I am at any given moment. When I'm in New York, I want to be in Europe. When in Europe, I want to be in New York.'

He never watches his old films and claims he hasn't read any of the forty or so books written about him. 'I don't want to waste time thinking about myself,' he says. 'And if I watch my own movies I only see what I could have done better.' Most directors take about four years to make a film. Allen is able to bring out one a year because, in the past at least, he has always managed to find indulgent patrons to back him – and give him complete autonomy over scripts and production. Also it only takes him between one and three months to write a script. This is followed by eight weeks of pre-production and three months' shooting. To his regret, though, he feels he has never made a *great* film – by which he means a *Citizen Kane*, *Bicycle Thieves*, or *Wild Strawberries* – and some of his films, such as *Manhattan* and *Hannah and Her Sisters*, he actually hates. Has he considered taking more time over his film-making, devoting five years to one project, say, in order to make what he might consider to be a great film? 'I don't think I could do it because when I finish with a script, even if I've written it in six weeks, I think it is the best I can do. I don't think, "If I coddle it for a year I might be able to improve it." I think, *"This is great."* I'm completely un-critical of myself as a writer. But when I translate the script to the screen my slovenliness takes over. When I see what I wind up with I think, "Where did it go wrong? I missed by ninety per cent." It's maybe lack of perfectionism or dedication. When it gets difficult I give up. I don't do enough takes and I only do these long master shots all the time because I don't have the patience for close-ups. People think it's a deliberate style of mine, but it's really just laziness.'

He's praising himself obliquely again. An indolent man could not make a film a year. Nor would a lazy man be rushing round the world promoting his latest film – he has just flown in from Venice, to be out of context here in London, and is just about to fly off to Paris. He looks around the room, points at himself, raises his eyebrows and says: 'Me?' He grins. 'Know something? I'm so lazy, if I get a really good idea but it has to be shot in Texas I throw the idea away – *just because I live in New York!'*

John Redwood

The aromatic whiff of a log fire and the sound of shoes crunching up a gravelled drive are all that disturb the drizzly Saturday afternoon air in this secluded, woody enclave of Berkshire. It is growing dark and the glow from the sturdy thirties redbrick house is welcoming. So, too, is the trim, fine-featured chatelaine with the twinset and silver-blonde bob who appears in the porch and opens the front door before there is need of a knock.

'I think there's one toasted tea cake left,' Gail Redwood says as she leads the way past a row of waxed jackets, around her husband's furry, clown-size reindeer-head slippers (a novelty Christmas present), and on into the drawing room. 'And there should still be a tolerable cup of tea in the pot.'

As P.G. Wodehouse might have said, if not actually disconcerting, this scene of charming domesticity is far from being concerting. For a question mark hangs over it like a bruised cloud: why on earth are the Redwoods inviting a journalist – *a journalist*, for goodness sake – into their gracious home for a rare and privileged glimpse of their soft furnishings? After all, the Majors never allow anyone within a hundred yards of their log fire in Huntingdon; the Blairs do, but only as far as the office at the back of their house in Sedgefield. The answer is obvious; and even more so when the 45-year-old Right Honourable Member for Wokingham – and leader of the Eurosceptic Tory right, since his challenge to John Major a couple of years ago – heaves into view.

He is looking casual (in slightly faded blue cords, open-neck shirt and woolly, speckled, cream pullover) and relaxed – or at least trying to look relaxed, because he has a gangly body and at first, as he stands by the fire, its language seems a little self-conscious. Perhaps to give his hands something to do, he turns and throws a log on to the fire, making it spit and crackle. More likely, though, he does this in order to offer a glimpse of the human face of a politician who has suffered more than most from accusations of appearing too cold, too logical, too, well, extraterrestrial – for, as we know, ETs don't throw logs on fires.

The face on offer, then, is the one he would like us some day to be watching on our television sets before we tuck into our roast beef and Yorkshire puddings of a Sunday: the leader of Her Majesty's Opposition, at home, in a jumper, by a fire, reacting to the latest Blair outrage. John Redwood doesn't say this, of course, but then he doesn't need to. The remark he does open with, however, suggests that he may still have some ground to cover on the road to looking more human, more ordinary, more of the people. Above the copper fireplace, framed by the dark wood panelling of the wall, is a painting of Elizabeth I. When asked about it, Mrs Redwood makes a topical joke: 'Now, she *was* the original Spice Girl!' And we all laugh. But when Mr Redwood takes up the theme – 'Yes. Made a fortune from the Spice Islands!' – the room falls silent, a gust of wind picks up outside and from somewhere in the far distance comes the melancholy sound of a dog howling.

The comment is just too brainy, too literal-minded, too academic. And it reminds you that, from the collar up, John Redwood stands alone. This is the man who, cursed with a First in History from Oxford, made matters worse by becoming a Prize Fellow of All Souls at the age of twenty-one and, worse still, by dashing off a doctorate in Philosophy in the evenings (while working during the day as a merchant banker). This is the man who, at thirty-two, was appointed head of Mrs Thatcher's Downing Street Policy Unit and, in an idle moment, worked out how to return Britain's nationalized industries back to the private sector. This is the man who, in order to relax, plays chess with two computers, one he knows he can beat, one he is sure he can't.

And as if the bulging forehead isn't enough to live down, John Redwood has also acquired, along the way, a reputation for being socially awkward – even socially unaware, to the degree that he cannot spot a political minefield when it's staring him in the face. On that fateful Monday morning in June 1995, for instance, when Redwood launched his impromptu leadership bid, the Crazy Gang, as represented by Tony Marlow (wearing his loud striped blazer) and Teresa Gorman (goggle-eyed in her fluorescent green dress), managed to insert themselves into Redwood's overcrowded press briefing. In the confusion – and social awkwardness – of the media scrum that ensued, the maladroit Redwood allowed himself to be photographed in front of Gorman and Marlow. The flashbulbs popped and the damage to his credibility was done.

But perhaps getting into awkward places is something inhabitants of Planet Redwood do simply for their own amusement. For in the drawing room there is a long blue sofa, which seats four people, and I find myself hovering near to the end seat. As Redwood invites me to sit down, he sits down, too, in the next space. Almost touching, and with our backs deep in the upholstery, we talk for a while without making eye contact, staring at our knees instead, like two strangers on a bus. After a few minutes, I perch on the edge of my seat, swivelling round to face him, and he – gratefully, I suspect – half-turns round to do the same, one ankle tucked under the opposite knee, his head propped up on his hand. Gail Redwood comes over and tactfully occupies the acre of space at the other end of the sofa.

At close quarters, John Redwood's speaking voice is measured and subdued, in contrast to the laugh he occasionally emits – haha! – which is short and strong. But there are none of the erratic shifts of pitch that characterized the voice we so memorably heard in his leadership press conferences. As one writer put it: 'The man has an unreal use of volume and emphasis, which he unleashes on words! without warning. He speaks like a man trying to stop himself falling asleep.' Mock him though they might, even Redwood's political enemies would not deny that he is an honourable man, loyal to his party. But when John Major challenged him, and others, to 'put up or shut up' he says he found himself left with no option but to resign. 'I took that comment to mean that the views I had been expressing continuously in private were no longer acceptable. I thought, "Well, I can't live with this. I can't work in a Cabinet where I'm not allowed to say that VAT on fuel is wrong or that we're not allowed to make up our own minds on a single currency." People were saying I was radical or risky and yet I was the one sticking to traditional Conservative values and, indeed, to our 1992 manifesto pledges.'

But 'risky' is not the adjective most used about Redwood in his leadership campaign: 'scary' was. Indeed, his cold intellect – along with his inscrutable, lupine features and quizzical eyebrows – earned him the nickname Vulcan, after the home planet of the emotionally challenged *Star Trek* hero, Mr Spock. At first, Redwood says endearingly, he didn't understand the joke, then a friend explained it to him and he found it funny. But to this day there still seems to be some confusion in Redwood's mind as to who Vulcans are and what they stand for. Thus:

Mr Redwood: 'I took it to mean that they didn't have any dirt on me and, because to err is human, I couldn't have come from this planet, but from another one. It was a backhanded compliment.'

Mrs Redwood (perhaps thinking about dead sheep or Welsh windbags): 'There are a lot worse things you can say about a politician!'

Mr Redwood: 'Yes, I don't think staying cool under pressure, keeping a clear head, is a fault in one who might be called upon to lead. Of course you have to understand how people feel about things as well. It was very mischievous of some journalists to suggest I don't have passions and feelings. I do have a sentimental side. I can be moved by classical music, for instance, although not to tears.'

Mrs Redwood: 'No, it's films that make John weep! He was in floods when we watched *Shadowlands* and *The Remains of the Day*!'

Mr Redwood checks his side parting with his hand, folds him arms, hunches his shoulders, and mumbles a few words of admiration for Sir Anthony Hopkins before taking the passion theme down a less personal route: 'I feel very passionately about the need to preserve a self-governing democracy in this country . . .' Alongside the sofa is a grandfather clock which the Redwoods commissioned, complete with a carved acorn, the symbol of Wokingham, on top. As Redwood's patriotic theme is developed, the grandfather clock announces that it is five o'clock and in so doing reveals itself to have the same arrangement of chimes as Big Ben.

'. . . and British identity is related to our lives together as a very successful people that has always been on the right side . . .' Ding-dong-ding-dong! Dong-ding-dong-ding! '. . . a people that has always gone to war to resist tyranny. British identity is related to one sovereign . . .' Bong! '. . . one church . . .' Bong! '. . . one parliament . . .' Bong! '. . . one set of laws . . .' Bong! '. . . and the English language . . .' Bong!

That's Vulcan humour for you – or so it would be nice to think, for Redwood, with the insouciance of the comic, gives no hint as to whether he is aware of the chimes that so affectingly accompany his speech. A more glaring example of Vulcan behaviour emerged on the Thursday that John Major resigned as leader. Westminster and Fleet Street went into a frenzy trying to find out whether Redwood would stand against him. For four days Redwood exhibited disturbingly alien cool: not bothering to answer his phone; nonchalantly choosing instead to play village cricket. Had the man no nervous system? 'Although I felt calm,' he now says, 'I agonized and agonized and agonized for those four days – apart from during the cricket match on the Sunday when I could switch off completely and enjoy the game. I went strawberry-picking on the Saturday, but they didn't spot me! Haha! I didn't make up my mind until I spoke to the Prime Minister on the Monday morning – he didn't seem to want to talk very much and I thought it was a time that maybe a conversation would have been a good idea.'

The Vulcan nickname, of course, owes much to his dogged love of logic. From 1973 to 1987, for instance, he worked in the City, first at Flemings, then at Rothschilds, places where employees often stay late regardless of whether they have deals to do. 'I used to work very hard,' Redwood remembers. 'I concentrated, got my work done and left at 5.30 p.m. on the dot because that's what my contract said. Yet colleagues used to criticize me for it.' He doesn't seem to see why. Any more than he sees the inadequacy of his answer to the unoriginal but morally imperative question about his support for capital punishment:

hypothetically, would he be prepared to pull the lever himself? Although the answer he gives doesn't actually start with a 'But that's illogical, Captain' it is, nevertheless, a response Spock would be proud of. 'I have no intention of applying to be a public hangman. I can see no circumstances in which I would have to do it or be expected to do it.' Try again. Surely, given his academic training, he can offer a sophisticated justification of the death penalty on moral or utilitarian grounds? 'Can I? My main reason for supporting capital punishment is that most of my electors do.' And again. Just because a lot of people believe something, doesn't make it right. 'No. But then it doesn't conflict with my view.'

Sometimes, though, a Vulcan's logical mind can get to the heart of an issue more efficiently than can the woolly, obfuscatory mind of an Earthling. Redwood, for instance, was the first to start referring to the innocuous sounding 'single currency' as the 'abolition of the pound', a phrase which has since entered the language and which, with its brutal clarity, brought home to a lot of people what a single currency actually means. Again, for many people, Redwood put his finger on the exact cause of the Church of England's current malaise when he said that it seemed embarrassed about its spiritual and moral role in the community. By contrast, John – and Gail – Redwood are anything but embarrassed about their enthusiasm for Christian family values. 'You can't trust people who say they believe in family values if they are doing the opposite at home,' Mrs Redwood says in a soft level voice. 'It would be so crass, so hypocritical.'

The couple met in the first week of their first term at Oxford and, although Gail Redwood says she doesn't think it was love at first sight, she does add, with a wry tilt of the head, 'Oh, I suppose it was fairly soon after.' Mrs Redwood is refreshingly scornful of the expectation that a politician's wife, even one who qualified as a barrister, should be seen but not heard at Conservative Party functions: 'Nothing worse than being introduced to people who make superficial conversation with you because they think you won't have anything interesting to say,' she says with a peeved arch of the eyebrow. Even so, she is – and John Redwood must know she is – a 'secret weapon' to rival even the Prime Minister's wife. For she combines the down-to-earth modesty and charm of a Norma Major – she will say, for instance, that she never has time to think about clothes and isn't even sure where the clothes she is wearing came from – with the high-powered career of a Cherie Blair (Gail is Company Secretary of British Airways, as well as being a mother to Catherine and Richard, the couple's two teenage children).

Drifting across the hall from Redwood's study is the sound of a television showing highlights from the Scotland v Wales rugby match. We are still sitting on the blue sofa and, as he pops into the study to hear the final score, I cajole him into admitting who he wants to win. With disarming honesty he says: 'Oh, I don't really care now that I'm no longer Secretary of State for Wales.' Then, pulling himself together, he adds: 'Oh, I suppose Wales!' A chance to examine the bookshelves in Redwood's study reveals few surprises: lots of history books, half a dozen video tapes of Commons debates, the odd book on wildlife and butterflies and countless volumes with titles so dull they swim before the eyes, blurring into one big, bedtime read from Hell: *Inflation; Nationalized Industries; Privatisation: Theory and Practice; Foreign Exchange Rates . . .*

Apart from a small Welsh coat of arms hanging up in an alcove, there is little evidence of John Redwood's time in the Principality. Dafydd Wigley, President of Plaid Cymru, once said that Redwood 'went down like a rat sandwich in Wales'. Presumably the feeling was mutual, given reports that Redwood only stayed one night in Wales during the first five months of his office, preferring instead to commute back to Berkshire. (He said at the time that he was the first politician to be criticized for wanting to sleep with his own wife – a pretty good and pretty human joke.)

But perhaps the real reason Redwood has so few tokens of Wales is that they remind him of the buttock-clenching moment he was caught on camera trying and failing to mouth the words to the Welsh national anthem. Although he was considered to have been a firm but fair Welsh Secretary, even his best friends could not claim that he ever really empathized with the Welsh people. 'The reason they said that was that I had no time for Welsh nationalism and I didn't learn the language,' Redwood says when this is put to him. 'I took a decision at the beginning that I was not going to have time to learn it to a high enough standard – and there is nothing worse than an Englishman wrecking the language. It was better to be honest.' Even so, Eric Howells, Tory chairman in Wales, once observed that Redwood has trouble relating to ordinary people. 'Well that is wrong,' Redwood tells me. 'I see myself as coming from the market-place.'

While it is true that his father was an accounts clerk and his mother a shop manageress, there is something a bit patrician about Redwood's manner. It is almost as if he, like Coriolanus, is secretly contemptuous of the many-headed multitude, as if his nature is too noble for the world. He doesn't see it this way, though. Indeed, he prides himself on his patriotic, Euro-bashing, hang-'em-high populism ('What's wrong with having popular views?' he says. 'I'm a democrat, for Heaven's sake!') But doesn't he empathize with Coriolanus just a little bit? 'No!' Redwood laughs. 'I did learn some of my politics from Coriolanus. And Macbeth. But I could never be Coriolanus. He is far too certain. I want to shake him and say, "Who the hell do you think you are? Get down there, boy, and talk to the people."' The thought is interrupted as Joe, the Redwoods' well-fed cat, ambles over for a stroke.

The grandfather clock chimes 7.30 p.m. and the Redwoods show me the corner of the drawing room they have devoted to watercolours of Oxford. In another corner there is a tape and CD collection which mostly features the sort of classical recordings that move John Redwood (though not to tears). There are quite a few middle-of-the-road tapes – Kate Bush, Elton John, Neil Diamond, Cliff Richard – and a rather alarming number of recordings of Andrew Lloyd Webber musicals. The most up-to-date album seems to be by Beverley Craven.

But there are no tapes by Lightning Seeds, which is surprising given that John Redwood once wrote an article for the *Guardian* in praise of them and other Britpop bands like Oasis, Blur and Supergrass. 'For me to be writing about Britpop,' it began, 'might seem about as likely as John Prescott writing an article on how much he appreciates the Latin verse of Virgil.' Much to the chagrin of Lightning Seeds, Redwood went on to quote their lyrics ('Everything's blue now, oh lucky you . . . there's nothing to lose') saying that it was a message to Tories. The *Guardian* columnist Matthew Norman, who had suggested the article, made it his mission in life to discover the boundaries of Redwood's Britpop knowledge. (Norman regularly rang him up to test him. And, even though Redwood lists one of his recreations as 'not reading the *Guardian*', and even though he knew he was being teased, he always played along, answering Norman's pop trivia questions as best he could. Norman believes that, had he not pushed his luck too far one day by calling Redwood out of an important meeting just so that he could ask whether the Smurfs could ever recover from the defection of Father Abraham, Redwood might still be the *Guardian*'s youth culture correspondent to this day.)

A cynic would say that, of course, this is what you'd expect from a politician who's trying to get elected: be human, not Vulcan; be normal, not desiccated; show you have a sense of humour, not that you are stuffed to the gills with serious purpose. A cynic would say that this is why he tells me he painted the ochre walls of his drawing room himself and that, since moving into the house three years ago, he has become quite handy at DIY. And that is why he says that, although he enjoys decorating, he prefers to unwind by chopping logs (like Gladstone, curiously enough). This is why he says he likes to do his own shopping at the supermarket and why, when the question that floored George Bush – Do you know the price of a pound of butter? – is tried on him, he has a ready answer. 'No, I don't because I don't buy butter. I buy Olivio. See! I even know the brand name!'

But the cynic would be wrong. John Redwood really does seem to enjoy doing these things. He does have a hinterland. The jumper isn't just for show. And, contrary to one's expectations, he is quite wry. On one wall of the dining room next door there are half a dozen large cartoons that chart the history of Redwood's political career. One shows John Major as a weathervane dressed in lederhosen with Helmut Kohl as the menacing raincloud overhead. Two depict John Redwood naked: one, captioned LOVE LOCKED OUT, shows him standing forlornly in front of Number 10; the other depicts him as The Thinker. 'I don't know why I always have to be naked in these,' Redwood says.

'I'm surprised they know what I look like without clothes on. As far as I know, it's never been revealed.' Again, not a bad joke.

Have these cartoons of a naked Redwood – a little vulnerable and innocent, perhaps, but with a certain moral purity and openness – got it right? He tells me that he believes he is not a calculating politician but one who acts on instinct. Perhaps the truth lies between the two: that he is a canny politician. After all, he did come away from the leadership challenge looking more courageous than Portillo and less treacherous than Heseltine. ('I wasn't an assassin because John Major put his job on the line. He invited a contest. As soon as I lost, I went on TV and said, "I admit defeat, long live John Major." You couldn't do more than that. I think that the party was sympathetic to me because I had done all in my power to have a decent, honest contest.')

And decent, honest contestants – like nice guys – often finish last, even if they lose romantically. On the opposite wall, above a mantelpiece with a bust of Beethoven on it, there is an exquisite oil painting on wood, dated 1756, which Gail Redwood inherited from her father, an auctioneer. The painting is of that other conservative young pretender, Bonnie Prince Charlie. As a history scholar, Redwood will not need reminding what happened when, almost exactly 250 years ago, that 'king o'er the water' raised his standard. Will Bonnie Prince John be any more successful in wresting the Tory crown from the leader's head? Perhaps it is too early to ask. The painting prompts another question, though: Do you suppose Bonnie Prince Charlie really was bonnie? Redwood's answer couldn't be cannier: 'He was to those who believed in him!'

A few days after this interview appeared, just before the general election in 1997, a psychiatrist contacted me. 'You may not have realized it,' he wrote, 'but your profile of John Redwood suggests that he has a number of characteristics which match those of Asperger's Syndrome, a form of autism. The literalism, the gangly body, the social awkwardness, the lack of eye contact, the dogged love of logic . . . It's the same symptom which the US press is hinting at for Bill Gates. For those of high intelligence it is by no means disabling, and might indeed bring enormous advantage because of the single-mindedness it generates.'

Bob Monkhouse

SEPTEMBER 1998

If Bob Monkhouse had bludgeoned his own mother to death with an entrenching tool, calmly burnt down an orphanage and then experimented openly with cannibalism during a Royal Variety Performance, it is doubtful whether the poor chap's critics could have come up with stronger words of disapprobation than those they have already levelled at him over the years. 'Despicable', 'slimy' and 'chilling' are typical examples.

While it is a pretty serious crime to spend a lifetime irritating people in the name of light entertainment, surely Monkhouse never deserved to be roughed up quite as excessively as he has been in the past – or indeed, despite his recent rehabilitation as a hero of comedy, as he still sometimes is today. He's an old man now. He probably wears carpet slippers. Being cruel to him just doesn't seem funny any more.

When I meet him on an overcast late summer afternoon at his sixteenth-century redbrick farmhouse in rural Bedfordshire, he is still licking his wounds from a mauling he had received a few days earlier. 'His delivery is like being touched up by a Moonie encyclopaedia salesman,' wrote A.A. Gill. 'Every mannerism drips insincerity and smarm. It's like having margarine massaged into your hair. No, it's like wearing marzipan socks.' Gill added that he hopes he is never introduced to Bob Monkhouse in person for fear of finding him terribly nice, amusing and thoughtful. 'A loathing of his every syllable and nuance is one of the cornerstones of my critical edifice,' Gill continued. 'If I ever found I liked him, my world would collapse.'

Inevitably, when you come face to face with Monkhouse, you do find him terribly nice, amusing and thoughtful. That is his tragedy. I don't think I've ever encountered anyone who needs to be liked quite as much as this man. Nor, with the obvious exception of Lord Archer of Weston-super-Mare, anyone quite so effortlessly capable of rendering his or her public persona unlovable. On stage, Monkhouse has some of the sharpest lines you'll ever hear: 'They laughed when I said I was going to be a comedian. They're not laughing now.' Or, 'I'm a hard man to ignore. But well worth the effort.' Or, 'I'd like to die like my father, peacefully in his sleep. Not screaming like his passengers.' But he just seems to try too hard when he's telling them. He shoots his cuffs, smiles and chews too much. His quick-fire patter is too polished and hammy. At home, by contrast, he speaks slowly and croakily in a subdued and wistful voice. He seems languid, gentle and relaxed – not at all repulsive. That distinctive mole on the chin is still there, as is the permanently arched eyebrow. But instead of a dinner-jacket he wears an embroidered beach shirt, its tails untucked, its buttons undone to reveal the sort of tanned, leathery chest you would expect a 70-year-old show-business personality to have.

'The irritant factor is still there,' Monkhouse says with a sigh, as he leans toward me across a wrought-iron garden table. 'In full. Apparently. I don't get upset about bad reviews from intelligent writers. What I hate is people like A.A. Gill who attack me personally and who are blisteringly unpleasant. I inhabit that persona he rejects – and it hurts. In the same way that someone refusing to shake your hand is hurtful. And, anyway, he misses the point when he complains that I am insincere. When did I ever say I was offering sincerity? I'm not coming out and saying, "I really mean that, folks." I'm not offering exhortations to be brave or patriotic or spiritually uplifted. The only thing I'm sincere about is that I sincerely want you to laugh.'

It would take Lake Windermere dropped from the sky to dampen Monkhouse's enthusiasm for making people laugh. Writing jokes is a compulsion for him. Throw any topical subject his way and, instantaneously, he will be able to turn it into a one-liner. His photographic memory helps. As Harry Thompson, producer of *Have I Got News for You*, has said, his skill is that he knows so many old jokes he can manufacture a new one for any situation using the component parts of others. But going to the grave obsessively thinking up jokes is one thing, attempting to perform them as you go is another. Monkhouse says he used to find it depressing when old heroes of his didn't know when to retire. 'I would see Flanagan and Allen trying to cavort on stage when they were clearly close to their dotage. The lower eyelid had fallen from the eye. Their timing was out. It was painful to watch. But now I'm seventy I can understand why they did it. They had nothing to fall back on. The joy I still get from confecting comedy is extreme.'

Every profession has terrifyingly ambitious types unfettered by obvious natural ability who, nevertheless, rise by virtue of their persistence and self-belief. Journalism is full of them. The Royal Navy had Lord Mountbatten, who was so mediocre and accident-prone that the Admiralty had to keep promoting him to get him out of its way. I suspect that Bob Monkhouse is the comedy world's equivalent. That's not to say he isn't an inspired gag writer. Nor to deny that he is probably the world's leading expert on the techniques of comedy, as is clear from reading his autobiography *Crying with Laughter*. It is full of self-deprecating anecdotes, salacious gossip and analysis of comic technique. At one time or another Monkhouse has worked with nearly all the big names in post-War comedy, so he is uniquely placed to dissect their work.

Sitting in his garden, the soothing bill and coo of wood pigeons in the background, Monkhouse becomes animated. He strips jokes down to show me how they work. He explains the principles of timing, 'the rule of three', and the Arthur Askey 'check step' you should take before delivering your 'topper'. Clearly, when it comes to tinkering around under the bonnet of comedy with the, um, monkey-wrench of laughter, he is a master mechanic. The trouble is, on stage, he's never learned to make it look as if he isn't – in the way that, say, the apparently rambling, vague and amateurish Eddie Izzard does. Even Monkhouse seems to know this in his heart. 'I actually can't watch myself on television,' he says. 'Yesterday I tried to sit through a tape of a new "best of" compilation that they are making. But I couldn't watch this man.' So why has he gone on punishing himself – and

A.A. Gill – for so many years? Given that his parents assumed he could never make a decent living from his profession, it might be that in the early years he was driven by a need to prove them wrong and – an almost impossible feat, this – win their approval.

Growing up in Beckenham, Kent, the closest young Robert came to his father – 'a prematurely balding chartered accountant who had a habitual dislike of people' – was when he was struck by him so hard he had to go to hospital to be stitched. The blow had been provoked by Robert accidentally dropping his towel while stepping out of the tin bath in front of the fire. His mother was told that he had fallen off his bike and, for a while, Robert and his father were 'co-conspirators, sharing a male secret, allied in a lie that only we knew about'.

His relationship with his mother was much less comfortable. When the 21-year-old Bob married against her wishes she didn't speak to him again until he was forty-one. Prove his parents wrong Monkhouse most certainly did. He left Dulwich College in London at the age of seventeen and immediately started writing gags for such music-hall turns as Arthur Askey, Jimmy Edwards and Max Miller. National Service interrupted his budding career but he used it to his advantage by conning his way into a job at the BBC – he duped an army psychiatrist into signing a letter requesting an audition on the grounds that it would be the only cure for Corporal Monkhouse's delusional psychosis. By the late forties and early fifties Monkhouse was appearing in his own television and radio comedy programmes as well as writing material for just about every big star, from Bob Hope and Frank Sinatra to Dean Martin and Jerry Lewis.

In 1958, he starred in *Carry On Sergeant*, the first Carry On film, and would have gone on to take the Jim Dale and Roy Castle roles in subsequent films had he not been offered three times as much money to play the lead in *Dentist in the Chair* (1959), something which seemed sensible at the time but which he now regrets. His career flagged in the mid-sixties only to take off again in 1967 with *The Golden Shot*, which at its peak had sixteen million viewers. Monkhouse went through a bad patch again in 1972, when he was sacked from the programme for taking a bribe (a photography book and a Wilkinson Sword razor). He has always been an obsessive collector – or rather hoarder – of things, from stamps to tins of food and old films. This obsession brought him to his lowest point: he was arrested in 1978 for conspiracy to defraud film companies by illegally importing films for his private collection (he was subsequently cleared of all charges).

In the eighties, Monkhouse hosted a string of game shows but by then he had become lumped in the public imagination with Jimmy Tarbuck, Frank Carson and Jim Davidson, the old school of unreconstructed and unfunny television stars. 'I thought I'd had my day,' he says, shaking his head at the memory. 'My career had slowed down. They'd cancelled *The 64 Million Dollar Question* and *Bob's Your Uncle*. There was nothing for me at the BBC. It depressed me. Briefly.' Then in 1993, against everyone's advice, he was interviewed for Radio 4's *In the Psychiatrist's Chair*, and everything changed. He cut a sympathetic figure. He was asked to write an autobiography; it became a bestseller. He appeared on *Have I Got News for You*, presented himself as a dry and poker-faced wit, and stole the show. Stephen Fry said how much he had always admired him, and his reinvention was complete.

Today, at seventy, Monkhouse has never been more in demand: presenting the Lottery, hosting *Wipeout*, a daytime quiz show, and packing out theatres again as a stand-up. An armchair psychiatrist might devise a theory about how Monkhouse, a comedian who can't stand watching himself, was driven masochistically by the need to win parental approval. But this won't quite wash. He seems to crave attention and admiration from everyone. And egomaniacs are often full of self-doubt. You can tell he's only half-joking when he describes himself as a shallow, selfish, cowardly liar. 'I'm aware of my own inadequacies but I'm not tortured by them,' he says with a shrug. 'I know that I've been a fool and made some stupid decisions in the past. As a performer I wish I had had a dark side. But tyranny was not within my compass. All I have is a perky mind. Not a mind of any depth. Which is another source of regret. I'm superficial. Skittering around on the surface all the time. I wish I had done a degree. Even sociology would have done.'

I had always thought the thing that set Bob Monkhouse apart from just about every other successful comedian you can think of was that he seemed so boringly sane and calculating. (Think how unbalanced Tony Hancock, Kenneth Williams and Benny Hill were. And look at John Cleese, Stephen Fry and Ken Dodd. Cuckoo to a man.) Now I'm not so sure. Neither is Monkhouse. 'Am I mad?' he asks. 'I don't know. It depends on your definition. Not mad. Just silly. And that's probably been my saving grace. Being silly. That's probably the nicest thing about me. I'm soppy, juvenile and I have a light heart. I'm desperately affected by emotions. But I have no angst.'

Another saving grace may be that he is too thick-skinned to develop a persecution complex or to wallow in melancholy. 'Self-pity is as habit-forming, corrosive to the spirit and delusory as any narcotic,' he believes. 'You have to concentrate on its absurdity and mock it out of your mind.' At school he had an obesity problem caused by a dodgy thyroid (it was later successfully treated). When he was mocked about it ('Fatty Arbuckle') he wouldn't get upset, he'd just withdraw into his own world and draw cartoons. His work was published by the *Beano* and *Dandy* while he was a schoolboy.

He still sees things in simple cartoon terms. 'It's a lovely way to see the world. If you can get away with it.' He says that he is constitutionally incapable of worry and that he nearly always feels happy. 'And sometimes I wonder whether I shouldn't shut up about it, because that might awaken a great deal of irritation and envy in itself.' A sunny disposition can be a defence mechanism against pain, though – albeit a healthy form of denial. In the past, Monkhouse has been so repressed mentally, he has reacted to traumatic events physically. When his grandfather died, the ten-year-old Robert lost the ability to speak for three months and was afterwards left with a stutter. He and his first wife had four stillborn babies before Gary was born in 1951. Gary had cerebral palsy, and Monkhouse began suffering from blinding migraine attacks which continued until Gary died in 1992.

When his wife went into labour with their next child, Monkhouse was so apprehensive he developed a strange burping complaint and thought he was going to die. (The baby was fine and the couple went on to have another healthy child and Bob stopped burping.) On one occasion while presenting *The Golden*

Shot he broke down in tears as he read out a letter sent in by a blind elderly widow who needed £20 to replace her beloved radio, stolen by thieves. Later in the same show, someone made him laugh and this turned into a bout of uncontrollable giggling that lasted for more than half a minute.

Has he trained his agile brain to be shallow and his outlook to be permanently happy for fear of falling victim to the dark emotional forces he suppresses? 'I had a great urge to be liked,' he says. 'I think I was absolutely two people. I was the child my parents expected me to be. Unemotional. But only because I suppressed that side of me. I became reserved. My mother saw all signs of emotion as being weak and despicable. Despicable. I would hear her speak of people who were loud or flamboyant, or who wept, with utter contempt. My father was the same: a joyless, lugubrious man. Eventually I escaped them and today I wish I could go back and embrace them and understand them and still be myself.'

He pauses and studies his fingers. 'I think I invented a facade. I didn't love the person I was. It wasn't until my first marriage failed and I fell in love with Jackie and she with me that I actually began to like myself.' Jackie had been his secretary for ten years before he married her in 1973. He describes her as being gregarious in ways which he is not, always on the phone and wanting to socialize. 'She has a more realistic view of people than I do. She says, "He isn't a very nice man; she's a bitch," and I can never see it. I'm always looking at how people react to me, not how they are themselves. Selfishness takes some strange forms.' Jackie is sixty-two, tall and blonde with apple cheeks and impossibly white teeth which she flashes when she smiles. As we are talking in the garden, she shouts across from the kitchen, 'Can I have a word, Bob?' 'Yes, darling,' he says, immediately rising and heading over to where she is standing in the doorway. I overhear her saying, 'And he was just so rude.'

When Monkhouse returns he is looking sheepish and explains that when our photographer arrived he had told him that it would be okay to have a look around the house for a suitable place to set up a shot, but that Jackie had found him upstairs in the bedroom. The photographer now emerges looking equally sheepish and begins looking for locations in the large garden instead. 'He's probably a genius,' Bob says shaking his head as he watches our man disappear from view behind a weeping willow.

Because his parents argued all the time, Bob Monkhouse hates confrontation. In the twenty-five years he has been happily married he has only had three arguments with his wife. About the same thing. He cannot keep his side of the house tidy. He snores and so the couple have separate bedrooms in different wings; they also have a shared room in the middle. With disarming candour he tells me his sex life improved recently after he started taking Viagra. 'It works after forty minutes and lasts for about ninety minutes. I'll give you one to try if you like, I've got them upstairs.'

He may now be a kind, fond and foolish seventy-year-old who says he is at the age where happiness is finding his glasses soon enough to remember what it was he wanted them for. But he is still obsessed with sex, or 'making love', as he always calls it. His memoirs were notable for their embarrassing frankness on this subject and contained a gripping account of his five-hour romp with Diana Dors and his subsequent terror when her husband, a gangster figure, found out, produced a razor and threaten to 'slit his eyeballs'. His encounter with a transsexual had an equally comic outcome: 'It was like plunging your feet into an apple-pie bed.'

Compared with what his generation got up to, the young stars of today must seem like a pretty tame bunch. 'Yes, my lot were at it all day long, as well as all night. They did it a lot more than the previous generation – they had all been too frightened of pregnancy. In my day syphilis had all but disappeared. There were various forms of reliable protection, condoms, the cap and so forth. I was fortunate with the timing. Just as I am fortunate with Viagra now.' He adopts a serious face. 'I was promiscuous. I think I did keep count. I could have said 137 at one point and virtually named them. But after a while it all seemed a bit vague. The press didn't know about what went on then and wouldn't have written about it if they did. Now, if I was on location in Manchester and I asked the porter to send a girl up to my room, the next day she would get £10,000 from the *Sun* for her story.'

Matter-of-factly he says of the serial adultery in his first marriage that he simply wasn't happy being monogamous. 'My first wife and I had only stayed together for Gary. He was the most important thing in my life for forty years.' Pause. 'I miss him so much. If he were here, he would be contentedly drawing over there with his right foot and would look at you and put his toe up to say it was okay you being here because he liked the look of you. But after an hour he would come over and tap you on the shoulder because he would think you had been here long enough. He was a martinet. But he had the personality of a star. And he was knock-down handsome. I'll show you a photo. But he could never speak nor hear nor stand or sit unaided. I would sit and talk to him for hours in that room there.' He points to a downstairs window. 'He couldn't hear me but I felt I could confide everything to him. He loved it and he would hug me with his legs.'

Gary Monkhouse was brought up at home but when his condition worsened he became a resident at his choice of centres for the disabled. In 1992, just before he died, he expressed a fondness for another occupant, a young woman whose physical impairments were even greater than his own. Because the local clergy would not agree to conduct a wedding because they couldn't be certain that both participants fully understood the undertaking, a church blessing was arranged instead. The *Sunday Mirror* ran a front-page story to the effect that Monkhouse, by not recognizing the occasion as a real wedding, was denying the woman her proper status as a wife. When Monkhouse read it he burst into tears. A few weeks later the paper printed a front-page apology and retraction. 'That was awful,' Monkhouse says, averting his eyes. 'I was horrified to see pictures inside which made Gary look disfigured and foolish. It upset me deeply and I felt utter contempt for the editor. I didn't want Gary to see that bloody paper. Some stupid bastard showed it to him.'

Denis Norden describes reminiscing as the most fun an older person can have without actually having much fun. For Monkhouse it seems to be as haunting an experience as it is a pleasurable one. Half of his old show-business friends are now dead, he says. 'Yet it's funny, you know. I can see Bernie Winters walking around that house now as clearly as I can see you.' His eye lingers on the ghost for an unnervingly long time before a twitch of his saturnine eyebrow brings me back into focus. 'The other day I went to the phone to call Tony Hawes [a writer on *The Des O'Connor Show*]. He's been dead two years. That wasn't just forgetfulness. It was an overwhelming urge to share a piece of information with him. I can't believe Tony's not there.'

Not so long ago, Monkhouse had an intimation of his own eventual death. 'I had a blip called a cerebral infarction where my face sort of slid south.' He pulls a lopsided face. 'It only lasted a week but I was sure I'd had a stroke.' He went for a CAT scan and when nothing showed up he asked if he had lost brain cells from alcohol abuse over the years. The doctor said he hadn't and added that his liver was in perfect condition, too. Monkhouse still drinks a fair amount of wine and whisky and never suffers from hangovers. I tell him he's a jammy bugger. 'Exactly! I've never told anyone that before because I was afraid that would be the reaction I'd get.'

The inevitability of his own death does not frighten him, he says, it just makes him curious to know what it will be like. 'I don't think there's going to be anything there.' If there is an after-life and he is called to account, could Monkhouse say that he had been a good man in this life? 'Oh, I think so. An inoffensive one. I think so. I've never done anything deliberately mean. I stole when I was a teenager but nothing considerable. I'm harm-less. I just tell jokes. I know I've irritated people but that's more about them than it is about me.'

Friendly, he certainly is. Although I doubt he is as irrepressibly cheerful as he claims to be. Guileless is a word that could be applied. He will try to answer any question you ask, however personal. For one who earns his living in a profession fuelled by high-octane ego, he even exhibits surprising humility. On the directions to his house which he had faxed to me he had written 'here are my directions' and then crossed out the word 'my'. And he is happier than most to regale you with stories which don't reflect well. Eric Sykes, he says, always hated him. When they met recently, Sykes said, 'I don't know, Bob, my memory's getting so bad. Can you remember why I have disliked you so much for all these years?' Monkhouse said he had no idea. 'No?' Sykes shrugged. 'Oh well, be bloody stupid to stop now.'

It is four o'clock, time for Monkhouse to take the Chinese remedy he hopes will cure him of his vitiligo, a skin condition which leaves his face and hands piebald, and which he covers up with masking make-up. The herbal cure is a sort of tea made of garden sweepings, he says. He has been taking it for six weeks, but it hasn't worked yet. On my way out I pause to admire a large Monet hanging in the hall. Jackie appears and points out that it's a fake. In their second home in Barbados they have a Picasso which is also a copy. Jackie makes light of having had a wobbly earlier about the photographer, 'But I just don't understand what he was doing snooping about up there. It's so untidy.' At the door, Bob Monkhouse says under his breath, 'Please be kind.' There is no laughter in his voice but I smile back at him. I should have said, 'Be bloody stupid to start now.' But the line doesn't come to me until I am halfway back to London. And anyway it would probably have stuck in my throat.

In 2001 Bob Monkhouse's estranged son, Simon, died of a heroin overdose in a guesthouse in Thailand. He was 46. Monkhouse was diagnosed with prostate cancer, the same year.

Charlton Heston

FEBRUARY 1997

Charlton Heston is pretty sure I'll know the story, but tells it
anyway. 'It's about – oh, nuts, who was that British actor in
Room at the Top? Laurence Harvey – it's about Laurence Harvey.
When he was doing Romeo he called Olivier and said, "You
must play The Chorus." And Olivier said, "No." And Harvey
said, "Why not?" And Olivier said, "Because I'm too fucking
grand."'

It's as well I do know the story, for Heston has propped his
crutches up against the table behind him and I have become
distracted by the sight of them slowly sliding down. (Is it im-
proper, I find myself wondering, to lean over a Hollywood legend
to grab his falling crutches? It's one of those questions upon
which *Debrett's Etiquette and Modern Manners* offers no clear
guidance.) There is a loud clatter as the crutches meet the floor.
Without blinking or looking round, Heston growls: 'All right.
Stay there.'

Composed, in a word.

It's nine o'clock in the morning – Heston can't get out of the
film actor's habit of rising for 6.30 a.m. shoots – and we are
sitting on a comfortable sofa in the stone and glass home he had
built for himself on the ridge of a mountain in California, while
he was away filming *Ben-Hur* in Italy thirty-nine years ago.
Below us is a swimming-pool, lined with poplars. Below that,
800 acres of forest. And below that, the rest of Beverly Hills.
Most of the books that line the shelves that take up the whole of
one wall are about Shakespeare. In the centre of the middle shelf
there is a space cleared for a signed photograph of . . . yes, you

haven't guessed it: Prince Andrew (Heston is a great Anglophile, and an arch conservative. Indeed, he was one of the few Hollywood celebrities invited to Lady Thatcher's seventieth birthday party).

On another wall there is a portrait of Laurence Olivier, his hero and friend. The reason he wanted to tell the Olivier anecdote was that he believes Olivier *was* too fucking grand to play minor roles in Shakespeare, while, he, Heston, is not. This is why he agreed to act in the comparatively modest role of the Player King in Kenneth Branagh's full-length, four-hour *Hamlet*. While he was filming it at Shepperton Studios in London last year, Heston slipped on a step. 'Didn't even fall,' he shrugs, his arms stretched out along the back of the sofa. 'Just jarred down, and that really hurt. It wasn't that I couldn't work. They just had to prop me up between takes.' Rather a come down, this; for such is the bruising toll that stunts have taken over the years that he has had to have a hip operation (which he had been putting off for fear of losing what mobility he had left). 'I can really walk without those crutches,' he now adds in a low voice like a sandbag slowly pummelling down a wooden staircase. 'But I'm not supposed to for a week.'

Inevitably, it must be harder for Heston to accept the ageing process than it is for the rest of us (he's seventy-two). We have not climbed mountains as Moses, scaled scaffolding as Michelangelo, nor been whipped as we rowed in galleys, our muscles oiled, wearing nothing but a loin cloth as Ben-Hur. In his day, the 6ft 3in Heston, with his broad shoulders and 45in chest, was an icon of virility, the great patriarch, a monumental presence on the screen. Indeed, our own Henry Cooper said of him: 'That's the only geezer I've met who makes me look like a poof.' Now, partly because of a stoop, Heston has shrunk a couple of inches. He has a creaky, bow-legged walk and his grey flannel trousers have been let out at the back. His weathered face is still handsome, though. That famous wide mouth still shows about forty-eight shiny front teeth when he speaks; and he still has those sculpted cheekbones, that finely chiselled broken nose, that strong, flinty jaw and those eyes that, though slightly watery and dimmed, are still a vivid blue. As for the hair . . . well, it fits.

Being immortalized on celluloid as a young demi-god must be the curse of the screen actor, mustn't it? 'Well, I'm certainly not going to be thirty again.' Heston smiles, recognizing that the question is a cue for the touching El Cid anecdote he relates in his autobiography. Again, he's sure I'll have read it but that I want to hear it from the Moose's mouth regardless. (Moose was his nickname when he was growing up in the Michigan backwoods. Now his friends call him Chuck. Except his wife who calls him Charlie. And his mother who called him Charlton. His staff call him Mr Heston.) Anyway: he has two (now grown-up) children, a son and a daughter, and when the daughter was eight, he (then forty-six) took her to see *El Cid* for the first time. Afterwards she wept and said: 'Oh Daddy, you were so beautiful then.' As he says this he emits a bass chuckle that makes the sofa tremble: 'Well, I guess I still was beautiful then. But what are you gonna do? It happens to athletes. Happily, actors can go on working. Athletes just run into a wall.'

In his tennis pavilion, near the house, there is a life-size poster of Heston as El Cid. You can't help wondering what goes through his mind when he contemplates it, especially in light of the story he goes on to tell. He was, he remembers, rehearsing in a production of *Antony and Cleopatra* that was just about to open at a Pittsburgh theatre. One dark winter night he went back to the theatre to check something on the stage and came across the huddled figure of the aged actress Lenore Ulric. Out of pity, she'd been given a job and cast – miscast – as Charmian, Cleopatra's handmaiden. She knew, as everyone else in the cast knew, that she was too old for the part. Heston found her kneeling in front of a life-size painting of her younger self playing her most successful role, and crying like a lost child. 'I slipped quietly out the stage door,' he says, nodding his head in rueful sympathy.

There, thanks to the grace of the Old Testament God he sometimes plays, he hasn't gone. Indeed, Heston says he has always kept his life in perspective. 'I did learn very early on that you shouldn't take yourself as seriously as other people are prepared to take you,' he says, compulsively patting his grey hair, presumably to prove it is real. 'The main thing is the work. If they like it, it's fine. If they don't, well, what do they know?' He keeps his feet on the ground by reminding himself of the

Byzantine emperors who employed servants to stand behind them and whisper, 'You, too, must die.' It's not that he suffers from Paradise Syndrome (a condition in which stars become hypochondriacs because their success has left them nothing to contemplate but ill health), but while he was filming *Ben-Hur* (in 1958) he was given to bouts of paranoia about dying young. They were triggered off by the sudden death that year of his fellow Hollywood star, Tyrone Power, who was only forty-five: 'His death hung in my mind, resonating with my own mortality.' Soon after, Heston hurt his hip in a fall – while trying to help Jesus carry his cross, as you do – and he felt sure he wasn't going to make it to the end of the film.

Now he says he would like to die quickly – like Caesar, naturally – but not before he has had time to say some famous last words. This qualification is revealing. First, it shows how much Heston identifies with the heroic figures – kings, cardinals, generals, presidents – he has spent a career portraying on screen ('One would like to hope that a tiny scrap of their greatness has rubbed off,' is how he puts it). Second, it shows the extent to which the real world has collided in his imagination with the illusory world of the cinema. When this is put to him, he shrugs. 'Unreal? I've been doing it for so long I feel at home with it. That's normality.' In his private twilight zone, he probably imagines there will be a camera rolling as he says his last words. After all, this is a man who once found himself talking to Tom Selleck at a bar and, seeing a shadow on Selleck's face, thought 'Shit. I'm in his key-light.'

The anecdotage could go on, and on. It's practised, perfect and charming. And, like much anecdotage, it serves instead of self-analysis. For it's telling that Heston so often talks about his roles only in terms of how physically suited he was to play them. He doesn't seem to believe that it is possible for an actor to play a character he does not identify with in these terms, just by acting. He says, for instance, that his height, deep voice and broken nose always precluded him from playing Hamlet: 'Even when I was young enough it was never a part for me, I had the wrong persona.'

Try and imagine the big, strapping Laurence Olivier, Marlon Brando or Daniel Day-Lewis being held back in this way and you will appreciate what an astonishing admission this is. The comment also shows, though, that Heston possesses an awareness of his own limitations. He probably knows he doesn't have the subtlety to play Hamlet (although he does recite for me, quite stirringly, the 'To be or not to be' speech, as an illustration of how accessible 'Old Will's' vocabulary is – only to ruin the effect by adding, 'See? Not really very complicated stuff'). He once perceptively observed that some film directors actually consider intelligence in an actor a drawback. And, even more wryly, that: 'Smoking a cigarette in a film can make you look cool and world-weary. Actually, I've learned to act determined and thoughtful. I can even throw in a dollop of anxious on top.'

Now, it may be that after many years of being gently ribbed by critics for his hamminess, he has learned to say such things to show he has a sense of irony. But I think not, for the first thing you notice about Heston is that he is neither precious nor pretentious but, rather, in possession of a lumbering sincerity. For example, when we discuss the dark, Freudian themes in *Hamlet* – sanity, guilt, self-doubt, shuffling off of mortal coils – I ask Heston if he couldn't perhaps relate to the character of Hamlet by contemplating his own mortality. 'No. Hamlet weighs up the advantages of killing Claudius as against killing himself. It has never crossed my mind to kill myself. Scots don't do that [although Heston, somewhat provocatively, likes to refer to himself as a 'Native American', his mother's side of the family was Scottish, and his father's English]. They may think of killing someone else, though.'

Heston has played both Macbeth and Antony dozens of times, because he feels he looks the part. But what about King Lear? Now that Heston is of a certain age, surely he is perfect for the role? 'As Olivier said, when you're old enough to play Lear you're not strong enough. Besides, I think you have to grow up with a role. I first played Macbeth when I was fourteen. I understand Macbeth. I understand Antony in both plays. But I don't empathize with Lear. I just think, what is this idiot doing? Why is he doing this? A bit like Othello.'

Ay, as Hamlet would say, there's the rub. Heston is probably the greatest epic hero Hollywood has ever produced. He has made more than seventy films and, alongside actors of the calibre of Olivier, Gielgud and Richardson, has performed in countless stage plays. He won an Oscar for best actor in a film which, to this day, still holds the record for most Oscars won (*Ben-Hur*, eleven), and which, in the chariot race, includes one of the most dramatic action sequences ever filmed. Yet, at the media screening of Branagh's *Hamlet*, the audience greeted Heston's initial appearance with a titter.

Was this because he is so obviously wearing a syrup on his head? Was it because he starred in the *Colbys* (the *Dynasty* spin-off) as well as in dozens of mediocre films in which he was attacked by killer ants or taken prisoner by apes? Was it because, in recent years, he has been trying to lighten up his serious image by appearing on such programmes as *The Dame Edna Experience* and in such films as *Wayne's World*? Or is it because he says he doesn't take himself too seriously yet so obviously does, especially when it comes to his far right political opinions?

Certainly, it's the seriousness factor – the lumbering sincerity factor – that lies behind the very public and very farcical feud Heston has been waging with the left-wing writer Gore Vidal over the past year. Vidal claims to have written a scene for *Ben-Hur* which, had it been in the final cut, would have explained the baffling rivalry between the Jewish Ben-Hur and his Roman rival Messala, played by Stephen Boyd: they had been teenage lovers and, when they meet again as adults, Messala wants to continue where they left off, but is spurned. Part of the reason Heston was so deeply rattled by this interpretation, I suspect, was that he identifies so strongly with the characters he plays. In some ways, the one he most resembles is Sir Thomas More (whom he played at London's Savoy Theatre in 1987), a noble soul with the fatal flaw of innocence. Heston sees himself as – and surely is – the archetypal family man. That the straight and honourable hero he portrays in *Ben-Hur* might be considered homosexual is, for Heston, an abhorrent notion. And as if this were not bad enough, Vidal has rubbed salt into Heston's whip welts by claiming that Boyd was allowed to know the homosexual subtext, but that the director decided not to let Heston in on it, for fear that he would fall apart. Vidal agreed, 'awed by the thought of so much wood crashing to the ground.'

If Heston really didn't take himself too seriously, he would have laughed the claim off. Instead, the naive, gentlemanly Heston decided to take on the street-fighting Vidal, describing him as 'a tart, embittered man' and firing off a letter of protest to the *LA Times*. When asked if he now has any regrets about rising to Vidal's bait, Heston emits one of those bitter, mirthless laughs. 'Poor Gore. Such . . .' He trails off, remembers the Marquess of Queensberry Rules, and recovers his air of resolution, superiority and dignity. 'No. I don't regret it because it's so easy to discredit him. He is a member of the Screen Writer's Guild. If he wrote any of the script, he would have been given a credit for it. But he wasn't. And how come he didn't bring it up for thirty years? No. It puzzles me because Gore has a respectable reputation as an essayist and novelist. I don't know why it's suddenly so important to him.'

When I suggest that Vidal might conceivably have told the story out of mischief, Heston says: 'Maybe. Or maybe he has a passion for me. Who knows? Maybe that's the subtext!' Now that's a good joke, and the answer Heston should have given in the first place. But it still leaves you wondering: does Heston really get Vidal's joke? Could it be that Heston is just so immune to malice and subterfuge, so decent, so, so solid, that Vidal's point o'erthrows his noble mind by several inches? Or is it that he is smarting because he does get it and he is only too aware that the Olympian heroes he played in all those epics now seem crude, stylized and kitsch? Worse, he recognizes that the point Vidal is making is that Heston – after years of playing characters who toss their heads, hold their chins high and leap from rock to rock in a leather thong – has, like the matinee idol Steve Reeves before him, become a gay icon.

Of course, Vidal's joke only works, and wounds, because Heston is the all-American, gung-ho male. Politically, he is probably more reactionary and hawkish even than his good friend Ronald Reagan. Indeed, in America he is now almost as well known as a champion of the right to bear arms as he is for his acting. (He keeps about forty firearms in his house, including a loaded one under his bed.) It was this reputation for rabid right-wingery that prompted the left-wing British journalist Christopher Hitchens to humiliate Heston on a live TV debate just before the Gulf War. Hitchens began by saying what an honour it was to be debating Middle Eastern politics with Moses himself. Then, suspecting that Heston was confusing Iraq with Iran, Hitchens challenged him to name the countries bordering Iraq. When Heston got them wrong, Hitchens said: 'Before you support bombing a country off the map, perhaps you should pay it the compliment of finding out where it is.' When Heston got angry at this, Hitchens retorted, 'Keep your hairpiece on.' Americans, Hitchens believes, still remember the debate because Heston was being so fatuous, complacent and self-satisfied. 'But upon reflection,' Hitchens tells me, 'I feel a pang of regret because it was like humiliating your own father. To be fair to Heston, he has shown a sort of bovine courage over the years in the way that he has stuck to his convictions, even when it has meant alienating himself from the liberal Hollywood establishment.'

When asked why he thinks so many Hollywood actors are liberal, Heston says it is because they make their living from their emotions, being called upon to weep for someone about whom they care nothing by sheer technique – just like that old pro the Player King, in fact. Liberals, he believes, tend to be emotional (and therefore irrational) people. This seems a dangerous line to take, given the inevitable conclusion that, because Heston himself is anything but liberal, he must be an unemotional and therefore wooden actor. But, of course, he is emotional, although he would call it following his conscience, or his heart. In 1961, for instance, long before the civil rights movement had become a fashionable cause in Hollywood, Heston joined Martin Luther King on a protest march because, in his heart, he knew it was the right thing to do.

More recently, again because he knew that it was the right thing to do, Heston stood up to the black gangsta rap singer Ice-T in order to get his infamous record 'Cop Killer' banned (when Ice-T threatened to kill Heston, the actor just growled, 'I'd like to see him try'). And even though he probably knew he would be ridiculed for missing the point, Heston criticized the violence in the films of Oliver Stone and Quentin Tarantino. When people did indeed laugh and ask if he had not realized the films were black comedies, he just shrugged and said: '"Didn't you get it?"

is a devastating question. Cool people cannot bear ever not getting a joke.'

As if all this were not enough to be campaigning about, Heston is vehemently anti-abortion and opposed to feminists because he believes they are responsible for the break-up of the family. Feminists can't be blamed, however, for the divorce of his own parents. 'I was still a child,' Heston recalls, 'and the loss of my father affected me greatly. I dealt with it, but I became a solitary, private child.' He says his parents' divorce was a terrible, dark secret he never told anyone about, saying instead that his mother's new husband was his father. This, he says, has left him shy to this day but he now has a public persona he can step into.

Perhaps it was the failure of his parents' marriage that made him want to succeed so much with his own. He married Lydia, his college sweetheart, when he was nineteen (after his first date, he tells me, he ran the three miles home along the dark streets shouting, 'I love her, I love her,' over and over again. 'I did, too,' he adds). Almost uniquely among the grandees of Hollywood, the couple have remained happily married for fifty-three years. Again, unusually, they have lived in the same house for much of that time. Wife? House? Politics? Stick to your guns. That seems to be the Moose's philosophy.

Lydia now appears for her morning swim. She is wearing a dressing gown, a bath hat and what looks like a facepack. 'Hello,' she says, waving cheerfully when she sees me. 'Excuse my clown make-up. It's just sunblock.'

It is time for Heston to make his way up to the tennis court where a photographer is waiting to take his picture. He is pretty nippy with his crutches. 'Learned to handle them playing Long John Silver,' he says over his shoulder. 'Although that was only the one crutch.'

The outside of the house has a faded appearance, bleached by the years of intense sunlight. Alongside a faded brass chariot and horse in the yard there is a sandpit with the words 'Jack's sandbox' daubed on the side. Further along the road towards the pavilion there is a faded sign which reads: 'Unauthorized visitors not welcome. Guard dog on duty. Proceed to house. Sound horn. Wait in car.' Another faded sign, at the back of the pavilion, says in more friendly letters: 'Do not enter this area. Santa and his elves are busy.'

All of this serves as a melancholic reminder that some of Heston's fame has faded, too. Inside the pavilion there is an even more poignant symbol of this: a beautifully hand-stitched leather director's chair with the name 'Charlton Heston' carved in it. While Heston waits outside for the shot to be set up, I run my fingers over the letters and think '*The* Charlton Heston used to sit in this chair. It should be in a museum. It must be worth a fortune to collectors of Hollywood memorabilia.' I almost forget that the genuine article is standing only a few yards away.

Outside, *the* Charlton Heston is growing impatient waiting for the photographer to finish his light readings. He has only had to wait about two minutes but he has started looking theatrically at his watch, shaking his head and sucking in breath. You can tell he hates having his photograph taken or, at least, that after so many years in front of a camera, he is bored rigid by it. After another few seconds have been wasted, he announces that he has a dentist's appointment in ten minutes. Root canal work. It has the desired effect. As the photographer's young assistant nervously shows the Hollywood veteran where to sit he makes the mistake of warning him to watch out for the light cables. 'One has seen cables before,' Heston sighs under his breath. 'One has seen cables.'

Once seated, Heston instinctively raises his chin, tosses his head and levels a look at the camera lens which is, yes, so fucking grand it gives you goosebumps.

Jeffrey Archer

APRIL 1999

The lift glides to a halt at the penthouse suite on the thirteenth floor. A butler leads the way along a panelled corridor and into a spacious, glass-walled living room. Lord Archer is standing in a rhombus of sunlight, his back to the glinting spires of Westminster. He raises his right hand, palm flat, and barks: 'Stop!'

My first thought is that he has gone mad. Actually nuts. He doesn't like to talk about it, but he used to be a policeman, spent five months in the Met before resigning in 1960. Now – clearly – the pressure of keeping this chapter of his life quiet has got to him. He has regressed. Thinks he's back on point duty.

I remain frozen to the spot. Archer continues to halt the on-coming traffic. He is riding the moment, enjoying the confusion and embarrassment playing across my face. The situation is too weird. Slowly, his Lordship closes all his fingers except for the index. This he tilts 180 degrees until it points to the bathroom scales at his feet.

Now I understand what the pantomime is about. He has remembered a passing conversation we had when we met here, at his London home, three months ago. I asked him how he had lost two stone in six months. He told me he went to his gym at seven every morning and worked out for eighty minutes. During the day he followed 'Jeffrey's food-combining chart'. He sent me away with my own laminated 'Jeffrey's food-combining chart'. I stuck it to the fridge, tried it for an hour, gave up. I now realize he thinks I've asked to see him a second time because I want to show him I've lost weight. Oh dear. I want to interview him again because, last time, I learnt a lot about his plans should he be elected London's first Mayor in May 2000 – enforce bus lanes, a commissioner for dirt, free milk to schoolchildren, and so on – and very little about what sort of a person he is, or thinks he is, and why he believes we can trust him.

Still cringing, I decline his offer to stand on the scales and we repair to the squashy cream-coloured sofas that surround a book-laden coffee table in the corner of the room. Though I'm sure he does the scales routine with everyone he puts on his diet, I feel oddly flattered he has remembered, as I'm sure I'm supposed to. I also feel grateful for the glimpse he has given me of the bully beneath the bluff surface. 'Wimp!' he says in a schoolmaster's voice as he gives me a mock stern look over his half-moon spectacles. 'Don't look so smug!'

Jeffrey Archer is obsessed with physical fitness. He's a sturdy, puff-chested 5ft 9in and though, at fifty-nine, there is something of the shocked sparrow about his looks – the bird recovering from moult – he has a strong nose, wide mouth and a firm jawline that is emphasized by a crew cut. But it wasn't always thus.

At Wellington School, Somerset, he was bullied for being a weed: nicknamed 'The Pune', he was the one the other boys held over the lavatory while it was being flushed. Everything changed when Hal Kenny, his PE master, encouraged him to take up body-building and become an athlete. After leaving school, Archer became a PE teacher himself. He was good at it. Turned his pupils into champions. But he was notorious for his bullying tactics. When I ask him if he thinks he is a bully he smirks impishly and answers in a booming but croaky staccato. 'Yes. Yes. But it's just enthusiasm, isn't it? I wake up wanting to do things. And want to encourage others to do the same.'

No one could ever accuse Archer of lacking enthusiasm. Or initiative. Or self-belief. Or nerve . . . He quivers with the stuff. Not only did he transform himself from a playground weed to a first-class athlete – an Oxford blue who represented his country at the 200 metres – as a student in the early sixties he helped raise £500,000 for Oxfam by cajoling the Beatles, Harold Macmillan and President Johnson into endorsing his appeal. In the early seventies a bad investment in a Canadian company, Aquablast, left him nearly bankrupt. He had to resign his seat in

Parliament but, instead of sulking, he decided to pay off his £427,727 overdraft by writing novels. He wrote ten. And even though reviews of them have included the phrases 'a true stinker', 'grindingly predictable', and 'flatulent banality', he has sold, he claims, 120 million copies of them worldwide – and earned himself an estimated £60 million.

The trouble is, there is so much else Archer can be accused of. He lacks judgement, he's vainglorious, he's a fantasist – or rather, as his wife Mary put it, he has 'a gift for inaccurate précis'. Everything about him smacks of invention. His whole manner is phoney. He's like a Donald Sinden of the political world, an actor so actorish he makes your teeth grind. Chief among his accusers is Michael Crick who, in 1995, wrote a biography of Archer called *Stranger than Fiction*. The book sheds light on the mysteries surrounding Archer's academic record, his father (a convicted fraudster and bigamist who died in 1956), and all the Archer imbroglios, from the libellous allegations made against him in 1986 (concerning the prostitute Monica Coghlan) to the accusations in 1994 of insider dealing in Anglia Television shares.

Although Archer is obviously insensitive enough to keep bouncing back when life slaps him down, it must have been painful for him to have his private life researched so meticulously and exposed so publicly. After all, as Mary Archer once noted: 'He's not as thick-skinned as people think. Criticism does get to him. He takes it personally and it hurts him.'

Candidates for the job of Mayor of London will have to convince voters they are honest, trustworthy and above reproach. To do this they will have to reconcile themselves to having their private lives scrutinized by the press. Archer says he feels psychologically prepared for the sniggering *Private Eye* lampoons and the Paxman interrogations that lie ahead. 'Well, I wouldn't be doing it if I didn't.' Still. Must be horrible having fellows like Crick pore over every aspect of his past? 'Horrible feeling? Hadn't really though of it in those terms. I mean . . . [pause] that's the way he makes his money. If you want to represent people on the public stage, you have to face that.'

When I ask Jeffrey Archer why he thinks people should have confidence in him, given his reputation, he gives a politician's answer. 'The reason I have worked so hard in the past two years on policy is to show people how seriously I'm taking it. To show I'm not being casual about it. That I'm not taking it lightly. I'm not standing for Mayor because I need a job. I don't. I want to make a difference, otherwise I wouldn't be bothering. It would be easier to write another novel.'

He seems to accept, though, that he has an image problem. 'I am very aware of . . .' he trails off again. 'Well, Michael Howard is a good example. I don't know of a better friend when you are in trouble. I don't know a nicer man with a more delightful wife. And yet he has a different public image and it's not fair.'

You have to wonder why Archer wants to subject himself to the torment of press scrutiny when he could so easily retire and enjoy his millions, his fame, his seventeenth-century vicarage in Grantchester. The obvious answer is that he craves power. Also, as he himself has said in the past, he feels he has been a failure. He wants to be more than just an amusing footnote in the history of the Tory Party. He managed to be a close friend – court jester – to both Margaret Thatcher and John Major. But he never advanced further than deputy chairman of the party, a post he held from September 1985 to November 1986, when the Monica Coghlan story broke.

But is there also a streak of masochism behind his willingness to run the press gauntlet? Those who are bullied often convince themselves they deserve to be. This theory would be consistent with the strong attraction Archer feels toward intimidating women. He worships Margaret Thatcher. And Mary, the chemistry don he married thirty-three years ago, is famed not only for her fragrance but also for being what the librettist Kit Hesketh-Harvey describes as 'a fantasy of most Englishmen . . . It's that idea of ice in the loins.'

Last summer, as a pre-emptive strike against his critics, Archer wrote an article for the London *Evening Standard* in which he offered explanations for the extraordinary puzzles surrounding his career. 'Yes, I was young once, and, yes, I have made a number of mistakes in my life,' he wrote. 'I'm neither genius nor saint.' He acknowledged that his father didn't win the DCM, as he had previously thought, and that his grandfather was never Lord Mayor of Bristol.

Archer used to boast that he was the youngest GLC councillor in 1967, and the youngest MP when elected in 1969, because, he explained in the article, he thought at the time that he was. He did walk out of a shop in Toronto in 1975 without paying for two suits – but only because he had wandered into another shop through an interconnecting passage. On the subject of the Anglia Television shares he bought for his friend Broosk Saib just days before an agreed take-over bid, he claims he did not receive information from his wife, a director of Anglia. There was an investigation. He wasn't charged.

The answers he gives in the article prompt other questions. Why was Archer dealing in Anglia shares on behalf of a friend who was used to buying his own shares through a stockbroker? I've been told by Anthony Gordon-Lennox, Archer's press adviser, that his Lordship is not prepared to comment on the Anglia shares story or on the recent scandal concerning his off-spring. Archer has two sons: William, twenty-seven, a theatre producer, and James, twenty-four, who was sacked from an investment bank for allegedly trying to manipulate the price of shares in a Swedish company.

Gordon-Lennox didn't say anything about Archer's academic record being off-limits, though. It might seem a trivial issue but, as Michael Crick has argued, we might all do better in life if we went around boasting of false degrees. Archer claimed to have a degree from an American university when he didn't. On his marriage certificate he was described as a 'research graduate' when he wasn't. He did go to Oxford (to do a one-year diploma in education at a teacher training college affiliated to Brasenose College) but he did not take any A-levels. The archives at both Dover College, where Archer taught PE from 1961 to 1963, and Oxford University show that he had three. In his *Evening Standard* article he wrote: 'I did not obtain any A-levels. Nor did I mislead Oxford University in telling them that I had.' So how did this false impression arise? Archer blinks. A rictus. A look of pain in his eyes. 'No, I did answer that and, forgive me, I'm not going over it again. I made a decision to answer all those things in one go. I want to be Mayor. I'm doing nineteen hours a day, working flat out. By all means read the Crick book and make your own judgement.'

William Archer, aka 'William Grimwood', died aged eighty when Jeffrey was fifteen. In an interview before the Crick revelations, Archer said he went to pieces when his father died, mucked up his exams, felt life was unfair. Now, when I ask what effect his father's death had on him, he says: 'That's forty-three years ago so I don't remember it vividly in that sense.' Pause. The smile is frozen on his face. 'My mother was the strong influence on my life. Still alive, God bless her, eighty-six years old. Saw her last weekend. She's still in fighting form.' He doesn't think his mother, Lola, spoilt him as compensation for losing his father. 'Hope not. Probably . . . I adore my mother. Very special lady. I suppose I would have stayed down in Weston-super-Mare if I had been that spoilt.' Lola wrote a weekly column for her local paper which featured her scampish son 'Tuppence'. Jeffrey doesn't think his being put in the spotlight in this way had any impact on his emotional development. 'I wasn't aware of it, to be honest. I don't think at nine I had a clue.'

The phone rings. LBC radio wants to do a two-minute interview, live, about the 'rolling manifesto' he is launching today. Archer excuses himself and barrels up a marble staircase to his mezzanine study. As I listen to him on the phone – 'Yes. It is the most *exciting* challenge . . .' – I cast an eye around the room. A sculpture here, a Monet there, a metallic Gothic chandelier over the dining table and, on the occasional table beside me, a framed black-and-white photograph of the young Jeffrey in running kit crossing a finishing line first.

Archer seems to have three main tactics for becoming Mayor: behave as if the job is his already; promise that if he's elected he won't write any more novels; wear Londoners down with his keenness so that they'll make him Mayor just to shut him up. Even the Tory grandees behind the 'Anyone But Archer' whispering campaign seem to be buckling under the Archer onslaught. They depict him as a ghastly overgrown schoolboy whose graceless, barrow-boy persona offends the propriety of the party. Yet Archer is tipped to win the Tory nomination for Mayor in the autumn. He will, of course, be insufferably bossy and pompous if he goes on to win the election. But even his enemies would have to concede he will probably get things done.

Baron Archer of Weston-super-Mare, of Mark in the County of Somerset, as he chose to style himself when he was created a Life Peer in 1992, thinks there is a mayor-shaped hole in his life. It is the job he was born to do. But he wants to become the Mayor of London so badly, one worries how he will cope if his main rival, Ken Livingstone, pips him to the post. Archer hasn't thought about losing, he says, because he's sure he's going to win. When I point out he was also sure the Tories were going to win the last election, he laughs and rocks back in his seat. 'You've caught me out there! But I had to say that. We knew we were going to lose. What shocked us was the scale. We honestly thought it would be seventy seats at most.'

An almost palpable air of frustration hangs around Jeffrey Archer. He's like a spermatozoid, constantly, frantically, selfishly swimming but not getting anywhere. He tells me he is easily bored and feels unfulfilled. When I suggest that it must be dreadful being him – because even if he did become Mayor the goalposts would only move again and the gnawing discontent would return to his soul – he nods gravely. 'Yes. I'll want to be captain of the England cricket team. I'm among that group of human beings who feel they have never achieved anything. One of my great heroes is Thomas Jefferson and he has written on his gravestone: "President . . . of the University of West Virginia."'

Rather grandly, Archer says he admires Jefferson for his intellect and Nelson for his physical courage. 'Would I be courageous if the enemy was coming towards me? Could I handle it? I don't know.' It's strange, but even when he's being sincere he sounds fake.

Four years ago Archer did, he says, stare death in the face. 'I nearly killed the whole family. I was driving down the centre lane at 70 mph in a brand new BMW. It turned two circles and went into a ditch. The police found a nail that big [he holds his hands six inches apart] in the tyre. All I remember is that for thirty seconds both boys went silent wondering what was going to happen.'

If the crash had been fatal, would Archer have died a happy man? 'Am I happy? Not really. But who is?' He says his money doesn't really bring him happiness – he's not even sure how much he's worth, not that interested. Even being the best-selling novelist in Britain doesn't seem to give him that much satisfaction.

'I know I'm no Graham Greene,' he says, rolling his 'r's. 'I know my limitations. Do I feel being a novelist is a proper job for a grown man? That's what Mary is always saying to me. Well, it's not a crime to entertain people.' He derives more pleasure, he says, from the auctioneering work he does for charity. He raised £3.2 million last year – he writes the figure down on a Post-it pad for me – and when he reflects whether he has been a good person in this life he concludes: 'I think I've put in more than I've taken out.'

He says he has no regrets, that it is pointless looking back. 'When I make mistakes I never feel sorry for myself. I might feel cross. I might think, *silly fool*. But even when I lost all my money – which was the worst time of my life – I tried to be positive. I hated being in debt. *Hated it*. Other than illness, it's the worst thing in the world. When you see a bill come through the letterbox and you know you can't pay it. I never want that again. I couldn't see a way out . . . Did I feel suicidal? No, I was too young. At thirty-four I knew I was young enough to dust myself down and start again.'

Mary Archer once said, 'Life with Jeffrey is never dull,' and this, perhaps, is his saving grace. He is a colourful character in a monochrome political landscape. He has other virtues. According to his friends, he has a generous nature. And he has good entrepreneurial instincts. Margaret Thatcher once described him as the 'extrovert's extrovert'. Today, though, there is none of the bluster and bumptiousness you would normally associate with him. He seems reserved.

The intelligentsia can never forgive him his Mr Toad-like resilience and popularity. He's a rabble rouser, a middle brow, a vulgarian. He has said that he will make an excellent Mayor of London precisely because he is vulgar. But when I ask him about this statement, he recants. Says he meant it as a tease. Perhaps it will take another twenty years before everyone gets the joke and finds him lovable enough to be declared a living national treasure. For the moment, for many, there is still something a little too weird about Jeffrey Archer.

He has a vulnerable side, though, and I see it when, the

interview over, an old friend of his drops in for tea. He has known Michael Hogan, a farmer, since they were at Oxford together. He greets him warmly and then, as he walks with me to the lift, Archer whispers, 'You know, Nigel, that man is one of only three people in the world I trust – my wife and my friend Adrian Metcalfe being the other two. He's such a fine man. Such a fine man. When I nearly went bankrupt he gave me £10,000, half his savings, to bail me out. A dear, dear man.' His eyes go rheumy at the memory and he stares at the lift doors, lost momentarily in his thoughts. They open. I step in. Just as they are closing, he snaps back into character and shouts: 'And lose some weight!'

Lord Archer became the Tory candidate for Mayor that autumn, only to withdraw, and cause huge, some would say irreparable, damage to the credibility of William Hague, the Tory leader who had backed his nomination. Unable to wrestle with his conscience any longer, Archer's former friend Ted Francis came forward to accuse the novelist of asking him to provide a false alibi for his 1987 libel action against the Star. *In 2000 Archer wrote and starred in a play called* The Accused, *loosely based on the case. In 2001, just before his trial for perjury opened, Monica Coghlan, the prostitute at the centre of the libel case, was killed in a car crash. At the trial he declined to take the stand. His wife Mary did. 'I think,' she said when asked about her marriage, 'we explored the further reaches of "for better or worse".' Archer's mother died the day before the verdict was given. He was found guilty and sentenced to four years in prison.*

Clive James

The dimly lit back room of the Japanese restaurant is empty save for some scruffy codger hunched up in the corner, sitting sideways on, lost in his thoughts. At fifty-six, it seems Clive Vivian Leopold James has become smaller than life. Only when I am opposite him, face to face, do the features of the man on the box lurch into focus. And this is just as unnerving. After we have been chatting for a few minutes, picking over a salver of sushi, I forget that we are mid-conversation. I have been watching his lips move, enjoying the performance, imagining the TV set framing that familiar face – a face once described by its owner as small and pointed at the bottom, like a talking turnip – when suddenly the turnip gets all interactive on me and asks, 'Have you read *Kim*?' Startled, I nod and shake my head at the same time. 'Well, you must. You must.'

This, I think, is Clive James as he likes to see himself: the pedagogue, at once avuncular and didactic. Had he not been a critic, poet, author, TV presenter, et cetera, et cetera, he would, you feel sure, have been that favourite English teacher at school. You know the one, pens in top pocket, tie over shoulder, infecting you with his sophistry – but always getting himself into trouble for teaching off the syllabus.

'I warn you,' he says. 'This will be the dullest encounter of your life. I'm a nightmare. Cantankerous. Tetchy. I'll either ramble or shut up.' He grins crookedly, offering a glimpse of shiny bridgework, and then starts to ramble. But it is one thing for James to allow himself to stray from the point. Permitting his syntax the right to roam is another. Even in discourse he

97

constructs his sentences with a precision bordering on the anal: he never has to search for the right word, but you can tell that he is listening out for a satisfying pitch and rhythm – even if it means, as his critics say, that he sometimes sacrifices content for form.

A detractor once described the TV column he wrote for the *Observer* for ten years as a cabaret turn. James took it as a compliment. But does he write as he speaks, or is it the other way round? 'First and foremost,' he says as nasally as the most unreconstructed Australian, 'I think of myself as a writer. Even on TV when I say something spontaneous I have written it in my head a few seconds beforehand.'

It can sound like it. A favourite Jamesian (he'll love that) device is to fold a sentence neatly in on itself, as in: 'Not everyone who wants to make a film is crazy, but almost everyone who is crazy wants to make a film.' A similar trick is to break one sentence into two and flip its tenses over until both sides are lightly browned: 'Breakfast was there for the taking. I rarely took it.' His own description is that he tries to 'turn a phrase until it catches the light'. That he resists the urge to add '*quod erat demonstrandum*' shows admirable, if uncharacteristic, restraint.

He has a more galling verbal tic: the rather anti-social habit of regarding conversation as an opportunity to pontificate – as Dr Johnson did, as James might put it. For that's another thing. He throws in references to playwrights, philosophers and men of letters the way other people punctuate. This could be intellectual bullying – he studied for a PhD, and speaks eight languages – but, equally, it could be his way of flattering, as opposed to patronizing, his interlocutor. Either way, he is well aware of the involuntary flinch that academic name-dropping elicits in the English nervous system. It is just that, after years of taking stick for it, he's past caring.

'Oh yes, I'm a raging intellectual snob,' he says, thoughtfully tapping the tips of his fingers together. 'But only because I see books, music, art and the life of the mind as a concrete reality. I can't separate them from nature. I don't just acquire knowledge to show off. I've read all my life. Devoured whole literatures. Why should I apologize for that? The English are embarrassed about learning. It's unique to these shores – a kind of Philistinism encouraged by the landed gentry.'

Landed gentry? It seems too easy and arbitrary a target. Could it hark back to the same smouldering resentment that once prompted the Kid from Kogarah to write that the principle effect of the sixties social revolution was to make young men who had been to Shrewsbury (the *Private Eye* crowd of Ingrams, Foot and Booker) feel less miserable about not having been to Eton?

Perhaps not. James gives an example of what he means: the time a journalist caught him reading Nietzsche in a restaurant in California. 'A piece appeared in the English press saying I was *ostentatiously* reading Nietzsche. There was no counter to that because the journalist was assuming you only read a book like that if you are trying to impress someone. I don't.'

There are other dimensions to this, I suggest: the British fear of appearing boastful, of being seen to try too hard. 'That's the influence of *Private Eye* for you,' he says, lightly conducting with his chopstick for emphasis. 'The assumption that if you are an intellectual you must be a bore. Perhaps the people who assume that should be more bothered for their souls. For their loved ones. For their children.'

James is talking in an untypically muted voice. As he does, he rests the side of his head against the wall to his right, as if to relieve his neck from the burden of all that weighty grey matter. It throws half his face into shadow, and this, too, seems unfamiliar: James as you never see him, away from the make-up and the harsh lighting of the studio. Someone once described his face as being that of a bank robber who has forgotten to take the stocking off. It is a cruel description – but not altogether unfair. Apart from two insouciantly raised clumps of wirebrush eyebrow, his face is curiously lacking in definition. It is something to do with the width of the nose; the corrugated shape of the lips that barely move, even when engaged in perpetual monologue.

That monologue is just one of the reasons why Clive James is almost impossible to interview. You feel you know too much about him already. What he has not told you on TV, he has in his novels and essays or in the three volumes (so far) of his *Unreliable Memoirs*. You know, for instance, that he sees himself as a wolf-whistling, red-blooded all-Australian male, but that his first sexual encounter – mutual onanism – was with a boy,

Gary. You can guess, too, why he doesn't open his mouth much when he talks: 'The last and hardest job was to clean my gums. After every few scrapes I flew around the surgery like an open-mouth balloon. The [dental assistant] pinned me with a body-slam and the job was done.'

What does not come across in his memoirs, though, is any real sense of his emotional geography. James will tell you that he is conceited, arrogant, pompous, naive and insensitive, but this, you suspect, is probably what he thinks other people think; it is not necessarily what he feels. He charts his motives at every turn, but instead of analysing what he finds in terms of his own condition, however painful that might be, he cops out and sweeps them aside with some clever-clogs aphorism or generalization that applies to Everyman. 'Christ died for our sins,' he tells me. 'It's rather presumptuous to think you have to die, too.' Yes, yes, you find yourself asking, but what about *you*? What, for instance, makes Clive James cry?

'I can be moved to tears by my own failures and failings in relationships,' he answers. 'But that's self-obsession. Usually when one weeps one weeps for oneself. That's the terrible truth. So I try to weep as little as possible.' He adds that the way he empathizes with a tragic novel is to imagine it happening to his children. 'People say it's impossible to imagine the Holocaust. But all you have to do is picture your own children being taken from you and gassed.'

James has been married to Prudence, a lecturer in modern languages, for twenty-eight years. They have two daughters – James says he can imagine dying in order to save their lives. 'I really hope I could. But you never know. In Germany, people killed their own children in order to save them from a fate worse than death in medical experiments. That took real courage.'

Just as we're descending into despair, James inadvertently flicks some raw fish across the table. 'Ah. Sorry about that. Always been a messy eater, especially when I'm talking.' He sees me prodding warily at what looks like a piece of pink wood. 'Try holding that ginger under your tongue and let the juice come out,' he says, playing mentor again. 'And wash it down with that sake. It'll do you the world of good. Clean up your sinuses.'

In an attempt to keep the mood light, I ask him if the sake will also make me fighting drunk. 'No,' he says. 'Sake only makes the Japanese wrap bandannas around their heads and charge when they are officially at war.' It is a surprisingly glib reference to a subject he is known to be haunted by. (His father was taken prisoner in the fall of Singapore in 1942 and died in an air crash while flying home at the end of the war.)

This, says James, was what spurred him to learn Japanese about ten years ago; it was, he felt, his best chance of coming to terms with his past. He has, too, been working for some years on an epic novel about the war in the South Pacific (along with a novel on Rio, and the next volume of his memoirs – no slouch, our Clive). Perhaps the epic may do something to atone for having single-handedly reduced the Japanese race to a crude stereotype in the eyes of the British viewing public. At best, I suggest, the mockery he made of *Endurance*, the masochistic Japanese game show, was entertainingly patronizing. At worst, it was racist.

He studies his nails, revealing liver-spotted hands and hairy fingers. 'It's almost impossible to avoid being accused of those things,' he says. 'You're wide open to it. All you can do is rely on the good sense of the public. It's true, I made my name on television making fun of Japanese game shows. But Japanese game shows are really like that. Hilariously awful. Most Japanese know that, too.' James showed he knew it with his last novel, *Brrm! Brrm!*. It was about Japan, or rather about an immaculately courteous and cultivated Japanese man who comes to England to acquire manners.

Brrm! Brrm! received favourable reviews, although, tellingly, most critics admitted that they came to bury it and ended up singing its praises. For the critics have never been particular kind to James. Auberon Waugh, another favourite schoolmaster, said of him: 'He pretends to be an irreverent figure but in fact is a cringing man on the make.' Such crushing comments have left James with a complex, or at least a feeling of insecurity. 'I've learned that the profile as a form does not favour me,' he says, screwing up his face in a stage grimace. He gives me an example. Earlier this year, a reporter from the *Daily Mirror* did a friendly ten-minute interview with him that was blown up into a double-page spread devoted to snide implications of serial lechery. 'They got a photographer to go up to Cambridge and photograph my house. They got someone else to trail my wife and my children. A rock came through the front window the morning after the article appeared. We were showered with glass. You don't have to be paranoid to find that a cautionary tale. The reporter wrote to me afterwards and said, "How can I apologize?", and I wrote back saying, "You can't. Get another job."' He laughs at this, lowers his chin and looks over the top of his glasses. 'I'm trusting you. I hate doing that. I've been stitched up by nicer-looking, more plausible, more literate people even than you.'

But because being sarcastic is what he does for a living, he knows that he cuts a less than sympathetic figure. Lest we forget, he did once describe the tennis player Andrea Jaeger as having a smile like a car crash (she was fifteen at the time and had braces on her teeth). And he is proud to tell you he once got a letter which said, 'You were so harsh about my translation of *Aeschylus* that I didn't write for a year.' And that he wrote back saying, 'Don't be a cry baby.'

Does James take his own advice? He tries to, but the truth is he bruises easily. Indeed, he once wrote that he enjoys a good joke against himself, before he goes quietly away somewhere to be sick. More recently, he failed to duck when the *Modern Review* took a swipe at him. 'I like to think I took the attack philosophically. With poise. The fact is it was designed to piss me off and it pissed me off. But I don't think you should punish yourself if you feel hurt. As a writer, a thick skin is the last thing you should grow.'

Having both dished out criticism and received it, he knows the thing you should do is ignore it – but that you never can. 'You always think the guy who is critical about you has got it right,' he says. 'Words are magical. If someone attacks you in print it wounds you grievously. Maybe you only get to see it all in perspective when you are on your deathbed.' Warming to his maudlin theme, he adds that the attacks in the *Modern Review* were so vitriolic he couldn't imagine what terms of disapprobation the writers would have had left if asked to condemn Hitler or Himmler. It is a line I remember reading in his memoir, *May Week Was in June*, where James used it to describe the personal attacks F.R. Leavis made on his rival academics, Hough and Holloway. For the sixth time during this lunch he makes a reference that has me flicking mentally to the appropriate page in one of his books – 'a 93-year-old Scots lady wrote to me saying that, when young, she had done all the same things I did'. Flick flick flick, page twelve, *Falling Towards England*.

It strikes me that the price of James' success is that he has become a pastiche of himself, formulaic, cruising on autopilot, or rather autocue. He has come to inhabit a fictionalized reality of his own making, a twilight zone in which he constantly re-reads the twenty-six books he has published and then, perhaps unconsciously, reiterates their tried and tested contents as part of his everyday speech. It makes me feel slightly cheated, but it doesn't change my view that he is, on the whole, a good thing. There, I've said it. I like his writing. He makes me laugh and pause for thought. I can't think of anyone else who could have come up with: 'I find myself left alone with an Iranian biochemist whose name sounded like a fly trapped against a window.' Or: 'My own transitional persona must have seemed as out of focus as a chameleon crossing a kilt.'

Yet I know plenty of people who do not share my enthusiasm. He knows plenty, too. So why is it, does he suppose, that he never seems to inspire neutral feelings? He gives an exaggerated blink: 'I might be just obnoxious, I don't know.' But even then he's hoisted by his transitional persona. When he's doing interviews on TV, his critics say, he isn't obnoxious enough – just sycophantic. I ask him whether his interviewing style is deceptively gentle or just gentle. 'Just gentle. I'm not very good as a probing interviewer – too easily embarrassed. I believe in bowling under arm, instead. That way they take a big swing at it and get caught out. There's far too much attention paid to the adversarial style of interview. Get them through their vanity instead. I took a lot of stick for my Ronald Reagan interview. But I knew that there were two ways of asking him about his connection with McCarthyism. I could ask outright, 'Were you a stoolie for the FBI in Hollywood?' – at which point he would have clammed up. Or I could say, 'How serious was the Communist menace in Hollywood?' – which I did and he opened up and told me everything.'

You don't get the feeling that Clive James tells you everything. Perhaps he expects you to read between the lines of his novels instead. Indeed, there are a number of parallels between the hero's life in his latest novel, *The Silver Castle*, and that of the young James. Both learn about the world through magazines and the cinema. Both fuel their ambition with envy and fantasize constantly about being famous. Both incorporate self-mockery into their armoury of devices for staving off wrath, even if it is not the way they really feel about themselves. Both are cursed by a sense that, even in their own country, they can never feel at home.

James has lived here for thirty-four years, yet still, I suspect, he does not feel as if he belongs, quite. He feels that he is still a bit of an outsider. An exile. 'I feel more Australian the older I get,' he says, yet he can't imagine fitting in there either. England – the motherland – is the only place he feels he could fit in, but, he says, he has never had the least urge to try. 'So cold in England,' he once wrote, 'even when it was warm.'

His friend Vitali Vitaliev, a Russian journalist, describes him as being too melancholy in his private life. Yet James himself once wrote that only self-discipline keeps his face straight. Which is true? The answer seems to lie in the chameleon reference. He is always playing a role, as he probably is here in the Japanese restaurant on the edge of Holland Park. In the *Postcard From . . .* series his persona is that of a wide-eyed amateur, charmingly lost, sometimes nervous. For one who lives his life in front of a TV camera, it can sometimes seem an implausible conceit. 'It's part genuine, part gimmick,' he shrugs. 'But it does answer a genuine need in my character. Egomania is not incompatible with extreme self-doubt.'

To his irritation, James has often been asked why he is wasting his learning – and talent as a writer – presenting populist TV shows. 'I'm very flattered that people assume I have talent to waste,' he says. 'I don't believe I am wasting it. I believe in mass communication, not art for the few. The short answer to why am I wasting my talent is that I never heard much about this talent before I started wasting it.' But when I ask him if he is happy, he gives a categorical no. 'On the other hand,' he adds, 'I'm happy to be alive. Happy to be here. But I won't pretend that I don't know what the question means. By keeping busy, I'm compensating for something – a sense of the world's arbitrariness that I acquired in childhood, perhaps. But I'm not about to burst into tears.'

His memoirs, he tells me, were written as a form of therapy. But writing something down, coolly and dispassionately (and later editing it, of course), is not the same as discussing it live, as it were, in the here and now. I am struck by the paradox that Clive James might actually feel uncomfortable talking about his favourite subject. 'No,' he replies. 'I don't mind talking about myself – because I can just offer the outer layer of the onion.' And with this he goes off in search of the chef, in order to practise his Japanese for a few minutes before it is time to go.

In my imagination, the onion analogy wrestles momentarily with that of the turnip, and then topples it off its throne. Onions have thin skins – those concentric layers of white succulent flesh that are bitter when raw, sweet when cooked. They also have a pungent odour which brings tears to your eyes, or makes you gag, depending on how you look at it.

Clive James said, after this appeared in 1996, that he would never agree to be interviewed again. He did, four years later, to promote a new collection of his essays as well as his internet site. He was much ridiculed in the press in 1997 when he wrote a long and heartfelt tribute to Diana, Princess of Wales, for the New Yorker.

Leslie Phillips

There's something poetic about the sight of an old man chasing moths around a room cluttered with antique bronzes, glassware and sepia-coloured photographs. The man is Leslie Phillips, the room is on the ground floor of his Victorian house in Maida Vale, north London, the moths are . . . well, they're just moths. Phillips claps his freckled hands together and opens them slowly to inspect. 'Missed,' he says gloomily. 'This one's a sod. I do hate moths.'

Even so, I can't help feeling that the moths belong here among the rickety chairs, sooty paintings and musty books stacked crookedly on shelves. They blend with the room's faded brown-and-cream colour scheme, rather like the 76-year-old actor himself, in fact. It is often noted how pets come to resemble their owners; Leslie Phillips, with dust fairies swirling around him, has come to resemble this room. He's at one with it. In harmony.

The cord shirt he wears is dark green, his hair is mousey, his smooth cheeks pink. But in the watery, mid-afternoon light, he looks quite frail and his hands shake a little, perhaps because he is just recovering from what he describes as 'a week on the lav. Nasty tummy bug I picked up while doing a speech for the WI in Scarborough.' The illness hasn't affected that refined, warm English beer voice of his. It's still unhurried, oaky and soothing. And it still makes his every utterance sound vaguely sarcastic. 'It's terribly distinctive,' he says. 'My voice is recognized as clearly as my face. When I phone, say, the electricity company, they always recognize my voice before I've said my name.' He gets requests to record himself saying '*Hel-low*', in that silky, suggestive way he has, for answering-machines. 'For some reason it brings a smile to people's faces,' he says.

The voice does make it difficult to gauge when he is being serious. Take, for instance, the business of his obituary. He has, he tells me, been brooding on it a lot lately. Why? 'A giant pie fell on my head a few weeks ago and it got me thinking. I mean, imagine the headlines. What an undignified way to go.' Did he say pie? 'Oh, it was a prop for a television programme. Left me with a stiff neck, but I didn't make a fuss, much to the relief of the producers who clearly thought I was going to sue.'

What really bothers him is that, though he has made more than one hundred films, the obituaries are bound to concentrate on the *Carry Ons*, those and the *Doctors*. And he only made three of each. He loathes talking about them; finds the way people associate him with them tedious; indeed, in the three hours I'm with him the closest he gets to mentioning the *Carry On* team is when he refers to 'the group I was with'.

Frustrated at being typecast as the suave, Brylcreemed Lothario who arched his eyebrow and purred the words 'ding-*dong*!' whenever he saw a pretty nurse, Phillips took the decision at the beginning of the eighties to accept no more broad comedy roles. 'My friends, my agent, my bank manager all thought I was mad, because I was at the top of the tree in comedy, but I knew I wasn't. There was an unnerving lull for a while, then I was offered a straight part in Peter Nichols's *Passion Play*. That's the role I'm most proud of playing. It changed everything for me. I wish the obituaries would lead on that.' He stares out of the window. 'But I don't suppose they will.'

After *Passion Play*, Phillips was offered numerous stage roles in Shakespeare and Chekhov and, last year, he starred in his own one-man play, *On the Whole Life's Been Jolly Good*, about the life and dalliances of a failed and ousted Tory MP ('I was tremendous in that, a great success'). He says he has earned more from his theatre work than from film, but the change in direction also led to his being given roles in 'serious' films such as *Scandal* (1988), *Empire of the Sun* (1987) and *Out of Africa* (1985). 'The past twenty-five years have been the most reward-ing for me. What goes on the tombstone might be . . .' He trails off.

When asked why he continues to work, long after the national retirement age, Phillips says: 'Work stops me feeling old. I don't normally think of retirement but the other day a black guy got up for me on the Tube and offered me his seat and I thought, "Oh shit! I must look old. It's happened." But my memory still works for learning lines. The fear of fucking it up helps, too.'

A cat wanders into the room and he begins stroking it. Her name is Pushy, he says, and she is a sixteen-year-old feral, the only one left of nine he brought back from Spain. He has a 200-year-old farmhouse there which he has been restoring for years. At one point his neighbours in Spain were his friends Terry-Thomas and Denholm Elliot. Both dead now, of course, like most of his generation of comedy actors. Of his friends from that group, Ronnie Barker is the only one he still sees regularly. Smashing bloke. 'I don't fear death,' he adds, 'just illness and senility. But I do sometimes forget I've grown older. When I did Lord Lane [in the docu-drama *The Birmingham Six*] I went in for make-up and they said I didn't need any, and I said, "But Lane was an old man!" I persuaded them to give me some eyebrows.'

The famous Leslie Phillips's moustache is white now – distinguished, as the euphemism goes. One of his catchphrases, from a scene in which he looked at himself in a mirror as he put on aftershave, was 'Oh, you gorgeous beast!' Perhaps dishonestly, he says he never thought of himself as handsome. 'I was never pretty. Pleasant-looking, that's all. As I got older my face looked fuller and more secure-looking. I looked like I had more savoir faire. I know some actors who can't accept that when they grow old they have to give up the romantic leads. I often advise them not to reach for the toupee.'

There is another reason why Phillips won't give up work. 'I'm an actor who wants to earn a living. All my money went on educating my children, sending them to very good schools.' He has four from his first marriage, a stepson from his second and fifteen grandchildren. 'Both my sons went to university, something I wish I could have done. One is a lawyer, the other a housemaster, they are both very successful, both lovely people. I was certainly marvellous with my children. *Terrific*.'

His being driven by a need to make money is understandable, given his background. Phillips was born in Tottenham, north

London, in 1924. His father, Fred, worked for Main Gas Cookers and suffered from rheumatic fever, eventually dying from it, aged forty-one, when Leslie was nine. 'That had a great impact. My father was a lovely man but he always seemed close to death. My mother was always having to look after him. She was my real role model.'

As there was no Social Security at the time, his mother, Cecilia, found it a struggle to bring up three children in the family home in Chingford, Essex, where the family moved. She took in sewing and, inspired by Leslie's victory in a beautiful baby competition, decided to put her son on the stage to bring in extra money. She answered a small ad for child actors, which led to Leslie appearing, aged ten, in a touring production of *Peter Pan* with Anna Neagle. From the age of fourteen, he was on tour more or less permanently. Actors such as John Gielgud, Laurence Olivier and Rex Harrison became his surrogate uncles. 'They were my family. Very kind. They encouraged me to read books and educate myself.'

As most West End actors were called up when war broke out, the fifteen-year-old Leslie found himself in demand, and at seventeen was appearing in two plays simultaneously. The following year it was his turn to be called up and, partly because he had lost his cockney accent and had learned, through elocution lessons, to talk with an upper-class voice, he was commissioned as an officer.

As part of his training he was shot at with live ammunition, an experience which left his nerves shattered. He was declared medically unfit for battle and put in charge of a base camp in Suffolk. 'The Army was an education for me,' he says. 'It toughened me up.' Not that the life of an actor in those days was soft, he adds rather defensively. 'You learned to cope with illness. You had to be dead nearly before you took time off. Nowadays actors stay in bed if they have a sniffle. The one occasion I took a break was when I had a stomach haemorrhage. My former Army MO discovered it. He's dead now, bless his heart. I told him I felt weak and had awful diarrhoea, and he asked me what colour it was and when I said, "Black," he said, "You're bleeding," and rushed me to hospital for a blood transfusion. I'd been taking too many aspirin, apparently, for my backache. I've never touched them since.'

Contrary to his screen image as a rake, there have been only four women in Phillips's life. The first was when he was nineteen and serving in the Army. The second was when he was twenty-four. Her name was Penny and, in 1948, they married. Their first child was stillborn. 'It was ghastly,' he says. 'Very difficult to get over.' The couple had four more children and then, in 1965, divorced after Leslie had an affair with John Mortimer's stepdaughter Caroline.

He never really wanted to get divorced, he says, Penny divorced him. 'I don't really know why it happened. There were lots of factors. I was very fond of her and remained so. The story of why things go wrong is complicated. But it wasn't a lack of love or care. Love is a very big word, isn't it?' He believes the divorce knocked Penny off balance. She wouldn't let him see the children and would ring his home and leave the phone off the hook so that no one else could get through.

Leslie and Caroline were together for nine years, but, partly because she wanted a baby and he didn't, they separated, and Leslie began seeing Angela, an actress twenty-three years his junior. ('The image of me as a womanizer was misleading,' he says distractedly, swiping after another passing moth. 'I always got on with women but I didn't really have them throwing themselves at me.' He grins. 'I much prefer being at home than in a nightclub. I do like my slippers.')

In 1981 Penny had a stroke. She died eighteen months later, in a fire at her nursing home. Phillips married Angela in 1982 and, for six difficult years, had to nurse her through clinical depression. Medication eventually worked and she is much better now. 'I became withdrawn when Angela was ill because of the stress,' he says. 'But our sense of humour held us together.'

In whom did he confide about his various marital problems? 'I didn't really confide in my mother. We were close, she kept cuttings about me, but never really understood my business. I sometimes thought this was a pity. None of my family have ever come into the inner part of my life. They wouldn't have been at ease there.' And perhaps he wouldn't have been at ease with them being there. Might he even have felt a twinge of embarrassment about them, having lost his cockney accent and re-invented himself as a toff? 'I don't think they felt betrayed.

Distanced maybe. They realized it would be virtually impossible to make a career without "talking proper". They admired me for it.'

In 1984 his mother, then aged ninety-two, was mugged by three boys at a bus stop outside her home in Chingford. When she clung on to her handbag, they battered her with their fists. She was taken to hospital, never fully recovered and died nine months later. For months afterwards he scoured the streets of Chingford looking for the youths, going on the only description police had, that they were black and one of them had been wearing a yellow sweatshirt. 'I still have strong feelings about that incident,' he says with a slow blink of his pale blue eyes. 'You can't suppress things like that. But equally you have to carry on, you can't dry up or commit suicide. My sister was closest to her. It ruined her life and she died of grief soon afterwards. They are buried near each other.' Phillips claps his hands at another passing moth. 'Oh bugger! Missed.' The movement makes a strand of his hair flap out of place, over his ear. He smoothes it back.

Leslie Phillips is not an easy man to figure out. There is ennui behind the bonhomie. He describes himself as bossy, though more tolerant now than he was as a young man. His immodesty is Olympian, but self-aggrandizement is often a device people use to counter low self-esteem. When he tells me how good he has been as a father, it is really himself he is trying to convince, I suspect, as if he is still judging himself for the break-up with his first wife. 'I don't go to church very often,' he says at one point, 'but I'm very good. I'm a good person. I'm not horrible to people.'

Similarly, what comes across as boasting about his career as a serious actor is probably just anxiety that his early comedy work will overshadow it. The role he really wants to play, he says, is *King Lear* – Sir Anthony Hopkins once promised to direct. 'I don't know whether I will get the chance now. I doubt it.'

He thinks his early comic roles were vulgar and undignified. He tells me he wanted to do more 'classy' roles. The word classy is revealing, especially as he goes on to say that he can't stand it when people don't speak clearly, with good diction. 'Everyone I've been associated with romantically has been middle-class. They have been well-spoken.'

112

He reinvented himself, but he can't escape the past. How cruel that, instead of being buried and forgotten, all those *Carry On* films are still being repeated, constantly, all around the world. And one thinks of all those terrible, scarring events from which Phillips can't escape: the deaths of his father, his mother, his first wife, his first child.

The extent to which he still lives in the shadow of the past is illustrated most clearly, and touchingly, in his attitude to children. 'I worry about seeing children at risk,' he tells me. 'Mothers not holding their children's hands in traffic, or near the edge of a platform when the train is coming. I can't stand it and have to intervene sometimes. I have to take the child's hand myself because I get so terribly anxious.'

Here is a man, then, who can demonstrate a deep understanding of the fragility of life and yet, the next moment, be chuckling to himself as he swipes at another moth. Which is what he does now. It escapes him and flutters in my direction. I grab for it. Success. 'Well *done*!' he says, with the same intonation he used for the words 'ding-*dong*!' all those years ago.

Roger Scruton

NOVEMBER 1996

I discovered Roger Scruton's true identity quite by accident, while listening to an interview I'd taped with him. There it was: a perfectly normal, if slightly lispy voice belonging to an earnest, sixteen-year-old public schoolboy. At first, I thought I had picked up the wrong tape. Only when my own voice came on – Mickey Mouse on helium, the normal sound of speeded up human speech – did I realize that I had flicked on the fast-play mode on my recorder.

Scruton, it seems, is a sixteen-year-old trapped in a 52-year-old body. As with Dorian Gray's picture, the exterior has aged while the inner voice, the 'identity of self' he so often writes about, has remained young. If you don't believe me, try taping Radio 4's *The Moral Maze* next time he's on the panel. Listen to his slow, ponderous monotone and then play it back at speed. I know it's childish, but I promise it will make you smile.

This discovery is only amusing, of course, because Roger Scruton is gravitas incarnate and he's quite intimidating to boot – and not just because he has a brain the size of Denmark (the double first, the professorship) and because he is a Renaissance man with a capital R (barrister, novelist, opera composer, journalist, author of twenty academic books on subjects ranging from architecture to sexual desire, and organist at his local church). It's to do, too, with his repertoire of facial expressions: he hasn't got one. Instead, his pale angular features are frozen in an impersonation of the sinister German dentist-torturer played by Laurence Olivier in *The Marathon Man*. As Scruton himself once

115

said of his inflexible face and voice: 'I can't simultaneously develop an argument and appear like a human being.'

He does smile occasionally, but even this is intimidating: more a tight grimace. Even his fiery hair is a bit scary. As for his name – well, Maurice Saatchi couldn't have come up with a more appropriate monicker for a right-wing polemicist who's been accused, over the years, of everything from racism to homophobia to, probably, global warming. Try saying it. *Roger Scruton*. It's brutal. It's stark. It almost snarls at you. Can it be just coincidence that the closest word in the dictionary is 'scruto', a trap door? 'Actually,' says Roger Scruton, as he prepares to drive off in his battered old Land-Rover, one of his rare, taut grins playing about his face, 'it's an old Yorkshire name. It means one who treats dandruff sufferers.'

***

Two hours earlier, Roger Vernon Scruton looks blank as he opens the door of his Wiltshire farmhouse. 'Forgot you were coming,' he eventually says in his Marvin-the-Paranoid-Android voice. This is as it should be. You wouldn't expect Britain's most famous philosopher to consult his diary every day. Nor would you expect him to dress up for the occasion, even if he had remembered you were driving all the way down from London to visit him on his remote 35-acre farm with its four horses, orchard and ducks. He hasn't, and he is wearing a blue moth-eaten tank top, grubby trousers and no shoes (but grey school socks that are threadbare and inside out). 'Follow me,' he says, and leads me through the kitchen and in to a sitting room that is – despite the log burner, the chairs that don't match, the hunting horn, the Wagner recordings scattered on the floor, the small painting of a saddleback pig and the large portrait of Lord Fairfax in long wig and armour – somehow austere.

On the window sill is a photo of two riders clearing a jump. One is Scruton, the other Sophie Jeffreys, the handsome, blonde 24-year-old he is marrying on 7 December. 'This photo,' he says, 'shows her competence and my incompetence.' You can see what he means: he has a shocked look on his bespectacled face and is joggling awkwardly out of his saddle; her seat is perfect. 'We met out hunting, believe it or not,' he says. Sophie Jeffreys is half-sister to Lord Jeffreys, a Conservative peer who shares Scruton's passion for country sports. She is also a descendant of Judge Jeffreys, whose enthusiasm for capital punishment you might expect Scruton to share. (Scruton is, after all, the man who once quipped on *The Moral Maze* that, 'Punishment is a good thing. There should be more of it, and it should be more severe.')

The couple are, by all accounts, smitten. The age difference seems not to be a barrier. Nor does Scruton's contempt for television (he won't allow a set in the house) nor his disdain for pop music. When asked if he worries that the marital home might be filled with the sound of Oasis, for instance, Scruton says: 'No. She is very much not that sort of person. She has the same outlook as I have. She loves, as I do, classical music, architecture and the countryside. Old-fashioned decencies. Not a television-watching type. I don't think there will be any conflict.'

No kidding. Scruton's latest book, out this month, was tried out on his fiancée first – and she suggested some 'vital improvements'. It's called *An Intelligent Person's Guide to Philosophy* and its modest aim is to rescue mankind from the trivializing uncertainty of science and to 'replace the sarcasm which knows that we are merely animals, with the irony which sees we are not'. In recognition of the improvements suggested, Scruton considered renaming the book *An Intelligent Woman's Guide to Philosophy*. Given that his last novel, *Xanthippic Dialogues* (1993), was essentially a send-up of scholarly writing in which Scruton draped himself in the clothes of Ancient Greek women the better to debate such topics as the role of the individual in society, you suspect that he may be only half joking.

All this might make you think that Scruton lacks the lightness of touch necessary to become a national treasure, in the tradition of 'Freddie' Ayer and 'Bertie' Russell. I'm not so sure. There is, for instance, a story about Scruton's time at Cambridge: when his girlfriend's clothes were discovered in his college room – a serious offence – he told his tutor the clothes were his, and that he needed them because he was a transvestite. In fact, it could be that his sense of humour is so dry it is misinterpreted as pretentiousness. As a teenager, while at High Wycombe Grammar

School, Scruton was accused of riding on the London Tube without a ticket. The case was made rather more serious by the allegation that he had given a false name to the police. This was solemnly read out in court as John Stuart Mill. And when once asked by the *Guardian* what phrase he most overused, he said, 'the transcendental unity of apperception'. He added that his favourite smell was the French Literature section of the London Library.

The Cambridge don John Casey once said that Scruton's philosophical armour-plating hides a quixotic, absurdist nature. It is an astute observation, even if the absurd aspects of Scruton's life are not always intentional. In 1989, for example, I heard him give the inaugural lecture of the Royal Institute of Philosophy in a lecture hall at Durham University. As he was talking, a choir began practising in the next room. The choir grew louder and louder, until everyone else in the hall had to bite on their knuckles to avoid sniggering. But Scruton was unruffled. He did not smile, raise his soft, low voice, or vary his measured, monotone delivery, as if it were for him an everyday occurrence to be accompanied by a heavenly choir. It got worse. Later that night, I gave him a lift back to Durham Castle where he was staying in the Bishop's Suite. Thinking I had got him back just before the Castle gates closed at midnight, I did not wait to see that he was let in. He wasn't, and next day the campus was tittering with tales of how Scruton's wan and wraith-like figure had been sighted flitting through the cobbled backstreets of Durham at two in the morning, still looking for a policeman to help him.

Scruton stares out of the window and, with limp fingers, drags on a fat cigar. 'What', he asks, 'would you like to talk about now?' Well, we could start with *Animal Rights and Wrongs*, a book he brought out in the summer. Or the First of June Prize, the award he was given this year by the people of the Czech Republic in recognition of the role he played in overthrowing communism. But we plump, instead, for *Modern Philosophy*, out in paperback this year. When it was published, *The Times* devoted a leader to it, not least because it is, unlike most books on philosophy, readable and lucid, conveying complex ideas in a conversational style – or, as Scruton puts it, expressing the problems of the head in the language of the heart. Judged in this light, Scruton has earned a place on the same pedestal as Russell and Ayer – for what they, too, had was a gift for sharing their wisdom with others. Unlike them, though, he is not the apple of academe's eye. Professor Ted Honderich of University College, London, for instance, went so far as to call him 'the unthinking man's thinking man'. (Scruton retaliated by calling Honderich 'the thinking man's unthinking man'.)

And if an Oxford chair once beckoned, it was off the cards once Scruton wrote *The Meaning of Conservatism* in 1980. 'After that book,' Scruton says, 'it was ruled out that I would ever gain the highest of academic honours. Even if I deserved them. Which I didn't. But being free from the possibility of those ambitions enabled me to write rude and disgraceful things about the intellectual establishment. It meant I was free to say some really enjoyable and unpleasant things and thereby give pleasure to others.'

He denies, though, that he makes his caustic comments solely because it excites him to do so. 'No, I don't enjoy being controversial, but it is enjoyable telling the truth about a conspiracy of silence or an established lie. If you are a right-wing academic, your colleagues think that you are not a proper philosopher at all. My right-wing stance has always heavily compromised my career. If you criticize the whole idea of human equality, which is basically what I do, you are going against a prevalent quasi-religious orthodoxy.'

His many enemies accuse him, though, of striking poses rather than expressing deeply held conservative convictions. The exhibitionist who subverts liberal pieties through ridicule, who declares unambiguously that there are no natural human rights, who describes democracy as a wildly raging contagion is, they say, exactly the sort of masochist who would take up fox-hunting at the age of forty-five simply because he knew socialists would hate him for it.

There is, undoubtedly, a combative side to his nature, but it's a mistake to suggest, as the *Guardian* once did, that his most controversial views – on multicultural education, say, or homosexuality – are just expressions of prejudice. Unlike true bigots, he welcomes serious debate and, you suspect, secretly wishes someone would come along and free him from his martyr's cross by persuading him that his 'offensive' beliefs are wrong. 'I don't want to be right-wing,' he says, 'but I just am.' He is similarly reluctant to set himself up as a moral arbiter, but he can't help himself. 'I have thousands of weaknesses and sins, like everyone else. I spend a lot of time regretting what I've done, feeling remorse for bad behaviour.'

It is depressing to consider the paradox implied by this. Here is an intellectual who feels he has to live with the indignity of upholding populist views that even some London taxi drivers might consider unsophisticated. Here is an essentially private, almost shy man who has felt obliged to court publicity all his life, even to the extent of appearing on television, a medium he despises. And here is a man who feels he has had no choice but to make himself unpopular with liberals even though he says he found the sack-loads of hate mail he has received over the years hurtful: 'You'd think I would get used to it, but I don't.'

It needn't have been like this. Roger Scruton's father was a socialist. And so was Roger Scruton – until he went to teach at a French university, just before the country was torn apart by the student revolution of 1968. After this, Scruton became vehemently anti-communist. Personal experience confirmed his views: 'When I started visiting Eastern Europe and acquired friends there, I became indignant and frightened on their behalf. I had an experience of evil: the systematic negation of the human spirit. If you wanted a description of the devil's work, that would be it: the world devoid of human spirit and freedom.'

In 1979, Roger Scruton was invited to address an underground seminar in Prague. 'In a communist society everything is forbidden unless permitted, the opposite of our assumption. Nobody had ever permitted anyone to gather in a private apartment and discuss philosophy, therefore it was considered a crime by the secret police.' Vaclav Havel, the first President of the Czech Republic, was one of the students Scruton taught. Scruton learnt Czech, helped set up a resistance movement and found himself cast in the role of Scarlet Pimpernel – before eventually being arrested and expelled.

Whatever kudos this might have earned Scruton among the *bien pensants* was dispelled in 1982, when he set up *The Salisbury Review*, a right-wing magazine, and published

Education and Race, an article by a Bradford schoolteacher, Ray Honeyford, which advocated that immigrants should be taught without respect for cultural difference. This established Scruton in the public consciousness as the natural successor to that other inflammatory right-winger Enoch Powell. Wherever Scruton went, demonstrators would be waiting. Some of his lectures had to be cancelled because city councils could not guarantee his safety.

Enoch Powell is one of Scruton's heroes, along with Kant and Wittgenstein. 'Enoch Powell suffered much more than me. He said things that all decent Englishmen in their hearts believe. But in the wrong tone of voice, and when it was so unfashionable. It became possible to label him . . .' He hesitates. 'In the most damning ways. I think he was very brave and stood for the right things, but he would not have made a good prime minister because he was totally unsound on the question of communism and Russia. He never saw what it meant. He had a romantic ninteenth-century view of how great powers worked. For him it was as if Disraeli and Bismarck were still dividing up the Balkans.'

Scruton doesn't think he would have made a good prime minister, either. 'I did put myself forward as a Conservative candidate, about twenty years ago,' he admits. 'I had an interview with some old blue-rinse at Central Office but I was judged to be far too intellectual and was told to go away. I think they were right. I didn't have the temperament to be a politician.'

One enduring myth about Scruton is that it was Powell who persuaded him to take up fox-hunting because to do so was every true Conservative's duty. 'He didn't really get me into hunting but he did sell me his hunting gear,' Scruton recalls. 'I happened to be sitting next to him at a dinner when he said he was giving up. I was a bit poor at the time so I offered to buy his second-hand clothes. I've still got his jacket but it never was quite big enough for me. It split down the seams.' The story goes that when someone asked Powell about the hunting clothes, he said, 'We're just about the same size. Physically, I mean, not intellectually.'

It's his physical being, really, that provides Scruton's strongest claim to the status of national institution. The subject of hunting suddenly reminds Scruton that he is supposed to be picking up a horse, even as we speak. As he rushes outside to hitch up a rusty trailer to his Land-Rover, he becomes distracted by a chicken that has escaped from its coop. It looks at him quizzically as he potters across the field towards it, making clucking noises. As he draws closer he spreads his arms wide and assumes a shuffling crouch, as though trying to hypnotize the bird. It is a comical sight. Gloriously undignified. And, yes, utterly endearing. Like the sixteen-year-old's voice on the tape, it serves to remind you of a sentence in Scruton's new book: 'We all know in our hearts, even if we never put the matter in words, that the human subject is the strangest thing that we encounter.'

Sophie Scruton gave birth to a son, Samuel, in November 1998. Roger Scruton declared that Sam would not enjoy his childhood but would be more enjoyable company as a consequence. Sam would not be allowed to watch television or listen to pop, instead he would hunt, learn Greek by the age of six, as John Stuart Mill had done, and learn the viola, because it is not much fun to play.

In 2002 the philosopher came unstuck briefly when he lost his column on the Financial Times, *after it was revealed he was receiving £54,000 a year to influence the media on behalf of a Japanese tobacco company.*

Andrew Neil

All heads turn as Andrew Neil enters the newsroom of the *Sunday Times* like a gunslinger moseying through the swing doors of a Wild West saloon. On his arm, dressed in the shortest of skirts, is the pouting Pamella Bordes. On his hip is the security pass to the newspaper's offices that he has taken to wearing like a holster. It's 11.30 on a Friday night, the early pages are being put together and, as he swaggers past cowering sub-editors and reporters, the editor points to various computer screens. 'Cut that intro,' he barks. 'Give me a better headline on this.' All eyes follow him as he now leads his girlfriend ostentatiously into the executive washroom at the end of the line of desks. He emerges twenty minutes later grinning like the cat who got the cream.

It is a story veterans of Wapping love to relate. And I am now reminded of it as I watch the great man approaching the entrance to Brighton's Palace Pier. He has a pigeon-toed walk which, combined with the rolling motion of his wide, forward-hunched shoulders, looks like someone doing a bad impression of Robert Mitchum.

Today he is not wearing the cowboy boots he sometimes favours, but he is carrying a six-shooter on his hip, disguised as a mobile phone. It is high noon. The sun is blazing down. And the Wapping Kid is back in town. I ask if he was followed. He grins and says that he doesn't think he was. *Full Disclosure*, his autobiography, tells of the time when he was tailed. By MI6, he thinks. In New York. It also describes the many death threats he received; the bodyguards riding shotgun in his car; and the attempts he claims were made by the Establishment to destabilize him.

On one occasion his new flat in South Kensington was burgled, and every drawer and cupboard searched. 'It was hard to avoid the impression that somebody was looking for some dirt on me,' he says, with a neutralized but still springy Paisley burr. 'It was no time to be paranoid. I knew everyone was against me! That was what hardened me. It brought out reserves of brutality I didn't know I had.'

Seagulls are wheeling and screeching overhead and, as we wander along the pier, past an arcade full of slot machines, their cries are drowned out by the sound of Madness singing 'I Like Driving in my Car'. Sportingly, Andrew Neil agrees to be photographed sitting in the tiny car of a brightly coloured merry-go-round in front of a huge grinning clown. It seems that Brillo Pad, as he is known to *Private Eye* readers, has a sense of the ridiculous. (The journalist Matthew Norman discovered this, too, after he started a campaign in his *Guardian* diary to find a suitable wife for Neil. The butt of his joke joined in the search and began faxing his own suggestions. Neil apparently enjoyed the whole caper, even when Norman's mother was revealed as the only applicant.)

A gang of shuffling old-age pensioners stops to stare. 'I know the face,' says one as she unwraps a treacle toffee. 'But I can't think of his name.' One's thoughts return to the time when Neil was asked by Mrs Merton on her television show if he had ever thought of having an allotment because it would do him good to get out and meet people his own age (Neil is only forty-seven, but he appreciated the joke).

The photos done, we stroll back along the pier and stop at a booth where palms can be read electronically. Ever since he dragged Fleet Street picketing and screaming into the computer age, Neil has been obsessed with new technology. Indeed, on the door of his downstairs loo is a framed page from *Private Eye* in which a disillusioned journalist from Wapping is quoted as saying: 'If Andrew Neil can't fuck it or plug it in to the wall, he isn't interested.' But the electronic palm-reader has gone to lunch, so we take a walk along the seafront to find a restaurant and do the same.

Andrew Neil edited the *Sunday Times* for eleven turbulent years. He was, he now claims, eased out of the job in 1994 for two reasons. First, the Malaysian Prime Minister demanded Neil's head on a plate, following a spat between the *Sunday Times* and the Malaysian government which threatened Murdoch's Far Eastern business interests. Second, Rupert Murdoch, the paper's proprietor, had become jealous of his celebrity. As if on cue, a middle-aged man lying in a deckchair recognizes Neil and shouts out to me, 'Are you auditioning him?' Neil smiles tightly, ignores the man, and continues his theme. The trouble was, he says, that in many people's minds he had come to personify the *Sunday Times*. 'Rupert didn't like that. He resented the independent celebrity I had. No one is allowed to outshine the Sun King.'

Neil portrays the Australian media mogul as a cross between an omnipotent Sun King and a foul-mouthed tyrant who has no real friends and who rules over his medieval court through authority, loyalty, example and fear. 'He can be benign or ruthless, depending on his mood or the requirements of his empire. It was part of his management style that he could leave you in deep depression or on top of the world.' Neil describes Murdoch as having a Jekyll and Hyde personality. In a later chapter of his autobiography, perhaps unconsciously, he uses the same cliché when writing about Pamella Bordes, the Parliamentary researcher who, after her fling with Neil was over, was exposed as a high-class call girl. I ask if he has a masochistic streak that draws him to such people. 'I'm not self-destructive. In fact there's a huge self-preservation streak in me. That was what stopped me falling head over heels in love with Ms Bordes, or getting besotted in the way our tiny friend [Donald Trelford, then editor of the *Observer*] did. The same applies to Rupert. The best advice I ever heard was: "Don't fall in love with Rupert. He turns on his lovers."'

Neil talks constantly of the breakdown in his relationship with Murdoch in terms of a divorce. 'It wasn't a love affair in the sense of being two intertwined individuals in a passionate embrace,' he says. 'But we were a team and we both knew our roles. I could see the divorce coming as early as 1990. But the decree absolute took until 1994. It was all about a clash of egos and, in a way, I'm surprised he tolerated me for as long as he did.'

There is a third version of what happened between the star-crossed lovers. According to this, when Murdoch offered the 34-year-old Neil the job of editing the *Sunday Times* he knew he was taking a big risk – critics said that because Neil came from the *Economist* rather than a newspaper, he was too inexperienced. But the Sun King's faith was rewarded when Neil rode into town for his shootout with the unions during the bitter Wapping dispute, one of the longest and most violent strikes in industrial history. And when Neil then went on to introduce the first multi-multi-section newspaper in Britain, as well as launch Sky TV, a strong bond was formed between master and servant. But in the early nineties, the theory holds, Murdoch began to accuse Neil of being gratuitously controversial, a parody of himself, guilty of *folie de grandeur*.

Worse, Murdoch feared his editor was so unpopular with the public that he was putting off more readers than he was attracting. (When Neil became editor in 1983, the circulation of the *Sunday Times* was 1.29 million – when he left in 1994 it was 1.22 million.) Murdoch's antennae may also have picked up on a feeling at the time that, under Neil, the *Sunday Times* had become mean-spirited, yobbish, too rabidly anti-Establishment. As a former colleague of Neil's puts it: 'The *Sunday Times* had become a perfect fake Rolex. Neil knew it, and each week he would pray that the gilt – his sensational scoops – would stay on until the lunchtime news. After that it didn't matter if the stories fell apart because everyone would have already bought the paper.'

And so, the story goes, Murdoch let Neil down gently by promising him the job of anchorman on a new prime-time current affairs programme in the United States. But it was a bone his pet Rottweiler never got to play with. The programme only made it to the pilot stage – amid plentiful stories of American terror at his untelegenic looks and impenetrable accent – so, when Neil returned to Britain six months later, tail between his legs, all his enemies were delighted.

Tellingly, some of these have been unable to keep up their animosity. As Ian Hislop, editor of *Private Eye* puts it: 'It is difficult to sustain a loathing of Brillo since the Dirty Digger stripped him of the apparatus of power and blew him out – or rather "offered him a job in television", as the euphemism goes.'

But Andrew Neil is canny enough to know that many people will still try. He is well aware of the enemies he has made over the years. 'The reviews for this book will all be hostile,' he grins. 'There will be a lot of retaliation from the diaspora of the dispossessed. You know, the old guard, from Hugo Young [a former *Sunday Times* colleague, now a big cheese at the *Guardian* and *Observer*] downward. But I don't mind. This book will sell on its controversy.'

And, judging by what is on the record, Neil's expectations are justified. Charles Moore, editor of the *Daily Telegraph*, finds him 'ghastly. It makes me laugh just to look at him.' Auberon Waugh says he associates Neil with a sort of whingeing enviousness: 'He seems to me like a wounded bear, ranting and raving inside his cave, a sort of Caliban figure.' Francis Wheen, writing in the *Guardian* this summer, seemed to sum up the feelings of many journalists when he wrote: 'I know of no spectacle so ridiculous as Andrew Neil in one of his periodic fits of morality. Come to think of it, I know no spectacle as ridiculous as Andrew Neil, full stop.'

Neil now thinks that the reason he made more enemies 'than was necessary' was that he had no patience or skill for massaging bruised egos. But there was more to it than that. Canvas the views of colleagues from *Sunday Times* days and you hear such descriptions as: 'A volatile man. Pugnacious and full of bluster. Eaten up with anger'; 'The key to understanding him is that he is very negative. He is driven by what he is against, not what he is for'; 'Working for him was nerve jangling; he created a poisonous, internecine atmosphere wherever he went'; 'He is chippy and gauche – all wing collars and red braces – but there is an attractiveness to his chippiness. And he could never be accused of being a hypocrite.'

Nearly everyone who meets Andrew Neil says that he can be relaxed, charming and affable. As we now sit down to lunch, he proves to be all three. But this, I suspect, may have a lot to do with the taut chuckle that punctuates his every sentence. He smiles a lot, too, which always helps. Indeed, over the years, his constant smiling has etched deep grooves on his face that run from the side of his nose down to the corners of his mouth. Combined with the cleft in his chin, these make him look as if he has been accosted by an over-enthusiastic, amateur make-up artist worried that those at the back of the village hall will not be able to make out her subject's expressions.

Actually, as he studies the menu, I can't help noticing that Neil *is* wearing make-up – orange powder that, presumably, has been applied in readiness for his televized conference report later that day. Despite this, his thick, rubbery skin still looks ruddy, as if his head has been boiled, and it strikes me that this may in part account for his Mr Angry image. He always looks as if his head is about to burst with rage.

I have to suppress a childish snigger when Neil opts for the brill (actually, his hair is not nearly so corrugated and bristly as legend has it – although it is a rather alarming mahogany tint). He doesn't want potatoes with his fish – just green salad and vegetables. Thanks to such restraint, he says, he has recently shed twenty-six pounds. He eats using just a fork, American style, and, returning to the subject of Murdoch, jabs with it for emphasis. 'What's Rupert going to think of the book? I don't know. I suspect he won't like it. But he's very unpredictable. It's not a hatchet-job, is it? It just reports what I saw. I suspect he'll pretend he hasn't read it.'

Murdoch still haunts Neil's dreams. This is not surprising given their symbiotic, almost preternatural relationship: Murdoch playing Frankenstein to Neil's Monster, or, more accurately, Mephistopheles to his Faust. At one point in the book Neil describes the way Murdoch 'descends like a thunderbolt from Hell to slash and burn all before him'. And you can almost smell the whiff of sulphur that lingers around Neil still. Indeed, I suspect the Wapping Kid still lives in fear of the moment when the ground will open up and the Prince of Darkness will return to claim his soul.

But it is a mistake to assume, as most of Fleet Street did, that Murdoch made Neil in his own Machiavellian image. Murdoch's attraction to Neil was narcissistic: he saw in him a reflection of himself. Neil was a fellow outsider, a mercurial Scotsman who hated the English Establishment and had an evangelical commitment to the freemarket economy. (A former *Sunday Times* journalist gives an example of how single-minded and one-dimensional Neil can be. He was once working on a nostalgic anniversary feature about the 1968 hippy counter-culture. Neil approached and asked what he was doing. 'Ah yes,' said Neil wistfully, "68 – the year of Callaghan's economic reform.')

Murdoch also recognized that both men are reckless gamblers: always acting on instinct and, almost addictively, taking risks. Neil compares his time with Murdoch to a ride on a rollercoaster. Again, he uses exactly the same comparison when talking about his time with Pamella (now Pamela) Bordes. He says he was genuinely frightened by what he calls her dark and evil side; yet, to echo Neil's cliché-rich writing, he was drawn to her like a moth to the flame. The thrill of the risk, the whiff of sulphur, was overwhelming. Bordes, he claims, told him that she thought she might be schizophrenic and this, combined with her bulimia, is what he now thinks accounts for the frenzied way in which she scrawled obscenities on his mirrors and took scissors to his suits and shirts. (She suspected him of being unfaithful because, according to Neil, she had listened to an answering machine message that was nearly a year old.) She would ring him constantly, send him dog excrement in the post and, one day, was even spotted by a caretaker waiting outside his flat with a bread knife.

'I found myself playing the starring role in the sequel to *Fatal Attraction*,' Neil recalls. 'The day I got back and she had wreaked all that havoc was terrifying. My friend Gerry Malone [now a Tory minister] joked that if I'd had a bunny rabbit it would've been a goner.' Until now, Neil has been leaning forward in earnest anchorman mode. As the conversation turns to Pamella Bordes he leans back as though trying to get away, one hand in his trouser pocket. He was flabbergasted when he found out that Donald Trelford was wooing Bordes as well: 'It seemed to me an incredible folly for, just as on Sunday mornings on the newsstands, it was a competition with me he could not hope to win.' The crude machismo of this comment reminds you of the answer he gave Mrs Merton when she sarcastically asked why women found him so attractive: 'Because I had the biggest organ on a Sunday.' It also helps to explain why, when the Bordes scandal broke out, Peregrine Worsthorne, then editor of *The Sunday Telegraph*, should have felt compelled to publish a leader accusing Neil of being unfit to be an editor.

In response, Andrew Neil sued *The Sunday Telegraph* for libel and won £1,000. 'I risked too much,' he now says. 'Winning by a thousand wasn't enough. I mean, it was better than losing, but £10,000 would have made it look more convincing.' In the press the libel case was presented as a clash of the Old Britain (Stowe and Oxbridge, stuffy, snobbish, pseudo-aristocratic, High Tory) versus the New Britain (Paisley Grammar and Glasgow University, brash, upwardly mobile, meritocratic, Thatcherite).

'The English Establishment thought it was a game,' he says. 'I didn't. They resented the fact that I couldn't be bought. I didn't want their cold country houses where you have to bathe in two inches of hot water. I didn't want one of their knighthoods. The hope of baubles and gongs in return for good behaviour is what is holding Britain back.' He adds that he would have refused a knighthood if one had been offered. 'But,' – that clipped chuckle again – 'I'm happy to say my resolution was never likely to be put to the test!'

Part of the reason he now regrets the libel trial, I suspect, was that it gave his press foes a second chance to snigger at him. He says he doesn't mind jokes being made at his expense. Indeed, he professes to enjoy *Private Eye*'s long-running gag of finding an excuse to reprint in every issue a photo of him in a vest and baseball cap with his arm around a young woman in a bikini. But Ian Hislop doubts this: 'Well, he has to say that, doesn't he? I heard that when the photo was first printed someone pinned it up in his office and he was hopping mad.'

When asked why it is always open season on Neil in *Private Eye* Hislop says: 'It's partly because his sense of himself as an outsider against whom the Establishment is always plotting is so absurd. The irony is that he *was* the Establishment in the eighties. That's the other funny thing about Andrew Neil. He's just funny. He says people like me are jealous of him because we live sad, pathetic lives with our wives and children. He's right, of course. How I would love to live his life! In the end, the best that can be said of him is that he is less ghastly in the flesh.'

Hislop is referring, of course, to Neil's reputation for working hard and playing hard. According to Fleet Street mythology you will find Neil in Tramp, the St James's nightclub frequented by minor royalty, celebrities and second-hand car-dealers, almost every night. 'I haven't been there for about three months,' Neil now says. 'But I don't want the mythology to be broken. As we say in journalism, it's a story too good to check.' But he does have an incredibly robust constitution. The model Nicola Formby, an old friend of his, says he is always the last to leave a good party. She recalls times when he and two drinking mates – a threesome known collectively as the 'Maltesers', cockney rhyming slang for old geezers – have still been going strong at 5 a.m., long after everyone else has slid under the table. And then Neil has gone straight to a studio to present an early morning radio programme.

Neil has a vulnerable side, though. He is never comfortable working a room, even if it is full of friends. And he describes how, when he was flying back from a holiday in America to take over as editor of the *Sunday Times*, he was so nervous he had an anxiety attack and began to hyperventilate. Again, when he was awaiting the outcome of the libel trial, he was so churned up with angst he couldn't swallow. 'They were the most miserable, loneliest two hours of my life,' he says.

The mood of the lunch having now changed, Neil tells me a touching story about the last time he saw his dying father, in 1988. 'I had just said goodbye to him. I kissed him on the forehead, but I don't know whether he heard me say goodbye. I was lost in my thoughts, keeping my head down as I waited at Glasgow airport for my plane back to London. Suddenly all these screaming banshees, SOGAT activists with East End accents, came from nowhere and started cursing me. I nearly punched one but, thank God, Gerry Malone happened to be on the same flight and grabbed my arm to stop me.'

He says it wasn't so much his father's death as his mother's, in 1993, that concentrated his mind on his own mortality. 'Ours was a small family and it made me feel very alone in the world. Just me and my brother left. You don't really appreciate how much you are going to miss your parents. I keep thinking of all the times I should have made the effort to go up and see them but didn't.'

Though there are stories of him dressing up as Santa and visiting orphans on Christmas Day, and of him being devoted to his seven godchildren, Neil has no immediate plans to start a family of his own. 'I never set out to get married and the way things have worked out I never have. I don't fall in love easily . . . But I do fall in love.'

Is he courting at the moment? 'Erm . . . I might be. We'll see how things go.'

Driving back to the conference, I ask him a final question. What is he like on the dance floor? 'Oh! A knockout!' he laughs, revealing a sprig of spinach caught on his tooth. 'Sensational! Whether I'm sensationally good or bad is another matter. But definitely sensational.'

The answer is as good a summary of the life and times of Andrew Neil as you are ever likely to hear.

Two days after this article appeared Andrew Neil wrote a letter to The Sunday Telegraph *to say that the anecdote with which this article begins is apocryphal, offensive and entirely without foundation. 'If this is really a true "story veterans of Wapping love to relate", as opposed to one invented by some fevered imaginations, did it never cross Mr Farndale's mind to consider why it has stayed unpublished for eight years? If anything remotely approaching such an incident had ever happened it would undoubtedly have been given due prominence in the next edition of* Private Eye. *After all, everything else I did at the* Sunday Times *was.'*

Andrew Neil went on to become the publisher of the Scotsman *and* Scotland on Sunday. *He made mass redundancies and, in 2002, his staff passed a unanimous vote of no confidence in his abilities.*

Paul McCartney

The soundcheck over, Paul McCartney – he rarely uses the Sir –
stares out across the empty seats of the ice-hockey stadium,
eyebrows raised in that way of his, lost in thought. In two and a
half hours these chairs will be filled with Americans waving the
Stars and Stripes; holding up lighters; crying, singing, hyper-
ventilating; greeting the latest concert of his nineteen-city tour
with what the press have been calling 'Maccamania'. He hands
his guitar to a roadie and picks up his jacket, flipping it over his
left shoulder in the same movement. Taking the stairs two at a
time, he steps down off the stage and greets me with a cold, dry
handshake. 'Art,' he says bluntly. 'You're here to talk about art,
right?'

'Here' is Long Island, New York, and it's news to me that I've
flown all this way just to talk about his paintings. 'Among other
things,' I answer, trying not to show the alarm in my eyes. What
about the juicy stuff? His children's feelings about his marriage
in a few weeks' time to a former swimwear model who lost a leg
and became a charity campaigner? His bitter feud with a dead
man, John Lennon? What about George? Linda? And, of course,
what about the Beatles, a band 'bigger than Jesus' that broke up
more than thirty years ago and yet still sells as many records
each year as it ever did, a billion at the last count? At least he
didn't add 'and poetry and classical music,' the other art forms
in which he has taken to dabbling.

As he leads the way along a corridor, a crowd – road crew,
hangers-on – mills around him briefly, jostling for position like
petitioners in a Tudor court. When we pass through a door at

133

the end, their progress is blocked by a security guard and I notice Paul McCartney's walk: it is loose, swaying, almost a swagger. He will be sixty next month but, apart from a few crow's feet around his bovine-big eyes and an interesting chestnut tint to his hair, he shows little sign of it. 'I think someone must have falsified my birth certificate,' he says, his flat Liverpudlian vowels softened by thirty years of marriage to an American. 'Joke! It's just I feel as youthful as I've ever felt. And pretty fit. I used to have to wring out my shirts after shows. Now I hardly sweat at all.' He is indeed looking lithe, tanned and moisture-free – and a little shorter than I'd imagined. I've read that he is 5ft 11in; but we all remember that conspiracy theory about how he died in a car crash in 1966 and was replaced by a taller double, only to give the game away by walking barefoot – a Sicilian symbol of death – on the zebra-crossing outside the Abbey Road studios.

Backstage we sit on sofas in an ashram-like room draped with black curtains, lit by candles, heavy with the smell of joss sticks. McCartney scoops up a handful of nuts from the coffee table. 'Excuse me if I eat these while we talk,' he says between crunches. 'I usually nibble at this time before a concert.' We have an hour before he has to change for the show – less if he feels the talking is putting a strain on that golden voice of his.

Alongside the bowl of nuts are copies of the *Sun* and the *Daily Mail*, just arrived from England. Both carry full-page features about how, after 11 September, Americans are saying McCartney is 'healing' them, just as the Beatles did in 1964 after Kennedy's assassination. Healing, Paul? *Healing*? 'I know! I know!' McCartney says, the puffy curves of his lips smoothing out into a grin. 'Better than bad reviews, I guess. Actually, I don't read them, because they have an affect on me: I either think I'm too great or I get paranoid.' The glowing reviews in the American press may have something to do with the fact that he has not toured for a decade; also that the show includes twenty-one Beatles songs; in the past McCartney has refused to play more than one or two of them at his concerts. 'I used to get pissed off when people called me "ex-Beatle Paul McCartney",' he says, tossing another handful of nuts into his mouth. 'Now I'm more comfortable with it.' He chews and swallows. 'JFK had died a few months before the Beatles' first tour and there was a sense then of America wanting to get back to normal after a world-shocking event. The same is happening now, though I feel more connected with it this time because I was in New York when the terrorist attack happened.'

Entering into the spirit of the thing, I ask if this tour is also about 'healing' Paul McCartney – after all, he has said that he 'cried for a year' when his wife Linda died of breast cancer in 1998. 'Yes, there is a lot of that for me. And I have a new woman in my life who I'm going to marry, so that's part of that, too. Heather has made me feel more at ease with things. After two full years of horror and doctors' offices and scares and diagnoses . . .' He trails off. 'In truth when you have been through that and come out at the end . . .' He trails off again. 'I'm grateful not to have to spend my days doing that any more. And I'm lucky to have found a good woman who is strong like Linda and beautiful and positive and funny.'

He found it odd dating again after so many years of marriage and he felt guilty, too, but soon rationalized that it would be what Linda wanted. With the 33-year-old Heather Mills, he tells me, it was 'big attraction at first sight'. Then, 'I really started to fancy her.' The marriage will take place at Castle Leslie in Ireland on 11 June, eight days after he performs at the Queen's Golden Jubilee concert at Buckingham Palace. His daughter Stella, a celebrated fashion designer, won't be designing the wedding dress. And there are rumours that his other children – Mary, James and, from Linda's first marriage, Heather – are not wildly enthusiastic about the union either. 'I think a second marriage is hard for the children,' McCartney says, nodding gravely. 'No matter who it is: people in my position are told not to worry, that time will heal. But it's very difficult. It's difficult for all of us. They find it difficult to think of me with another woman. But it's how it is and how it must be, and I think that, more than anything, they want me to be happy – and this is what makes me happy.'

It's a steely remark, as cold and dry as his handshake. McCartney once said, 'I'm not really tough. I'm not really lovable either.' He was half-right. You don't stay at the top for as long as he has without being pretty tough and single-minded. His comment about how his children will just have to lump it seems to reflect this, as do his thoughts about his reaction to George Harrison's death last November. Looking distraught, McCartney went before the cameras to pay tribute to his 'baby brother'. Was he wanting to make amends for the flippant comment he made in 1980 when John Lennon was shot? 'It was definitely to do with that, yeah. I was conscious of that. I was just as distraught when John died, probably more so because it was a shocking murder. I knew George was going to die. I'd seen him and I knew. He had terminal cancer . . .' He shakes his head at the memory. 'But you're right. When John died I didn't know whether to stay at home and hide or go to work. I decided to go to work, as did George Martin, and at the studio we talked about John and cried and when I was leaving that night, in the dark, in the London traffic, I had the window slightly open and someone pushed a microphone in and asked me what I thought about John dying. I said, "It's a drag." I couldn't think of anything else to say. And, in print, it looked so heartless. When I saw it written down I thought, "Jesus Christ."'

It was not just in print. He said it with a shrug, as if in an attempt to be cool. And the callousness of the comment seemed to confirm what many suspected McCartney really felt about Lennon. When the Beatles broke up in 1970 the world blamed Yoko Ono. But John, George and Ringo blamed Paul, partly because he had, they thought, become too bossy, partly because he refused to work with the band's sinister new manager Allen Klein (later imprisoned for tax fraud), partly because he was the first to tell the press – much to the annoyance of John Lennon, who had already told the others in private that he was planning to leave the band and wanted to break the news himself. Feeling angry, unemployed and bewildered, McCartney retreated to his farm on the Mull of Kintyre, grew a beard, drank too much and had what he later described as a nervous breakdown. Eventually he recovered his composure, became a vegetarian, sued the Beatles, recorded the gorgeous 'Maybe I'm Amazed', formed Wings – with Linda on keyboards and vocals, much to everyone's amusement – and had a long run of chart-topping singles and albums. He also wrote 'The Frog Chorus'.

Lennon, meanwhile, moved to New York, became a junkie and revealed himself to be the borderline psychopath many had always suspected him of being. He embarked on a hate campaign against McCartney, comparing his former partner to the cabaret artiste Engelbert Humperdinck. McCartney would try to patch things up and have 'very frightening phone calls' with Lennon which always ended with one telling the other to 'fuck off' before slamming the phone down. In 1976 Lennon said of McCartney: 'He visits me every time he's in New York, like all the other rock 'n' roll creeps.' McCartney felt hurt, not least because, as he said in 1987, 'I always idolized [John]. We always did, the group. I don't know if the others will tell you that, but he was our idol.'

If George was his baby brother, was John his big brother? McCartney smiles, causing crinkles to arc downwards from his hazel eyes. 'Yes, definitely, although not in the Orwellian sense. John was older than me and, in the good sense of the phrase, he was a big brother. He was a lovely guy. But we were very competitive. Looking back on it, I think it's . . .' He purses his lips. 'It's awkward. You don't always say to people what you mean to say to them when they are alive. And with John, we had a guy relationship, loving each other without saying it. We never looked at each other and said, "I love you," but people would ask us, "What do you think of the rest of the Beatles?" and we would say, "I love them." So we knew indirectly, peripherally.' He rubs his hands together to brush off some crumbs. 'We were brothers. Family. Like an Irish family. It's not unusual to get brothers fighting, but we did it in the spotlight – everyone got to look at the O'Malleys arguing. We gave and took a few good blows. But with John, we made it up by the time he died and I was very thankful for that. We were talking normally about baking bread. And cats – he was a cat man. He would talk about going round his apartment in his "robe" as he called it by then, dressing gown to us. So, ordinary stuff.'

But there's more to it than that. For years now Lennon's role in the Beatles has been talked up and McCartney's down. Lennon is portrayed as being deep and cool, McCartney shallow and cheesy. Yoko Ono has played a large part in this. Most witheringly she said four years ago, 'John was the visionary and that is why the Beatles happened. Paul is put into the position of being a Salieri to a Mozart.' McCartney has been trying to counter this, to make his version of the Beatles story the official one, most notably in an authorized biography, *Many Years From Now* by Barry Miles. He wants it to be known, for instance, that he, not Lennon, was the one who introduced the Beatles to Stockhausen and the avant garde.

Does he feel he has finally set the records straight? 'I became more comfortable that my contribution was being recognized, yes. And George's. Sad that he had to pass away before people really saw it . . . There was a re-writing of history after John's death. There was revisionism. Certain people were trying to write me out of the Beatles' history, as well as the other two. George was reduced to the guy standing with his plectrum in his hand, waiting for a solo and, as John would have been the first to admit, George was very much more important than that, as a character, as a musician. And Ringo is now being sidelined because he wasn't a composer. We all needed each other. We were four corners of a square. There were people close to John saying, "Well, Paul just booked the studio," which was galling. The trouble is', he says, scooping up another handful of peanuts and speaking indistinctly through them, 'I became worried that the John legend would totally wipe out any of our contributions. I'm sure I got paranoid about it, but, hey, that's normal for me.'

Such was McCartney's paranoia he even tried to have the Beatles songs he wrote retrospectively credited to McCartney-Lennon (as opposed to Lennon-McCartney, a brand as revered as Gilbert and Sullivan, or Rodgers and Hammerstein). Yoko Ono, who inherited Lennon's estate, refused to give permission for this. 'I didn't want to remove John,' McCartney tells me, 'just change the order round. I don't mind Lennon-McCartney as a logo. John in front, that's OK, but on the *Anthology* (1996), they started saying "Yesterday" [a tune that came to McCartney in a dream] by John Lennon and Paul McCartney and I said, "Please can it be Paul McCartney and John Lennon for the sake of the Trade Description Act? Because John had no hand in that particular song."' He jiggles his knee up and down in agitation. 'I recently went to a hotel where there was a songbook and I looked up "Hey Jude" [another McCartney song] and it was credited to John Lennon. My name had been left off because there was no space for it on the page. Do I sound obsessive?'

Just a bit. Everyone knows who wrote which Lennon-McCartney composition because the songwriter always took the lead vocals. And he's Paul McCartney, for goodness sake. His boyhood home has been preserved for the nation by the National Trust. According to the *Guinness Book of Records*, he's the most successful popstar in history. Bigger than Elvis. Bigger even than John, now. How can he possibly feel insecure about his reputation? 'I know! That's what people say to me. *Because I'm fucking human.* And humans are insecure. Show me one who isn't. Henry Kissinger? Insecure. George Bush? Insecure. Bill Clinton? Very insecure.' It's a curious crew to compare yourself to – the model for Dr Strangelove, a Texan to whom English is a second language, a philanderer – but perhaps it makes sense in light of something McCartney said at the height of Lennon's war of words: 'John captured me so well. I'm a turd. I'm just nothing.'

Improbable though it may seem, Paul McCartney appears to have suffered periodically from low self-esteem. Linda McCartney once said: 'I don't dwell on what people say about me. I dwell on what people say about Paul, for some reason. Maybe it's because he can't handle it.' For all his chirpy optimism, mannered blokiness and double thumbs-up gestures, he is, it seems, prickly about his reputation. As *Private Eye* discovered when he reacted with cold fury to the inclusion of one of his poems in Pseud's Corner recently, he takes himself very seriously. His 'fucking human' comment is intriguing in another respect: it suggests that, in his professional life at least, he suffers from Paradise Syndrome: having a perfect life he needs to find something to feel anxious about. It's not enough that he's credited jointly with writing the soundtrack to our lives, he wants his name to come first. It won't suffice that, since he was twenty, millions of his fans have been calling him a genius – he needed to hear it from his 'big brother', his musical equal, his idol, John Lennon.

But you can't help feeling that he should be, that he can afford to be, a bigger man. He shouldn't rise to Yoko Ono's bait. It looks so petty. Worse than that, his attempts to control not only the Beatles' history but also their mythology have come across as boastful, petulant and self-serving. Perhaps it is just that, for all his gifts as a lyricist, he frequently expresses himself badly in conversation, often hitting the wrong note, not saying what he means. His mother died when he was aged fourteen: his first response? 'What are we going to do for money now?' He has regretted that line all his life. Even his heartfelt tribute to his 'baby brother' George seems a little patronizing and ill-considered. He must have known that Harrison always hated being thought of as the baby of the band, not least because when the Beatles first formed Lennon used to refer to 'that bloody kid hanging around' – and Harrison, long after the Beatles broke up, said he thought that was how Lennon still regarded him.

Perhaps McCartney's insecurities only seem undignified – even indecent – because in so many other ways he is such a dignified, decent man. He pays his taxes, he doesn't wear leather shoes on principle, he sent his children to the local comp, he was faithful to his wife for thirty years (something almost unheard of in the priapic world of rockstardom), he does his own shopping at Selfridges, he travels on the Underground. The superstar next door image he has tried to cultivate may seem like a tragic affectation given that he is thought to be worth £713 million, but at least he tries. 'You said I have this thing about wanting to be seen as an ordinary man: well, I'm sorry *but I am*,' he tells me. 'It's just too bad, I can't be anything other. I'm a *lucky* ordinary guy, it's true. I've done a lot of things and fulfilled a lot of my dreams, but it doesn't mean . . .' He smiles ruefully. 'I assumed, like you, that when I met someone who had done well that they would be saintly and just say, "Thanks, I know I am OK now." But it doesn't work like that.'

Yet, to the outside world, he seems so positive and well-adjusted. 'Yeah, but my worst fear is being found out . . . I don't want to elevate any higher than I am now. Sir Paul McCartney is as elevated as I ever wish to go – in fact, it is a little too high. It was a great honour and all that but . . . I need the people around me to know I am still the same and I want to feel the same, because I like who I am. A bit insecure. So I don't go, "Fuck you! How dare you tell me that. I'm better than you." It would be easy to do but I don't want to get like that. Know why? Because I'm working class [his father was a cotton salesman, his mother a nurse, and he grew up on a council estate]. If I got like that now, people, the crew out there, would be doing this [he flicks the V-sign] behind my back as I walk past.'

He checks his watch pointedly. 'Now,' he says. 'The Walker Gallery, Liverpool.' There is an exhibition catalogue for it on the coffee table and as we flick through the paintings – bold colouring, some abstract, some figurative – I nod approvingly. Pretty disturbing, though, some of them. 'Oh. Yeah, a lady friend once walked through my studio and said, "Paul what would a psychiatrist make of all this?" Here,' he says stopping at one. 'It's red, so I suppose you could say "demonic, red, hell," but I just like red. In the Rorschach test, some people see a butterfly, some see a devil. You are supposed to betray yourself in painting. But that's OK. I don't try and hide anything about myself.' He turns to a warmer image. 'These beach paintings aren't disturbing, though. That was just a memory. Shark on Georgica is somewhere I used to sail. I knocked the paint pot and a shark appeared. I like that accident. Perhaps it betrays some hidden fears.'

Freud said there are no accidents. 'Exactly.' He flicks on a few more pages. 'The curator picked this one out and says it's very sexual. I'm not sure what he means but I'll go along with that. That could be phallic.' He gives a thin laugh and moves the page round to view the painting from a different angle. 'When I was a kid I used to draw nude women and feel guilty. Now when I look at nudes in photographs and paintings I don't giggle. I had to get over that block, get over the smutty stage. I started painting seriously when I was forty, when I had children, and that was when I got over it. To have babies we do have to do *certain things* . . . Here's a nude of Linda. Why not? I was married to this woman for thirty years.'

Has he painted any of Linda from memory since she died? 'No, I haven't painted too much in the past couple of years. Well, I've done one or two and they are a bit disturbing. But they would be, wouldn't they? I *was* disturbed.' He grieved properly for Linda, he says, something he didn't do when his mother died from breast cancer. 'I certainly didn't grieve enough for my mother. There was no such thing as a psychiatrist when I lost her. You kidding? I was a fourteen-year-old Liverpool boy. I wouldn't have had access to one and I do now. I saw one when Linda died and he said, "A good way to grieve is to cry one day and not cry the next, alternate days so as you don't go down one tunnel." I took his advice.'

McCartney has said that in the months following Linda's death he thought he might die from grief; did he mean he considered taking his own life? 'No. I was very sad. In deep grief. But never suicidal. I'm too positive for that. After a year . . . It was as if the seasons had to go right through, as if I had to feel like a plant. A couple of months after the end of that cycle I began to realize I was also having other feelings, that I was emerging . . .'

That all you need is love? 'Mmm. I am a romantic. I like Fred Astaire.' Me, too, I interject. 'That's good,' he says. 'Now I feel I can open up to you. I always say to young guys, "Be romantic," because not only do women love it but you'll love it, too. English men are so reserved, though. The idea of being caught with flowers on the bus! You hide them under your jacket.' He mimes hiding a bunch and looking nervous. 'Well, I'm not like that any more.'

McCartney looks at his watch again. Nearly time to go to his dressing room. Presumably the big difference between touring America in 2002 and 1964 is the seats; audiences today don't wet them quite as much. 'I think the main difference is the age range of the audience,' he says with an easy laugh. 'The Beatles audience was essentially our age or younger, a lot of screaming girls. Now the audience is layered: people the age I am now, but also their children and grandchildren. They were holding up babies the other night, which was like, *What*?'

I say I imagine people bring their babies along because they want them to have a stake in history – like watching the Queen Mother's funeral procession. 'Yeah, there's probably something in that. People want to be able to say, "I was there."'

Later I make my way upstairs to take my seat for the concert. The excitement of the crowd is palpable and infectious. And when a giant silhouette of Paul McCartney's violin-shaped Hofner bass appears on a screen on the stage, everyone goes nuts. The screen lifts, the crisp, heavy, opening bars of the Beatles song 'Hello, Goodbye' are heard, and thousands of hairs on the backs of thousands of necks stand on end, mine included.

Dave Lee Travis

JUNE 1997

Driving towards Tring on a drizzly morning with the radio tuned
to 828 medium wave is like travelling back in time. On the M25
the signal is still too faint and crackly to make out that sonorous,
diluted Mancunian voice once so familiar. Then, as you turn off
at Junction 20, it really starts comin' atcha through the wind-
screen wipers: 'But just to get serious for a moment, folks. Let's
not forget that the police do a really great job . . .' It ebbs again,
lost to the atmospheric hiss as the four-wheeled time-machine
enters a cleavage hewn through what must be the only hill in
Hertfordshire. On the other side, the signal surges back across
the ether, down the years, and washes over you like a warm,
runny, medium wave of nostalgia.

Dave Lee Travis is taking a call from a woman who has a dog
that can talk, or at least growl the sort of 'hello' sound made by
tracheotomy patients with voice boxes. 'You must be mad!' Lee
Travis splutters. 'What's the dog called?' The woman who must
be mad is also laughing now. 'Buddy,' she says. 'I've got two.
Buddy and Olly.' The old pro, now giggling, pauses just long
enough to wipe away a tear. 'That's okay. I have two cats called
Flap and Mandu! Oh dear. I'd better play the next track. This is
Fleetwood Mac.'

Of course it is. The track is a paradigm of the sort of mouldie
oldie that the 52-year-old Lee Travis plays every morning on his
Classic Gold show. This programme, in DLT-speak, 'comes atcha
through the cornflakes' if you live in the Reading area (or Bristol
or Carlisle or any of the dozen or so other regions to which the
show is networked). He wasn't always a 'Radio Mould' man,

though. In the halcyon days of Radio 1 – the seventies and early eighties – Lee Travis bestrode the airwaves like a bell-bottomed colossus, pumping out a billion megawatts of p-p-p-power! to his nine million 'completely bonkers' listeners.

As I wait round the back of the Rose and Crown in Tring, chewing over the significance of this fall from grace, I don't notice immediately the dark blue Ford Scorpio that has pulled up a few yards away. Then I see the door swing open and a fleshy, hairless hand framed by a chunky gold bracelet emerges to beckon me over.

Once inside the Ford, I can't help noticing the air: a robust brand of freshener is at work on it. The second thing I notice is that the generous size of the driver's pale, moon face is exaggerated by a chiaroscuro of salt-and-pepper whiskers and that famous mane of hair which, in 1980, moved the National Hairdressers' Federation to name Dave Lee Travis Head of the Year. As we stop at some traffic lights five minutes later, Lee Travis turns and eyes me suspiciously through the tinted lenses of his glasses. 'So what's this interview about, then?' he says. It's a fair question. It's partly, I suppose, about that lost generation of 'completely bonkers' DLT listeners out there in radioland.

The listeners were the sorts of people who had those bonkers dayglo cards which said 'you don't have to be mad to work here – but it helps!' pinned above their bonkers desks. People who want everyone to think them endearingly bonkers usually do so because they fear they will be otherwise thought dull, something which they suspect they probably are. Pinning the card above the desk was like buying an off-the-peg personality. So was listening to DLT.

For DLT was bonkers, too. Or rather he was 'zany', an altogether more self-conscious proposition best summed up by his choice of car – a Pontiac Trans-Am called the Flying Banana – and by his gravelly voiced jingle offering 'close encounters of the hairy kind'. But there was more to it than zaniness. Like those other Radio 1 jocks whose names – Batesie, Noelie, Readie, Wrightie – always ended in a chummy vowel, DLT-ie was an egomaniac. Treated like a rock star by his fans, he felt obliged to behave like one. Until things turned sour.

It's now four years since Lee Travis made his melodramatic resignation from Radio 1. 'There are changes being made here which go against my principles,' he had intoned gravely, live on air. And not since Geoffrey Howe stood up in the House of Commons in 1990 to declare that 'The time has come for others to consider their own response to the tragic conflict of loyalties with which I have myself wrestled for too long' had a resignation speech resonated across the land, caused jitters on the stock market, made everyone chuckle.

The comparisons with political life do not end there. Enoch Powell once observed that all parliamentary careers end in failure. The same can be said of a DJ's working life. Indeed, theirs is one of the few professions where long years of faithful service – twenty-six in Lee Travis's case – more or less guarantee the sack. But if, as the saying ought to go, old DJs never die, they only change format, what becomes of their bouncy-castle-sized egos? Do they die of malnutrition?

'So what's this interview about, then?' Lee Travis has asked. The 'what happens to giant inflatable egos?' answer seems too rude – so reassuring things about the nation's interest in him being sempiternal are muttered instead. Satisfied with this, Lee Travis starts talking in general terms about how the country is going to the dogs – but you just know he is thinking about Radio 1. 'I feel strongly about the fact that people are paring everything down to the bone,' he says. 'In every walk of life. It's sad that good people who have a feel for a job are replaced by youngsters because they're cheaper.'

Lee Travis often starts his sentences with 'I feel strongly about'; and years of having people in radioland listen to his opinions has left him assuming that if he feels strongly about something everyone else will, too. It also means that he now no longer needs a second person present when having a conversation. His mono-logue about good people being replaced by youngsters lasts until we reach the 250-year-old farmhouse in Hertfordshire where he lives with Marianne, the Swedish blonde he married twenty-six years ago.

The outside of the house is painted ochre which complements the black leaded windows. A couple of sheep are grazing in a paddock and, in the garden, waddling around a rusting seed drill, are a dozen Indian runner ducks. Because Lee Travis feels he is too old to look after them properly, he no longer keeps the pot-bellied pigs he was wont to talk about on air. 'I remember one listener writing in to say that no one wanted to hear about my stupid farm and that I should remember that not everyone could afford one,' Lee Travis recalls as he brings the car to a halt and opens the door only to have it whipped from his hand by a gust of wind. There is a loud crunch as the metal on the door axis buckles and this is followed by an equally loud 'Bollocks!' from DLT.

'Where was I?' he says, running a finger over the paintwork. 'That's right. This letter. It was venomous. And I was really annoyed because it wasn't signed. So I went on air and said, "To the man who wrote this letter, you didn't give me a chance to reply. Will you phone in?" He did and we had a long conversation. He went away happy.'

You can see why. Lee Travis has an earthy, engaging manner and a quality – decency? lack of pretension? – which can probably be best defined as blokishness. Perhaps it is something to do with his being called Dave. (Try and imagine him being called David. It just doesn't work.) Or maybe it's the quaint words and phrases he uses. He'll say things like 'not firing on all cylinders', 'you pilchard', 'hitherto', and 'the old grey matter'. Possibly the best illustration of this Factor X comes when the burglar alarm goes off with a nerve-jangling whoop (there is a maintenance man testing it). It prompts Lee Travis to say how paranoid he is about anything happening to his wife. 'It's not your professional thief that worries me,' he says, every inch the bloke in the pub. 'It's the amateur because he might be armed with a knife and might use it on Marianne. If any thief comes in while I'm here, I'll do anything to put him on the ground. I get annoyed very easily and when I do I get strength from somewhere.'

It reveals the bluffness that always set Lee Travis apart from the other Radio 1 jocks. Not for him the mawkish sentimentality of a Simon Bates or the relentless, smirking fatuity of a Noel Edmonds. And, unlike other jocks, he never spoke with an ex-clamation mark after every word, that grammatical equivalent to canned laughter. Instead there was always something excitingly dark, bullying and edgy bubbling underneath his warm affability. Here, you felt, was a DJ who'd give you a good kicking if you crossed him. And, indeed, he was prone to losing his temper or, if he got worked up about a subject, launching into a long tirade about it. On one occasion, when he felt compelled to put the nation off its breakfast by delivering an impromptu lecture, in gory detail, about the evils of seal culling, it nearly cost him his job.

'I have a reputation for diving in feet first when I feel strongly about things,' he now says with a shrug. 'Being outspoken. But as far as I'm concerned the boss of the station always has the last word. Nowadays, if someone says something really out-rageous people say, "This will be good for ratings." There is a very obvious example of this, and I think that was probably plotted from day one.' He is referring to Chris Evans, the DJ who briefly staunched the haemorrhage of Radio 1 listeners before leaving the BBC under a cloud in January.

'I think Chris Evans is a very talented guy on television,' Lee Travis says. 'I just never felt he was right on the radio. He did what was expected of Channel 4 late at night on a national radio breakfast show at seven in the morning. I mean two guys in the toilet peeing and telling dirty jokes, followed by a quiz in which nine-year-old kids win prizes for getting the wrong answers, just isn't on.'

Lee Travis adds that when he meets people who haven't heard him since he left Radio 1 they always say, 'Oh it all went wrong when they fired you, you know.' This makes him wince because, he says, he wasn't fired. That came later when he broke his contract – which he intended to honour for the few months it had left to run – by talking to the press. Lee Travis decided to sever his connection because he thought it was a mistake to replace old DJs with young ones, because it would mean aban-doning listeners aged twenty-five to forty-five. The station's version of events is different: Lee Travis had become a dinosaur and a Luddite who wanted to play album tracks all the time instead of chart music, and he would have been pushed anyway if he hadn't jumped. Either way he claims he's not bitter: 'It's just that I knew Radio 1 was going to collapse and it did. [Today Radio 1 has half as many listeners as in Lee Travis' heyday.] The same way I know that, in five years' time, we're going to come full circle and want real broadcasters again, instead of kids who save you money in the short term. Radio 1 will have to get back the people who know how far they can and should go. People who can go into a studio which has a live microphone and, when all the other equipment stops working, talk for two hours and entertain people without having to resort to swearing.'

Lee Travis's two labradors, Spike and Sam, wander in to the room for a pat and, as he obliges, he warms to his theme. 'Knowing how far you can push things, what things you cannot say on air, takes experience. Barriers of decency are coming down. Anything sexual or involving bad language will make the press nowadays.' This moral indignation does not sit comfortably with the Lee Travis sense of humour – he keeps a collection of books on the theme of farting in his downstairs loo – nor with the series of photographs he once took of 'Page Three Stunnas' for the *Sun*. But this does not necessarily make him a hypocrite. Though he swears freely in private, he never does on air. And though he is probably a long way from being a feminist, this seems more to do with his passive conservatism than any sense of active political antagonism.

Lee Travis seems instead to be a victim of his emotions. When he says, for instance, that he doesn't have children himself but if he did he'd want to be able to walk with them in the park without worrying, he almost shakes with passion. 'I feel strongly about the law and the way criminals are given better treatment than their victims,' he says. 'I want someone to stand in front of me and explain why we can't list the names and addresses of all the paedophiles that they've got.'

This tendency to break off from the usual stream of inane DJ chat 'just to get serious for a moment folks', was so savagely and wittily satirized by Harry Enfield, it seems mean to dwell on it. Equally, though, you get the feeling that Dave Lee Travis will not feel comfortable until the subject of Dave 'Nicey' Nice is out of the way. 'Was it hurtful?' Lee Travis repeats. 'Well, that question had to be in there, didn't it? No. You're fair game. You have to see the funny side. It was a funny period. Not arf! We were all there wearing medallions and flared trousers. I never want anyone to think I take myself seriously. I'm not a brain surgeon, after all. I'm a bloody disc jockey. But it didn't matter to me as Smashie and Nicey were based on Alan Freeman and Tony Blackburn.'

There is some evidence to the contrary. What about that one-off 'popumentary' in which a bitter Dave 'Nicey' Nice reflected upon his career as he walked about his farm? In it, Nicey recalled his first break on pirate radio (Lee Travis, too, began on Radio Caroline); his hitmungous single 'I'm a Rocking Crackers Pilchard' (Lee Travis's novelty band, Laurie Lingo and the Dipsticks, had a hit with a song called 'Convoy'); his tobacco industry award for Pipeman of the Year (Lee Travis won it in 1982); and, finally, the hatred Dave Nice has felt for young people ever since being ousted from FAB FM.

And then there is the way Nice jokes constantly about the fragile state of his own interlobular region. Lee Travis, too, will say: 'What has kept me semi-sane – I'm not sure that I am – is that everyone deals with me as a friend in the home. There is an ego trip. I love people to come up and greet me with a "Hiya, Dave, how y'doin'?" but it's not a fame trip like a pop star. I've never had that hot and cold of being in and out of favour. I've always just been warm. Although there was a period in the seventies when DJs were almost pop stars, that was just a silly phase we were going through. Sounds like a pop song, doesn't it?' He sings a bar and then adds: '10cc: "I'm Not In Love".'

By any standards, though, Lee Travis is pretty much a popular cultural icon; and not just in Britain. For twenty years he has presented *A Jolly Good Show* for the BBC World Service. It gets the biggest mailbag in Bush House, including one letter that arrived on Lee Travis's desk from India, simply addressed to 'DLT, England'.

Marianne breezes in, wearing jeans and big green pully, and places a tray of cheese sandwiches on the table. Speaking in a Swedish accent which, fascinatingly, incorporates flattened Northern vowels she has picked up from her husband, Marianne explains that she turned DLT into a vegetarian, persuaded him to give up his pipe, and is now lobbying him to have a wind turbine installed on the farm. 'I've given up watching *Top of the Pops,* too,' Lee Travis chips in. 'It drives me potty. I prefer to listen to Radio 4 these days.'

Glenda Jackson

The transport minister opens the door, plucks the cigarette from her lips and says: 'Be with you in a sec. I'm just on the phone to Cherie.' As she hastens back to her desk she steps out of her shoes and hops on one stockinged foot while massaging the toes of the other. 'You were saying?' she croaks, cradling the phone between chin and shoulder. Her office is still cluttered with unpacked crates bulging with personal effects. These include what looks like the long black Cleopatra wig she wore on the 1971 *Morecambe & Wise Christmas Special* and the smooth golden head of an Oscar protruding decadently from an art nouveau flowerpot. Along one wall of the room there is a Louis XVI chaise longue against which is propped a large, luminous painting by and of Gilbert & George in the nude. Next to this there is an ice bucket in which is chilling a bottle of Veuve Clicquot. Catching my eye, Glenda Jackson cups her hand over the receiver, nods at the bottle and mouths: 'Be a love and open that would you? It's been a hard day . . .'

No.

Of course it isn't like this.

Power has neither corrupted nor mellowed the 61-year-old Labour MP for Hampstead and Highgate. Nor has it compromised her reputation for being cold, puritanical and, as she herself once put it, totally charmless. Her office is barren – no pictures, no fronds of green rubber plant, no homely touches. She is, by her own reckoning, not at all sentimental – and she can't stand untidiness. The only shred of authenticity in this opening scene is that Glenda Jackson has had a hectic day. She rises at 6.30 a.m. every morning and it's now a quarter to six in the evening, forty-five minutes later than the time originally scheduled in her diary for this her final meeting of the day.

We are six floors up in Eland House, the gleaming new glass-and-steel-fronted building into which John Prescott's merged departments of the Environment, Transport and the Regions moved this year. From this height you can appreciate that a remarkable number of roof tops around Victoria have flagpoles – which fly Union flags and cast long shadows in the low autumn sun. When Jackson invites me to sit down she shivers, rubs the arms of her magenta and black dog-toothed jacket, and mutters something about the new air-conditioning. 'God, it's so cold,' she adds in that distinctively deep and flat vowelled voice. 'My blood has stopped circulating.'

She isn't even smoking, which is a bit of a disappointment given that she is said to get through forty Dunhill a day, and there is a rather wonderful rumour doing the rounds that she has requested a special £4,000 air-recycling unit for her new hi-tech, smoke detecting office so that she can puff away at her desk rather than waste valuable ministerial time by trekking back and forth all day along the corridor to the smoking room.

Small talk about the smoking story is dismissed by the minister with the word 'allegedly'. Mention of the clean and shining new offices is given similarly short shrift: 'Have you looked out of the window?' she asks. There is a thick layer of grime on it. Tch! That's London air pollution, I say with an ingratiating nod that leads me more abruptly than planned onto the topic of traffic fumes.

'Only today I was talking to someone about the inequities between providing company cars and season tickets for employees. One is regarded as a perk on which tax has to be paid, the other isn't. I also raised the issue of employers offering interest-free loans for their employees to buy a bike and this guy said, 'I'd buy them all bikes now if I thought that I wouldn't be taxed for it.'

I raise the point that one of the advantages of being in opposition is that you can make extravagant demands based more on ideology than practicality. Once in power, funds have to be found to implement big ideas, and targets have to be set in order to establish whether they work. Given that the Government is still pretty much enjoying its honeymoon period, Jackson is surprisingly defensive about this truism. 'You talk about targets,' she says with a short, forced smile that scares rather than re-assures. 'But there can also be aims you can have. And it is important to have them, otherwise nothing is achieved, nothing develops, nothing is shown to work. That in itself is bad. But it also breeds a sense of helplessness.'

It has to be said, though, that Glenda Jackson does not sell well the Integrated Transport Strategy – or ITS as it is bound to be known. It would be ungracious to quote verbatim one of her statements on the subject – not least because, on the occasion we meet, she seems fraught and distracted. And, though I've never met her before, in comparison even with recent photographs, she seems weary, drawn and under-nourished. There is no passion in her delivery. Her answers seem stilted, repetitious and, at times, quite inarticulate. The way she can get tangled up in a sub-clause, by slipping in expressions such as 'by virtue of' or 'which is a movable feast' (three times in one answer alone), makes the syntax of her boss, John Prescott, seem positively lucid.

All politicians are, of course, trained in the art of not giving proper answers to questions you never asked. It's just some are better at it than others. When you hear flannel from, say, Kenneth Clarke you want to believe it because it's said with a mixture of cheery confidence and bluster. He's a performer. Why then, you find yourself wondering, does Glenda Jackson not call upon some of her formidable powers as an actress to do the same? We know from one performance at least, *A Touch of Class* (1973), that she can act flirty, personable and funny when she has to; why then does she not deploy a little of this to counter her apparently natural freezing manner?

The only answer that makes sense is that she overcompensates for the bohemian image of her first career. After all, as Gudrun in *Women in Love* (1971), she seemed to capture the Dionysian spirit of the late sixties, early seventies. She symbolized all the hedonistic urges of which politicians are supposed to disapprove, in principle if not practice. But what's the problem? Hers was a distinguished career. She was appointed CBE. It wasn't as if she was a call girl or a game show host in her previous incarnation. She feels, you suspect, that her flamboyant past undermines the authority of her dour present.

Her acting career, of course, is the prickly subject which dare not speak its name. There's not much she enjoys in life, she has said. She's not really the enjoying sort. But her life in acting is something she seems to have actively not enjoyed. She found it artificial and strained. Now she looks back on it with neither affection nor regret. And her two Oscars lurk unloved in a box somewhere at her sister's house.

There is then a perverse, giddy pleasure to be had from daring yourself to ask about it. Will the eyes narrow and the lip curl as they did so chillingly in *Elizabeth R*? As an actress Glenda Jackson was unconventionally beautiful, and then only when she was playing the part of one who was angry. Hers was the dark, Promethean beauty of the mountain range that could be truly appreciated only by the sufferer of vertigo who forced himself to look down from its peak. My question, then, when it comes, is so cunningly obtuse it seems not to be about acting at all – the equivalent of lying on your back with just your head over the edge of the abyss, looking down at the plunging precipice through a mirror held at arm's length. Ahem. If she had gone straight into politics from working at Boots, would she have been a different kind of politician?

(Glenda Jackson, it should be explained, is the eldest of four sisters brought up in the small seaside town of Hoylake on the Wirral. Her father, Harry, was a bricklayer, her mother, Joan, cleaned houses. She left West Kirby Grammar School at fifteen and, before getting involved in amateur dramatics and then going on to RADA, she worked for two years at Boots. On the laxative and bilious attacks counter.)

'I honestly don't know. I don't know,' she says without any sign of hostility. 'I think people's attitudes to me would be different.' But presumably she learned some presentational skills and actorly tricks that have proved useful when performing in the House? 'You say that but the most salutary lesson you learn if you are fortunate enough to act a lot is how little you know and how easy it is to act badly. And how hard it is to act well. Yes, I suppose there are benefits. I'm not bowled over by the

154

thought of having to speak in front of a room full of strangers. But then again I never considered acting a process of covering up. It was more a process of stripping away. I think the best drama aspires to be truthful and so does the best politics. I am not frightened by speaking in public. The thing people are most frightened of, after dying, is speaking in public.'

Glenda Jackson does have fears, she says, of flying and of dentists. But she is not afraid of being alone. She was married at the age of twenty-one to Roy Hodges, a theatre director. They divorced in 1976 and then she lived for five years with a lighting engineer, Andrew Phillips. She now lives in Blackheath with her 28-year-old son Daniel Hodges, who worked for a while as her parliamentary researcher before taking a job with the Road Haulage Association.

'I think we generate our own fears,' Jackson says. 'And sometimes they can be useful and sometimes they can be crippling. I used to worry when I didn't get stage fright. You have a heightened awareness which you can trace to physiological things. But you have to be as ready as you can be. If you watch an athlete, I noticed this particularly in the Olympics, I found I could know who was going to win in the single events because the people who won, and we are talking about minuscule time differences between winning and coming second, but the person who a fraction of a second before the gun went off just let go. Some inner voice, and that is a process I can relate to. It's not about becoming free of self-consciousness, it's just about, well, letting go. Harder to explain than to do.'

Despite recognizing the need to let go, Jackson has said in the past that she feels the lack of a brain trained to work in a particular way. For her, she said, things are a really hard slog. Has this ever made her doubt her abilities as a politician?

'Of course. It would be a sad day if you didn't. Just think what you are as a constituency MP. To represent the needs of 68,000 people is a huge responsibility. Surely you have to do the best you can just in terms of the hope people invest in you. If being up to it can be achieved by dint of hard work and acknowledging you don't know everything and having no pride about saying to people that you don't know what they are talking about then . . .' she trails off. 'The people around you are very good about helping you get on top of the information. And, of course, you are informed by the principles of your particular party . . .'

Her party has principles? 'My absolute belief that this country is the best by virtue of its people is very clear to me, and as I said, one of the things I found most heinous under the Tories was the sheer waste of this country's greatest natural resource. Its people. Their energy. Their imagination.'

Jackson resents the idea that she has only been engaged in politics since she won her first seat in 1992. 'I've always been a supporter and voter for the Labour Party. And I'd been asked to do things by them because I had a high profile. When I was approached to become a prospective parliamentary candidate I was motivated by an overwhelming desire to get rid of Mrs Thatcher because she was trying to turn the country in which I was born, and which, please God, I will die, into a country I couldn't identify with. And turn vices into virtues and virtues into vices. And I think this is probably a myth I've created for myself – because I don't think the timing is right – but I'm convinced that it was hearing that speech about there being no such thing as society which made me so angry I walked into a post. But anything I could do, anything to get rid of that appalling, immoral philosophy and to get a Labour government.'

When she first started canvassing to become an MP, people would ask her for her autograph because she was a famous actress. Now that she is a government minister has she noticed a difference in the way people treat her? 'To be honest,' she says, 'One of the big differences about becoming a Member of Parliament was that people can talk to you as a representative. You do have that. There is no pretence that you are not who you are. There is no blurring of who you are. There's none of that, "Oh I expected Queen Elizabeth and then you arrived." There's none of that. So, no, people always speak their minds to me.'

This said, she says she is aware of her hard image and thinks it has a lot to do with her portrayal of Elizabeth R. But her reputation for being cold and frightening is unfair, she thinks, because she is not like that royal sourpuss in real life. She doesn't believe she has ever experienced an uncontrollable passion, for instance. Although she does lose her temper, she doesn't lose it often, and then only over some minor irritating thing that has come at the end of a lot of other minor irritating things.

An abrupt manner is often a defence against feelings of insecurity. At school she suffered badly from acne and was self-conscious about being overweight. She had, she says, no sense of herself being physically attractive in any way at all, either then or now. No wonder she didn't enjoy the close scrutiny of the cameras when she became an actress. Ironically though, the social awkwardness, brittleness and discomfort she often brought to her screen roles were precisely the qualities that made her such a compelling, sultry, unpredictable actress to watch. And they are exactly the same qualities which limit her appeal as a politician. She has no bonhomie about her, and this makes the attempts by her Transport press office to turn her into Our Glenda look farcical (GLENDA LAUNCHES SAFELINE SCHEME IN SHEFFIELD ran a headline on a recent press release. Not Jackson. Glenda.)

Perhaps a more rewarding tack would be to play to the minister's transport strengths and cite the description Oliver Reed gave of his co-star: 'Working with Glenda was like being run over by a Bedford truck.' Or, perhaps, the one given by Les Dawson, that hers was the face that launched a thousand dredgers.

In terms of appearance, then, the minister for transport (and shipping) seems to have overcompensated for the ephemeral image of her youth by becoming Labour's answer to the gloriously uncompromised Ann Widdecombe. Even Barbara Follett MP, who was charged with giving New Labour MPs a makeover, couldn't remove the whiff of carbolic that lingers about her. She has strong cheekbones, her mousy-auburn hair is cut in a severe Bauhaus style and there is something about the arrangement of her teeth that makes her smile look like a snarl. Last year when Glenda Jackson – wearing a suit with temperatures in the eighties and looking like she'd just sucked a lemon – did her photo-opportunity walk on the beaches of Benidorm, in order to tell startled British sunbathers why they couldn't trust the Tories, Sir Tim Bell, the Tory PR guru, was tempted to run the picture of her as an advert saying: 'New Labour: less style more substance.'

Glenda Jackson finds such considerations trivializing. As well she should. She says she sees herself as female rather than feminine, which is something she equates with being 'frilly and pink and frothy and lacy'. And she cannot understand the fuss always being made in the press about what Ffion Jenkins or Cherie Blair is wearing.

'I wonder why we waste time worrying about it,' she says. 'It is actually an impediment to the work being done. It really acts as a bar to women achieving what women are capable of in virtue of their abilities. But again I don't think it is serious. And I don't think we should allow ourselves to be trapped into an agenda which is irrelevant. And why should women be trapped into not being attractive or not being interested in fashion or not being interested in those kind of things? Why should we be? That's got nothing to do with images, be they powerful or weak, it's got to do with the story of the day. It's coming from a different angle. It's a different kind of scenario. The whole thing about image and image-making is in itself an artificially created area, I believe, for another scenario as well.'

Even so, she did take part in the group photograph of what the tabloids dubbed 'Blair's Babes'. Presumably she agreed because, like her famous, goosepimply nude scenes, the plot demanded it. The Prime Minister didn't feel the need to have a group photograph taken of himself with all his male MPs, but perhaps to raise this point is to miss a greater one. After all, as Glenda Jackson points out, the number of women MPs now elected to the House of Commons represents a brisk stride forward. 'I think it's wonderful,' she says. 'But I would like to see an equal gender split sitting on those benches. What are we now? 658 MPs? There are certainly not 329 women sitting there. But I think it has made a difference already in the atmosphere of the place. It can make a difference in the practical reality of the place.'

You can just imagine that atmosphere when the female (not feminine) Jackson is around. The real essence of her intimidatingly graceless manner was defined by a long-serving Hampstead party worker who said: 'She can be very cold and hard work. Even by the standard of the Labour Party she hardly has a sense of humour.' There is evidence of wryness, though. On her first day at Westminster, she says she kept getting lost but no matter where she walked she seemed to end up next to a statue of Winston Churchill. She names her chief pleasure as reading *Hansard* in bed. And she once laughed approvingly when she heard that her ex-husband had said of her: 'If Glenda went into politics she'd be prime minister. If she went into crime she would be Jack the Ripper.'

It is now dark outside and Jackson leans forward, squints at a clock on the opposite wall and says; 'It's quarter to seven. We've got to make a move.' As she walks over to her desk in the corner of her office a light comes on above it. 'They are movement-sensitive to save energy,' she explains. 'Sometimes when I'm working late and sitting very still they turn off.'

It leaves a melancholy image lingering in the mind. Glenda Jackson sitting very still at her desk, long after everyone else has gone home. She is looking thoughtful, determined. Her pen is poised in her hand. Suddenly the lightbulb above her head dims and she is left in darkness – without even the orange glow of a cigarette for comfort.

Glenda Jackson was pushed before she jumped from the Department of Transport. She then unsuccessfully attempted to gain the Labour Party nomination for the London mayoralty. In the end she gave her support to Ken Livingstone and, in her modest way, became a backbench critic of government policy.

Gore Vidal

On a cliff-top high above the Amalfi coast an awning flaps lazily, stirred by a welcome breeze, and then is still once more. It shares the temperament of the aged American bachelor standing under it, on his balcony, pondering the cobalt-blue sea half a mile below. 'You know,' Gore Vidal says with a heavy sigh, 'every morning at ten a tourist boat sails past and I have to listen to a woman telling my life story over a tannoy.' Pause. 'It is followed by another boat which tells the same story in Italian.'

Quite useful, though, should he ever forget who he is. 'Yes.' The sigh again, a wan stare into the middle distance. 'There are such mornings.'

For all the affected world-weariness, it is safe to assume that Gore Vidal is secretly delighted to find himself, at the age of seventy-five, a tourist attraction. He is, after all, a man given to Olympian, if usually wry, displays of condescension and arrogance – 'There is not one human problem that could not be solved if people would simply do as I advise,' he once half-joked. For thirty years, he and his companion, Howard Austen, have divided their time between a house in Los Angeles and this place, a five-storey palazzo in Ravello, a place once considered sacred to the god Pan and now a shrine to Gore Vidal; it is a museum in which he is the prize exhibit, a reminder to himself of what he might have been and *who he is*. The house was built by an English peer in 1925 – 'the same year [sigh] I was built' – and is set in terraces of olive trees, grape vines, cedars and cypresses. It is not accessible by car, but is approached along a corniche path, through three sets of security gates.

Inside, hanging on the walls, there are dozens of caricatures, photographs and magazine covers featuring Vidal's saturnine face and what he calls his 'flaring Gore nostrils'. On the bookshelves in his study there are more than forty different volumes with his name on the spine: collections of essays, plays and screenplays, twenty-four novels and an autobiography. By the window is a hand-carved chessboard, at which he and Howard sit down to play every day. Pass through a hall hung with seventeenth-century Neapolitan canvases and into a high-ceilinged drawing room, and the eye takes in tapestries, a Greco-Roman head of Zeus, a flaking Buddha and a first-century mosaic floor mounted as a wallpiece. Among the framed photographs on the table by the door is a serious-looking image of the woman he claims he introduced to dark glasses, his step-sister, Jackie Kennedy – 'whose boyish beauty and life-enhancing malice were a great joy to me'. There are other pictures, ones that chronicle Vidal's life as a failed politician but transcendent political observer and gossip: Vidal on the stump with Harry S. Truman; Vidal sharing a joke with his friend John F. Kennedy; Vidal with Hillary and Chelsea Clinton, taken when they came to stay and inscribed with the words, 'To Gore, with thanks for letting us trespass'.

Though the writer does occasionally hold court here, entertaining a circle of friends that includes Sting, Princess Margaret and Paul Newman, visitors probably do feel as if they are trespassing, because this is where he comes to write, on a chestnut-wood table, in longhand. For the past three months he has been working on an essay about the execution of Timothy McVeigh, the man who, in 1995, killed 168 people when he blew up the FBI headquarters in Oklahoma. The two men began a correspondence. Vidal found McVeigh to be intelligent and sympathetic. McVeigh invited Vidal to attend his execution, in one of the seats reserved for his friends and family; in the end Vidal stayed in Ravello.

Il Maestro, as he is known locally, is wearing green linen trousers and a pink gingham shirt, the buttons of which strain against his paunch. He shuffles in from the balcony, eases himself into an armchair and crosses his legs stiffly, causing the bottom button to give up the struggle. The pleats of skin on his cheekbones smooth out as he raises his eyebrows, a prompt for a question.

Doesn't it worry him that many Americans find his sympathy with McVeigh offensive and traitorous? 'Fuck that,' he says with a mirthless laugh. 'I know how opinion is manufactured in the United States,' he adds. He speaks slowly, languidly, with an oaky, vowel-rolling Ivy League accent. 'The *New York Times* is for us what *Pravda* was for the Soviets. McVeigh was part of a much larger conspiracy, but they wouldn't go after it. They wanted to demonize McVeigh as a madman who killed children. They wanted another lone, crazed Lee Harvey Oswald.'

So why didn't he go to the execution? Had he caught a diplomatic cold? 'Well, I tried to go. I was all set to go to the first one: just as I got off the plane there was a stay of execution so I came back. His lawyers had 4,000 documents to go through and I assumed they would allow at least a month for that, but they didn't – they were so eager to get him off the scene. So I had three days to get from here to there and couldn't manage it.' Wouldn't it have given him nightmares to watch McVeigh die? Long pause. 'I don't think old people get these nightmares. Old people are nearer to death themselves. Most of one's friends are dead.' He doesn't suffer from mortal panic, then? 'It depends on your nature. Those of us who went into the army at seventeen expected to be killed. Half the boys I trained with in the infantry were killed in the Battle of the Bulge.'

Vidal's first love, Jimmie Trimble, was killed fighting the Japanese at Iwo Jima in 1945. The two met as twelve-year-olds at St Albans boarding school in Washington, DC. Vidal likens Jimmie to Rosebud in *Citizen Kane*, the secret that explains everything. He also compares their relationship to that of Achilles and Patroclus and describes Jimmie's sweat as smelling like honey, 'like that of Alexander the Great'. When he heard the news of Jimmie's death did he feel suicidal? 'It confirmed what I suspected would happen to all of us. At the time I was not the least stoic about it. But no, I wasn't suicidal. And love is a very evasive term. Let us say we identified with each other. I don't want to put it in romantic terms. It was stranger than that. More like a twinship. That sort of thing is numbing but you must remember I had heard of a dozen other deaths before what happened on 1 March 1945, at four in the morning.'

Did it harden his heart? 'I have never checked my heart for morbidity of any kind.' Has he been in love since? 'I don't know what the phrase means.' Pause. 'That is a question to ask people who really care about themselves. I'm more interested in the present-day crimes of the Supreme Court. In American history.'

I'm not convinced, I say: his memoirs, his novels, all are an exercise in self-analysis. He is, after all, his own best subject. 'That's nice to hear but it's not true. Philip Roth writes about Philip Roth. I write about Lincoln.'

And yet it seems he never did fall in love again. He has a giant picture of Jimmie, aged seventeen, in his bedroom here and he still has recurring dreams about running through the woods to the Potomac river, where he and Jimmie used to play. By the time he was twenty-five, he had given up hope of finding the other half, the twin, that would make him whole again and so had settled for 'a thousand brief anonymous adhesions'. Vidal has an ecumenical approach to sex and believes that only acts, not people, can be described as homosexual or heterosexual. When asked by a journalist once whether his first sexual experience was gay or straight, he replied, 'I was too polite to ask.' He has written of a woman in his life, an actress with whom, off and on, he has 'kept loving company'. And, in 1950, he met Howard Austen, a raspy-voiced Jewish boy from the Bronx who was working in a soda store to put himself through New York University. The two have lived together ever since, but, according to Vidal, sex has played no part in their relationship.

Vidal always portrays himself as emotionally remote. 'There is no warm lovable person inside,' he says. 'Beneath my cold exterior, once you break the ice, you find cold water', and yet he and Austen have reserved themselves a plot at Rock Creek Cemetery in Washington, DC, yards from the spot where Jimmie is buried. Isn't this evidence of a sentimental streak? 'I don't feel self-pity. I inherited my stoicism from having spent my youth with a blind man, reading to him. By the age of ten my grandfather [T.P. Gore, an Oklahoma senator] had lost both eyes. You don't feel very sorry for yourself when that is your role model.'

When Gore Vidal was ten years old his parents divorced, and he went to live with his grandfather. His father, Eugene, was a national sporting hero who became an aviation pioneer, a founder of three civil airlines, including TWA, and a member of Roosevelt's cabinet. His mother, Nina, remarried the millionaire financier Hugh D. Auchincloss, who then left her to marry Janet Lee Bouvier, Jacqueline Bouvier [later Kennedy]'s mother. His father was, he says, charming and serene, but his mother was a 'perfect monster – a lush twenties flapper prone to thunderous rages'. He cannot remember a time when he loved her. At seven he began setting fire to things and stealing watches in protest. At eleven, he would vomit when he saw her. For the last twenty years of her life he refused to see her. Vidal is something of an autodidact – he never went to college, and has always read books fanatically. His mother didn't like him reading. Does he see the connection? 'She would rather have had a Martini than read a book and I must say I would too, now, but not at 10 a.m. No, the most important figure in my life was my grandfather, and my mother was scared to death of him. There was a terrible genial coldness that you sometimes find in masterful politicians. He started to turn to marble before your eyes and I used to enjoy that when he did it with my mother.'

He has, I suggest, been unforgiving in his portraits of her. 'I don't think unforgiving. Accurate. I don't think about her. She was a comic character but she also had enormous charm. She was better-looking than Tallulah Bankhead but they were the same girl. Politicians' daughters.' She would answer the door naked? 'Oh yeah, and receive you on the john. It didn't embarrass me. I was used to her doing it. She had no self-consciousness.'

Which parent is he more like? 'I don't think I am like either, I'd like to think I am more like T.P. Gore. He was a sharp observer. Great comedian. He always gave good advice. He said, "When someone does you an injury, turn the other cheek, bide your time and one day he will put his head on the block; then you get him." I wait, too.'

He certainly does. Gore Vidal is as well known for his feuds as he is for his writing. Among others, he has done battle with Bobby Kennedy, Truman Capote and Norman Mailer (on one occasion Mailer head-butted Vidal, on another Vidal bit Mailer's hand). His reputation as an acid-tongued provocateur was made during a televized debate in 1968: Vidal called the journalist

William F. Buckley a crypto-Nazi, to which Buckley shouted in reply, much to Vidal's mocking pleasure, 'Listen, you queer, stop calling me a crypto-Nazi or I'll sock you in your goddamn face.'

Are these feuds his lifeblood? 'Of which there have been practically none. Mostly they come from journalists and writers. I used to keep the company of writers when I was young but I try not to now because in this age . . . [sigh] . . . everything is about, oh, prizes and reviews and fellowships, all of which bore me. You must remember I have had to deal with a lot of freaks. Imagine being a contemporary of Truman Capote. He was a pathological liar. The bigger the lie the darker the pair of sunglasses he would wear. The Gores are an extremely combative family, with the exception of cousin Albert [Al Gore, the presidential candidate] – sadly, he was the only one who did not inherit the family love of a fight. People who engage in feuds tend to take everything personally. If someone attacks me, I shall attack them back.'

Like many arch-teasers, Gore Vidal doesn't like to be teased back. He ran unsuccessfully for Congress as a Democrat in New York in 1960, and for the Senate in California in 1982. Absurdly, he claimed he could have won California had it not been for a homophobic article Auberon Waugh wrote for *The Spectator*. 'Teased is not a synonym for insulted,' Vidal says. 'But I never took Auberon Waugh seriously, aside from . . . did I kick his ass in *The Spectator*?' Sort of, having been given the right of reply. He uses the word 'insulted': given the insults he has dished out over the years, isn't that a bit rich? 'Give me one line that you regard as vicious. Just one . . .'

He has a point. Vidal might have described Ronald Reagan as 'a triumph of the embalmer's art', but that was pretty playful stuff. Most of the epigrams for which he is known have offended not because they were genuinely insulting but because they were annoyingly well-timed. When the novelist Richard Adams accused Vidal on television of being meretricious, he retorted: 'Mere-tricious to you and a Happy New Year.' On being asked what would have happened if Khrushchev, rather than Kennedy, had been assassinated in 1963, he said: 'I think I can safely say that Aristotle Onassis would not have married Mrs Khrushchev.'

I settle for something he said on hearing that Truman Capote had died – 'a good career move'. Whatever Capote's own last words might have been, they were certainly overshadowed by that. Vidal smiles. 'Well, first he was dead, so he didn't care. And it *was* a good career move because he had been dying in public for a long time, collapsing with drugs and so on. Besides, it was a private comment.'

Has Vidal considered his own last words? 'We all have last words but we don't know what they are. How about: "To be continued . . ."' Doesn't quite square with his atheism, though. He smiles and mouths the word 'no'. But he has thought about his own exit. 'All of you will go with me because I'm a solipsist. I've just imagined you. When I go, all will be blank.' Maybe he thinks there's immortality in books? 'I would doubt it now. Do you see anybody reading anything in the near future? The book is almost irrelevant. Poetry has the best chance. Fiction, I'm not so sure. I see the essay as probably the last necessary form of prose. I can imagine Montaigne outlasting Shakespeare, who will become too difficult.'

It is hard to judge whether Gore Vidal's own books will stand the test of time. As a novelist he is respected but not revered. A sequence of seven historical novels, which began with *Washington DC* (1967) and ended with *The Golden Age* (2000) – a chronicle of American public life from the Revolution to the present viewed from the perspective of one family – has earned him the unofficial title of the nation's biographer. But none could be said to be required reading in the way that novels by John Updike, Saul Bellow, even his old sparring partners Mailer and Capote, are. He is philosophical about this: 'For those who haven't read the books,' he says, 'I am known best for my hair preparations.'

Has he thought about gaining immortality through having children, a condition many aspire to? 'Aspire and perspire,' he says without missing a beat. 'They have my sympathy. We are programmed to replicate in order for the species to survive. But what happens when there is no more planet and no more human race? The arrangement of atoms that makes up you and me will one day be disarranged.'

In the early fifties, it is said, Vidal had an affair with a waitress at Key West – she became pregnant and had an abortion. If this is true, does he now brood upon what might have been?

'Ask me about the euro.'

Hypothetically then, would the thought of his genes continuing not be a comfort in old age? 'You mean having someone to challenge my heirs and assigns?'

There is little evidence today of Vidal's legendary vanity – 'a narcissist,' he once countered, 'is someone better looking than you' – and his carelessly shaven face is grizzled with patches of white hair. As a young man he was considered something of a dish: Harold Acton found him 'aggressively handsome', and the novelist Elaine Dundy said, 'Just the sight of Gore had the effect of instantly cleansing my palate like some tart lemon sorbet.' Does he look at photographs of himself as an epicene youth and weep for his lost beauty? 'No. I was never my own type, so I see no great loss. I was hardly epicene. That was Evelyn and Auberon Waugh.'

He shows me a photograph of himself shaking hands with a grinning Jack Kennedy. 'He's probably saying to me [he bares his teeth and adopts a Kennedy voice], "Find out who that girl is in the yellow dress over there." He could talk while smiling, you know.' It's a funny impersonation, doubtless a party piece. In terms of Kennedy's place in history, does Vidal think it was almost a kindness that he was assassinated before his promiscuity and drug dependence were exposed? 'It is the United States of Amnesia. No one is remembered. I should think half the people don't know who he is now.'

According to Vidal, Kennedy liked to have sex in the bath with the woman on top, because he had a bad back. Once, with an actress, he suddenly pushed her backwards until her head was under the water, causing a seizure for her and an orgasm for him. 'She hates him still.' I tell Vidal I shall never be able to look at a picture of Kennedy again without thinking of that story. 'He was promiscuous, it's true. There was a different woman every day. He was pretty candid with his friends. The artist Bill Walton was a great friend of his – as indeed was I – and Bill and I did worry about him the first year, we were worried someone was going to shoot him. Not Lee Harvey Oswald but an angry husband while Jack was escaping down a drainpipe. Jack said to Bill, "They can't print any of this while I'm alive. And when I'm dead I don't care." He didn't expect to live long and there was speculation among his friends that he wouldn't get through the first term because his health was so bad. He was on so much medication, especially cortisone which affects your judgement.'

Has he been following the Senator Condit case? A nod. What is it with these politicians? Why can't they keep it in their trousers? 'I think that is true of most males who have the opportunity. My father thought otherwise. He found politicians sexless. The difference now is that the press feel they have every right to know about private lives.' Don't they? 'Of course not. What has sex got to do with the administration of the country?'

Well, if you have an impulsive leader who is incapable of controlling his sexual appetites and is unfaithful to his wife, the logic goes, how can you trust him to act responsibly and truthfully toward the country? 'So there goes Julius Caesar, right? I guess he was a bad leader. Closer to home, yours not mine, Lloyd George wasn't too bad.'

Is a sexual appetite a prerequisite for good leadership, then? 'It's irrelevant. It's as if you've got someone who has a tendency to overeat. It has nothing to do with anything, except in peculiar countries like England and the US where there is so much hysteria roiling around. Have you ever had the slightest interest in the sex life of any politician of your time?'

Absolutely!

'How morbid.'

The Monica Lewinsky affair was the most riveting political drama to have unfolded in the past ten years.

'I assure you it wasn't, and I spent quite a lot of time attacking Mr Starr for the sting operation he pulled on Mr Clinton. Perjury in a civil suit means nothing. The whole system was poisoned in the process, ending with the crash of the Republic last fall. The electoral system has got to change or we may see a Pentagon committee governing – preferable, I suppose, to the Supreme Court.'

He must be very, very proud to have George W. Bush as his president. He laughs. 'I wouldn't wish my country that much ill,' he says. 'That he's ridiculous is humiliating for the United States. But things are stirring. There is even talk that Bush may not serve out his term. It has become a lawless country. The constitution has broken down. We have no enemies except those we elect and select and direct toward the nearest nuclear bombs. They need an enemy to provoke, a diversion. This is the mentality of these tenth-rate people who are now in politics because corporate America likes them. They are malleable. They give them contracts to build missile shields that will never work. It's deeply corrupt. The un-bright Bush was born into a system he takes for granted. His father was equally corrupt. At least with Kissinger, the world-killer, you had a very brilliant man who knew how to tiptoe in and out of a room. These people just fall on their faces.'

Writers, Vidal believes, must tell the truth, or try to, and politicians must never give the game away. As a writer he has been consigned to the fringes of power; he was never the one in the White House making the decisions about the Cuban missile crisis, or Vietnam, or the oil crisis. Does he think he didn't realize his potential? 'Every now and then. It crossed my mind two days ago: my grandfather's last secretary sent me some letters. One was about Senator Gore's plan to establish me in New Mexico, get my name on the ballot and have a conventional political career. When I published *The City and the Pillar* [a novel about homosexuality] that was the end of it. I had made a choice. I haven't regretted it. Writers can actually influence history if they don't confine themselves – as many journalists do – to [writing about] private lives.'

He would probably have been hopeless as a politician anyway, because he has a dangerous addiction to revelation. 'Like Portillo, eh?' He pronounces it the Spanish way, Por-tee-o. 'No, I like to think I have depths of insincerity as yet un-plumbed.' Was it homophobia that did for Portillo? 'Maybe. Maybe it's just that old thin-lipped Conservatives don't like full Iberian lips.'

Norman Mailer once described Gore Vidal as being shameless in intellectual arguments. 'He is absolutely without character and moral foundation,' he said. Does Vidal think he is a good man? 'I never think in those terms. "Useful", I would like to say.' Is he happy? 'Oh yes, very serene.' He doesn't suffer, as one has been led to believe, from bouts of melancholy? 'You do as you get older. It's the medicine we have to take. Five pills a day. [He suffers from diabetes.] They are mood-altering. Doctors have no idea how one pill is affecting the other pill. I'll give you a little tip, never trust one doctor.'

***

In the palazzo on the promontory overlooking the coast, five hours have passed. The evening air now carries the scent of lavender as well as the sound of cicadas and the peal of bells from a nearby monastery. Howard has appeared in his dressing-gown to say hello and disappeared again. An offer to use the swimming-pool – 'We have no need of bathing suits here, it is very private' – has been made and accepted. A full bottle of scotch, VAT 69, has been brought out, two glasses have been poured with a shaky hand, two more, and two more, and now it stands empty. With the tape recorder off, another side of Gore Vidal has been seen: less imperious and self-regarding, more bohemian and mischievous.

Sitting in a cool steady light, he has told me about how he once tried opium but it made him nauseous; how he enjoys pornography, but only as fiction (he wrote the screenplay for *Caligula*, then, when he saw Tinto Brass's film, demanded to have his name taken off the credits); how he used to go cruising with Tennessee Williams and Tom Driberg and once had a fling with Jack Kerouac, but only for the sake of literary history; how he held his own against the Mitford sisters amid the 'savage dialogues' at Chips Channon's dinner parties.

In many ways Gore Vidal is everything you hope he will be: the garrulous, supercilious gadfly. His manner is Augustan, his tone amused, his pursuit of urbanity strenuous. His conversation crackles with sardonic humour, as you would expect from the man who once said, 'Never miss a chance to have sex or appear on television,' and, most famously, 'Whenever a friend succeeds, a little something in me dies.' But I can't decide whether he is at ease with himself. I suspect not. He has, he says, met everybody, but not really known anybody. There seems to be a gnawing discontent to him, or at least a restlessness. Perhaps it is to do with his, as he once put it, not having caught his own attention.

The actress Susan Sarandon, a friend, believes he was 'de-vastated' not to be elected either to Congress or the Senate because, if he stands for anything, it is a belief in the purity of the Republic. The disquiet may also be because he still feels like an outsider – this is perhaps why he is so drawn to Timothy McVeigh. In a way Vidal has become everything he despised in his youth: a snob, a puritan and the epitome of the settled 'family' man. He will tell you shocking stories about JFK in the bath, but then add loftily that what people get up to in their private lives, his included, is no one else's business.

I ask about his feud with Charlton Heston. Vidal claims to have rewritten an early scene of *Ben-Hur* to give it a gay subtext, one that would explain the stormy relationship between Ben-Hur (Heston) and Messala (Stephen Boyd). Boyd was in on the subtext, but William Wyler, the director, told Vidal not to say a word to Chuck or he'd 'fall apart'. When Heston heard this story for the first time in 1996 he took the bait and growled: 'It irritates the hell out of me.' He called Vidal 'a tart, embittered man'.

I interviewed Heston shortly afterwards. 'Poor Gore,' he told me, 'I think he must have had a passion for me. Perhaps *that* was the subtext.' When I mention this to Vidal, his face clouds over. 'Such an unattractive man,' he hisses. A lot of teeth, I agree, but surely the barrel chest, the oiled muscles, the height – 6ft 3in – qualified him as a pin-up. 'He wasn't that tall,' Gore says with a peeved expression. 'We are about the same height.' We change the subject, but later return to it. Vidal picks a photograph off a table by the door. It shows a beaming, towering Heston, his arm around a shorter, more brooding Vidal. 'Now,' he says triumphantly, 'tell me, who is in love with whom in this picture?'

D.M. Thomas

AUGUST 1999

Luminous white hair, dandruff on black polo neck, florid complexion, thick lips cracked and bruised, fingers stained yellow from smoking . . . The 64-year-old Cornishman drinking Rioja and chain-smoking Marlboro Lights at the table by the window is either a broken-veined pervert or a literary genius. As it happens, D.M. Thomas has been described as both – female critics tend to favour the former theme, male critics the latter. Actually, what he looks most like is the survivor of a bomb blast, emerging blinking and disorientated from the rubble, white with plaster dust.

It's a rainy afternoon in Truro. The clouds outside the pub are black. We're on our second bottle and Thomas is hunched forward, avoiding eye contact, telling me about the topic that preoccupies him at the moment – his wife Denise, who died at the age of fifty-three last October. 'She had kidney cancer that went to her vertebrae,' he says in a subdued, mildly Cornish burr. 'Most people try to avoid thinking about death because there is nothing you can do about it. But when it happens to someone close to you, you can't escape it. You know that half of you is dying and will die. You feel sorry for her but also for yourself because everything she knows about you dies with her.'

Donald Michael Thomas, D.M. Thomas to his readers, Don to his friends, has a first in English from Oxford. He began using his initials as a pen name when a contemporary at the university, another Donald Thomas, beat him into print with a collection of poetry. D.M. Thomas went on to publish six collections of verse, twelve novels, an autobiography, translations

173

of Pushkin and Anna Akhmatova, and, last year, a 550-page life
of Alexander Solzhenitsyn which A.N. Wilson described as the
most impressive literary biography he had ever read. But it is for
his third novel, *The White Hotel*, that D.M. Thomas is best
known. When it was published in 1981 it became a surprise
bestseller, first in America, then in this country, where it was
short-listed for the Booker Prize. When the author heard that
Salman Rushdie had won that year, his response was com-
mendably honest: 'Fuck!'

The commercial success of *The White Hotel* was – and, as it
has never been out of print, still is – something of a mystery to
the publishing world. Though it is considered a 'difficult' novel,
it has sold more than two million copies. And like most of
Thomas's fiction, it is about his obsessions with Sigmund Freud,
the Holocaust, dreams, myths and the sex-death parallel – grand,
over-arching themes which have earned the author a reputation
as the dirty old man of literature. Does D.M. Thomas like himself? He sighs. 'Yes and no. What does Hamlet say? Neither
terribly good nor terribly bad. I sometimes have monstrous ideas,
but I don't think I'm a monster.'

Feminist critics of *The White Hotel* disagree with this analysis.
They consider one chapter in particular to be the work of a
monster. Lisa Erdman, the clairvoyant opera-singing heroine of
the novel, becomes a patient of Freud in the Vienna of the
twenties. Together they explore her sexual fantasies and her sense
of impending catastrophe. Twenty years later, Lisa is among the
multitude at the massacre of Babi Yar, the ravine near Kiev where
200,000 Jews, gypsies and Slavs were machine-gunned by the
Nazis. The careful attention Freud pays to Lisa as an individual
in the first half of the book is contrasted shockingly with the
way the Nazis dehumanize her in the second. She ends her life
on a pile of naked corpses as a soldier uses a bayonet to simulate
sex with her.

Feminist critics have accused Thomas of fantasizing about
being that soldier. 'People are afraid of what Freud had to say
about the inner-self and sexuality,' Thomas says when I put this
to him. 'They would rather explore things on sociological and
political terms than confront their own demons. That scene was
an exploration of the good and evil in every human con-

sciousness. I have no desire to put a bayonet in a woman's vagina. But I do want to try and understand the destructive and sadistic impulse that makes some other men want to.'

The White Hotel is a metaphorical place where all that is good and beautiful in the world coexists with all that is evil and brutal. In her recurring dream about it, Lisa longs to go there yet dreads it as well. 'I'm willing to accept that I am a White Hotel,' Thomas says. 'We all are, if we are honest. Even Freud admitted he had good and evil impulses. But most of us can leave those impulses under the surface. I have never beaten or ill-treated a woman in my life, but I accept the world of fantasy where these things can happen. And perhaps it's the people who don't explore these impulses as an abstraction who are the most likely to act upon them in real life.'

D.M. Thomas says he has always tried to be faithful to the truth in his writing, but in his private life, and that of his family, he admits he has engaged in 'every colour of lie from white to grey to black'. As we shall see, his amatory career has been extraordinarily complex and he has been, at best, evasive about it. But the death of his wife has taught him that such deception is pointless. 'Oh, what does it matter any more?' he sighs. 'Let's get drunk. Ask me anything. I'll try and be honest.'

And honest he is: about sex, drugs and infidelity. But such is his suicidal frankness and his clear vulnerability that you feel protective towards him. When he stubs a cigarette out, he taps it against the ashtray about fifteen times in rapid succession. Rat-tat-tat-tat. It is a compulsive gesture, agitated, wounded. He does this now and immediately lights another cigarette. He managed to stop smoking five years ago, he says, but the stress of watching his wife die made him start again. She was a smoker, too, and towards the end he would have to guide her hand to the ashtray.

Lately he says he has found it very easy to cry. Although he has written a few poems, and has recently been commissioned to write a novella, he has had neither the energy nor the inclination to write fiction. 'It's been a struggle just surviving. I wrote a few poems about Denise tending the garden when she knew she wouldn't complete it. They were a feeble attempt to pay tribute to someone who wasn't known to the world at large.'

In the mid-eighties Thomas suffered a nervous breakdown and was unable to read or write for a year. He still suffers periodic bouts of depression. 'It feels like a terminal illness, too,' he explains. 'It is almost as powerful as travelling with your wife on her road to death. I feel terrible for saying that – but in depression your life is totally without meaning. Chaotic. Every moment is enormously painful. There are no parameters and you are convinced that every day until your death you are going to be miserable. I didn't actively seek death. I lacked the energy to commit suicide. But I certainly felt it wouldn't matter if I didn't wake up.'

Living a life of deception may have contributed to his breakdown. At one stage he would divide his time between his first wife Maureen, with whom he had two children (Caitlin and Sean), and his second wife Denise, with whom he had one (Ross). Maureen and he grew up in the same tin-mining community near Redruth in Cornwall. They met while he was home on leave during his National Service and married in 1958, when he was 23-years-old and still a student at Oxford. 'At the time in Methodist Cornwall if you slept with someone, you married them,' he says. 'But I wasn't mature enough for marriage and I'm sorry I put her through so much. Then again, I don't really regret it because children came out of it – and I wouldn't want to wish them away. Maureen and I both went through a long period of uneasy, unsatisfactory compromise, in which she knew about my mistress. To her infinite credit she said in her late forties: "I've had enough of this, I'm leaving." We are still on friendly terms. When she remarried I felt relief. Then panic.'

After graduating in 1958, Thomas become a schoolteacher and then, in 1964, a lecturer at Hereford College of Education. He remained there until 1978, when it closed and he was made redundant. Instead of looking for another teaching post he decided to try and earn a living writing fiction. He met Denise, an engineer's daughter, when she joined Hereford College as a student teacher in 1966.

'Denise and I had a very unconventional marriage. It was all to do with a piece of paper. She wanted a child. She taught at a church school and in those days, the seventies, it would have been a scandal to be a single mother. We decided to marry so that she could have a child and keep her job. It would be treated as a formal arrangement and, then, as soon as we could – three years is the minimum – we'd get a divorce.'

Ten years and one divorce from Denise later, he was back with her. The couple moved to Cornwall and began living together. When they discovered that Denise had cancer they went to see their solicitor to check what provisions the original divorce settlement had made for their son. 'We were told that the divorce had never gone through. We had the decree nisi but someone at Hereford Crown Court had neglected to issue the decree absolute. We were unexpectedly still married after twenty-four years. We were flabbergasted. And glad. It was like fate had stepped in. Even Thomas Hardy wouldn't have got away with such an improbable twist.'

Thomas says he has been haunted all his life by Freud, whose writing style he consciously imitated. He also seems to have taken inspiration from Freud's promiscuity. In his autobiography, *Memories and Hallucinations* (1988), Thomas alludes to affairs he had during both marriages, as well as to his penchant for seducing big-thighed students. Did he suspect he would be an unfaithful husband right from the day he married? 'No. I drifted into it. It was like I was in a dream state. I wanted to be loyal but I did feel, selfishly, that if I wanted to be a writer I would need more experience of life. But my being unfaithful was a contradiction because though I wanted self-fulfilment I also felt a root loyalty to look after my family.'

When in turn his mistress found out he was being unfaithful, she seems to have taken it in her stride. 'I think Denise knew no one else would be a real threat to her. She led her own life and we understood each other.' Thomas doesn't think that his literary fame gives him a feeling of empowerment, a sense that normal moral codes don't apply to him because he is an artist. 'No. I sinned and accepted that I was a sinner.'

So much for his private life, in his professional life he has been labelled a 'devilish misogynist' (by the *Guardian*). And one *Observer* reviewer has compared him to 'some raddled seducer, tweaking his passive conquest with absent-minded fingers'. He plays up to the image to an extent. For a few years he ran an erotic writing course from his home – until the *Modern Review* sent a female journalist on it, under cover, to see if he would try and seduce her. She claims he did. He says he didn't.

D.M. Thomas denies the misogyny charge. On the contrary, he says, he feels at home in a feminine psyche. When I ask if he is Lisa in *The White Hotel* in the same way that Flaubert is Madame Bovary he answers: 'Yes, although I didn't realize it at the time. It's great fun writing as a woman because it is the unknown. It didn't occur to me until years after I had written *The White Hotel* that the Don Giovanni poem at the beginning is a representation of my own turbulent sexuality. The extreme puzzlement, wonder and frustrated longing I felt as an adolescent. I think it is easier for men to write about women than for women to write about men because we've all been inside a woman – our mothers.'

Thomas recognizes that he probably went through an androgynous phase. 'Around puberty I became something of a hermaphrodite. I have a sister who is ten years older than me and I would wear her clothes sometimes. It felt liberating because I couldn't get close to real girls at that age and yet I had a strong sexual instinct to turn myself into one. I'm sure my sister played a vital role in fostering my weird imagination.'

Don Thomas and his sister had a peripatetic childhood. Their grandfather was a carpenter who worked in the copper and tin mines around Redruth. Their father, Harold, would have done the same had the mines not been closed after the First World War. Instead, he travelled to California to construct film sets at Twentieth Century-Fox, only to return to Cornwall during the Depression. When Thomas' sister married an Australian serviceman and moved to Melbourne in 1949, he and the rest of the family followed. Thomas, his father and mother, lived there for two years before returning again to Cornwall.

'I never got on with my brother-in-law,' Thomas reflects. 'I was in my early teens when we moved to Australia, and maybe there was some Oedipal jealousy there. I never went through a homosexual phase – although I did sleep with my father a lot from the age of seven to fourteen, because I was afraid of ghosts. My mother would be turfed out of bed. I definitely had Oedipal fantasies about her.' When his father died in 1960 Donald took comfort by sleeping the night in the same bed as Maureen his wife and Amy his mother. When his mother died fifteen years later it triggered an obsession with death, which was to become a recurring theme of his writing.

Thomas has always wanted to revisit the place where his family lived in California. But because a clairvoyant told him twenty years ago that he would die there, he has never dared go. Now that Robert Geisler and John Roberdeau, the producers of *The Thin Red Line*, are making *The White Hotel* into a film, he might have to. There have been several unsuccessful attempts in the past to bring the novel to the big screen. First D.M. Thomas wrote a screenplay, then two more screenwriters tried and failed before Dennis Potter had a go, which is the version being used.

At one stage David Lynch wanted to direct it. 'Lynch thought the opera singer was too highbrow and so should be a trapeze artist instead. He also thought that his then girlfriend Isabella Rossellini should play the role. When she left him he went off the idea. I suppose because of my parents' connection with Hollywood I shall enjoy going there,' Thomas reflects. 'But I feel superstitious about dying there. The stress might bring on a heart attack at the première. Actually, that might not be such a bad way to go. It would be terrifying – but what publicity for a film about clairvoyance!'

We leave the pub and head across Truro, up a hill to the converted coach house where Thomas has lived for the past twelve years. Currently in residence is Sean, Thomas's 35-year-old son from his first marriage, a former heroin addict whose taste for S&M led to a rape charge (of which he was acquitted) in 1988. He is also a published novelist. We greet him briefly and then head upstairs to the study. The walls are lined with shelves carrying various editions of D.M. Thomas's many books, including more than twenty translations of *The White Hotel*. The computer is switched on. There is a sculpture of a unicorn with a broken horn, a photograph of Denise and, above his desk, a painting of Akhmatova, the Russian poetess whom he says is his muse. Thomas lights up another cigarette and, shrouded in smoke, his eyebrow arched, he looks demonic. I ask him whether he has ever been tempted to experiment with drugs. He has had the odd joint, he says, but nothing stronger. 'I know I have an addictive personality so I don't want to risk heroin. But part of me would like to try it just once. If I knew I was going to die, I would try it.'

Perhaps when he goes to California? We are back on the subject of death. He is beginning to feel old. His body aches from sciatica. He has another drag from the cigarette he holds between blotchy fingers and, as he starts the process of stubbing it out fifteen times, he tells me he has a religious consciousness but finds it difficult to accept the notion of an afterlife. 'I hope there is one. I fear there isn't. Denise and I talked about it when she was in the hospice and I tried to be more optimistic than I felt. When someone is desperate you put the best gloss on things.'

How should an artist die? Thomas tells me he once experienced the death of a novelist. William Golding used to live near Truro and the night before he died he had a party. 'I stayed after the other guests left and his daughter brought out his two best bottles of wine. This upset William a bit and there was a certain tension. But then he suddenly told her he loved her. He looked out of the window and remarked upon how much he enjoyed living in this house. He squeezed his wife's hand affectionately. I said goodnight, drove back seeing double, and he died of a heart attack half an hour later. That was a good way to go.'

Like William Golding, D.M. Thomas will probably be remembered for just one novel. He is philosophical about it. 'Some writers can do it again and again and it's wonderful. Others have to resign themselves to never producing anything as good again. At least I did it once. I didn't get angst-ridden when later novels weren't as commercially successful. *The White Hotel* is the novel with which I am most satisfied. I was almost in a dream state when I wrote it. It flowed automatically and needed little revision. It was the book where all my themes and obsessions found their absolute objective correlative.'

The phone rings and the answering machine clicks on. A young woman's voice, well-spoken. 'Hi, my darling. I'm at home. Call me when you get in. Bye, darling.'

The author and I exchange a glance.

'Oh, my God,' D.M. Thomas says from behind a blue veil of smoke. 'An unexpected intrusion of reality.'

Who was she?

'A friend of mine. Yes. A friend.' Silence. 'Life has to go on.' Silence. 'Do you want to ask more about her?'

No. That's all right.

Eddie Izzard

OCTOBER 1997

Transparent and inflatable, Eddie Izzard's sofa is not so much a piece of household furniture as a plaything in a crèche. It's a bouncy sofa. A comedy sofa. One that makes rubbery squeaking noises whenever you move. I've been invited to sit on it by the enigmatic blonde who answered the door, explained that 'Eddie is running late' and then left. As I'm waiting, I try to work out a technique for rising from the sofa with dignity. There isn't one – you're either pitched violently towards the floor or wobbled sideways – so I move to the inflatable armchair opposite. It envelops me. And with arms forced up and forward looking like a no-necked sleepwalker, I take in the interior with eye movements only. The walls are painted silver. The phone is in the shape of Mae West's lips. There is a guitar, a packet of Rizla papers and a curtain of beads on strings hanging from the doorway through to the kitchen. All as you'd expect really.

Inky afternoon rain is sluicing down in Soho and Eddie Izzard, the 35-year-old comedian who looks twenty-five and acts fifteen, emerges from it bedraggled and drenched. He has a few days' stubble on his face but no make-up. His normally tousled and fluffy Meg Ryan haircut is lying flat and lank against his scalp, roots defiantly exposed. While I'm still struggling to rise, he slips off his leather trenchcoat, gives it a shake and lopes across the room to proffer a hand in greeting.

You have to be careful how you press the flesh with Izzard. He hates, no, hates is too strong a word for this amiable man, he isn't particularly fond of those crusher handshakes, the ones you're never expecting and that etiquette dictates you're not allowed to react to. Izzard thinks that the world's hand-crushers should be taught a lesson – whenever you encounter one, you should either scream or collapse silently to the floor, getting a friend to point out to the horrified crusher that you suffer from 'hand-squeezy death'.

Apparently satisfied that my shake is equidistant between firm and limp, Izzard flops on the sofa, dangles his black spiky-heeled boots over the end and talks about the party Tony Blair threw at Number 10 this summer for his coolest, grooviest supporters. Izzard, the heppest pussy-cat with the shiniest PVC trousers of them all, was there. And to prove it, the next day, the *Daily Telegraph* ran a picture of him arriving. The deliriously terse caption under it read, TRANSVESTITE: IZZARD. And, human nature being what it is, one can only assume that this haiku-like summary of a complicated life will appear on his gravestone as well.

That there is more to Izzard than his transvestism – and his gift for reducing his clucking audiences to jelly – is the point he's trying to make by taking on more serious roles (having already played three on stage, Edward II among them). Then, again, even as he tells you this, you can't help but smile. 'Yeah. Well,' he says, languorously contorting his vowels, 'I can do both comedy and serious. I've got spare energy. It's some sort of "I'll show you" thing. Not wanting to be pigeonholed. Because then you become a pigeon. And even pigeons don't want to be all put in the same hole. They want to be, er, um . . .' He pursues this feathery theme for perhaps twenty seconds, grinds to one of his familiar 'mumble, rumble, scrumble' halts and then grins impishly.

'Hey!', he blurts, as if just struck by an Archimedean revelation. 'Don't you think these sofas are great? You can just sort of slide off them.' He just sort of slides off the sofa, springs back up on his stacked heels, sits and just sort of slides off it again.

Watching his performance – the uninhibited, hyperactive child at play – reassures you that, for all his aspirations as a serious actor, Izzard means it when he says he will never be able to give up live comedy. He clearly derives far too much pleasure from making himself laugh. And for us as well as him the real appeal of his comedy lies not in the subtlety and sophistication of his allusions but in its exuberant, sniggering puerility, his cheerful cartoon land of talking animals and pre-teenage innocence, his ability to talk to the child in us all when he says that people who consume too much calcium should tell their doctors they feel 'all cheesy-bony'.

But what might otherwise be just endearingly childish flights of fancy are rendered irresistible by Izzard's appearance: with his footballer's legs, sturdy body and square head he looks like a giant toddler, or a seven-year-old who has found an unguarded bottle of steroids. As it happens, the comedian remembers his wild, seven-year-old self vividly. 'He was a very bad loser,' Izzard says with a thoughtful scratch of his stubbly chin. 'Always throwing tantrums. Tennis rackets through windows. Ridiculously competitive. But my dad was a live-and-let-live kind of guy and I suppose eventually I got on board with that.'

Izzard grew up in Bexhill-on-Sea which, he admits, doesn't sound all that exotic but – as he was born in the Yemen, is descended from Huguenots in the French Pyrenees, has one grandfather who was a shepherd, another who was a bus driver, and a German grandmother – he feels that exotic has been taken care of. His father aspired to a 'middle-class sort of thing' and became an accountant with British Petroleum, sending Eddie and his brother to a minor provincial boarding school where pupils were taught to vote Tory. Although his father gave him 'space to take risks', he also impressed upon his son the motto 'be happy, but preferably as an accountant'. The young Izzard flew various flags of convenience, such as Civil Engineering and Accountancy, but, eventually, after dropping out of a degree in Maths and Financial Accounting at Sheffield University, he came clean with his father and spent the second half of the eighties as a street performer in London and Edinburgh.

Upon reflection, the comedian sees his father's reluctance to put pressure on him to get a proper job as having a lot to do with the bond the two struck when Eddie's mother, a nurse, died of cancer. He was six and he says he cried continually until he was eleven, and after that he never really cried again. The fact he was sent off to boarding school may well have had something to do with it. 'The only way to survive being a boarder is to get rid of your emotions, basically,' he says with a shrug. 'The whole atmosphere is geared towards convincing you you have to be a captain of industry. That you have to run things. They don't say, "You've all got to go away and become transvestites". They wouldn't even say the word. People never say the word. They would say instead, "he's one of those".'

Remembering the caption TRANSVESTITE: IZZARD, I have been trying to avoid the subject. But it's not just because it pigeon-holes him, it's because, well, it feels like we've heard a little too much from Eddie Izzard over the years on his right to express himself through his clothing. That Izzard feels the need to bring it up himself, though, and in such an abrupt and clumsy way, seems to point to some lack of resolution in his own feelings towards being 'one of those'. And judging by the way he equates his being a transvestite – rather than his being a comedian – with other people's sense of themselves as lawyers, doctors or teachers, his urge to cross-dress seems to have become the skeleton on which he has fleshed out his whole self-identity.

Although he may describe himself as being two lesbians trapped – but cohabiting happily – in a man's body, Izzard actually takes his heterosexual brand of transvestism most seriously. At one point there was rumour of a steady girlfriend, Vanessa Jones, the beautiful daughter of the Bishop of Sodor and Man, but at the moment Izzard says, 'I'm kinda loose. Which is fun. At some point I'll settle down, but not tonight.'

He wears lipstick and skirts, he says, because it makes him feel comfortable. 'I don't choose to look this way. It's a built-in thing that tells me to head down this direction.' And he isn't particularly fond of the expression 'women's clothes' because, he says, they are *his clothes*. He has bought them, not borrowed them.

Even when he talks about being 'TV' – his preferred expression – as part of his stand-up routine, he does so only to make a serious underlying point. The 'dick-head men' on the building sites who shout out 'bloke in a dress' when they see him coming, and continue shouting it as he walks past, should, he believes, show more respect for other people's inclinations. They should, as his father taught him, live and let live. Does it follow, then, that Izzard should also show some tolerance for those people, even the dick-head men, who simply find it odd that a bloke should want to wear a dress?

'Oh yeah,' he says, with a slurring, public-school delivery. 'I totally understand it. Perhaps they feel threatened by it. Perhaps they are suppressing a desire to do the same. But I think basically there are those people who hate themselves and those who feel good about themselves. If you feel good about yourself, you have to take the risk of giving out positive energy in the hope that people who hate themselves will give something positive back. I wanted to like myself. I didn't want to be a coward. I wanted to be able to walk down the street as a TV and, if I got beaten up, I wanted to be able to stay on my feet and afterwards take them to court. I wanted to be the person who wasn't scared.'

Earlier this year, Izzard did get into a fight, in Cambridge. And he did stand his ground and, for the first time since he was twelve, he did exchange blows. Afterwards he went to court and the man who fought him was fined £370. Like many people who have taken strength from facing their fears, though, Izzard seems to have become addicted to the scary challenges he sets himself. Almost masochistically, he defies his fear of drying up on stage by improvizing much of his material (when I ask him how much, he gives me a look you would give a village idiot and says, 'Er, exactly seventy-two per cent'). But he takes his therapy further. He does gigs in Reykjavik just to see if his sense of humour can cross cultural barriers. He is a passionate pro-European who speaks French and German (and Latin) but not fluently. That doesn't stop him testing his courage, though, by doing his Paris gigs in French. And, though he can fill London theatres almost indefinitely, he likes to do gigs in Bexhill-on-Sea, scene of his most humiliating and painful adolescent moment, because, he says, it helps him put 'a large ghost in pink lipstick to rest.'

When he was fifteen, he was caught stealing make-up from the Bexhill-on-Sea branch of Boots. Thinking he might get asked awkward questions if he bought some lipstick, he hid it under a loaf of brown sliced bread instead and walked out. That way, he says, no-one would know – apart from the police and the judiciary system. He was let off with a warning from the chief constable which, in his fevered imagination, became: 'That eye-shadow is never going to work with that lipstick. You want more russet colours. That's light blue, that is. A death colour for an eye shadow. No-one could get away with wearing that . . .'

That Izzard keeps stressing the 'whatever else I might be, a coward I am not' point is curious. It's a manly aspiration. And he reinforces it constantly by slipping into the high-testosterone language of the rugged, outdoor type. He will tell you that he was a fanatical footballer at school: 'You know. First eleven. Right half. Played thirteen. Won one. Lost one. My main thing was football. And make-up.' Then, talking over his shoulder a few minutes later as he makes some fresh coffee, it's: 'I wanted to be in the Army, you know. I really did. The only reason I was put off is that they always eat potatoes. Remember those films? "Stephens! You're on potato duty! Peel those potatoes!" But I love the climbing trees and jumping over rocks side of soldiering. Invading countries and the shooting people dead stuff I skip over.'

He pauses for a second to emit a thoughtful, sighing 'Yeah' and then he's off again, telling me about his time in the Scouts, and giving vent to a deliriously juvenile stream of consciousness. 'We had this Scout master who was an incredibly energetic, organized and listy-type person, and he drove around in an MG and came from Mars really. Or Kenya. We were eleven guinea-pig kids to him and we did everything. Going down waterfalls, and lead mines and potholes. Outward boundy-type things. Loved that. Want to get back into all that.'

In fits and starts, Izzard chatters away on these masculine topics for a good twenty minutes. He does so charmingly, amusingly and largely unprompted, unspooling anecdotes in the same free-form style that he adopts on stage. He is dyslexic, which may account in part for his babblingly rhythmic speech patterns, padding out hesitations with 'dum-di-dums' or 'bingy-bongy, dingly-danglys' when he can't find the right phrase. Then again, it could be that, with all that febrile energy and those highly charged hormones, he is simply too impatient to wait until the right word comes along.

He doesn't agree, though, that he possesses any unconscious urge to prove that he has all the normal red-blooded aspirations. 'Do I find I need to mention them? Well, not really. Because it's not very hip to say you wanted to be in the Army.' It is a refreshingly unpretentious answer to a pretentious question and it reminds you that Izzard's comic persona does not hide – as those of so many other comedians do – an introspective, self-punishing and melancholic alter ego. But that's not to say Izzard cannot relate to the comedic tradition of looking to childhood for certain blame associations. He talks, for instance, of the links between his craving for an audience's approval and his mother's death. 'There really are,' he says. 'It's the strongest thing. I love that rush of endorphin off the audience. It's an affection fix, which I analyse back to my mother dying. A lot of people think the TV thing is linked to that, too. But it's not. I knew I was TV before she died. I haven't really sorted out my feelings towards my mother though. Never had therapy. There's still emotion there.'

What his transvestism did give him, of course, was a ready explanation – an excuse – for the times when he felt unpopular. And he took this safety mechanism further with the theory that 'people won't reject you if you appear not to give a damn whether they reject you or not'. As his confidence in his own popularity has grown, however, his appearance has become more compromised and 'acceptable'. When, in the early nineties, he first came out as a transvestite on stage, his look was, by his own estimation, frumpy. Now he has acquired a much more sophisticated and androgynous look; shiny black PVC trousers, burnt orange velvet frock coat, spiky stilettos and a swagger that reminds you of John Travolta in *Saturday Night Fever*. It suggests that what he has really come out as is not a cross-dresser but a narcissist.

'Oh yeah,' he says. 'But it depends how you define narcissism. I found by looking in the mirror that my posture was terrible. I was all bent over. Now I've corrected all that by doing Pilates and stuff.' He demonstrates straightening his back. 'Because I wasn't caring what I looked like, because comedy is a mind/speed thing and I thought it doesn't matter what you look like – but it's better if you get the whole visual thing working.' Pause. Scrunching of eyes in attempt to pick up thread again. 'What were we talking about?'

The psychoanalyst Heinz Kobut says that for a healthy self to develop, to gain balance and cohesion, the infant needs to feel affirmed, recognized and appreciated, especially when he displays himself. If those needs are unsatisfied, mirror-gazing in adulthood is a belated attempt to obtain the reassurance that he's there, whole and in one piece.

We were talking about narcissism, Eddie.

'Yeah, narcissism,' Izzard says. 'I feel more confident when I look kicking. I started out in Jesus sandals and combat trousers. They had lots of pockets that I couldn't help stuffing full of things. It made me look like a weird hamster whose jaw had slipped. The Italians have the right idea. Lots of pockets. But sew them up because if you put things in them it will ruin the line of the suit.' He stands up and runs his hands over his hips to demonstrate what he means by the line of a suit.

The interview continued in this vein for three hours, filling up two C90 audio tapes. When, a few weeks later, I came to transcribe them, I discovered that one of the tapes, the first, had gone missing. I searched everywhere for it, accused everyone, but eventually consoled myself with a remark that Mother Theresa made to Sir Cliff Richard after he returned from recording an interview with her only to find the tape was blank: 'God must have had a reason for not wanting the tape to be heard.'

Perhaps I was going to misquote Izzard and he was going to sue me for libel. Perhaps it was destiny. Karma. A Zen thing. And, come to think of it, these were some of the subjects Izzard talked about on the missing tape. He's a big believer in being 'centred', he told me. It's something that practising yoga has taught him. It's what enables him to Flow rather than Struggle, to feel his way through one of his elastic, improvised stories on stage, rather than worry about where it is going or whether it is about to snap.

I suppose I could have asked Izzard to go over the areas covered in the missing tape. He is, after all, extremely accommodating and friendly and he loves to natter. On stage he will meander from subject to subject, occasionally giggling at his own jokes. He will doodle and embroider with words, spinning shambolic webs around random thoughts and surreal juxtapositions. He will give you a rush of cerebral vertigo one moment and grind to a standstill the next. 'I've forgotten what I was saying,' he will say typically, with a smile of such innocence it must have been calculated to beguile.

His comedy washes over you, sweeps you along in its undercurrent and afterwards, when you come up for air, it leaves you feeling almost blue as you try to recall quite what it was he said that made you laugh so much. When I tried to describe this post-performance tristesse to Izzard, he gave me a hurt look. When the lights come on after a show, I said, digging myself deeper, you feel sort of deflated, leaden and unfunny. He described a figure of eight with his head, half nodding it and half shaking it in a pantomime of wounded confusion.

And that's the main reason you can't do justice to Izzard in a written profile, and why it doesn't really matter about the missing tape. He's an inspired mime artist. He can conjure up a queue of murderers at a petrol station simply by walking backwards and giving occasional flicks of his hips and a shrug of his shoulder.

He demonstrates it to me now. If you have one imaginary character talking to another, you have to spin yourself a full 180 degrees to face them. As he swivels back and forth, one character standing behind and above the other, his inflatable sofa squeaks against the seat of his black denim jeans.

Beneath all the garrulous vagueness there is a certain cunning, a certain technique, then. Off stage, too. He produces his own videos. He gives exclusive interviews to rival papers. He stands in for Paul Merton on a whole series of *Have I Got News For You* and then insists that he never does television. Like a child who has learned how to get his own way with adults, Izzard is a skilled manipulator.

And, however random and rambling his routines may seem, they always come to a neat full circle. As the interview draws to a close, we find ourselves back on the subject of Bexhill-on-Sea. I ask if he thinks the town will ever put up a statue to its most famous son. 'No,' he says, widening his eyes. 'You must never have that. Because pigeons will poo on it. Pigeons understand the vanity of humans. They say, "Oh here's another trophy to a human ego." And they never poo round statues, they poo on them. No matter how high the pedestal is. That's the pigeon's job in life . . .' And so on.

William Hurt

Mathematicians say that if you halve each pace in crossing a room you will never reach the opposite wall. I'm beginning to think this true of crossing the Charles Bridge in Prague with William Hurt walking beside me. He has a slow, flat-footed gait and, every few yards, he lurches to a halt, turns to me, head cocked, and asks if I agree with him. I mentally pinch the bridge of my nose, try to ignore the headache I feel coming on and wonder, in an abstract way, whether I shouldn't just make a run for it and leave him standing there – rather as you would if you found yourself cornered by a wild-eyed man with a sandwich board on which the nighness of the end of the world was proclaimed.

We have been talking for about twenty minutes, and our conversation has so far been largely one-way and desultory. I've introduced myself and asked him something inane like how is he enjoying filming on location in Prague? He has answered with a thesis on the interconnectedness of quantum mechanics, Tibetan Buddhism, infected blood, the Gulf War, Chaos Theory and Third World population growth. Which is unsettling.

Although he doesn't believe in using a short word (such as 'religious') when there is a longer, more confusing one available (such as 'religiosity'), he does use recognizable words. It's the way he deploys them that throws you. One writer compared the unruly Hurt sentence to a balloon being folded into a matchbox. To be fair, Hurt himself is aware of his condition, apologizes frequently for 'the length of his wordings' and, jokingly, I think, puts it down to his being logorrhoeic. And, in fairness, he doesn't seem pretentious – earnest, sweet, friendly and steeped in liberal angst, but not pretentious. It's all part of the William Hurt Experience: what you get when you ask to go on the full, white-knuckle, loop-the-loop ride.

The tip of the fat Cuban cigar he is holding glows red and, so close does he stand when he talks, I can smell its smoke on his breath. It's gone eight on a clear and still evening and the floodlit view of Prague from the bridge is beguiling: the spires of the St Vitus Cathedral to the northwest are lit in ghostly green, the castle is yellow, the Church of St Nicholas pink. Halfway across the bridge there is a statue of the blind St Luitgarde kissing Christ's wounds; when eventually we reach it, we turn back and head for a nearby Spanish restaurant the actor knows and likes.

Once inside, he recovers his equilibrium a little. He's less distracted. The words no longer pour out in a convoluted stream. He's a bit more like those dry, poised, detached characters he played in all those intelligent eighties films: *The Big Chill, Children of a Lesser God, Gorky Park* . . . But it is, of course, always a mistake to confuse an actor with his roles, especially a versatile one like Hurt. One thinks of the gullible, seedy lawyer he played in *Body Heat*; or the shallow and self-absorbed anchor-man he played in *Broadcast News*; or the fluttery, sensitive, soft-shouldered transvestite in *Kiss of the Spider Woman*, the role for which he won an Oscar in 1986. Anyway, he looks more relaxed now. He takes off his chunky sweater, switches off his mobile phone, grins broadly.

His movements are more graceful, his speech more languid and . . . elliptical. His looks are more familiar, too: that dramatic cleft in the chin, the intense blue eyes behind metal-rimmed glasses, the mouth that turns up at the corners so that it looks as though it's half-smiling, even in repose. William Hurt is a few days shy of his fiftieth birthday but the years have dealt lightly with him: he's still handsome, lean and tall – 6ft 2in – and his fine, thinning hair is still dirty blond. 'I have changed,' he protests with a throaty laugh. 'I creak and rattle when I get out of bed in the morning. I try to work out but actually I'm falling apart like everyone else. My body is going. I've had cataracts and hernia operations and I've got a bad back.'

He orders gazpacho, pesto spaghetti and mineral water. I order vegetable lasagne, on his recommendation, and beer. When it arrives, I ask if he minds me drinking alcohol in front of him. He used to have a serious drink and drugs problem – remarkably, he was a vodka and lithium man and, since checking out of the Betty Ford clinic in 1986, he hasn't touched a drop. 'Doesn't bother me at all,' he says in his resonant yet sleepy American drawl, stretching out the vowels hypnotically. 'Though someone told me it's illegal here for me to chin-chin with you if you're drinking alcohol and I'm not . . . Ahh, to heck with it!' We clink glasses and he tells me about a phone call he's just had with his children. 'I have four, aged seventeen, ten, nine and six. It's easy to keep in touch with them when I'm working abroad. Less with the oldest one because of things that have happened. But the boys [the nine- and ten-year-olds] live with me now. The custody thing was hard. The kids are not responsible . . . Well . . . This is a big question. Are they responsible for your fame? I don't know, there's a sentence that says no one is innocent.'

The 'things that have happened' are – complicated. William Hurt married his first wife, the actress Mary Beth Hurt, in 1972; the couple separated after five years and divorced, amicably, after another five. From 1981 to 1984 he lived with Sandra Jennings, a ballerina with the New York City Ballet. They had a son, Alex. Hurt then lived with Marlee Matlin, an actress with whom he co-starred in *Children of a Lesser God*. In 1986 at the Hazelden Dependency Treatment Center in Minnesota he met Heidi Henderson. They married and had a pre-nuptial agreement which tied alimony payments to the ability of both parties to stay sober and clean. They had two sons, Samuel and William, but divorced acrimoniously after he claimed she had broken the agreement; he later won custody of the children. Then in 1989 Sandra Jennings reappeared, claiming that she and Hurt had had a common-law marriage, and accusing him of, among other things, violence, religious hallucinations and urinating on the sofa.

The hearing, which was held at Room 1254 of the New York Supreme Court and followed daily on television by millions of viewers, became one of the most notorious 'palimony' cases in American legal history. Hurt won the case but compared the experience to having his skin steamed off in public. In 1993 he met the French actress Sandrine Bonnaire, by whom he had a daughter, Jeanne. Disillusioned with America, Hurt decided to reinvent himself as a European and that same year moved to Paris. 'I prefer it when people don't look at me cross-eyed when I speak of other peoples or of mortality or spirituality or transcendence of the material,' he says, leaning back in his chair. 'I've always felt that way about America. I don't feel like an American. When I was young I used to break out into a sweat of embarrassment getting off a plane in Europe that had come from America. It was very hard for me because I had lived overseas. My best friends were Ivo in Guam, Sandy in Samoa; my mother's best friend was Chinese; and in America no one knew these people existed. They can be so insular . . . I have a map of the Balkans next to my bed, so as I can follow what's going on.'

William was six when his parents divorced – for a while, he lived with his mother and two brothers in a small apartment in Hell's Kitchen, New York; his father worked for the US Agency for International Development and directed a number of foreign-aid programmes around the world. 'He was a remote figure when I was growing up,' Hurt says. 'But when I was older I went back into a computer that I had thrown away and culled out of its dormentness much of my father. In his last years I would take him on films with me. He felt proud, I think. He was extremely charming and bright but didn't give himself any credit for the ways I found him to be brightest – his childishness, his sweetness, his sense of romance. It was funny about him, not until he was dying did he acknowledge his great spiritual side. It was like it lived with him there by his side all the time and he disavowed it.'

His father died in 1996, aged eighty-six, of complications from liver cancer. 'I held his hand as he died into the light.' When Hurt was ten, his mother, Claire, a secretary, married her boss, Henry Luce III, son of the founder of *Time* magazine. The family moved into a twenty-two-room apartment on the Upper East Side and William was sent to Middlesex, an expensive Massachusetts boarding school. He felt lonely there but discovered a talent for acting. He won a scholarship to the Juilliard School of Performing Arts in New York, where Kevin Kline and Robin Williams also studied, and went on to read theology at Tufts

University. After this he took to the stage and performed in some sixty repertory and off-Broadway plays – David Mamet described him as the best Hamlet he had ever seen. In 1980 he starred in his first film, *Altered States*, directed by Ken Russell.

'What would I have done if I hadn't been an actor? I think I might have been a pretty decent teacher. I could have worked on boats. Maybe I would have ended up in a monastery. In fact, I do that. I go away. Being in a monastery would be a good way of life but I can't imagine not being a father and not being with my kids. I would give anything to go back to school right now, or start a theatre laboratory, so that you don't get into the gossip end of the business, so that you can work with people who aren't afraid of the idea which I see as emotion. The problem is we don't trust our emotions because we are so out of whack. But if you are in balance you can trust your feelings because they are your mind. I mean, this is part of your mind.' He strokes my hand. I lean over my microphone and say: 'Let the records show that William Hurt is stroking my hand.' 'No,' he laughs. 'Touching it. And that's part of your mind. Everything. Every sense and interpretation. You can't separate the thought. Look at Spinoza. Look at William Blake. I think Blake was very much there, very much home. He accounted for himself. He didn't preoccupy himself with how misunderstood he was. He was integrating his consciousness. The yin and the yang . . . Discovering the feminine sensitive side of yourself doesn't preclude masculinity at all.'

While William Hurt was on honeymoon with his first wife, his mother died from pancreatic cancer, aged forty-seven. Of his imminent fiftieth birthday he says: 'It's something . . . a milestone . . . I'm grateful to my mom, who didn't get much mileage out of the trip but . . . her wheels turned well.' His stepfather, a strict Presbyterian, seems to have been a more influential figure in his formative years. 'He was a churchgoer. Big time. I had connected up to my father's lack of religiosity and began my contest with doctrine in my stepfather's family.'

Our food arrives. 'Excuse me,' says Hurt. 'I stop before I eat. I don't mean to embarrass anyone, but I stop. And it's not so much a prayer but a sort of commemoration of something else. So excuse me. I'll be gone for about fifteen seconds.' He closes his eyes. Thirty seconds pass. 'Thank you,' he says. I ask him what form his commemoration takes. 'Whoever you are, thanks, thanks for the company, thanks for the food, thanks for reminding us to look for what is right . . . That's why rehearsal is my flag.'

Hurt always requests six weeks rehearsal time before filming starts. He rarely gets it. This sometimes makes for tension between actor and director. Hector Babenco, the director of *Kiss of the Spider Woman*, is quoted as saying: 'Hurt promises you a bad time and he delivers. How he made me suffer. Would I work with him again? Tomorrow.' Hurt resents his reputation for being 'difficult', he argues that it is not a crime to try to deliver the best performance you can by rehearsing thoroughly. 'You experience states of concentration,' he explains. 'Like hitting a golf ball. You have to think about it for a long time before you can stop thinking about it and do it.'

The characters he plays often seem lost in their thoughts, dreamy. Is this because he has become possessed by the role? 'No. It's technique. But I do try to be lost in something. I don't think you're co-ordinated until you stop telling the various parts of your body what to do . . . Acting is not lying. It's not false emotion. Doesn't everyone decide when and where and for whom to shed their tears? I'd like to act one more time in something where no one recognized me. I'd like to immerse myself in the craft, not in a schizophrenic way but by becoming the fabric of the conversation; where you occupy every cell instead of being self-conscious; where you walk through a mirror and it's not you any more.' He seems to have returned for a moment to the Hurt I first encountered – random thoughts and academic references spilling out, spiralling off, making him less fluent than jagged. Is this the authentic Hurt, I wonder, a man ill at ease with himself, or at least with his fame?

When asked if William was ever happy, his first wife once said: 'How can you be happy if you never have a quiet mind . . . Most people will just eat a hamburger, he will want to know where the cow was born.' Hurt doesn't think success has brought him happiness, necessarily, which is why he feels wary of it. 'Success isn't going to help you deal with loneliness or help you make your peace with solitude. There are times when someone on the street says, "Are you William Hurt?" and I will say, "No, not at the moment." I'm more myself when I'm whittling wood or doodling, doing something with my hands. That leaves me free to be played on. Played through.'

He has trained himself not to look in mirrors, he adds. And he never watches his old movies, he sees them once and that's it. 'There were many ancient words for vanity,' he says. 'It doesn't just mean being self-centred. I don't want to be my ego's fool.' Glenn Close, his co-star in *The Big Chill*, says that when Hurt stopped drinking he became more accessible, more forgiving of himself. 'When you hate yourself it's pretty hard to deal with other people,' she said. His self-loathing seems to have been connected with a sense of rejection he felt as a child. I ask him if he likes himself more these days. 'I get along better with myself than I did then. I had a hard time for a while. There were a lot of things I didn't like about myself. I was trying to assimilate con-flicting impulses. I mean, a neurosis is defined as mutually ex-clusive goals, so how do you get everything going in the same direction? I came out of an environment where there was lots of conflict. My mother grew up in poverty on the prairies of eastern Oregon and was abandoned by her parents.

'My grandmother was self-destructive to the point of suicide . . . She did commit suicide in a very gruesome way when I was fifteen. [He tells me how but says he would rather not see it in print.] It was a shock. I later worried that I might have inherited the urge to suicide. Your job in life is to accept a way of being that is not defined as conflict . . . Growing up I missed my father a lot. Had separation anxiety. Worried that people I loved would always leave . . . I used to have a terror dream. No story, just formless, infinite minglings of darkness. Even as I began to craft a sentence that would tell me who I was, it would be eaten away. Years later, when I stopped drinking and began to reconstruct, I had waking dreams that I hadn't had for many years, and suddenly I would be in two realities at the same time. I would be talking to someone and this dream would be going on at the same time. It was a very visceral experience. It went on for two years.'

I wonder what effect his parents' divorce had on his own relationships, whether it prevented him from falling in love completely. 'How many times have I been in love? Really really really? There was some love in all my relationships, but twice it was more than other times. One changed everything for me. One did and still does give me nothing but strength and gratitude.' (He prefers not to tell me who the one is because 'private is private and things are not as good if they are not . . . kept for oneself'.)

It is nearly one o'clock in the morning. Hurt apologizes for talking too much, says it's only because he gets nervous, and he quotes a fourteenth-century rabbi who said, 'If you can hear yourself talking, shut up: leave the talking to God.' It's raining as we walk back to our hotel along tiny lanes, over the wet cobbles of a square and past gloomy baroque buildings with sloping roofs and crumbling facades. I ask him if he ever feels as if he has sold his soul in order to become famous. I see his sad smile in the orange glow of the street lights. 'How could I admit that? It would be like damning myself. But it isn't necessarily good fortune to be a success. Fame is a vacuum. It doesn't necessarily bring you pleasure.' His pleasures in life, he adds, come from fly-fishing, playing chess and flying small planes. 'The ones I fly are more like kites than proper planes, but I enjoy doing it because when I'm up there I have my destiny in my own hands. I always carry a compass,' he says, unzipping his coat to show me it. It's a big one, the sort you use for map-reading. 'That's north,' he says, holding it up. 'Which means we're heading to the river.'

In the morning, over breakfast, he tells me he slept badly because he was worrying about whether movie stars really are just narcissists who make a pact with the devil. It is only when he picks up the threads of the previous night's conversation that I realize he doesn't suffer from intellectual dyslexia, as I had assumed upon first meeting him. Once you tune into his wavelength you see there is method in his madness, a structure to his thinking. It's just that, like William Blake, he is sometimes overwhelmed by his thoughts.

This morning he is obsessed with the theme of shame: how Clinton gave in to his; how Jesus went to the cross despising it. Is this evidence of a guilt complex about something formless and dark in his life? Or a Christ complex? Or impostor syndrome?

It's anyone's guess. A few days later, as the e-mails start arriving, I discover that there's one complex he definitely suffers from: persecution. The letters are very long, thousands of 'wordings', and he writes like he speaks, with the same dramatic pauses and labyrinthine syntax. In one he broods upon how the media take famous people hostage in their own space, how interviewers always betray the interviewee. For a few days I wonder if he is being manipulative, trying to compromise me, then I conclude he is just being insecure. After all, he writes also of 'the old nightmare times' when the press went through his rubbish bins and people spat on his window outside courtrooms and tracked him down in London while his wife was pregnant and feeling hysterical. It had been cruel of the judges to hold the trial in front of the cameras, he adds, because adults know things that children are not ready for. 'They never once thought of the effect it would have on our six-year-old son.' He adds that Sandra Jennings has turned out to have 'much of the qualities and loyalty and love to our son that I valued in our love, before it got bruised'.

The letters make me suspect that part of William Hurt never fully recovered from that legal battle with Jennings. 'Whatever good I have done as an artist is obscured by it,' he writes. It has left him vulnerable and raw, delirious and disconnected, desperate to be understood. That defining trauma has also left him hypersensitive to criticism – yet unable to resist the chance to expose himself to scrutiny in this interview. Perhaps it is Stockholm syndrome he suffers from, the psychological condition that describes the mutual dependence between kidnapper and victim. But the letters are touching, too. In one he tells me it's his birthday. In another he quotes from the book about Augustine he is reading at the moment. In a tender one, from Paris, he writes: 'People cry alone and they can laugh alone too. My daughter laughed and laughed in her sleep the other night. It wasn't for anyone else. She was just laughing.'

George Best

Gone are the bloated and waxy features of the career inebriate; gone the grey beard, the lank and lifeless mullet, the shell suit, gone, all gone. Indeed, as George Best steps out of his dark-windowed Range Rover he looks lean, tanned and casual in black jeans and a black T-shirt. Sunglasses hang from his neck. At fifty-five, the sculpture of his cheekbones, dimples and sulky lips is dramatic once more.

It's lunchtime on a flat and sunless day in Belfast. Alex Best – blonde, lithe, 29-years-old – is by her husband's side and, as the couple enter the hotel where we're meeting and walk through its Victorian-Gothic hallway, they acknowledge with nods and shy grins the guests who stare at them. George Best coughs raspily to clear his throat and, with a tight Ulster accent, orders a pot of tea. Alex says she'll leave us to it and heads off to read a newspaper.

On closer inspection, I see a vestige of George Best's former fashion sense – a gold bracelet – and I note the mysterious absence of laces in his lace-up shoes. I also see that his skin is not so much sun-tanned as sallow; that below those distinctively long and dark eyelashes the whites of his eyes are yellow; and that, presumably because chronic liver damage stops you absorbing protein, he is not so much trim as thin.

Whenever John Diamond was asked how he was feeling – and people always did ask – he would smile and answer, 'I've got cancer.' It seems a similarly daft question to ask Best, but I find myself asking it anyway. 'I'm feeling good, thanks. Yeah. Really good. I'm starting to . . .' He doesn't finish the sentence.

'The longest problem has been with jaundice. It's been showing in my eyes a bit. Well, a lot. But the last couple of weeks it has started to clear up. You can try and help it along, but it decides when it goes.'

We are sitting by a window overlooking Belfast Lough. A ferry is sailing past on its way out to the Irish Sea. In 1961, when he was an 'unbelievably skinny' fifteen-year-old, George Best boarded a similar one. Matt Busby had invited him to join Manchester United as an apprentice after one of the club's scouts had telegrammed from Northern Ireland, 'I think I've found you a genius.' Wee Georgie from the Cregagh Estate, as he was known, felt so homesick he returned to Belfast two days later.

A fortnight passed before he summoned the courage to go back to Old Trafford. There he remained for the next eleven years, scoring 137 goals, mesmerizing the crowds with his repertoire of skills, becoming a pin-up, a superstar, a legend before abruptly, it seemed, announcing his retirement, two days before his twenty-sixth birthday. His team-mates weren't that surprised. For some time, Best's playboy life had been getting in the way of his football – he had been missing training sessions and even matches. The transition from heavy drinker to alcoholic followed swiftly. He came back from retirement every so often to play for any club, however lowly, that would pay him – Dunstable Town, Stockport and, for a year, the Los Angeles Aztecs. He gambled heavily, dated actresses, pop-singers and two Miss Worlds. In 1978 he married Angie Macdonald Janes, who was Cher's personal fitness trainer, had a son, Calum, went bankrupt and, in 1984, after driving drunk and assaulting a police officer, spent two months of a three-month sentence in Pentonville Prison and Ford Open Prison (where the warders asked for his autograph). Angie grew tired of George's drinking and philandering – in one furious row she stabbed him in a buttock with a carving knife – and, after eight years of marriage, the couple divorced. In 1990 Best appeared on *Wogan* as a giggly, boastful and, above all, pitiful drunk. In 1995 he married Alex, a public school educated air stewardess for Virgin Atlantic. The reception was held at a pub near Heathrow Airport, and one guest recalled that Alex's parents 'stood in the corner, looking shell-shocked'.

In March last year George Best made the headlines again when he was rushed to the Cromwell Hospital, west London. He had barely eaten for ten days, drinking wine with brandy chasers for breakfast instead. He remained in hospital for six weeks and was told that his liver was so severely damaged one more drink could kill him. Four months later, after a row with Alex, he went on a binge and, according to news reports which he has since denied, was found at 7 a.m. lying on a bench in Battersea Park clutching a champagne bottle. In February this year he was diagnosed with bronchial pneumonia and admitted to Belfast City Hospital, where he was constantly disturbed by autograph hunters. When he got out he went on another binge, this one lasting for three days. He then took the drastic measure of having Antabuse pellets – which will make him violently sick if he touches alcohol – implanted in his stomach. So far they seem to have worked. The tea arrives, and Best pours it with a steady hand. 'I found it hard not drinking at first,' he says with a nervy smile, wide enough to show the boyish gap between his front teeth. 'But the longer it goes the easier it gets.' He gives a short, soft, sad chuckle, a tic of his. 'This is probably the first time I haven't felt like a drink, whereas before, when I've been getting better or recovering, I've always thought that at the end of it I would have a drink. I once went a whole year without booze and then, with the logic only an alcoholic could understand, I went out to celebrate with a bender. Even in AA meetings I would be looking at my watch wondering when they would end so I could get out and get the drinks in.'

He and Alex are here because, in October, the couple rented out their Chelsea flat and moved to a four-bedroom house on a hill overlooking the beach at Portavogie, near Belfast. Dickie Best, George's 82-year-old father, still lives in Belfast – he was an iron-turner in the Harland & Wolff shipyard – indeed, he still lives in the same house, on the same Protestant estate where he has always lived. 'Dad's got himself a bird now,' Best says. 'His "lady friend" he calls her. He goes dancing once a week.' Two of Best's sisters live on the estate, too (he has two more sisters, and a younger brother who is in the Army). 'My sisters have been supportive. They have never preached to me, even though one of them is very religious.' Does he think, in retrospect, that perhaps they ought to have preached a little? 'It wouldn't have made any difference.'

When Best became ill last year strangers began offering him advice – and they haven't stopped since. 'It drives me nuts, to be honest. Most of them haven't been through what I've been through, so how can they know how to help me?' The soft chuckle again. 'I've been told to try deep-sea diving, jumping off bridges, and eating a melon in the morning to stop the craving.'

Best believed he was almost indestructible. Given that he once went without food for thirty days, surviving on drink alone, and that, with the grandiosity of the true alcoholic, he will boast that he has outdrunk every hard drinker he has ever met, this seems an understandable delusion. But in 1998, he tells me, he planned to commit suicide by taking a bottle of Nurofen tablets but didn't go through with it because he couldn't bear the thought of Alex finding him dead. 'Yeah, when I'm on my own I do get depressed,' he says. 'It doesn't last long, though, and things always look better in the morning. But when I was in hospital last year I did feel suicidal.' If someone had offered him a cyanide pill, would he have taken it? 'Yeah. The pain was dreadful, as though a knife was being twisted in my stomach. When Alex took me to hospital I couldn't stand up, I couldn't move. I was coughing up blood. And when I came out, for a long time I couldn't do things like get out of the bath. When you've been fit for most of your life, that's hard to deal with.'

Ann Best, George's mother, drank herself to death in 1978. She had worked in a cigarette factory all her life and died at fifty-four, almost the same age George is now, having turned to drink only ten years earlier. She is still a sensitive subject for her son. Although she could become vicious when drunk, she was, for the most part, a shy and private woman who felt threatened by her son's fame and later notoriety. 'She couldn't handle it. Found it very difficult when strangers came up to her. My dad could fob them off – he found it easy to adjust. But my mum found it impossible. At first her death affected me terribly because I thought it was my fault. It's a terrible thing, guilt.' Why didn't the shock of his mother's death put him off alcohol? 'Even then I didn't know I had a problem as well.'

George Best's fame meant he couldn't see as much of his parents as he wanted to – whenever he came home to Belfast he would be mobbed. His sister Carol once said, 'We always loved it when George came home but found it a relief when he went away again.' Best shakes his head at the memory. 'I tried to get them to move to England, but they didn't want to leave home. My visits became a nightmare. We were just a normal, quiet family, and whenever I arrived that would be disrupted – people would be banging on the door, there would be cameras flashing, reporters shouting questions.'

In the 1960s George was often called the Fifth Beatle. He wore stripy flares and velvet Nehru jackets. He was pictured at parties surrounded by mini-skirted models, filling pyramids of champagne glasses from foaming bottles. He opened his own fashion boutiques and nightclubs, drove an E-Type Jaguar, was screamed at by teenage girls at airports, and employed three full-time secretaries just to answer his fan mail, as well as a hairdresser to blow-dry his hair. His dark hooded eyes, grooved chin and mischievous grin became framed by long sideburns and a mane of luxuriant black hair. On the field, he cultivated a distinctive look – socks rolled down, shirt untucked, face unshaven – at a time when footballers were still soberly turned out, on and off the pitch.

Sir Alex Ferguson, manager of Manchester United, says of George Best that he was 'unquestionably the greatest'. So do Pele and Maradona. And when you watch footage of George Best in his glory days – the two goals he scored in the first twelve minutes when Manchester United beat Benfica 5-1 away in 1966; the crucial second goal he scored in extra time when the team again beat Benfica two years later, this time 4-1 in the European Cup Final at Wembley; the six goals he scored in one match against Northampton in 1970 – you can see why. His elasticity was freakish, his balance and control of the ball almost supernatural. One commentator compared him to a dark ghost because of the way he could start a shimmying run from the halfway line and glide past half a dozen men before gracefully sliding the ball into the net. The Manchester United midfielder Pat Crerand remarked that one of Best's markers, Ken Shellito, had been turned inside out so often he was suffering from 'twisted blood'.

Was Best's skill down to hard work or does he think he was born with a gift? 'I can't analyse it. It was just natural, not something I ever had to work at. When I coach kids and they ask me how I did it, I can't tell them. I cheat a little and say it is just hard work, but I know it's not. Maybe I was blessed.' He's talking about genius, isn't he? He takes a sip of tea before he answers flatly: 'Yeah.' On one level this is a remarkable boast, but from Best it sounds banal.

George Best is an intelligent man. He has an IQ of 158 and was the only child in his class to pass his eleven-plus. But this 'yeah' is clearly, understandably, a tired answer to a question he has been asked far too many times. He has, after all, been told he is a genius so often that it seems unremarkable to him. Other players of his generation, such as Bobby Charlton and Denis Law, had great skill but you would hesitate before using the word 'genius' to describe them. The fact that Best combined his genius with glamour, as well as a raft of all too human flaws, perhaps explains why he was deemed a superstar, and why his fame, unlike that of many of his sporting contemporaries, has lasted.

The years of being analysed by other people, as well as his own occasional attempts at self-examination, have left George Best with a singular lack of curiosity about himself. People who have known Best a long time often comment upon his detachment. He will become lost in his own thoughts; seem remote and self-contained, as though on autopilot. 'Whatever I do,' he has said. 'I can always find a way to be there but not there.' He doesn't really want to know why he has been so self-destructive, he just accepts that he has been. Even so, he will trot out theories for you about how he was a lonely and introverted child who always played truant from school, and about how he always ran away from his problems, he will tell you, never confronted them. His nervousness about speaking in public was such that he would sometimes avoid having to make an after-dinner speech by climbing out of a lavatory window and running away. He even missed his own birthday party once and his own wedding (Alex forgave him, and the couple were married a few weeks later). Shyness may be one explanation for his drinking. He also cites escapism, guilt and boredom. The boredom theory is the most convincing. Though he felt inspired on the pitch, he found football too easy and the routine of football life – the training, the team politics, the travelling – boring. Life after playing for Manchester United seemed like a dreary anticlimax to him. It must have been hard for him to adjust to normal life after the vertiginous heights he has scaled. 'Well, that is why so many footballers struggle when they retire,' Best says, taking a sip of tea. 'Because they can't replace it. You feel empty. I've never replaced it.' Was it the applause he missed, the approval of the crowd? 'Success I crave. Funnily enough, I teach my son the opposite. I tell him there is nothing wrong in coming second. But I don't actually believe it.'

Best also became tired of seducing women, probably because he found that became too easy as well – in one night alone, he once told a tabloid reporter, he slept with seven. Does he think his promiscuity was a way of filling the vacuum left by football? 'No, nothing ever comes close to scoring goals.' Did sex become meaningless for him? 'No, I was a normal healthy male and I enjoyed it as much as the next man. Well, I say the next man but nowadays you don't know, do you?' He grins. 'It was still a challenge because women didn't always throw themselves at me. It could be the opposite of that – because of who you were, even if they wanted to, they wouldn't.' Did he keep count? 'Nah. There was no way you could keep count. Well, I certainly didn't, anyway.'

He never became bored with drinking, but did he really enjoy it? Did he like himself more as a drunk? 'I can't analyse it in those terms. It's like, why can my dad go out with his pals for a drink and have two drinks and stop? Whereas someone like me has to stay out with his pals till three in the morning?' Best's wife says he did most of his drinking on his own. Was it that he feared facing reality again when the night ended? 'No. I don't know. There are no easy answers. I've tried everything – private sessions, meetings, pills. I've gone through it all. Alcoholics Anonymous might have worked for me if I had been anonymous, but I wasn't. People kept asking for my autograph.'

Even a charitable assessment of George Best's character would have to allow that he has been immature, self-centred, vain, bloody-minded and possibly cynical in the way that he has made a lot of money out of talking about his illness: 'I use the press as much as it uses me,' he says. But if he has behaved like a spoilt child at times, it is only because people have always spoilt him. And low self-esteem may be as much a part of his alcoholism as the lying, the stealing cash from handbags and the blackouts, but he never seems to have felt self-pity.

Meeting him is disconcerting because he is like a ghost from a different era. He is the man on the faded posters, in the history books, on the black-and-white television screens. It seems like a corruption of folk memory that he is still with us. I tell him that I remember singing songs about him on the bus on the way to primary school: 'Georgie Best, superstar . . .' He finishes it: 'Walks like a woman and he wears a bra.' He laughs and then starts coughing. 'Hopefully those are two things I've never done.' But he did once advertise a bra, didn't he? 'Yes.' Grin. 'Playtex. I've done everything. Aftershave, chewing gum, Spanish oranges, milk, sausages . . .'

Why does he think his fame hasn't faded? 'Apart from the sporting side of it, I don't think I've ever been . . .' Pause. 'Nasty to anyone, or hurt anyone, except myself. I've never beaten anyone up or molested somebody. I just got drunk!' It's not quite true. In a fit of jealousy he once dangled a girlfriend from a third-storey window, and he was once found guilty of hitting a woman in a nightclub (she was drunk and abusive and ended up with a hairline fracture of the nose). His wife Alex has also said that while he is lovable most of the time, he can have a Jekyll and Hyde personality when drunk, becoming vindictive and even violent. Isn't this the case? 'Well, drink does change your character. Aggressive people become subdued and subdued people become aggressive. But I only ever got aggressive with people who were aggressive with me.'

There is a story that George Best tells when he is giving an after-dinner speech. One night, while out with his girlfriend Mary Stavin, who was Miss World 1977, he won £15,000 in a casino. Later, in his room, with his girlfriend down to her underwear and the notes spread on the bed like a counterpane, he rang room service and ordered a bottle of champagne. When the waiter arrived he looked at the money and the semi-naked Miss World sprawled on the bed, shook his head and said: 'Where did it all go wrong, George?' At the time the waiter was making a good joke. But later . . . Where did it all go wrong, George? 'Well, people still think I'm struggling, apart from the illness. People think I'm begging and going out and doing things for money, well, I don't have to. I don't have to work again for the rest of my life if I don't want to. I do it because I don't want to get bored.'

The Antabuse pellets only last for three months at a time and this is the fourth time George Best has tried them since 1981. Though he doesn't drink at the moment, he says he cannot imagine going the rest of his life without another drink. 'I've started sketching again,' he says, changing the subject. 'Alex and I are talking about moving to the sun somewhere. It would be nice to sit and paint. I could knock 'em out. I could sell them for 100 quid a go because they would have my signature on them.' I point out that he could probably charge more, given that his first pair of football boots are now thought to be worth at least £50,000. He smiles. 'The boots and the medals and so on are for Alex and Calum. Eventually. That will be their legacy. But they are not going anywhere yet. They are stuck in a bank. I often thought about selling them but I know what people would say.'

Alex rejoins us. They are planning to have children, she says. 'For the moment though we have an 18-month-old red setter as a child substitute.' George touches her hand. 'We'd love to have children,' he says. 'But that'll be, well, we've decided that that is for when I get fit again.' With this he stands up to leave, and a hotel guest, who has clearly been waiting for this moment, approaches and asks for an autograph.

George Best's autobiography became a bestseller. In 2002 Calum Best ran away after charging a huge hotel bill to his father's credit card. In July that year, having been given three months to live, Best had a liver transplant. During the ten hour operation, he required forty pints of blood.

Jocelyn Stevens

The chairman is running late. Half an hour. His PA has been popping her head around the door every ten minutes to convey his apologies. The sound of him barking out orders carries through the walls and, alongside me on the squeaky leather sofa in the corridor, I sense the spectral presence of employees past: broken and wretched minions summoned here to squirm a while before finding out if they're to be sacked. There is a chill in the air and, to the imagination, the cough of a nearby secretary becomes a hollow groan; the tapping of a keyboard mutates into the rattling of a chain.

It must be quite something, being mythologized – even if it is as a foul-tempered bully who could kill rats with his teeth and think nothing of impaling 500 work-shy personnel on pikes before breakfast. For one thing, it must be a hoot watching the way strangers react to you. And it must be so good to know that, thanks to the negative expectations they must harbour, their first impressions of you are bound to be positive. Sir Jocelyn Stevens, the 66-year-old chairman of English Heritage, certainly revels in this reputation. And when you meet him he does indeed confound your presumptions by being all backslapping heartiness and bonhomie. He is a tall, barrel-chested man with smooth, pink skin that looks freshly scrubbed. There is a manly cleft in his chin and his nose is broken, a constant reminder of the Public Schools' Boxing Championship final he lost in 1949.

The next thing you notice about him is that he is wearing a watch on each wrist. And with his thick white hair and blustering, distracted manner this eccentricity morphs him momentarily into the hopelessly late but time-obsessed White Rabbit. You are taken further through the looking-glass when Sir Jocelyn ushers you into his office on the fourth floor of an imposing thirties-style building in Savile Row. There is a wooden dog the size of a pony next to his desk. It is the sort of object which your instincts scream at you to ignore in the hope that it will go away (a reaction psychologists call perceptual defence).

For the first forty minutes my side of the conversation goes like this: 'I'd like to start by . . .'; 'Yes, I see, but . . .'; 'Wouldn't it be . . .'; 'You say that but surely . . .' Sir Jocelyn does not brook interruption – just shouts you down – and when you do manage to lob in a question he sighs impatiently, gulps air and fidgets until you've done asking it. Although his delivery is clipped and plummy, he slurs odd words and, in his eagerness to crack on with the next thought, he doesn't always finish his sentences. He has no volume control, emphasizes words erratically and punctuates his monologues every so often with a friendly, snuffling laugh.

At the moment, he says, his mind is focused on the grand unveiling of the Albert Memorial by the Queen. As he warms to this theme it becomes clear that Sir Jocelyn considers himself to be a living embodiment of the Victorian spirit. He is half-right. He does get on and do things; and he is sentimental. He often catches himself weeping when he listens to military bands. And recently, when he visited a community of immigrants who were living in a formerly derelict Victorian square in Brixton, he felt moved to tears. Thanks to a conservation scheme he had introduced, they had formed a square committee. 'The civic pride they had. You wouldn't believe it! Absolutely splendid people. Newly arrived from the Caribbean. They laughed and laughed and laughed. And afterwards they did this tin-drum song about Queen Victoria.'

But the image he is stuck with is that of the free-marketeering, union-bashing, archetypal Thatcherite. While it is true that Margaret Thatcher admired the Victorians for their enterprise and their family values, she had no time for their liberal paternalism. And neither does Sir Jocelyn. Though he says so himself, his career has been all about saving great institutions – *Queen* magazine, the *Evening Standard*, the *Express*, the Royal

College of Art and, since 1992, English Heritage – by making them more efficient and commercially viable, for which read clearing them of the dead wood. He knows he has made a lot of enemies doing this, but he says he doesn't mind. 'Not at all. I think you have to make enemies. England is in a funny state at the moment; a lot of people who talk a lot and not many who do a lot.'

In order to make English Heritage work, Sir Jocelyn offered voluntary redundancy to 700 members of staff. But being ruthless in the name of efficiency is one thing. Appearing to take pleasure in humiliating people who work for you, or whom you are about to sack, is quite another. According to clause 384, subsection ii, of the Journalist's Code of Conduct, there are certain stories about Sir Jocelyn's ferocious temper tantrums which must appear in any article pertaining to his life and times. So let us dispense with them: (1) The time he got so angry with a fashion writer he threw her typewriter out of a fourth-floor window. (2) The time he got so angry he snipped a telephone wire with a pair of scissors in order to cut a caller off. (3) The time he got so angry he sacked a secretary over the tannoy. (4) The time he got so angry he roared to someone: 'Get out of this office! And what do you mean by bringing this ghastly little man with you?' (The ghastly little man was a highly regarded City surveyor who was hunchbacked from having had polio as a child.)

'Most of the stories that you hear are true,' Sir Jocelyn says with a shrug. 'But in a long working life, which is now forty years, people only remember . . .' The sentence is unfinished. 'I mean, the lady with the typewriter is now dead. So often printed. Very boring. They're things I can't escape now because they're in every cutting. It doesn't allow one to mature very much. And people do exaggerate. I was once called before the Permanent Secretary because they were worried about morale at English Heritage and Peter Brooke said in my defence, "You don't know him as well as I do. When he was at the Royal College of Art he once sacked nineteen professors in an afternoon. It was wonderful!"' Sir Jocelyn gives a wheezy chuckle at the recollection of this. 'Well, that was an exaggeration. You see it was only eleven. *And they were all useless.*'

It seems a bit rich that Sir Jocelyn, the arch self-publicist who will gladly dress up and act the clown for a photo opportunity, should complain that he is a prisoner of his cuttings, even if he does add, 'I suppose it hasn't hurt me. People tend to ring me up to ask me to do things because they know I will get them done.' He is obviously pretty thrilled with himself and with his belligerent public image. This, after all, is a man who once wrote to a paper to complain that it had libelled him by describing him as charming. Only someone who is sure he can charm if he wants to would joke about that. But it does reveal a curious paradox. On the one hand you have to assume, given his spectacular rudeness, that Sir Jocelyn is someone who genuinely doesn't care what people think about him. On the other, he cared enough about his image to go around every newspaper library removing any cuttings file about himself (in the days before cuttings could be called up on computer). 'I've never confessed to that before!' he says with a snorting laugh. 'Terrible of me, really. But I wanted to be able to start again, otherwise anything you've done in the past is constantly repeated.' It makes you wonder what dark secrets from his past he wanted to erase. Was he worried that people would find out about his two musically gifted brothers, Shakin' and Cat, the ones he kept locked in the attic at home? More likely he wanted to play down his image as a sixties dandy and playboy because it undermined his eighties reputation as a fire-breathing monster who *gets things done*.

On his twenty-first birthday he came into his inheritance – £750,000 – left him by his mother, whose family had made its fortune in newspapers, owning the *Evening Standard* in the twenties and *Picture Post* in the fifties. He immediately bought himself an Aston Martin and wrote it off the same day. On his twenty-fifth birthday he bought himself the ailing *Queen* magazine, and called in his chums Marc Boxer and Tony Snowdon. When bored with that, he says, he sold it off to a man who happened to be sitting at the next table at Claridges.

Vain enough to reinvent himself, then, and reportedly to storm around his office shouting and slamming doors whenever a hostile profile is written about him in a newspaper. That is, whenever a profile is written about him in a newspaper. Yet, whenever there is a new milestone in his career to commemorate, he always agrees to be interviewed about it. It could be that he's a glutton for punishment, or an optimist. Or maybe it's that all he really cares about is getting attention in whatever form, and by whatever means, including screaming for it petulantly like a baby. The obvious Freudian reading of this is that he craves the attention he never received from his father, the late Major Greville Stewart-Stevens. When his mother, Betty, went into labour with him there were dangerous complications. The child lived but she died a few days later. His father, Jocelyn believes, never got over the death, blaming it on the Roman Catholicism of his wife's family, and always regarded his son as the murderer of his wife.

As a small child, Jocelyn was sent to live in his own flat, off Baker Street in central London, with his own nanny, priest, cook and maid. He was driven around Hyde Park every day by his own chauffeur in his own Rolls-Royce. His father lived in another house and, when he remarried four years later, Jocelyn went to live with his stepfamily in Scotland. Although his stepsisters claim that Jocelyn exaggerates this rejection, it is clear that the boy never felt close to his father. After Eton, he did his National Service in the Rifle Brigade. Though he won the Sword of Honour, his father declined to come to the passing-out parade.

Sir Jocelyn Stevens does not see a connection with his unorthodox upbringing and the need he feels today to always get his own way. He does not believe he was spoilt. 'I don't think so. Not particularly. I don't think it's about getting your own way because quite often you win by going someone else's way. I don't work alone.' Given the privileges he was born to, it would have been understandable if Sir Jocelyn had opted for a life of idle luxury. Instead he became a workaholic, regularly putting in fourteen hours a day, and in 1979 this took its toll on his marriage of twenty-three years, to Jane Sheffield, Lady-in-Waiting to Princess Margaret.

He has been with his present partner, Vivien Duffield, for eighteen years. With an estimated fortune of £45 million inherited from her father Sir Charles Clore, she is one of the richest women in Britain. And with her own assertive and unembarrassable manner she is said to be more than a match for Sir Jocelyn. When kept waiting in reception for him once when he was managing director of Express Newspapers she sent a message saying if he did not come down immediately she would buy the paper and fire him. The couple divide their time between houses in London, Hampshire, Scotland, Geneva and Gstaad, and are known for their extravagant parties.

You have to wonder, then, where Sir Jocelyn gets his motivation to carry on working as fanatically as he does. 'It's just that I have always been very determined and have always hated losing. Very bad losers, my family.' He is not sure why this is. 'One is born that way or not. I don't think it happens.' Not nurture then? 'No. I don't think so. Although it may have had something to do with being brought up in the war, quite a tough upbringing.'

His account of how he was offered the job of saving English Heritage is telling. He was in Scotland cleaning leaves out of the gutter when Michael Heseltine rang. 'There was a thunderstorm and I was soaked to the skin and took ages to come to the phone. He asked me what on earth I'd been doing and when I told him I'd been cleaning the gutter because the house was leaking all over he said, 'Very appropriate to the job I am about to offer you: chairman of English Heritage.' I said I didn't know much about English Heritage except that I hated it and he said, "Got it!" They wanted a fox in the chicken coop.'

It is obvious why Michael Heseltine admires Sir Jocelyn. They are both protected by the same armour of the deliberate philistine. In his new history of the Tory Party, Alan Clark describes Heseltine's aggression and vanity; he also refers to his unpredictability, cunning and low intellect. There are other parallels. Both are self-parodying, single-minded and ruthless in their pursuit of power. Both are electrifying orators. Both love it when they are the victim of satirists or cartoonists. Heseltine tried to buy his *Spitting Image* puppet. Sir Jocelyn has on his office wall several large cartoons which depict him as a tyrant. All the staff I talked to referred to Stevens as 'The Chairman,' presumably at his insistence. Heseltine liked to be called 'The President' (of the Board of Trade) instead of the more usual 'Minister' (for Trade and Industry).

Above all, both men are as hyperactive as children. You can see Sir Jocelyn getting more and more excited as he talks. He is sitting in an armchair which whizzes around on its rollers as he rocks back and forth. The mental image of one of those toy cars which you wind up by chaffing its back wheels against the carpet is irresistible. Any moment now I fear he may stop rocking and the armchair will scoot off to the other side of the room.

Even on brief acquaintance it is obvious that Sir Jocelyn is a force of nature: that this is why no one has ever dared to stand up to him and why he assumes he will always be forgiven for his vile behaviour. He could never be accused of being a dull conformist and this – along with his vitality and brio – is his saving chracteristic. He seems civil enough to me, jolly in fact; perhaps, dare one say it, even a little charming in his way. But having never witnessed him become incandescent with rage, I have no claim to objectivity. That's not to say I haven't heard first-hand accounts of his tantrums, though, including one occasion when he was overheard on a street corner screaming into his mobile phone at his chauffeur who was late in picking him up: 'You are a worthless fucking worm.'

Mercurial, then; and volatile. But it is difficult to gauge whether his bluff manner and irrepressible enthusiasm conceal extreme cleverness or bestial stupidity. Although everyone thinks of Sir Jocelyn as an arch Tory, Tony Blair was happy to see him re-appointed as chairman of English Heritage for another three years, which suggests that Sir Jocelyn has good political instincts. It is clear from listening to him that his passion for conserving England's heritage is genuine. He believes that a nation which doesn't care about its past has no future. 'I am an old-fashioned patriot,' Sir Jocelyn says. 'Always been. Love this country. Hugely proud of it.'

The trouble is when I ask him whether he would have been equally committed and enthusiastic if Michael Heseltine had rung and asked him to save a football club instead of English Heritage, he says, 'Yes. Anything.' For him it is not the cause that is really important, it is the not losing. He's competitive; not a good sport. 'Yes. One is in competition with oneself, in a way. One is not racing against someone else's monument. It's inbuilt. I can't bear people who don't finish a job. You have to overcome the carpet of bureaucracy in England. If you look at the people who succeed in beating it, it is usually impatient people.' He means angry people. 'Well anger, I am afraid, is sometimes the only way to *get things done.*'

It is comments like this which make you suspect that the anger may sometimes be an act. 'Well, now it's mostly controlled,' Sir Jocelyn admits. 'It wasn't before. I was quite proficient in the martial arts and I would get physically angry. Even now if someone rammed into the back of my car I would get out and shout, "You fucker!" at whoever did it. It's a sudden thing. But I have no instinct to throw my weight around any more. One is helped by one's growing reputation when one arrives at a new job. When I arrived at the RCA, a lot of resignations were already waiting on my desk. These were professors who hadn't been working. Turning up and getting paid for nothing. They knew they wouldn't last. They knew that when I arrived here, too.' He springs from his chair, marches across the room and peels off a sheet of paper that someone has Sellotaped anonymously to the back of his door. 'Terribly funny, this,' he says as he hands it to me. Written in black felt-tip pen are the words: 'We must create an environment where everyone knows and feels that a failure to fulfil orders means death.'

What seems to worry people most about Sir Jocelyn is that he might be a genuine sadist, that he really does enjoy being a bully. 'No,' he says. 'No pleasure. But I do get annoyed. If one is harsh on people, it certainly isn't with juniors. Most famous example, I suppose, was when Miss Page, now chief executive of the Dome, was stolen from us by the hapless Stephen Dorrell. I was so angry that he hadn't bothered to tell me that I stormed round, crashed my way in and said, "Right, that's it. I work like a bloody dog. I expect to be treated civilly." Someone should have rung and told me. I was angry because it offended my code of trust. He had made a massive breach. I said, "I'm attacking you for bad manners and I will not sit down again in your company, to remind myself of what a shit you are." So for a month when everyone was sitting down in meetings I would be standing up. It is eccentric but it had an enormous effect. He knows I don't fear anybody. I've never been frightened of anything.'

To overcome your fears in adversity means you have courage. To have no fears in the first place means you are just odd. Does Sir Jocelyn acknowledge that there is something a little inhuman about his fearlessness? 'It does sometimes puzzle me. In the military I was never frightened. Not at all afraid of dying. Maybe something is missing. I've never been to a psychiatrist. Never felt the need to. It's just the way one sees things. It's just . . .'

Frenetic people who throw themselves into their work sometimes do so because they dread being left alone with their own thoughts – for fear of discovering that they are the empty vessels who make most noise. Anything that will distract them from contemplating their inner life will do. 'No, I don't have a fear of that,' Sir Jocelyn says, twiddling one arm of his half-rimmed spectacles. 'I just want to win. I have obsessions. I'm a perfectionist. That is the curse. It means one is permanently unhappy.'

Another curse seems to be that he always feels bored and restless as soon as things start running smoothly. Like a successful wartime prime minister, he feels disconnected and aimless in peacetime. His feeling of permanent unhappiness, though, is a surprising admission. You'd think he might feel just a teeny bit fulfilled from time to time. 'I don't think I'll ever be content because there is always something to do. I mean, as exciting.'

All this is not to suggest that his life has been without its black days. As a young man he got into Trinity College, Cambridge, on the strength of his rowing prowess, only to be sent down for bunking off during term time to go skiing and sending his tutor a postcard from the Swiss Alps saying, 'Wish you were here.' He was sacked from the *Express* in 1981 when he attempted a management buy out. He had four children, two boys and two girls. One of them, Rupert, was disabled with palsy and died at the age of twenty-two in 1989. When another, Pandora, became a drug addict, Sir Jocelyn broke into her squat, carried her out, checked her into a rehab clinic and then had her dealer hunted down and arrested.

'Oh, you can't help but get depressed some times,' he says blithely. 'God, I feel low some times. But my first reaction is not to take things personally or give up but to pick myself up and start again.' But if you are thick-skinned enough to keep bouncing back, does that not make you shallow? Sir Jocelyn pinches the bridge of his nose. 'I'm not that thick-skinned. One does have bad moments but not very often. One has been very lucky.

Come and have a look at this.' He jumps up again and shows me two giant rectangular photographs of Stonehenge; one shows the site with a road, one with it airbrushed out. 'See how much better it looks.'

He looks at the watch first on his right hand, then on his left, he really must get on and finish proof-reading his report on Stonehenge *right now*. The nagging question still has to be asked. Why two watches? It turns out this is the first day Sir Jocelyn has worn both. He is trying out an old one, which he doesn't trust. The only other person he's ever known to wear two was Lord Mountbatten. Sir Jocelyn was being driven by him one day in his Land Rover when he made the mistake of asking the time as they were approaching a gate. He mimes Lord Mountbatten taking both hands off the steering wheel to check his watches. 'Crashed right into the bloody thing!'

He roars with laughter, slaps me on the back and sends me tottering unsteadily into the pony-sized wooden dog which I have been trying so desperately to ignore.

Stephen Fry

DECEMBER 2001

Upstairs at the Café de Paris, a nightclub in Piccadilly, an unattended mobile phone is ringing. More accurately, the mobile is barking out the words, 'Stephen, *answer* the *sodding* phone. Stephen, *answer* the *sodding* phone. Stephen . . .' The velvety bass voice is unmistakably that of its owner, Stephen Fry. He emerges to retrieve it a few minutes later – nine feet tall, jawline like the prow of a ship, a physically awkward, middle-aged schoolboy checking his side-parting with his hand – and apologizes profusely for keeping me waiting. 'The, um, photographs took longer than, er. Do accept . . .' It's wonderfully effective, and completely unnecessary. I haven't been kept waiting and, anyway, it was our photographer he was posing for. In fact, the only reason he is in this dingy nightclub in the middle of a cold December afternoon is that we have asked him to be.

As the club's management are busy hammering and cursing and shifting in preparation for the evening's revelries, I lead Fry to a quiet, brothel-red backroom I have found, behind plush red curtains, lit by red light bulbs. He sits down in the corner and, even though his eyes are darkly hooded and one side of his face is bathed in a demonic red light, and though he is chain-smoking full-strength Marlboros and wearing a black polo neck and a leather jacket, he still comes across as being a big, gentle, eager-to-please bear. He does realize, does he not, that when I come to write this interview I'll have to lie and say that he was wearing tweed, from his pocket handkerchief to his socks; that he was smoking not cigarettes but a tweed pipe? 'Absolutely, yes, indeed. No no. Goes with the turf. Exactly. Goes with the territory. Yep.'

223

Since Radio 4 broadcast Fry's eight-and-a-half-hour-long reading of *Harry Potter and the Philosopher's Stone* last Boxing Day, the reformed juvenile-delinquent-cum-Cambridge-graduate-cum-comedian-cum-actor-cum-best-selling-novelist-cum-charity-fundraiser seems to have amplified another role he's developed for himself: that of favourite uncle to the nation and the nation's children. Hugh Laurie, Fry's best friend and sometime comedy partner, once said, 'I've never seen a child who isn't thrilled to be with Stephen, probably because in many ways he is very child-like himself.' Fry himself once said, 'It would be lovely to turn into a teddy bear for the young, a kind of amiable eccentric.' How can he say things like that without blushing? 'Well being a multiple godfather and uncle, one feels that that's one's role, really. I'm not going to be a parent so I think to be a more or less ursine avuncular figure is my role.'

But why shouldn't he become a parent? Being homosexual didn't prevent Oscar Wilde – Fry's hero and the man he played in the film *Wilde* (1997) – from procreating. 'Well, that's true, yes, I suppose. Never say never, obviously. And, um, who knows these days? You just have to leave a toenail behind and the next thing you know there are five million of you marching across the countryside like killer ants. But for the moment I'm satisfied being a godparent and some of my godchildren are getting to the age now where they need a godfather who's not going to sneak to their parents when they confess that they've started smoking. I had such a turbulent teenage myself that most of my godchildren probably know that they're never going to be quite as disastrous as I was.'

Disastrous is the word. Stephen Fry grew up in Norfolk, the middle child of well-off parents – his father, Alan, was an electronics engineer and inventor. He went to Stouts Hill, a prep school, as a boarder at the age of seven (where he still wet the bed and where an IQ test revealed he was 'approaching genius'); and at his public school, Uppingham, he developed a passion for cricket, chess and Wagner, passed all his O-levels, became infatuated with 'Matthew', a fellow pupil, began stealing, got expelled and saw a psychiatrist who diagnosed him as having 'developmental delay', all by the age of fourteen. He was expelled twice more, and, following a mad adventure with some stolen credit cards, ended up serving a three-month prison sentence. His 'turbulent teenage' had a happy ending, though. Pucklechurch remand centre – where he was known as 'the professor', not only because he could read and write but also because, every day, he would complete *The Times* crossword in about ten minutes – proved the making of him. After his release, he sat his A-levels at a crammer and won a scholarship to read English at Queens' College, Cambridge (he was still on parole when he arrived there). It was at university that he met Hugh Laurie, with whom he went on to find television fame (in, among other shows, *A Bit of Fry and Laurie*, *Blackadder* and *Jeeves and Wooster*). And, while still in his twenties, Fry became a millionaire – thanks to the libretto he wrote for the musical *Me and My Girl*.

In his autobiography, *Moab Is my Washpot* (1997), Fry writes about his formative years in an amused matter-of-fact way, but fails to offer explanations for his behaviour. What, for instance, does he think was the trigger for his kleptomania? 'I don't know – and I do say at some point in my book that it's not my business to say why – but I never believe people who explain themselves, who say they know why they are like they are. You're in danger of sounding post-therapeutic aren't you? You know, the kind of, "Oh, it's because I had low self-esteem when I was this age", or, "I was in denial" which, as you know, is a river in Egypt.' He sweeps his hair back from his forehead. 'I mean, my brother Roger was fed on the same food and had the same parents and was close enough in age to have been said to have had the same upbringing, and yet you couldn't ask for a more decent law-abiding fellow. I could sit and talk about my relationship with my parents as an explanation to some extent, but it wasn't that different from my brother's relationship with them.'

No? In his autobiography Fry portrays his father – who's still alive – as a misanthropic and arrogant man with an 'infuriatingly cold, precise ratiocinating engine of a brain fuelled by a wholly egocentric passion'. He adds that whenever his father was in the house 'instantly fun, freedom and relaxation turned into terrified silence.' After one argument with his father – he claims not to remember what it was about – the seventeen-year-old Stephen attempted to commit suicide. He took a combination of Paracetamol and Lentizol and woke up in hospital having his stomach pumped.

Frankly, his father sounds a nightmare. Formidable, to say the least. 'Yes, he was, he was indeed formidable. Though I describe him as being like a Sherlock Holmes figure and . . . urm. But er . . . [sigh] . . . what you have with parents, especially when you're kind of happy with them . . . when all the troubles have slid away, or just about, the past doesn't matter. That's the huge surprise of the past. So I don't think either of us felt that personally involved by retelling a story [in the autobiography] that no longer had relevance – in fact, you know, we laugh at how appalling I was.'

Crushingly, his father once said, 'Stephen spends a lot of energy doing things that aren't worthy of him.' Has this left him with a feeling that he's wasted his life? He rolls his eyes and gives a mock grimace. 'Of course, all of us feel that sometimes. I mean, whatever platonic paradigms are up there as things to be achieved are never going to be. Perfection is unachievable and we're all going to be on our notional deathbeds saying, "Why didn't I climb a mountain? Why didn't I see an opera? Why didn't I lick breast milk from the armpits of a Nepalese maiden?" And that's just the trivial side of it. There's the bigger side – what kind of a person was I? It's the curse of being human.' He takes a deep breath. 'That sense of consciousness that animals so manifestly appear not to have. One of the nice things about looking at a bear is that you know it spends one hundred per cent of every minute of every day being a bear. It doesn't strive to become a better bear. It doesn't go to sleep thinking, "I wasn't really a very good bear today." They are just one hundred per cent bear, whereas human beings feel we're not one hundred per cent human, that we're always letting ourselves down. We're constantly striving towards something, to some fulfilment.'

Is this what Wilde was referring to when he said there are two forms of tragedy, not getting what you want and getting it? 'Absolutely, yes.' He wrings his hands. 'I do feel a bit like someone who is returning footsore from a golden city which was appalling, cold, hostile and unattractive, and scrambling up the hill passing me are people on the way to it and one wants to say, "Why? Don't go there! It's pointless! There's nothing there! Fame and money are hollow shams."'

Yes, but as hollow shams go, they're two of the best. 'Well, true. We all suspect fame and money can't buy happiness but we still want to find out for ourselves.'

There's something else Wilde said that seems relevant here: 'I have put my genius into my life; all I've put into my works is my talent.' Arguably, Fry's best work has been as a comedian on television and radio – *Saturday Night Fish Fry* on Radio 4 in the mid-1980s was sublime. In his various film roles – such as *Peter's Friends* (1992) and *IQ* (1995) – he has rarely seemed more than adequate. In Robert Altman's *Gosford Park* he was embarrassing. Perhaps directors have difficulty disguising his physical appearance and tweedy voice, for he often appears to be playing himself (a criticism he hates). Though his four novels have sold well, none of them could be considered a literary masterpiece. They show his talent, not his 'approaching genius'. Perhaps if future generations remember Stephen Fry it will not be as an actor or writer but as a dazzling conversationalist – 'the e-mail of the species is deadlier than the mail,' for instance. The vocabulary is P.G. Wodehouse with swear words, the sentences are both finely wrought and meandering, weaving an array of subordinate clauses and philosophical and literary allusions. Does he ever wonder whether his monument will be the ephemeral conversation of a dinner-party – or worse, a talk-show – guest? 'Perhaps, yes. Yep. Someone whom I greatly loved as a man but whom before that had admired enormously as a comic genius was Peter Cook. You could say that of him, too. When he fully achieved his Peter Cookness it was as likely to be when buying a newspaper and observing something to the person he was handing his money over to. He was in that sense profligate with his wit, he didn't store it up for professional packaging and presentation.'

The comparison with Peter Cook is intriguing. Whereas Cook held the Establishment in contempt, Fry with his clubbable, over-English Englishness has often seemed beguiled by it – the Prince of Wales is one of his closest friends. While at university Fry said, 'I sometimes think if I wasn't Jewish and queer I would be the most appalling right-wing person.' As it is he is, broadly speaking, a socialist who would like to pay more tax, but he is also pro-foxhunting and he would never dream of travelling anything other than first-class. And, as a wit, Peter Cook could be savage. Fry's early comedy seemed by contrast safe and cosy; he could be mildly iconoclastic but seldom dangerous.

Yet Fry's dark side is apparent in his novels. You suspect he is capable of Cook-like cruelty but holds back from it because, ultimately, he wants to be liked too much. He rarely loses his temper, he says, having inherited from his mother Marianne an abhorrence of confrontation. 'Yes, [Fry adopts an E.L. Wisty voice] Peter would always speak as he found. But also he had a patrician laziness to him. You know, he would talk about writing a book or doing this or doing that but never get round to it. Whereas I have, for whatever reason, um, and again your guess is as good as mine – perhaps it's my Jewishness – this desire to prove myself and to do things, however lazy I feel.'

Does he throw himself into work as a way of avoiding self-absorption? 'Yes, I believe in the Socratic idea that you should "know thyself" but I also realize that to know oneself is a very strange journey. And it isn't necessarily best achieved by sitting and thinking about oneself.'

If people want to understand him, he says, they should read not necessarily his autobiography but his first novel *The Liar* (1991), in which the hero is accused of living by pastiche and pretence, and having an intelligence which renders his emotional life meaningless and makes him callous. Fry, it seems, thinks of himself as a dissemblingly cheerful impostor who cleverly cons people into liking him.

But wasn't the autobiography written at the time it was, a year after his nervous breakdown, precisely because he needed to 'sit and think about himself'? Wasn't it a Socratic exercise in trying to know himself? 'An exercise and an exorcise. It's true, I did feel the need to stop and reflect. I had a feeling of someone who'd been in an expensive and exciting car in the fast lane but who had never actually once stopped to look at the countryside around him. I had never even consulted a map to work out where I might actually be going. The ride was all and then the moment the engine went phut! I found myself shivering on the hard shoulder with the bonnet up wondering what the hell it was all about. You know, it was a, a piddling midlife crisis compared to those of many, but . . .'

Piddling! It was so dramatic it made front-page news. In 1995 Fry walked out on a production of *Cell Mates* – a play by Simon Gray in which Fry co-starred with Rik Mayall – partly prompted by the bad reviews the play and his performance received. He came close to committing suicide – sat in a garage with a duvet against the garage door and his fingers on the ignition key of his car – but decided against it because he couldn't bear the thought of upsetting his friends and family. Instead he fled the country, taking the ferry to Zeebrugge. English tourists spotted him in Bruges wearing a black beret; they informed the press, Fry contacted his family by e-mail, and his father drove to Belgium to collect him. Fry then spent a few months in California, seeing a psychiatrist and working out in a gym. He grins shyly. 'Well, yes, I suppose it was dramatic because of course I'm well known but, I mean, it's probably happening, even as we speak, to someone somewhere. Someone saying, "I'm just off to the Post Office, dear," and she will never see him again. You know, it's a very common story.'

But wasn't it harder for him than it is for most people who aren't famous? Even if he had phoned the Samaritans, wouldn't they have recognized his voice? 'That's true, and you just feel you're not getting a proper shake at it. Not that the Samaritans aren't very well trained – I'm sure they wouldn't betray any confidences or, or, or say, "Ooh, what's it like working with Rowan Atkinson?" in the middle of a conversation about how miserable one is but, erm. Of course it's harder to some extent if you have some kind of whatever it is – somewhere halfway between a wobble and a breakdown – in public because of the intense scrutiny and the fact that so many people are aware of it. But there are compensations in terms of the warmth and kindness of strangers. I received hundreds of letters and e-mails from people making a direct emotional connection with me. The people who wrote seemed to understand I was not the supremely confident and secure person full of self-knowledge I previously seemed to be. They could see I had been in as bad a pit of despair as anyone. And that was strangely comforting.'

Presumably he didn't receive a letter from Simon Gray? (The playwright wrote a book about the episode and said, 'I hope I never see him again.') 'Oh yes! Yes! We did exchange letters, and he was very kind in his, but, um . . .' He's never really forgiven Fry? 'I don't know if he's forgiven me. I think that once he knew I was sort of OK and had been discovered and was recovering it started to irritate him, the fact that his play had collapsed. And I don't blame him.' Pause. 'It's just, you know, if I could have chosen when I would have a breakdown, I'd have had it before the play started, but of course I couldn't.'

Does Hugh Laurie understand why he felt he couldn't talk to him before his 'trip to Bruges'? 'He probably found it hard at first, thinking, "Come on, what are friends for?" but I know he understood. That's the nature of friendship. If he did the same, I would understand it, too. Most of us, if we had some weird wart growing on the end of our genitals, we would not want to show it to our best friend.' Throaty laugh. 'We'd be much happier to show it to a complete stranger, a doctor that we'd never met before. Otherwise I would find it embarrassing and so would the friend.' He impersonates Hugh Laurie: '"Yes, yes, of course you can show me . . . *Woah there*!" You know? And one feels the same about the emotional warts, one's unsightlinesses.'

Do Laurie and his wife now keep a close eye on Fry, looking for early signs of another breakdown? 'Yes, and fortunately the one great saving salve, lubricant, whatever one wants to call it, of all these kinds of things, is humour. That's sort of what humour is for. "We laugh that we may not weep." I sometimes say, "I can see you looking at me with that *sliiiightly* worried expression." And they will giggle, and I will giggle, and that makes things a lot easier.'

As of six years ago, Fry has another best friend he can giggle with – as well as share his house in Hampstead, apartment in New York and Georgian manor house in Norfolk. After fifteen years of celibacy, Stephen Fry fell in love. The man – Fry prefers to keep his name out of print – is ten years his junior and not in show business. Fry's friends say this relationship has made him a lot calmer, and Fry himself says that it has helped him discover the real root of his previous problems: loneliness. 'Yes, indeed. Who'd have thought it? I've finally come on in and found the water is lovely. It's terrific. I'm thrilled with it. Still have to pinch myself. Can't quite believe it's true. Excuse me.' He blows his nose. 'Damn, I thought I'd shaken this bastard off, sorry.'

Part of the reason for Fry's celibacy had been his loathing of his own body – he said the thought of inflicting it on others repelled him. But he was also chronically insecure about his looks, convinced that everyone thought him an ugly Caliban. It was partly to do with his lopsided nose, which was badly broken when he tripped up at school. Was he never tempted to bolster his self-esteem by having it cosmetically corrected? 'I was, yeah. When I was twelve I went to see an ENT specialist with my parents and he said, "Young man, we'd better wait until you've grown. So come back when you're eighteen or nineteen." But when I was eighteen or nineteen it was when I was doing stuff – got into Cambridge – and it just didn't seem to matter any more.' He folds his arms. 'The fact is if I straightened my nose, I wouldn't suddenly look like Gregory Peck, I'd just be Stephen Fry with a slightly straighter nose.'

His broken nose has left him with a sinus problem which was aggravated by his heroic drug abuse in the late 1980s and early 1990s. At one stage he was hoovering up £1,000 worth of cocaine a week. Did he not worry that cocaine would disfigure that beautiful alpha brain of his? 'Absolutely! It is one of the daft things about taking coke, you know it can't be good for your intellectual capacity, yet . . . In fact, in my coke-taking days, I used to do stupid things like, the next morning, I would make myself do *The Spectator* crossword, just to reassure myself that I could still do it.'

Has he been prescribed any medication for his depression? 'No, I resisted Prozac because I had a few friends on it and I really didn't like what it did to them. I took Lithium for a time, when it was quite bad, otherwise no. I mean really I'm not that bad. Many people have it – a bi-polar affective disorder, they don't call it manic depression any more – much worse than me. I try to get through the depression by thinking that it's like the weather. If it's raining, you can't pretend that it isn't raining – "No, no, the sun is shining!" – you have to accept that it's raining, that you are feeling really low. But you keep somewhere inside yourself the belief that, absurd as it seems at the time, the next day the sun may pop over the horizon with a joke, and a brass band may play and a bluebird may twitter and everything will be, if not perfect, better. Like the weather, it is something over which you have no control. That's the point. You know it's time for an umbrella but you must not lose faith in the idea of sunshine. That sounds pathetic, doesn't it?' He laughs and mimics himself in an American voice: 'Do not lose faith in the idea of sunshine.'

The sodding phone rings again. 'Stephen, *answer* the *sodding* phone. Stephen, *answer* the *sodding* phone. Stephen . . .' Fry says, 'So sorry, please excuse me,' and picks it up. It's about his next appointment, in ten minutes at the Groucho Club. He is casting someone there for a film he is to start directing in March, an adaptation of Evelyn Waugh's novel *Vile Bodies*, for which he, Fry, has written the screenplay. I walk with him, through the dark backstreets of Soho, and as I do I notice that, like a lot of tall people – he's 6ft 5in, actually – he keeps one arm folded across the front of his body to create a horizontal that breaks up the vertical, and he stoops and bends one knee and cocks his head to disguise his height, to disguise himself, to become one hundred per cent bear. But people still stop and stare at him as he passes, mouthing the words, 'Wasn't that Stephen Fry?'

Matt LeBlanc

Perhaps it's the pain that blurs and distorts Matt LeBlanc's appearance. Perhaps it's the painkillers. Either way, he's pretty much unrecognizable as he slouches into the dimly lit bar in Beverly Hills. No big entrance, no swagger, no boyish grin in camera-conscious three-quarter profile. Instead, that firm jaw-line is diffused by a week's stubble, and the leather jacket he's wearing makes his shoulders look rounded, his physique stocky. I squint uncertainly and give him one of those vague hand signals that can be turned into a stretch and a yawn if identity proves mistaken. He sits down at my table, orders a Stoli with soda and lime, sinks it and signals the waiter over for a second one. He's just come from the gym, he explains in a voice so soft and low against the background chatter, I have to lip-read to get the gist. He dislocated his shoulder while doing laterals. 'If you move a millimetre, it kills you,' he mouths slowly. 'The pain is so bad you get light-headed.'

It's the eighth time this has happened since his shoulder bone first parted company with its socket during a rehearsal for *Friends*. Matthew Perry collided with Matt LeBlanc when – as Chandler and Joey – they were racing to occupy the same chair. For the following half a dozen episodes, while LeBlanc was in a sling, the injury had to be incorporated into the script.

At first, as we sit and talk, the actor is subdued and earnest, fixing me unblinkingly with eyes that seem ninety-six per cent pupil, four per cent iris. This keeps distracting my eyes from their lip-reading duties and, as a consequence, our conversation becomes stilted. The thought bubbles above LeBlanc's head are

233

reading: 'Jeez . . . stuck with . . . goddam English stuffed shirt . . . keeps looking from my eyes to my mouth like a moron . . .'

He orders another vodka. Along with the five Advils he's already taken, this relaxes him enough to bare a broad smile that features teeth so impossibly white and even I find myself involuntarily covering my own mouth with my hand as I smile back. To compound this, I'm veering between feelings of paranoia that I'm the dullest person he's ever met, and, as I get better at deciphering his mumbled words, mounting panic that it might be the other way round.

Without the sharp, deadpan one-liners the *Friends* scriptwriters put into his mouth, LeBlanc has all the social buoyancy and grace of a seal out of water. Still cute, still in possession of the big, sleepy brown eyes but now clumsy and inelegant with it. I order another beer. Telepathically, we have agreed that the best way for both of us to survive this evening is to get steadily drunk.

Later at the restaurant, we are led to a table in the middle of the room and LeBlanc requests that we be moved to one in the corner where he can have his back to the other diners. 'I used to enjoy eating out,' he says, and then loses the train of thought. He munches on a bread stick and furrows his brow as he studies the menu for about forty minutes. 'Yeah, I used to enjoy people-watching,' he says, suddenly returning to his subject and making me jump. 'Now I can't do that any more because people just end up watching me, do you know what I mean?'

I'm about to tell him I know exactly what he means because, the previous year, I had sat a few tables away from him and the rest of the cast from *Friends*, in a restaurant not far from here and – ha ha ha – I hadn't been able to take my eyes off them. Luckily I don't get the chance before he adds, 'And I hate that. No, I don't hate that, because it has made me financially comfortable. New house and car for mom and a new smile on my face. It's made me feel like Elvis.' He says that he is not very good at 'this whole celebrity thing'. You can see why: jealous men are want to approach him in bars and punch him for no reason. And he is constantly harassed by predatory women. 'It's not that it makes you feel vulnerable. Just unreal. Being stared at all the time. There was this one girl, thirteen or fourteen-years-old, and she just gaped at me, then started shaking. I freaked out because I didn't know what to do. I felt really guilty because it was like she was so overwhelmed she didn't know how to react. The trouble is, people have an imaginary relationship with you, especially when they see you on television. It's more intimate than the cinema. You are in their house and often they are watching you in bed, you know?'

Although in recent years Matt LeBlanc's name has been romantically linked with his manager, Camile Cerio, Goldie Hawn's then sixteen-year-old daughter, Kate Hudson, porn star Jenn Jameson, *Playboy* model Tonya Poole, Minnie Driver, Jennifer Aniston and Amanda de Cadenet, the actor doesn't have a steady girlfriend at the moment. 'Now I'm thirty, though, I suppose I'm thinking about marriage,' he says. 'Sometimes I think, yeah, that's what I want – but you can't look for it. It's got to find you. I saw this girl one time on the freeway and she saw me and we both pulled over and ended up going out for a year.'

Not all his assignations are so charming. When dining at a Hollywood restaurant with some caddish companions, he took a female admirer off to the washroom after being introduced to her just fifteen minutes earlier. He came back to his table grinning and soaking up the laddish applause and then all but ignored his latest conquest for the rest of the evening before leaving without saying goodbye to her.

'It's difficult with girlfriends,' he says ploddingly, in his barely audible bass, 'because I will go to a premiere and when I get home she asks, "What's the matter?" and I say, "I just signed a hundred autographs" and she doesn't know how I feel about that. That's why a lot of actors end up going out with actresses. I don't know what she wants me to say, "I'm a freak?" My shoulder hurts, I feel mortal. Yet I have people screaming at me and I think, "What's real and what's not real?"'

A fine example of this state of unreality could be witnessed on a visit he made to London in April. He was with the cast of *Friends*, filming an hour-long special which included a chance meeting with the Duchess of York. *Friends*-mania ensued, with British fans following the cast everywhere, waiting at the airport, and camping outside their hotel.

Refreshingly, LeBlanc is under no illusion that he is adored by his female fans simply for his acting ability. His foppish black hair, bee-stung lips and wing-mirror cheekbones also enter into the equation. Much to his chagrin, the same features seem to appeal to men, too – which is why this high-testosterone, all-American heterosexual has become a gay icon. A photo of him even appeared on the cover of *Spartacus: International Gay Guide for Men*. He went to court to stop further copies being printed. It has since become a collector's item.

This said, there is no denying his gifts as a comic actor. His timing and delivery are good. But his theorizing about them is less so. In an eerie echo of the sort of cool and opaque self-analysis you would associate with his new best friend the Duchess of York, he says of his acting technique that it's really just a matter of thinking of himself as a dozen eggs. To do *Friends* he takes eggs two, four, six and eight. To do something different, maybe he would use eggs one, three, seven, nine and twelve.

Presumably for his first starring role in a $90 million Hollywood film, he has utilized eggs five, ten and eleven. In *Lost in Space*, which opens this summer and co-stars William Hurt, he plays the hero, a clever, ruthless engineer who saves the spaceship from the on-board psychopath, played by Gary Oldman. He says that he is surprised to find himself being cast in such a major film, alongside such distinguished actors, but he can at least relate to Gary Oldman in terms of his wild, hard-drinking life as well as the hardship of his upbringing. Matt LeBlanc was an only child brought up by his divorced mother, Pat Grossman, who worked in a factory making circuit boards. The young Matt knew that his father had gone to Vietnam but had been too frightened to ask his mother whether or not he had been killed there – because she made it clear she did not want to talk about him. 'Ours was a blue-collar, Italian-American household in Newton, Massachusetts,' he says. 'I met my father when I was eight. Ran down the stairs and there was this guy wearing army fatigues with long hair. He looked like Jesus Christ and I could see LeBlanc on his shirt. But he never came home to stay and my mother remarried. Am I in touch with him? Yes and no. It's a sore issue though, and I don't really want to talk about it. The way I am is because of my mom, not my dad. She was there always, always, always.'

LeBlanc's first job was a paper round, then he stacked shelves in a convenience store and worked in a burger bar. He had, he says, no real ambitions. He enrolled on a construction and technology course only to drop out of it soon after. He never studied at drama school but was spotted one day in the street by a woman and asked to try modelling. This lead to him appearing in a series of high-profile TV commercials for Heinz ketchup, Coca Cola and, most notably, as the Levi's 501 man. His attempts to get into acting were less smooth. He spent a year in New York looking for work and even had to sell his furniture to pay for food. 'I kept looking at other actors and saying, "What's he got that I ain't got? Some fancy drama-school diploma?" I know I will never be the best actor in the world. But then, I don't see it as a race to the top.' Eventually he landed some small parts in soaps and sitcoms, and then in 1994 came the big one, *Friends*, which soon went to number one in the ratings in Britain and America.

While most American television comedies are pitiful and cringe-making, over the years a handful have been outstandingly well-honed: *M*A*S*H*, *Taxi*, *Cheers* and *Frasier*. *Friends*, with its crisp metropolitan humour, is in this category. And as the self-obsessed, dim-witted but amiable womanizer Joey Tribbiani, Matt LeBlanc gets some corking lines. 'Do you know what blows my mind?' he'll muse. 'Women can see their breasts any time they want. How they get any work done is beyond me.' Or when giving advice on dating he will say, 'Why do you have to break up with her? Be a man and just stop phoning.'

In terms of delivery, of course, it helps that in real life Matt LeBlanc himself seems to be a self-obsessed, dim-witted but amiable womanizer. I had heard reports of his reputation as being the moody one among the cast of *Friends* and of his prima donna-ish behaviour, but there is none of that this evening, and when the conversation turns to his favourite pastime – snowboarding – he seems positively animated. Any dangerous sport will do, in fact. He collects fast cars and motorbikes and says, 'I'm an adrenaline junkie. Love speed. I ski-dived – ski-dove? – as well. It's like banging your head against a wall just because it feels so good when you stop.' He pauses, 'God, I've had a brain failure, where was I going with that thought? Oh, here we go; afterwards it's so life-affirming. "Oh man, you think. I'm still alive. Wow!"'

The restaurant is on the ground floor of the Four Seasons, the hotel where my wife and I are staying. She has declined my suggestion that she join us for a drink after dinner because she thinks LeBlanc will think that she, like every red-blooded female, must be desperate to meet him – and she does not carry out her threat to approach us at the bar, pretend not to know me, turn her back on LeBlanc and chat me up. We are joined instead after dinner, by a female friend of LeBlanc, who is also a friend of Kirstie Alley, and by one of his snowboarding chums who has the obligatory permatan, dazzling white teeth and chiselled jaw. A lissom young woman with dyed blonde hair and a spray-on skirt approaches and introduces herself to LeBlanc. He says hello rather curtly and then turns back to his friend to continue their analysis of a recent snowboard jump they have done. Another woman, almost identical, approaches and says that she cannot believe it is him and that if she had known he would be here tonight she would have worn more make-up. Ignored she goes away and another, with long black hair this time, approaches, giggles flirtatiously, and says she is called Melody or Misty or one of those Californian names. She hangs around for a few seconds, ignoring LeBlanc's peeved expressions, and says that she is sitting at a table in the corner if he fancies company later. Over the next hour or so about half a dozen more long-limbed women do the same thing.

Good grief.

In January, a law was passed in California banning smoking in restaurants and bars. LeBlanc and his chum head for the French windows that lead out on to a garden to have a smoke. Two skeletal pouting blondes appear from nowhere and make for the door with such indecent haste that the fronds on a nearby rubber plant bend over in their slipstream. I watch their body language as they ask LeBlanc for a light. It's not subtle. I assume that this is the last I will see of the actor. But small talk over, cigarettes stubbed out, he and his friend mosey back over. I ask what he thought of the girls who had followed him out. He shakes his head wearily and sighs, 'They're not exactly rocket scientists.'

Well, I suppose by his standards the night is young. They are about to head off to hear a guitarist they know play in a nearby club. Kirstie Alley is going to be there, apparently. I'm welcome to join them, to discuss the latest developments in Space Shuttle heat-shield technology, presumably. I thank them awfully, yawn conspicuously, look at my watch and, like a goddam English stuffed shirt, decline.

Marc Almond

OCTOBER 1999

My idea of living dangerously is staying up until 2.30 a.m. watching television and drinking whisky when I know I have to drive to Wiltshire next morning for a wedding. Marc Almond's idea is to jump on a plane to New York, consume a wheelbarrow-full of LSD, heroin, crystal meths, Quaaludes, opium, mescalin, Ecstasy and cocaine, and then spend a week crawling from one S&M club to another, before bursting into tears and making his mascara run.

Concerted self-abuse of this sort takes its toll. The 42-year-old pop star attributes his liver damage, blackouts, panic attacks and mood swings to his hedonistic lifestyle. And he found the chronic memory loss a distinct drawback when it came to writing his memoirs. There is a period which began in 1981 with Soft Cell's number one single 'Tainted Love' and lasted for about five years that he can only recall through a haze of hallucination – it was, he explains, a nightmarish blur of events, places and faces.

'My twelve-year addiction to benzodiazepine [sleeping pills] didn't help either,' he adds in a confidingly camp but stentorian tone. 'I can never remember anyone's name. An hour after meeting someone, I've forgotten it. The memory loss is all part of my stammering and dyslexia, too. I get my mords wixed up.' A peel of nervy loud laughter at this. 'Luckily, I have an obsession with keeping lists, notebooks and diaries, so they helped with the chronology of the book – getting things in the right context.'

Today, sitting under a bust of Harold Macmillan in a publisher's office in Chelsea, Marc Almond looks out of place. He is 5ft 6in, with a wiry physique – his own description is that he looks like a nose on a stick – and, as you would expect, he is wearing black clothes, black sideburns and black eyeliner. Tattoos run the length of both sinewy arms, and creep up his neck like tendrils from under his T-shirt collar. On one finger there is a heavy silver ring in the shape of a skull. There are chunks of metal in his nose and his ears, too – and there appears to be a little glittering something on his front tooth. He has had cosmetic surgery to remove the bags from under his eyes.

It is midday. We were supposed to meet at 11 a.m. but a panicky Almond realized at the last minute that that meant having to do something in the morning – and he simply can't do anything before lunchtime. He's cheerful and funny, hyperactive if anything. To keep his stutter in check he speaks in a torrent – words tumbling out breathlessly – and he repeats himself to maintain the rhythm of his sentences. As I listen to his cautionary tale of rock-and-roll excess I grip the sides of my chair and try not to look too startled.

He first got a taste for shocking people in 1979, when completing a degree course in performance art at Leeds Polytechnic. For one exam show he sat at a mirror, naked except for black boots and a swastika thong, and shaved half his body. He then smashed the mirror and, with a shard, cut himself, drawing blood. For the climax he lay face down on a large mirror and simulated sex. All he remembers about this now is that the mirror was very cold.

Around this time, the beginning of the New Romantic movement, Almond met the synthesizer player Dave Ball and formed Soft Cell. Their first appearance on *Top of the Pops* caused, as the saying goes, the BBC switchboard to jam – 'I look back on those early performances and I even embarrass and shock myself in a way, they are so kind of, "Please love me, please love me", and I'm trying so hard. I can imagine why it would have got people's backs up – too much eyeliner, too much leather, too fey, too mincy.'

Nevertheless, 'Tainted Love' sold more than a million copies in Britain. It was also a number one all over Europe, and in America it was in the charts longer than any other record in history – and so gained a place in the *Guinness Book of Records*, replacing Bill Haley's 'Rock Around the Clock'. Ball and Almond received no publishing royalties for the single, however, because it was a cover version. 'We were so naive,' Almond says with a raucous laugh, 'we put a cover on the B-side as well. If we had used one of our own songs on the B-side, we could have shared the royalties fifty-fifty! Instead we lost around £1.7 million.'

Even so, the first half of the eighties were extremely lucrative for Britain's first 'synth duo'. They had a succession of hits and Almond developed an addiction to spending money: £500,000 on drugs alone. He bought a Mercedes convertible on a whim as he passed a car showroom – even though he can't drive. On another occasion, while recording in Bavaria, he developed a craving for sushi and, unable to find a sushi restaurant nearby, flew back to London for the night – 'When you have to have sushi you have to have it.' Accountants were despatched to devise saving schemes that would prevent Almond getting his hands on his money. 'Then one day came the terrifying realization that the money was coming in faster than I could spend it. The addict with an endless supply of money can remain indefinitely in denial.'

Through the haze Almond recalls that around this time he was groped by George Melly at a party; Rowan Atkinson did a sketch about him on *Not the Nine o'clock News;* on a night out with his friend Molly Parkin he drunkenly tried to seduce the boxer John Conteh; Madonna stayed at his bedsit in London; and, in New York, Andy Warhol invited him to his studio, the Factory. They filmed each other. 'It was Polaroids and Super 8s at fifty paces, a strange stand-off.' Almond's recording history after Soft Cell split up in 1984 has been chequered. He would announce his retirement in a petulant fury – on one occasion storming into the offices of *Record Mirror* to bull-whip a journalist who had been critical of him – only to retract the announcement next day.

Over the years his distinctively off-key voice mellowed and improved. He signed to half a dozen record labels, reinventing himself variously as a Latin, jazz or R&B artist, a torch singer and even a Vegas crooner. There have been hits, notably a couple of duets (with Jimmy Somerville for 'I Feel Love' in 1985 and Gene Pitney for 'Something's Gotten Hold of my Heart' in 1989) and 'The Days of Pearly Spencer' in 1992. But his sexual promiscuity and drug-taking got worse and he took to hanging out with underworld figures: criminals, prostitutes and gun-carrying drug dealers.

Then in 1993, he confides, something happened which forced him to change his way of life. Two acquaintances tried to throw him from a sixth-floor balcony window. A neighbour intervened and the police arrived to find Almond mutilated and unconscious on the floor. Instead of pressing charges for attempted murder he decided it was time to check himself into a drug rehabilitation clinic, the Promis Recovery Centre, just outside Canterbury. The therapy included a regime of rising at 6.45 a.m. to scrub floors, followed by hours of intensive group therapy.

'My life started collapsing in the mid-nineties,' Almond recalls. 'I didn't know why I had been taking the drugs. Someone had to point it out to me. I had been in this selfish, self-absorbed world and all I knew was that I had to keep taking them and spending money and having love affairs and moving house and changing record company. Each time I realized there was something horribly wrong with each new situation – me.' He stutters as he says this, and he pronounces Rs as Ws. In conversation he peppers his vocabulary with psycho-babble in that way people who have been through therapy do: lots of self-analysis about being damaged, having low self-esteem, needing affirmation, craving attention, confusing sex for love. 'I did see a psychiatrist,' he explains helpfully. 'But I was bored by it, quite frankly, because I have an attention span of about two seconds.' More likely, the psychiatrist, faced with the bewildering array of traumas associated with Almond's childhood, didn't know where to start and had a nervous breakdown.

Peter Marc Sinclair Almond was born in 1957 in Southport. He moved constantly from house to house and school to school around the northwest of England and, wherever he ended up, he was bullied – often chased by gangs of boys chanting the word 'queer' at him, before catching him and beating him up. He was a sickly child afflicted by asthma, bronchitis and pleurisy. To avoid being attacked in the playground he learned to hyper-ventilate and black out. His nickname was Pwune. His father, an unemployed former Army officer and salesman, was an alcoholic who would sometimes slap his son. The laziness down the right side of Almond's face is, he claims, caused by his father hitting him with a telephone. 'I hated him,' the singer now says, matter of factly. 'Haven't seen him for years and there is no chance of a reconciliation. He saw me as the source of his short-comings and failures. There was always an edginess. A dark anger behind his eyes as secretive as those bottles he hid away.'

The twelve-year-old Almond was a bed-wetter by night and a shoplifter by day. When his parents divorced in 1972, Marc and his younger sister Julia were overjoyed – not least because, says Almond, their father had, allegedly, just found their savings and spent the money on alcohol. One day his father stormed into his school and demanded to know from the teacher if his thirteen-year-old son was a homosexual. He was, as it happened, but the teacher didn't know that. Although Marc Almond says he wanted to like girls – and he actually lost his virginity that year to a 'big-boned, galumphing, sweaty girl called Hilary' – he was always drawn to boys.

Almond left school with two O-levels, talked his way on to an art college course and promptly had a nervous breakdown. He tried to commit suicide by throwing himself off a balcony – someone grabbed him – and he was sectioned for a month at Ormskirk Mental Hospital. 'Oh, I cried and cried and realized I had been bottling up tears for years,' he says. 'I'm still like that to an extent. I become introverted, keep all the feelings back and end up exploding.'

Given his emotional scars, it is amazing that Almond coped as well as he did with the sudden fame and fortune that was heaped on him as a 24-year-old. And though he barely coped at all, at least he didn't kill himself through a drug overdose, a sexually transmitted disease or, in one of those fits of romantic anguish that pop stars are prone to, a suicide attempt. He came close, of course, and he says now that he feels a shiver when he realizes quite how close. I tell him that he makes me feel as though I've lead a very dull life indeed.

'Pop is very disposable by nature and so are pop stars,' he says with an uneven grin. 'We are put on pedestals so people can watch us being damaged on everyone else's behalf. And the record companies encourage us to be excessive. You are told to go to the parties and take the drugs because you have to get into the gossip columns. Then you become a liability. You don't turn up for your TV performances. You're brought before the chairman of the record company to have your wrists slapped.'

Clearly his relationship with his father was not an easy one but does Marc Almond now consider that he might owe some of his success to this same relationship – in that he was desperate to prove his father wrong? 'Definitely, that's the double-edged thing. He gave me my weaknesses but also my strengths. Success is revenge. Sometimes you have to use your bitterness – as long as it doesn't consume you it can give you a feeling of being alive, it gives you an edge. I always felt he hated me. He blamed his own problems on his sensitive, effeminate son. But if success meant having to go through my childhood again, I wouldn't want to have it.'

Since he spent most of his schooldays hiding from his father and running away from bullies, why does he think he had a need to draw attention to himself by performing on stage? Was it masochism? 'I'm a shy extrovert, but I think that's quite common, isn't it? On stage I say, "I'm here to give you songs and you're here to give me waves of love over the footlights and the sooner we can give each other these things the sooner we can all go home." It's that reaffirmation thing. Every time I go on stage I have to overcome a fear. It hangs over me like a black cloud beforehand. I'm sick and nervous – until I put on the make-up, you know, the mask, and I become this monster called Marc Almond.'

Even so, he recognizes that some of his psychological problems stem from his inability to differentiate between his public and private personas. 'It does get confused and you do start to become this other person. Out of guilt. Because you don't want to disappoint people. It's a silly camp old idea but I don't want to let the public down. I'm aware that I've become a gay institution and so when I go out I have to put on this Marc Almond drag. But the flamboyant glittery image is sometimes hard for me to reconcile with the person I am at home – unshaven, in my slippers, watching *Coronation Street*, with a microwaved dinner on my lap.'

As a child he had always craved approval but when he got it as an adult, he could never accept it. 'I think it was guilt. I felt an impostor, a fake, a phoney. I felt it was all so false. I couldn't understand why everyone was making a fuss over me. I'm not worthy. I felt out of control of my own life, you know, completely. That I wasn't in control. Self-loathing clung to me like rust. The worse thing was that I had to lie about my sexuality. My record company was saying you must invent a girlfriend. In the early eighties if you said you were gay, it was a career destroyer. Pop stars were never really openly gay. It was always that bisexuality thing. A cop out.'

His homosexuality has been a mixed blessing. He has happy memories: nights at the London nightclub Heaven, for instance, when Freddie Mercury would pick him up and carry him over his shoulder on to the dance floor. But he has also had to endure being spat at and punched in the face by strangers. Until his twenties he was very confused about his sexuality. 'I was attracted to anyone who would pay any attention to me, or anyone who would show me love. Love had to be sex. But I never felt comfortable with my homosexuality. I couldn't be open about it. Even now I'm only ninety-five per cent sure. I think homosexuality is genetic but there are still doubts.'

In the late eighties, Almond took to visiting female prostitutes. 'It was all part of that adventure thing,' he says. 'It had to be done. I also felt because I was singing about this life – all the cigarettes and neon and satin sheets and regret – I ought to immerse myself in it. I did like it and it became another addiction for a while.' There are people who want to be spokesmen for gay issues, he adds, but he has never wanted to be one of them. 'I would like to think there is much more to me than a sexuality. People don't say "the heterosexual artiste Rod Stewart", do they?'

Almond doesn't get attacked in the street as much as he used to. 'It's changed now because everyone becomes mainstream in the end, even me. It doesn't matter how rebellious you were, whether you were John Lydon [Johnny Rotten of the Sex Pistols] or whatever, you know, you become cuddly. Occasionally I'll hear, "Marc Almond you queer bastard," and someone will spit at me, and I will shout, "Well, actually, it's Mark Almond millionaire queer bastard, if you don't mind."'

That said, does he feel guilty that he might have lead people astray, that, as a public figure, he set a bad example? 'The one thing I felt uncomfortable with was having a young teenybopper audience. I thought of Soft Cell as a dark, arty band. I never set out to write for kids. I did try to keep things secret but, ultimately, if you are an adult, you have to take responsibility for your own actions.'

Analysis of Marc Almond's character is problematic, in that, once you have digested the things he says about himself you struggle for anything more insightful to add. By his own estimation he is an emotionally immature, chippy, bitchy, self-pitying neurotic who is addicted to everything, frustrated, self-flagellating, self-destructive and narcissistic. Oh, and he says he always sounds pompous and gets out of his depth whenever he tries to be intellectual. The therapy-speak and self-loathing may well all be part of the tortured drama-queen act, but few of us can claim to be as self-aware – and honest – as Marc Almond is. And he is at his most endearing when he is sending himself up. He describes, for instance, phoning *Smash Hits* one day and screaming at them for putting his photograph in between Clare Grogan's and Adam Ant's, adding, 'Well, wouldn't you?' And his observation about group sex deserves including in a book of quotations: 'I've never been one for threesomes. Inevitably someone ends up making the tea, and knowing my luck it would be me.' It seems a fitting epitaph.

Max Clifford

You know that creepy feeling you sometimes get of being watched? Well, that's what it's like all the time when you're with Max Clifford. It's not him doing the watching, it's hidden cameras, as if you're taking part in *The Truman Show*. The acting is stilted, the colours unnaturally saturated and the shadows don't quite correspond to the movements of their subjects. Things seem suspiciously ordinary, tidy . . . staged.

The master illusionist and his family – Liz, his wife of thirty-two years, and Louise, his 28-year-old daughter – recently moved from a house in suburban Raynes Park to a chalet-style bungalow set in private parkland near Weybridge in Surrey. There is a spotless silver Jaguar in the driveway, a hanging basket above the door and, in the leafless trees surrounding the bungalow, songbirds. You can hear them but – how *Truman Show* – you can't see them.

It is a mild morning, the sunlight is watery and I could swear that the middle-aged woman walking her dog is the same one who passed by, heading in the same direction, two minutes ago. Max Clifford is wearing sports casuals: a white tennis shirt and tracksuit bottoms. When I leave at noon, he will play tennis with one of his old schoolfriends, Dave, because it's a Wednesday, his tennis day, the one day of the working week he doesn't go in to his London office in New Bond Street. Clifford is a thickset but fit-looking 56-year-old. The most alarming thing about his appearance is the area between his eyes and his thick thatch of silver hair. His eyebrows are so black and dense they look as though they've been bought from a novelty shop as part of a

Groucho Marx kit. He has never considered pruning or dying them, he says, even though his wife and daughter have made constant mocking reference to them over the years. The close proximity of the black eyebrows to the silver hair has earned Clifford the nickname 'the lugubrious badger'.

But he has been called other names. At school, he tells me, he was Maxi Tree, because he had legs like tree trunks. Edwina Curry called him 'the little turd'. David Mellor preferred 'the sleazeball's sleazeball'. I'm not sure how I expected the interior of his house to be decorated. Framed tabloid front pages of his PR triumphs, perhaps. FREDDIE STARR ATE MY HAMSTER!, I'M GOING TO HAVE MY EIGHT BABIES!, MELLOR MADE LOVE IN A FOOTBALL STRIP! Or maybe there will be Tory scalps presented in glass cases: Piers Merchant's shrunken head, Jerry Hayes's beard, Jeffrey Archer's impish grin. But I suppose chintz, family photographs in frames, and a mantelpiece laden with china spaniels is about right. Clifford has a cocker spaniel called Oliver. It sits in his lap and he strokes it as he talks: this twilight zone's equivalent to Blofeld's cat.

I don't suppose little Oliver would be much use against intruders, but I bet Clifford could handle himself. He is, after all, a great believer in defending property. In the next few weeks, when the case comes to trial, you can expect to see him on the evening news most nights as he throws his weight behind Tony Martin, the Norfolk farmer accused of murdering a sixteen-year-old convicted burglar last August. He is working for Martin free of charge because, he says, he feels sorry for him. 'If someone broke into my home in the middle of the night and I had no electricity and I'd been burgled several times already, I wouldn't make them a cup of tea,' Clifford says in his softly spoken and ponderous south London twang.

Clifford likes to see himself as an arbiter of public morality. Last autumn, just days before he acted as stork and brought us news of the Blair baby, he broke the story of Jeffrey Archer's false alibi and represented Allison Brown, who made accusations of sex abuse against Gary Glitter. (The Glitter case failed when it was revealed that the contract Clifford had brokered for Allison Brown with the *News of the World* was worth £10,000 plus an extra £25,000 if Glitter was convicted.) Clifford likes to boast about how he played his part in bringing down the last government. 'I do think I contributed to the word "sleaze" being attached to the Tories,' he says. 'There were other stories I could have brought out about them. But if I am going to bring out, say, my Portillo story, it will be much further on, nearer the next election, when the public need to be reminded of Tory sleaze. The reason I brought out Jeffrey Archer when I did was the Tories were becoming more popular. I tried to warn Archer six months earlier that he shouldn't run for mayor – Ted Francis, the man who gave Archer his alibi, is a friend of my brother – but he carried on and I have no sympathy for him. He's as hard as nails, and I find his arrogance and hypocrisy ugly.'

Max Clifford doesn't go to church but he considers himself to be a Christian and he does pray. He also talks to his mother, Lilian, who died twenty-four years ago. 'I'm very close to her now. When I'm in situations I know she is smiling and laughing. I feel it very strongly.' He attributes his unflappability to his mother's influence. 'It's a matter of how you look at things. She was a very capable woman, very loving and caring. Everyone came to her with their problems – whether it was laying some-one out who had just died in the night, or sorting out abortions, whatever. She would get on with it and then cook us breakfast as if nothing had happened. Mum was a giggler – fat, jolly and flatulent. Dad was more reserved and distant. Didn't think the flatulence was funny. He wasn't the type to say he was proud of me. He was forty-three when I was born. A very good classical pianist.'

The late Frank Clifford, Max's father, had come from a pros-perous Tory family, which owned properties around Wands-worth. His job had been to collect rents on these but, being a 'natural socialist', as his son puts it, he could never bring himself to evict tenants who couldn't pay. His family turned their backs on him and he moved to a poor part of Wimbledon – tin bath, outside privy, no car. Frank also gambled, which may be why Max has always feared compulsions: he has never drunk alcohol, smoked or taken drugs.

Max Clifford is the youngest of Frank and Lilian's four children. He has a sister, Eleanor, whom he describes as 'terribly, terribly' and 'a natural Tory', and two brothers, Bernard (or

Bunny, because his ears stick out) and Harold (or Cliff, because he doesn't like his Christian name). Last-borns, it is believed, resent their elder siblings' power and authority, and they are said to be far more likely than first-borns to challenge the status quo. This has certainly been the case with Max Clifford, whose hatred of the Establishment borders on the pathological.

Sir Peter Harding, the defence chief and Establishment figure *par excellence*, was an archetypal Clifford victim. He felt obliged to resign in 1994 when the publicist's client Bienvenida Buck kissed, told and earned herself £300,000 from the tabloids. But any authority figure deserves a good kicking as far as Clifford is concerned. 'I resent anyone telling me anything at all,' he says. 'I'm that kind of person. I don't think I'm arrogant but I've got an awful lot of faith in my own ability . . . There's no one I've been in awe of – if the Queen or the Pope was sitting here, I wouldn't treat them any differently to the way I'm treating yourself.'

There are three recurring themes in Clifford's conversation. One is that he 'doesn't want to seem arrogant'. Another is that he has never pitched for an account in his life: he tells me at least five times that stars always come to him, he never goes to them. The third is that he can't stand people with 'affected', that is, 'plummy' voices – and this seems to stem from a need he felt as a teenager to prove he was just as good as 'the snobs at the top of the hill' in Wimbledon Village (he lived at the bottom).

'I always resented being talked down to. And I hated arrogance and pomposity. I had my first experience of it on my first day at junior school. I was kicking a ball about and this boy began speaking to me in a very affected voice, telling me to clear off, so I hit him. He turned out to be the headmaster's son.' Clifford left his secondary modern school at fifteen and went to work at a Wimbledon department store called Elys. He hated being patronized by the 'snobby customers' there and was sacked after a year for putting glue on his manager's chair. He had three passions at the time – boxing, football and water polo; aggressive, competitive sports which, he says, taught him to stand up for himself. It was writing match reports about the latter that won him a traineeship as a reporter on the *Merton and Morden News*. He started a record column there and in 1962 talked his way into a job at the publicity department of EMI. He always uses the same pat phrase to describe what happened next: 'My first job was to promote an unknown band from Liverpool. The Beatles.' Hmm. It sounds like a claim worthy of Jeffrey Archer. Clifford glibly acknowledges that he lies all the time when promoting showbiz stars – because it doesn't matter, because they are 'light relief' – so it follows that his recollections of his own career might also be clouded. 'I learnt early on that by window dressing, by colouring, you get the big coverage,' he says. 'I would always exaggerate record sales and get the big headlines. I was always instinctively good at lying, you know, telling someone they look really nice when they looked in a right state. As long as your distortion of the truth isn't harming any-one, it's fine.'

He went on to promote Jimi Hendrix ('he was so out of his head, he didn't know what he was, let alone where he was') and Bob Dylan ('a miserable sod') but found rock stars boring and irritating because they never turned up for the PR junkets he had organized. Maybe they just found his brassy manner a bit uncool. Clifford is vague about precise dates and times but he believes he set up his own PR company, Max Clifford Associates, when he was about twenty-seven, in 1970. Neither myth nor history really relates what happened in the years between then and his great fictitious scoop in 1986, the Freddie Starr story, but presumably he was busy learning about the perverse nature of fame – how it can be manufactured out of very little substance, how it can take on surreal forms, how you can use one client to promote another. Freddie Starr never ate the hamster, but the publicity the story generated helped him sell out his tour. Derek Hatton, the former militant and would-be pantomime star, didn't really have a torrid affair with another of Clifford's clients, Katie Baring, the aspiring actress and merchant banker's daughter.

One of Clifford's more memorable triumphs was making the world believe that two of his clients, the supermodel Claudia Schiffer and the magician David Copperfield, were having a passionate romance when really, until Clifford introduced them, they hardly knew each other. Clifford, who reckons he makes about £750,000 a year, describes the PR world as empty and sycophantic. I ask him whom he has more contempt for, the stars who are prepared to prostitute themselves shamelessly at his behest or the media which is prepared to swallow the scraps of gossip he throws? 'I don't think you can generalize,' he says. 'Neither really. Some journalists loathe me, others love me. Which is fine. It works well for me. And I don't have contempt for the stars because I know most of them are only really in love with themselves. I don't mean to sound arrogant but stars generally need you more than you need them, so they are nice to you.' Well quite, who would have heard of those fly-by-nights Hendrix and Dylan, or Lennon and McCartney, had it not been for the sterling work of their junior press officer? 'What I mean is that I can keep things out of the press that will destroy them. I do it by calling in favours with editors, by being aware of a problem in advance so that I can take care of it. If Hugh Grant had been a client of mine and I'd known about his weakness for going off with ladies in cars, I could have dealt with it. I could have supplied the cast list from friends of mine who are madams, worldwide. Or I'd have fixed things with my friends in the LA police department.'

Can almost any compromising situation be recovered through PR? 'I don't know about that,' says Clifford, speaking in the slow voice of one on Mogadon. 'I'd hate to represent Gary Glitter right now. But you can make things better, yes. Jeffrey Archer would be easy to turn round. One year or two, provided he played the game and did what I asked him to do. I could present him as a lovable rogue, an Alan Clark figure. He hasn't done anything that we find too odious. He's been economical with the truth, but aren't all politicians? It's often a matter of damage limitation. Look at Mellor and Paddy Ashdown. Both caught out at about the same time. Paddy turned it to his advantage and if anything it made him more popular. He showed humility. He didn't blame anyone else. Mellor did the opposite, tried to hide behind the very family he betrayed. He came out crawling. The garden gate picture. That's revolting.'

Although Clifford denies it – he says he doesn't want to risk being sued – it seems unlikely that David Mellor ever made love to Clifford's client Antonia de Sancha while wearing a Chelsea FC strip. But it was this inspired detail that made the story funny and marketable – de Sancha made £100,000 from it. Clifford grins and says, 'All I will say is that it made a lot of sense that he would wear that because anything that would draw attention away from his face would be an advantage.'

He does admit, though, that he put Judge James Harkess up to saying that he wanted to horsewhip Alan Clark who, having languidly confessed to serial-womanizing in his diaries, was forced by Clifford to face the 'Harkess coven', the South African mother and daughter who were his mistresses. 'The Harkesses? They came to me, I didn't go to them, and said we want to stand up and put our side of the story and make money. What a pantomime that was. Alan Clark loved it, sold more books, and the mother and daughter got what they wanted too. They didn't think they were making fools of themselves.'

So, as Clifford sees it, his clients usually emerge from their dealings with him happier and richer and that's all they care about. Their total humiliation is never an issue. De Sancha never lost her dignity, he says, because as an out-of-work actress who hated the situation she was in, she didn't have much dignity to lose. And Mandy Allwood, who became pregnant with octuplets only to lose them? 'Mandy approached me, as everyone does, I don't ever approach anybody. I did a very quick deal with the *News of the World* that was never about how many babies but about paying her a lot of money for her story.' And her threat to sue him for the £350,000 she claims he still owes her? 'There's no substance to it. All the accounts were there. Her people have seen everything and in point of fact, having looked into it, they discovered they owed me money.'

Max Clifford is friendly enough but he has cruel, thin lips and he doesn't use them to smile much. He is, I suspect, driven as much by chippiness as he is by moral indignation. He can sound sanctimonious on the subject of his charity work: visiting the sick and elderly, donating the money from all his television appearances to the Marsden Hospital. And there is something of the Dickensian humbug about him; protesting too much about sleaze, when clearly he needs to keep us interested in it in order to promote himself.

All this makes it very difficult to gauge the purity of his motives when it comes to the subject of his daughter, Louise, who has been disabled since the age of six with rheumatoid arthritis. She has had twelve major operations – hip and knee replacements, a rod fixed into her spine – and at one time was in hospital for eight months. It was at this point that Clifford came to hate the Tories for what they had done to the NHS. 'I set out to do everything I could to embarrass the last government because of the NHS,' he says. 'Because of what I saw daily, going in and out of hospitals with Louise, talking to nurses, seeing the effects of shortages.'

As if on cue Louise appears and sits on the arm of her father's chair. 'How's mum getting on?' Max asks her. Fine, she says in a small voice that is just as soft as her father's. Then, turning to me he explains: 'Louise has been told she needs a kidney transplant and we've been having tests. Unfortunately I'm the wrong blood group but Liz is OK so she's out there today on a treadmill at the hospital. And she's not sporty like I am!' I ask Louise – who has a degree in Communications from Bournemouth University and who plans to take over her father's company when, if, he retires – if she ever felt uncomfortable about being, well, used by her father as a weapon against the Tories? 'It really wasn't an issue,' she says, 'because it was something we were passionate about. When you care about things you want to talk about them. His attitude to the NHS wasn't entirely shaped by me, it came from talking to nurses and doctors as well.'

I ask Max if he has ever felt that he was over-playing the Louise card. 'No. This is my life, and if I'm going to point the finger at the Tories, I have to be prepared to stand up and say how it is. I know what they did to the NHS. I've had first-hand experience of it. I'd sleep on a mattress by Louise's bed after her operations because one of the after-effects of the anaesthetic was that it made her sick and there would only be one student nurse on duty. And Louise would be bound up like a little mummy, in traction, unable to move. I wasn't using Louise. This is how it is. The more attention we can draw to this cruel disease the better. I didn't blame the Tories for arthritis, I blamed them for the lack of nurses, beds, care.'

He adds that if the present government fails the NHS as badly as the last government did, he will queer their pitch too. He claims he was the first to tell the world about Ron Davies and his nocturnal walks on Clapham Common. And more recently he set up the chocolate-eclair-in-the-agriculture-minister's-face wheeze (the self-styled 'socialite environmentalist' Birgit Cunningham had sought his advice). In a week when the news was full of real stories, such as the IRA failure to decommission arms and the Shipman serial killings, the stunt made the front page of every single newspaper, broadsheets included. Does New Labour have skeletons? Clifford gives an amused sigh. 'At the moment I should think there are about twenty affairs I haven't brought out, because I couldn't justify exposing them. But if they start lecturing us about back to basics, who knows?'

Sounds like blackmail: a Max Clifford tactic. Although he has a short fuse – he once had to be pulled off the Tory MP Roger Gale during a heated exchange on Kilroy – there is an eerie passivity to him. Like Bridey in *Brideshead Revisited*, he floats with log-like calm on the ripples of social discomfort he creates. He never gets nervous, he says, and is not easily embarrassed. Like most bullies, he is a very sentimental man. 'I can watch films and have tears,' he says. 'I've spent a lot of time up at the Marsden and I often come away feeling moved. You see tots of two or three with leukaemia, and when I'm driving my car away I have to stop and cry because sometimes life can be very cruel. I suppose the reason I go up there a lot – and have done for twenty years now – is that you can cheer people up a bit. Give them a lift. Put something back.'

The paradox about Max Clifford is that, while he clearly needs the approval and love of his family, and wants to be appreciated for his charity work, he seems not to mind if what he does as a publicist makes him unpopular with the general public. 'If I'm sleazy for exposing sleazy people, so be it,' he says with a shrug. 'I don't mind if people who don't really know me hate me. I'm the only white person in this country who thinks O.J. Simpson is innocent, for instance, and I've had death threats about it.' (One of his more surreal stunts involved bringing O.J. over to England and having him appear on the *Richard and Judy Show* and then, even more bizarrely, debating at the Oxford Union.) 'So, if you see what I'm saying, I've always had the courage of my convictions.'

He certainly has. He stuck up for Geoffrey Boycott when the former cricketer was accused of beating up Margaret Moore and didn't seem to have a friend in the world. He also advised the five suspects in the Stephen Lawrence murder case to appear on ITV's *Tonight* programme. 'I told them to put their case live on television because in a fair society you should hear both sides. My instinct is that one or two of them had nothing to do with it. These are not very bright boys who were acting on the advice of their lawyers not to answer any questions.'

And now Clifford has joined forces with that honest fellow Mohamed Fayed to promote Fulham FC. Hmm again. It occurs to me that Judge Clifford, the PR man who has become as famous as his clients, actually represents the new establishment, the new spirit of Britain: hollow, cheesy and spiteful. I ask him if he thinks he is a good man. 'I'm extremely happy to be the person I am. I'm happy generally. I never get depressed. You get your moments, a few tears, but the laughter always outweighs them.'

He is easily bored, he adds, doesn't read much, eats out three times a week and likes to walk around the house naked. I notice he drums his fingers a lot: is this because his calm exterior hides a tense and frustrated man? 'No, I think it's to do with an epileptic fit I had when I was forty-eight. It was quickly sorted out with tablets and after a couple of years I was told I didn't need to take them any more.'

'It could just be another twitch to add to his repertoire,' Louise adds. 'All his siblings are twitchers. It's like being at the zoo when they get together. Bunny is a grunter as well.'

Three hours have passed and the inscrutable Max Clifford has proved to be such an engaging talker we have strayed un-wittingly into his tennis time. As I'm leaving he tells me, apropos of nothing, that Bobby Davro lives next door but one. The Clifford devil is in the surreal detail.

Shortly after this interview appeared I bumped into Max Clifford at a party. 'Thanks for saying I used my daugher,' he said in that chilling way of his. 'Thanks a lot.' In 2001 he (allegedly) set up Neil and Christine Hamilton in a sting operation which resulted in them being charged with rape. The charge was later dropped.

Will Carling

His family, in a spirit of affection no doubt, nicknamed him The Little Shit. One of his first long-term girlfriends called him Big Willy, or at least that is how he signed himself in letters to her. The players in the England rugby team he captained for eight years knew him as Bumface – it was to do with the curious shape of his chin, a firm pair of buttocks hewn with a wide chisel. But the name that seems to have stuck for Will Carling is the one conferred on him by the *Sun* three years ago: Love Rat.

'I suppose it was the perfect story,' Carling says, lowering his voice, as well as his eyes. 'As far as the media was concerned.' He gently kneads the velvety ears of a dark chocolate labrador, staring at his fingers and thumbs as if they were not his own. 'It had everything.'

It certainly did. Carling had already put the press on high alert in 1996 when his two-year-long marriage to his first wife Julia ended in divorce, following very public speculation as to the exact nature of his relationship with the Princess of Wales. When two years later he left Ali Cockayne, Gary Lineker's sister-in-law, for another woman – Lisa, the wife of his former Harlequins team-mate David Cooke – he also walked out on their eleven-month-old son Henry. According to Ali's version of events the first she knew of Will's decision to leave was when she came across a revised draft of his autobiography in which all references to their relationship had been changed to the past tense. As far as she was concerned, they were planning to marry. She had even chosen her wedding dress. Pictured sobbing outside her house, baby in arms, she said, 'I just hurt – I really hurt. No one could have done more damage to me than this.'

Overnight Carling went from sporting hero – he is the most capped and, with three Grand Slams to his name, the most successful captain England has had – to pantomime villain. His testimonial match was cancelled at short notice, as were various endorsements, after-dinner speaking engagements and a nineteen-theatre tour of *An Evening with Will Carling*. Signed copies of his autobiography gathered dust on the shelves of bookshops. He had expected to make £1 million that autumn. Instead he ended up having to sell his £800,000 house in Berkshire. It was a modern morality tale.

Will and Lisa Carling married on the island of Fiji in 1999. They live in a rented house – fourteenth-century in parts, leaded windows, beamed ceilings – on the edge of a village green in Surrey. Outside, under a light blanket of fallen leaves, a Range Rover and a Jaguar are parked. Inside a log fire is burning, Lisa – blonde, trim, friendly – is making coffee for a BT engineer in the hope, she whispers to me, that he can be persuaded to fit an extra line which wasn't part of the initial order, and Jack, the couple's fifteen-month-old son, is asleep upstairs. Will, his eyebrows and gelled hair as black as the Devil's heart, is sitting on a deep sofa in the drawing room, his legs crossed.

He can do this now. There was a time when his thighs were so hefty – a build up of lactic acid in the muscle caused by punishing workouts on a Cybex exercise bike – he couldn't. At thirty-six, he is still a solid 5ft 10in but, if anything, he looks top-heavy now, as if substance has been transferred from his legs to his head, a balloon squeezed at one end that bulges at the other. Though he no longer plays rugby – 'Nah, I don't miss it. I miss the players but not the playing' – he does still exercise regularly, mostly on his mountain bike, and he does do a little yoga, when not watching *Coronation Street*, his favourite programme, or listening to the Bee Gees, his favourite band.

Behind him is a stack of memorabilia which he displays in the marquee that Will Carling Management, his corporate hospitality company, runs at Twickenham: his old rugby boots in a glass case; a moody black-and-white blow-up of him leading the players out of the tunnel; framed cuttings about the 'fifty-seven old farts' affair – the time in 1995 when 'Greedy Carling' was sacked temporarily as England captain for saying, off-camera, that the members of the RFU committee were old farts because they disapproved of his plans to make money by turning international rugby from an amateur sport into a professional one.

Is he still having a hard time financially? 'Well, everything is relative,' he says with an ambiguous smile. 'What is a hard time?' Losing a million. 'Yeah, but the weird thing is, it was never about the money for me. The lost million has never bothered me. Relatively, I did go through a hard time. At one point I did wonder how I was going to earn a living. I even thought of becoming a taxi-driver. It has been hard because we have school fees to pay for Tom and Tali [Lisa's children, ages fourteen and twelve] and there was a lot of pressure suddenly. But, touch wood, it's all right now.'

How did he live with the humiliation of having his testimonial match cancelled? Long pause. 'Personally, it was never a great ambition of mine to have a testimonial match. Other people suggested it.' He leans forward. 'So when it got called off, for me, it was like neither here nor there. I'd have liked to have played in it. Lots of players have said to me since that they wish it had gone ahead. I saw Jonah [Lomu] last night and he was saying it was a shame. But, yes,' Carling sucks in air between his teeth, 'at the time it was horrific. I mean, *really* horrific. For Lisa, for Lisa's family, for my family. Unbelievable. I think back to it now and I get this horrible churning in my stomach. But, you know, you make your decision. Whether people agree with . . . I mean, if people want to judge . . . It's the sort of decision that people make every day. The relationship is over. But the way it ended up being portrayed . . . The momentum behind it was just, just frightening. I'm not whiter than white, by any stretch of the imagination, but . . .'

Given his sporting achievements, Will Carling ought to have enjoyed huge popularity. Perhaps the public's coolness was to do with his self-satisfied manner, his flat voice, his clichéd speech – 'Like I say', 'at the end of the day', 'she was a special lady'. It may also be to do with the way he smiles on one side of his mouth, a manly, patronizing smirk. Even as a rugby player he was never lovable. Together, he and Jeremy Guscott were great centres because they complemented each other: Guscott, the rapier, had grace and subtlety; Carling, the blunt instrument, played a more brutish game. He had, as the joke went, the hardest tackle in rugby. In post-match analyses Carling always came across as a complainer, a bit whiney, a bit aloof. He was aware of this, but put it down to his own shyness and insecurity. He was always introspective, he says, a loner.

Now, though, as he talks haltingly about the events of three years ago, his eyes water and, well, I find myself feeling sorry for him. Either he is a very good actor, which seems unlikely, or he was, is, genuinely traumatized by what happened. He tells me that when he saw the tabloid headlines getting worse by the day he felt as though he no longer knew who the real Will Carling was. But crises of identity were not so unusual for him. 'I've seen that stranger since I was twenty-two [the age when he became the youngest-ever England captain]. A comic book hero that isn't me. I didn't quite become a recluse but I became very private. The only people who come here now are very close friends, otherwise I don't see many people.' He declines invitations to dinner if there will be people there he doesn't know. 'I can't go. I don't want to have to spend two or three hours answering questions as people try and work out what I am really like. It's so tiring. My heart sinks.'

He doesn't regret his decision to leave Ali and Henry, but does he at least regret the timing? 'Well, this is the thing. I could have been really callous and waited until after my testimonial year, after I had made a lot of money and then done it. If I'm meant to be the real shit people say I am, why wouldn't I have thought that through? Put on a facade for nine months then run with the money?'

Well, maybe he didn't expect as much fuss to be made about his love life as was made about it. Maybe that was what he didn't think through. Maybe, as a comic-book hero, a captain who had squired a princess, he believed he was above criticism. But, giving him the benefit of the doubt, why did he feel under so much pressure to take such a drastic step at the time he did? 'Because I was so unhappy.' He was so unhappy he couldn't stay a moment longer? 'Yeah. You get to the point where you think this is not right. I was very, very unhappy.'

Are we automatically entitled to happiness? Don't we sometimes have to sacrifice our own happiness for the sake of others? Is that something he thought through? 'Er, just a bit. Yes.' He grins ruefully. 'But . . . [*sotto voce*] but is it better to spend years and years and years living with someone you don't want to live with for the sake of the child? Children are not stupid. Of course they pick up the fact that mum and dad are incredibly unhappy but are putting on a front. Then dad leaves as soon as the child is eighteen, and when the child asks, "Why?" dad says, "Because I haven't been happy since you were a baby." How much guilt is the child going to feel then?'

But still, eleven-months-old. If he had waited until Henry was three or four, when his mother might have found it easier to cope on her own, might the public reaction not have been different? Carling eyes me narrowly, leans forward and turns off my tape recorder. After a long sigh he tells me his side of the story. It is quite specific – eye-poppingly so – and the gist of it is that the baby was far from being planned. The word blackmail is used. We have not agreed to anything being off the record, but his turning the recorder off is a canny move. I turn it back on. Why didn't he say all that at the time? People would have been more sympathetic. 'Yeah, but Henry is four-years-old now. At some point, when he is old enough to understand, I will have to sit down with him and explain all this. I don't want him to have to read about the specifics in the press first. I love him. It would have been a lot easier for me if I'd gone to the papers and told them what I have just told you. People would have sat back and thought, "Oh well, that's different." And I have all the proof. Ali's story is that we were having a perfect relationship and I suddenly got up and went. My story is different. You've heard it now: which has the ring of truth? Who ever leaves a perfect relationship? You don't just decide, "Oh I'm bored now. I don't care. I'm off." I can't be quoted on the details of this because Henry's feelings are the most important thing. Not mine. Not Ali's. Not those of the press.'

Given that we did only hear one side of the story, though, does he understand why we were so shocked by it? 'Yes, absolutely, and it was being stoked by people close to me. I can understand why it made a great story. Maybe you can now understand why I found it incredibly painful to watch it being played out. How come if I really don't care about Henry . . . how come I have spent the past three years fighting to see him?' He has access? 'Yes, I do, but only because I went to the High Court.'

Ali now lives with David Ross, the multi-millionaire co-founder of the Carphone Warehouse. Do Will Carling and Ali still speak? 'Not a lot. She's a very unhappy lady. It's a very sad situation.'

Carling's mouth is bracketed by grooves so deep they make his face look like a ventriloquist's dummy's. They also make him look drawn and doleful. Has he come close to a nervous breakdown? 'I don't know. I did get very, very depressed. Very down. But I have some close friends. And whenever people came up to me in the street they were sympathetic. If they had spat in my face and said, "God, you're a disgrace," I would have been devastated, and I probably wouldn't have kept my head above water. As it was it got very close. I felt I was the worst person in the country. That's how I felt. My self-esteem plummeted. I don't think it will ever recover.'

He has seen a psychotherapist, Alyce Faye Eichelberger, John Cleese's wife: did it help? 'Yes. It helped a bit. It helped me see that I had made a choice and I had to live with it. You said to me earlier that maybe we aren't meant to be happy. That sometimes we have to make sacrifices. Well, possibly. But. I don't know. I'm happy now.'

Did he consider leaving the country to go and live, say, in South Africa or Australia, rugby-loving countries where he might have felt more appreciated, less of a pariah? He props his head up on one hand. 'To do what? I wouldn't be able to see Henry. I couldn't just leave him.'

Is Will Carling a moral man? 'Apparently not.' But what does he think? Pause. Tight smile. 'I have the same weaknesses as everyone else. But I think I have certain standards, too. When most people think of morality it is in terms of marrying one person and staying married. Never committing adultery. Well, I can't claim that that applies to me. I've been married twice and have had another relationship that has broken down. But, even so, I don't think I'm the great womanizer I'm portrayed as being. I've challenged the tabloids to find women I slept with on tour. It didn't happen.'

Hang on, was that an admission of adultery? His 1994 marriage to Julia Carling, née Smith, broke down after she gave him ultimatums that he must end his close friendship with the Princess of Wales. The idea of a captain of England having an affair with a future Queen of England proved irresistible to the press. Were they? Weren't they? Speculation became so intense Carling went into hiding in a flat in Covent Garden. He couldn't even take a taxi to his door for fear of being followed, and only two people, male friends, were allowed to know his phone number. He has said in the past that he loved the Princess as a friend. He has also said that even if he had had a sexual relationship with her, he would never have dreamed of telling anyone. He has never confirmed that he did – equally, though, he has never really denied it. Are we to assume from this that he did have sexual relations with the Princess? 'Ach!' he says, shaking his head peevishly and folding his arms. 'I've been over this so many times and I've said, you know . . . People want to keep bringing it up. Time after time. How many times do I have to say it? She was just a good friend.'

So that *is* a denial? 'Absolutely! I don't know why people think I haven't denied it. It's like, "For goodness sake. She – was – just – a – good – friend." I felt privileged to know her. She was good fun. End of story.'

James Hewitt once told me in an interview that, before her infamous *Panorama* appearance, the Princess struck a deal with Martin Bashir: he was allowed to ask about Hewitt on condition that he would not ask about Carling, because she was negotiating her divorce settlement at the time. Does that surprise Carling? 'That's what Hewitt thinks, is it? Well, I don't think James Hewitt is in a position to make theories about anyone. I have no idea about any such deal.'

At the time of their divorce, Julia Carling said of Diana, Princess of Wales, 'It would be easy to say she's ruined my marriage. But it takes two to tango, and I blame Will for getting involved in the first place.' Why would she say this? 'Yeah, but I don't think Julia was in a great frame of mind at the time. If she did insinuate anything, she was out of order. I think Julia got a bit carried away about trying to have a go at the Princess. It wasn't on. I understand she was unhappy but that wasn't great.

Not great. Anyway, this whole subject is dangerous ground because the Princess is no longer around to put her side of the case. We should be more respectful.'

Quite so. As Carling would say, it's out of order. In 1988, after his first game as captain, when England beat Australia 28-19, Carling walked back to the changing rooms and burst into tears of relief. He cried again, this time into his socks, apparently, after England lost to France in the World Cup in 1995. In touch with his emotions then? 'Very. I weep easily, just not in public. When Jonah Lomu was doing *This Is Your Life* his little sister, six-years-old, came on and said, "I love you, Jonah," and I cried then. I cried when I watched *Gladiator*, too, that bit where the servant brings him back the miniature statues of his dead wife and son.' He smiles the one-sided smile. 'Doesn't quite fit the image, though, does it? As I say, just not ... Not in front of people. It dates back to school.'

When, at the age of seven, Carling was sent to board at Terra Nova, a prep school in Cheshire, he would crawl under the blankets at night to cry. He soon settled in, though, and even admits he became a bit of a bully. 'When I first went there I knew I wouldn't see my parents for three months. But my parents had no choice because, being an Army family, we moved house practically every year. I would never contemplate sending a child to boarding school at seven. It was hard. But I think people do use it as an excuse later in life.' (Perhaps his therapist has suggested his behaviour in recent years points to a fear of being alone – one which often springs from childhood experiences of being abandoned, or living with the prospect of abandonment. Just a thought.)

Carling's talents on the rugby field were spotted when, at thirteen, he went on to Sedbergh, a very rugby-minded public school on the edge of the Lake District. He was made to play for the year above his, which made him unpopular with his contemporaries. 'I hated it. Hated it. I was terrified. Every game I was like, "Oh God."' He, nevertheless, became captain of the First XV and carried on playing at Durham University, where he went on an Army scholarship and from which he graduated with a pass. 'My degree was a joke. No one ever got below 2:2 in the Psychology Department and I didn't even get a third. I think

they are still debating whether I should have had a degree at all.'
While at Durham he joined Harlequins, and was selected to play
for England. He was due to follow his father into the Army, as
an officer in the Royal Regiment of Wales, but bought himself
out for £8,000 when the Army's demands clashed with his
England training schedule. Those still being the days of
amateurism, he had to make a living, so he founded Insight, a
company offering business leaders advice on motivation (the
company later ran into financial difficulties). The seeds of his
conflicts of interest with English rugby were sown.

His father, Bill, a lieutenant-colonel in the Army Air Corps
who had played rugby for Bath, was something of a martinet.
'He is quite military. I remember when I was thirteen, Dad told
my brother Marcus and me, "If you ever get into trouble with
bullies, find out who the leader is and hit him as hard as you can
in the face."' In a sense, this advice stood him in good stead on
the international rugby field, where his courage in taking on big
brutal forwards with misshapen faces was legendary. But, he says
disingenuously, he cannot understand why people still assume
he must also be a hard man away from the rugby pitch. 'They
say, "Obviously I wouldn't have a go at you, Will," and I just
look at them and think, "Why?"'

He never shied from confrontation off the field, though,
especially where RFU committee men were concerned – he once
grabbed a senior administrator by the throat, and had to be
restrained by Rob Andrew. He has had epic spats with, among
others, the England manager Jack Rowell, the Lions manager
Fran Cotton and even his mentor, the former Harlequins coach
Dick Best. His career at the club ended in acrimony when Carling
led moves to replace Best with Andy Keast, whom he also then
fell out with. In recent weeks he has been accused of leading a
conspiracy to oust Clive Woodward, the current England
manager. He doesn't see it this way, but, still, poisonous atmos-
pheres do seem to follow him around. Wasn't he always the
common denominator in these disputes? 'For sure. I am very
difficult. I've never denied it. That's what you had to be to make
England successful. That was my strength and my weakness. I'm
not a politician and I'm not a diplomat. I was twenty-two with a
burning ambition. I was a bull in a china shop.'

Temperamentally, Carling reminds me of Geoffrey Boycott, of whom Dr Anthony Clare once said, 'I thought no man was an island, until I met Geoffrey Boycott.' Boycott never cultivated friends within his sport, indeed he seemed to go out of his way to make enemies. Like Boycott, Carling always blames everyone else. A close acquaintance of his suggests to me that Carling has a ruthless, almost delusional capacity for reinventing the past. Perversely, though, the main lesson he seems to have drawn from his therapy sessions was that he spends too much time trying to please other people, and not enough on his own happiness. He discovered that, deep down, he always felt guilty for everything. Or so he says: contradictorily, he also realized that he had developed a system whereby he would stop speaking to friends if they notched up a certain number of black marks in his book – unpunctuality, his pet hate, presumably being an example. This was the way his mother, Pam, had behaved with him. She rarely explained why she was angry or upset.

Though this self-analysis – helped by professional analysis – doesn't deal with the possible contributions of what some might regard as his selfishness, immaturity and self-pity, it does bear out his claim that he is more sensitive than people assume him to be. He contemplates daily his own mortality, for example. 'There are books of philosophy all over the house. I'm fascinated at the moment with religion, especially Buddhism. How you enjoy life. If you can wake up every morning and accept that one day you will die, that gives you strength and energy and you enjoy your life more. I remind myself every day. It sounds morbid but it's the reverse.' Carling squares his shoulders. 'I was brought up Church of England but now I find myself asking how can you have a forgiving God who damns you for eternity in hell if you do anything wrong? How loving is that?'

How indeed. The labrador has gone to sleep in front of the fire, and, upstairs, Jack has awoken. Will goes out and returns grinning a minute later, with Jack in his arms. 'He hasn't got my chin,' he says. 'But he has got my distended belly. I bought him his first shoes the other day, and he was so excited about them. He just kept walking up and down the kitchen. It was a lovely sight.'

Tim Rice

It's all that Andrew Lloyd Webber's fault. If it hadn't been for his soppy influence, Sir Tim Rice could have been a serious rock 'n' roller: helping Keith Moon throw television sets out of hotel windows; hanging out with John and Yoko as they lived off a diet of champagne, caviare and heroin; and generally having some phreaked-out phun with the children of the revolution. But, oh no. What was Tim Rice doing in 1968 instead? Touring provincial schools with *Joseph and the Amazing Technicolour Dreamcoat*, that's what.

These aren't Sir Tim's exact words but, as we sit sipping coffee on a drizzly Sunday morning in his Thameside house in Barnes, you can tell that's what he's thinking. Suddenly feeling rather sorry for him, I suggest that Joseph was a *little* bit trippy, what with all that psychedelic dreamcoat stuff.

'Not really,' he says, in his mild, buttery soft voice. 'The lyrics were more influenced by fifties semi-cabaret numbers like "Mud, mud, glorious mud."' Then, regretting the admission, he adds: 'Oh, I suppose we were vaguely influenced by all that sixties stuff. I mean, I was really a rocker at heart.'

There. He's said it. He may be fifty-two, the thinning hair brushed over his ears and forward over his brow may have silvered, and he may be wearing a blue pully, comfortable shoes and pressed jeans that ride up to expose pale grey socks when he sits down. But in his daydreams, Timothy Miles Blindon Rice is still twenty-two, his hair is shoulder length and he is wearing leathers.

In fact, he thinks that if he hadn't met Lloyd Webber in 1965 he might have become a rock star. 'I did sing with one or two

269

bands,' he says. It's true. Whang and the Cheviots, for one. But they disbanded because none of the members could agree on who was supposed to be Whang. Not that one feels they'd have got too far in the Age of Aquarius – one musician at a *Superstar* recording session was chided by Rice with the words, 'Oh, good heavens! You're not stoned again?'

But the point is taken: Rice was in the right place at the right time. EMI records. As a management trainee. 'In one sense,' he recalls, 'I was at the centre of what was going on. The whole of EMI revolved around the next Beatles single. Even a junior employee like me got to hear the acetate of *Sgt Pepper* a week before the common herd got it!'

Then again, if he hadn't met Lloyd Webber, he wouldn't be celebrating the twenty-fifth anniversary production of *Jesus Christ Superstar*, which opens soon at London's newly restored Lyceum Theatre. '*Superstar* holds up wonderfully,' Rice says. 'But almost every work of art is about one thing – getting old. Everyone over the age of forty is aware of time rushing by. At least one has the consolation of knowing one made it.'

In material terms, Rice has certainly done that. The three musicals he wrote with Lloyd Webber – *Joseph, Superstar* and *Evita*, as hep cats everywhere shorten their titles – have made him rich beyond the dreams of avarice. The *Superstar* album alone sold a staggering six million copies. 'I get so many Americans come up to me now and say "Gee, when I was at school *Superstar* was the record we played all that year." In its way, it was just as big as *Sgt Pepper*.' And, as if all those royalties weren't enough to retire on, Rice co-wrote *Chess*, co-founded Pavilion Books, wrote the *Guinness Book of Hit Singles*, carried off two Oscars for songs in the Disney movies *Aladdin* and *The Lion King*, and – may the Lord have mercy on his soul – has now written the lyrics for Cliff Richard's *Heathcliff*.

His genius for satisfying the demands of popular but middle-of-the-road culture have made him very comfortable indeed. In fact, as one looks around the conservatory in which we are sitting, the words 'cosy' and 'comfortable' keep popping back unbidden to mind. Hanging from the ceiling are cuddly toy parakeets. On one wall, there are pen and ink drawings of Victorian cricketers. On another is a glass cabinet containing nine international caps, signed by nine international cricket captains.

We are even on a comfortable sofa. And though Rice occasionally clasps his hands together on his lap, and though he rarely makes contact with his pale blue eyes, preferring instead to address his comments to a large, comfortably cuddly toy lion sitting on a chair opposite him, for the most part he looks pretty comfortable with himself, sinking languidly into the cushions, and stretching his arms out along the back of the sofa.

But making it in material terms is not the same as making it spiritually – ask any true child of the sixties. Rice once, for instance, shrugged off the failure of *Blondel*, a medieval extravaganza for which he wrote the lyrics, with the comment: 'It's only rock 'n' roll, after all' – only then to blow it by un-hippily adding, 'And it doesn't really matter a hoot.' But it was the 'It's only rock 'n' roll' line, from the Rolling Stones song, that was significant. Much as he wanted it to be, his work has never been 'only rock 'n' roll', as well he knows. It was 'only a musical'. And, as he himself once confessed: 'The trouble is, I'm not really the sort of bloke who likes musicals that much.'

We start talking about The Rolling Stones' *Rock and Roll Circus*, a film made in 1968 but not released until now. Rice has just seen it – 'So many people at the height of their fame, success and beauty,' he sighs. Not, alas, including Rice. Nor was he present when, soon afterwards, guests at Mick Jagger's birthday party drank from huge silver bowls of Methodine-spiked punch and nibbled at hash brownies. Such sixties hedonism passed Rice by. 'I was fairly straight, I guess. I don't remember anything wildly outrageous. I had my odd little moments, I suppose, but nothing much. I would have a few drinks and would live a wild existence in some ways. But the sixties were four guys somewhere having a great time and everyone else running around trying to find them.' Everyone else, presumably, including him and Lloyd Webber, who at the time favoured tunics buttoned up to the collar, trousers tucked into knee-length leather boots and a Louise Brooks bob.

Part of the reason Rice makes such an unconvincing rocker is, of course, that he is simply too nice, too decent, too gentlemanly. With his lanky, ambling walk, his boyish looks and his amiable, diffident air, he will always be the well-mannered but over-enthusiastic public school boy playing air guitar at the disco. He will say, 'That twerp [the photographer] turned up fifteen minutes early this morning – before I'd had a chance to go for some milk.' Then, feeling guilty, he will spoil his stab at prima donna-ishness by saying: 'Actually, he was a rather nice bloke.' It is this trait, too, that ruins Sir Tim's efforts to be cynical; because he is always afraid of hurting someone's feelings, he qualifies every comment he makes. When he talks about his inability to say no, for instance, he says: 'It's definitely a problem. I find I've agreed to have lunch in the West End knowing it will wreck the entire day, that it'll be a waste of time and that I won't really enjoy it. Having said that, I do like, you know, there's nothing I like more than a, sort of, good meal. Some wine and a good time out with good pals, but, um, um, there's always a danger of agreeing to everything.' Again, when talking about relationships: 'I quite like being on my own. But there are times when I don't like being on my own.' Everyone happy?

The same confused wholesomeness applies to his weird and wonderfully complicated love life. On the glass coffee table in front of us, nestled between copies of *Variety* and *Mojo*, is this morning's *Sunday Times Magazine*. On its cover, looking like a drag queen, is a photo of Elaine Paige, Rice's lover for eleven years. His wife Jane 'sort of' divorced him in 1990 after sixteen years because the marriage was 'full of question marks and very strange'. Yet Rice still goes on holiday with Jane and their two children. And, though he split up with Paige shortly after he divorced his wife, he still sees her. 'Had dinner with her last week, funnily enough', he says blithely. He adds that he is now in a 'very relaxed sort of situation' with another woman.

Also on the table is another colour magazine, containing a lurid – if disputed – account of another public figure's love life. 'I wish someone would make up some interesting stories like that about me,' chuckles Rice. 'It would give me some street cred.'

Along with the status of a true rock 'n' roller, street cred is something that has always eluded Rice, in part because he still uses such expressions as street cred. His is a nerd's vocabulary. He uses the sort of expressions fathers use to embarrass their children. 'I'm a chart freak,' he says at one point. 'I quite like this Kula Shaker lot.' He describes something else as being 'all over the shop' and, elsewhere, talks of 'numero uno' and 'all that jazz'.

For all his obvious warmth and charm, it is possible to see why Rice rubs some people up the wrong way. Craig Brown, for instance, has dubbed him Tim Rice-But-Dim. 'He's the luckiest man alive, after Ringo,' Brown says. 'I mean, for a man with such modest talents to be given an Oscar . . . I suppose he hasn't actually killed anyone. It's just his professional niceness that gets me.'

When I ask Rice if such criticism annoys him, he says: 'Yeah, suppose so. Well, yes and no. I mean Craig Brown has had a go at me from day one. Not quite sure why. He obviously thinks I'm crap. Which is fair enough. I think he's one of the greatest writers this country has ever produced.'

Ooh. Controversial. 'Whenever anyone says anything bad about you, you always say, "I'll get him,"' Rice adds with promising menace. 'But then you forget. You see someone like Craig Brown and think, "Was he the one who was rude about me or was he the one who thought I was great?" It's a bit difficult because you don't know whether to go up to him and be friendly or hit him.'

But his niceness is not, as he implies, simply a matter of being absent-minded. An hour or so after the subject of Craig Brown has come up, Rice is still smarting from it. '*Superstar* will be around for a few years to come. The only one-up I have on the brilliant Craig Brown is that I've written a few pieces that will be around for a long while.'

So there are chinks in the armour of Sir Tim's niceness. He hates people poking fun at his lyrics. And his relationship with Lloyd Webber has not been entirely smooth, either. Indeed, there has been much speculation about their respective professional and emotional jealousies. When I ask Rice if his dealings with Lloyd Webber are more harmonious now, he chuckles and says that they had dinner together in New York only the other day. (Elaine one night, Andrew the next. The napkins of peace were being puffed pretty hard in the Big Apple.) But he adds: 'The only thing that pisses me off is when people keep saying Andrew Lloyd Webber's *Evita*. In the musicals he did after we broke up, no one knows who did the words. They all get billed as Andrew Lloyd Webber's *Sunset Boulevard,* or whatever. And that's what's happened with *Evita*. The guys who wrote it should have equal credit. Even Madonna seems to think Andrew wrote the plot to *Evita*. Actually it was my idea and it took me a year to persuade him to do it.' (Incidentally, Rice says he would have given the film role to Elaine Paige. But then, in a rush of niceness, he adds: 'But I can see equally good reasons why Madonna should have been given the part. And I'm delighted for her'.)

He gives me another example of how the craving for equal billing haunts him. He was once on a Concorde which juddered for fifteen seconds and then let out a big bang. 'Bryan Adams, the rock star, was on the plane and I remember thinking seriously for about twenty seconds that this was it: if this plane goes down, it will be BRYAN ADAMS DIES IN CONCORDE CRASH and I'll just get mentioned in *Wisden Cricket Monthly*. I would have been the Richie Valens of the Buddy Holly plane crash'.

This is Rice at his most self-deprecating, humorous best. But it also displays an insecurity that probably explains why he never misses a chance to point out that lyric writing is an art form on a par with writing music. 'Writing music is a talent,' he says, 'but it's not a time-consuming talent. That's why Mozart produced so much stuff. He could just do it. Writing with words is a much slower job. And it takes a long time.'

Like the other virtuoso of non time-consuming talent, Andrew Lloyd Webber, Rice was given his knighthood for services to the arts. At the time, this prompted the *Guardian* journalist Francis Wheen to ask if a peerage for Pam Ayres could be far behind. But most people suspect he was knighted because he is pally with John Major. After all, referring to his campaigning work in the 1992 election, Rice did call himself the Jeremy Irons of the Conservative Party. 'I didn't really get the knighthood for my lyric writing,' he now says. 'It was more for my involvement in sport.' Neverthelesss, Wheen's slight has stuck. In the public imagination, Tim Rice earned millions, and was given a knighthood, simply for rhyming district with biscuit in *Joseph*. Rice believes that people who say this do so because they are jealous (and he's right, of course, in my case anyway). If it's so easy, he has been known to ask, why don't you try?

On the way over to his house, I had done just that. 'Tell me what you think,' I say, and offer this: Tim Rice / quintessential Englishman / Is John Major your biggest fan?

'Well, it rhymes,' he says with a smile. 'But it would depend on the music. A lot of my stuff has been written to music, you know. So you have to be concise, saying a thought in twelve syllables. No more, no less. And the danger of writing lyrics on their own, and I do enjoy that, and it's very nice to do it that way round, with Elton [John] in particular, the danger is that you do become too long-winded. Because you've got nothing to stop you and you think, "Well, I want to get this point over and I can't say it in eight words so I'll say it in eighteen." And then it might become long-winded. So that's the danger you have to watch. I usually set myself, if I'm writing words without a tune, I usually set myself a little, um, pattern for the first four lines and of course then you have to repeat it.'

Quite. I try again. Tim Rice / Superstar / Do you think you're what they say you are?

'What do they say I am?'

Mr Nice Guy.

'Incredibly accurate, that is.'

But is there a dark side?

'Well, obviously, everybody, obviously, there are many things I do that I'm not too, that I wouldn't advertize. I mean, I don't go round molesting goats or anything. But yes, I mean, er, I think I'm quite laid back in my approach to most things.'

Is that because he is six foot four? You know, the gentle giant never having to worry about being beaten up in the playground as a child? 'Yes, I'm sure that's right,' he smiles, his face wrinkling up like a labrador puppy's. 'But I was never into fights anyway. Doesn't apply to everyone who's tall, of course. I mean Robert Maxwell was very tall and he wasn't very laid back. And my brothers. I probably don't need to go around thinking, "Gosh, I'm tall." Ha ha ha. It allows one to assert oneself.'

Part of his Mr Nice Guy image, of course, comes from his obsession with cricket: the fancy blazers, the committee membership of the MCC, the Heartaches XI, the team he founded in 1973 and which he is still captain of today. I ask him how he would convince an alien that the game of cricket wasn't boring. His answer is too long-winded and, yes, all over the shop to repeat in full, but the overall thrust of it was that cricket is like an art gallery rather than a movie, I think. For this is what Sir Tim's discourse is like. You find yourself adrift in it, floating on a seat of cotton wool, deprived of all sense of time and space. I try to steer it back on course by asking Rice if he would rather have been Keith Richards or David Gower. 'Well, both those characters are fascinating. It would've been great to have been either. They're both marvellous.'

From which life would he have got more satisfaction, then? 'Very interesting question. Very interesting question, indeed. But I think possibly David Gower, because I can't contemplate being good enough to do what he did. Of course, I can barely play guitar but I can contemplate a situation where if things had gone differently, I might have become a figure in the rock world. The thought of being Keith Richards is not quite so ludicrous as being David Gower.'

He's on to something. Indeed, Keith Richards, who was once described as the world's most elegantly wasted human being, has, in a curious way, become more like Tim Rice over the years. It is as if their lives have been lived in parallel. Jekyll and Hyde. Rice and Richards. Both men, after all, are fantastically wealthy. Both men have had rich and varied love lives. Both have songwriting partners who've attracted all the glory. Both have had complete blood changes – or perhaps not.

But both, certainly, are appallingly lucky. Rice once nipped off an express at Newcastle for a sandwich, and the train left without him. He then picked up £200 at a betting shop on 18-1 winner Gay Traveller and used the cash to hire a car for the rest of his trip to Edinburgh. During the war, Keith Richards was evacuated from his home in London, two hours before it was hit by a Doodlebug. Could it be that some alien force is guiding their lives? After all, Rice is a passionate stargazer. He has even built an observatory at his secluded Edwardian house in Cornwall. 'I would think,' he says, 'almost certainly there is life somewhere else in the universe. Almost certainly. Equally, the odds on them arriving here are tiny. That said, aliens could well have landed on the earth millions of years ago, not found any life forms and sodded off back to Betelgeuse.'

See that? Notice how specific he was? Betelgeuse. It all makes sense now. Don't be taken in by his 'brought up in Hertfordshire, father worked for Hawker Siddeley company' line. Tim Rice came from Betelgeuse. Consider the evidence. When someone once called him 'Rock Brain of the Universe' he said, 'I'm not sure I deserve this title – there was nobody from another planet in the final.' And what about that song, 'A Whole New World'? What else can explain Sir Tim's supernatural powers?

You think I exaggerate? Well, just before I left his house, he played me a song he wrote which he thinks 'is rather nice' but which, he says, no one will ever hear because it never made it into a show. It's called 'Ziggy' and it's about a girl who is in love with a boy who is gay. It goes like this: 'Ziggy / I call him Ziggy / I'm so hot for him / He's not like all the rest but there's no doubt he's the best / Ziggy / I call him Ziggy / I'm so hot for him / When I saw him that day I gave myself away / Ziggy / My crazy Ziggy / He lives a life that I don't share / I don't know why but I'm not there . . .' You get the picture.

As he was playing it, I didn't know where to look. At the end, there was a silence. What could I say? 'I've never heard anything quite like it', maybe. Yet, in the car on the way home, there I was singing along to this inane lyric: 'Ziggy / My crazy Ziggy.' And now I can't get it out of my head.

This is a dangerous man. Like a cult leader, he plays with people's minds – he sucks out their brains, steals their souls and leaves them with a goofy, joyful smile on their faces. So don't be taken in by his onslaught of bonhomie, by his pose of the amateur who never has to try too hard. Don't be seduced by his breezy English charm and innocence. Those mawkish, drippy lyrics he writes are a travesty of nature. This is a man who abetted the celibate Cliff Richard in his absurd fantasy that if he put on some designer stubble and a long black wig, he could transform himself into that smouldering Gothic sexual inferno, Heathcliff. Only Rice could have made Heathcliff sing: 'Oh Cathy – the game you played / Oh Cathy – you've paid / I've been betrayed.'

You need only look at the queues of middle-aged women trying to get hold of *Heathcliff* tickets to see that I am right. Look at their vacant eyes. Observe their slow, zombie-like movements. All has become clear. Rice didn't need to experiment with LSD in the sixties because he knew what he was taking, and peddling, was far more potent: he was on musicals, the opiate of the masses.

Today, he has given us a sanitized *Heathcliff*. But do you think he'll stop there? Of course not. Next year, he is doing a musical about King David and, in another collaboration with Elton John, *Aida*. And after that? Can *Keith Richards – the Musical* be far behind?

Oh, the horror! The horror! Pass the Methedrine-spiked punch.

David Starkey

The dumb waiters either side of the pink marble fireplace speak eloquently of the man Dr David Starkey believes himself to be. So do the fresh carnations, the dainty silver spoons arranged on a side table, and the mildewed pages of Shakespeare left lying open near the antique magnifying glass. Here, they say, is an aesthete, a history don, a dandy, even, who can afford to surround himself with 1830s opulence.

In vain does the eye search this drawing room in Highbury, north London, for a hint of Starkey's northern, working-class roots – for a grainy, sepia photograph, perhaps, that will show the lonely lad clumping down a cobbled street in baggy shorts, flat cap and the callipers he had to wear to correct his club feet. And this absence of pathos is surprising, for the 52-year-old Starkey generally likes you to know how tough he had it as a child. 'The early years,' he reflects, 'are when we become what we are.' So, we must conclude, it is the early years which explain why Starkey was dubbed 'the rudest man in Britain' by the *Daily Mail*. And it is the early years which allow him to get away with being the intellectual bully who, at five past nine on Thursday morning – when *The Moral Maze* returns to Radio 4 – will electrify us with his wit and poison us with his venom.

Today, though, the monster is purring, his claws are withdrawn. This, you suspect, is the real David Starkey: friendly, incorrigible, a good laugh. Like the oak-framed French Charles X chair which he sits upon, his robust nature is disguised by a delicate appearance: neatly pressed cords, a lamb's-wool cardigan and knotted silk cuff links. Perched on his retroussé nose are tortoiseshell Armani glasses that match the cornelian intaglio ring on his finger. His backcombed hair is silver, his hands are small and, when offered in greeting, warm to the touch. Starkey's polished brown leather shoes are small, too, and, when he is concentrating, he crosses his legs and points one of them at you, like a terrier pointing a cocked foreleg as it picks up a scent.

It is inadvisable to mention size in Starkey's company. When the *Daily Mail* columnist Paul Johnson did this – addressing Starkey as 'little man' twice in the same show – Starkey went into flame-thrower mode: 'The only things I have that are smaller than yours,' he hissed, 'are my liver and my nose.'

But he doesn't really mind being called a monster. Indeed, when he is, he emits a wheezy, almost dirty chuckle. 'Monster? Well, I'm very well aware that all the combative head-butting exhibitionism could be construed in that way. But I just see it as a role I play on the programme. Michael Buerk [the chairman] is the long-suffering parent and I am the naughty juvenile lead. Obviously, I'm a licensed fool, but I don't think I go over the top. I've never been sued for libel, I suppose because most of what I say is true!'

This is a cue for him to remind us of his greatest hits: the time he infuriated Dame Jill Knight, a witness on *The Moral Maze*, by asking her how 'ladies in hats' like her are now the central defendants of the Christian tradition; and the occasion he said of the Archdeacon of York, another witness, 'Doesn't he genuinely make you want to vomit? His fatness, his smugness, his absurdity.' He recalls these moments with obvious relish, over-enunciating every word but talking with the haste of the insecure person who fears his audience will walk away if given the chance by a pause for breath.

It's a memorable voice: managing somehow to be clipped and rolling at the same time. Starkey describes it as being that of a 'high duchess' and says he picked it up from listening to the Home Service. Before learning to lengthen his vowels, he adds, he sounded 'as camp as custard', his accent stranded somewhere between the flat, soft Lancashire vowels of Oldham, where his parents came from, and the coarse, almost Scandinavian northern English of Kendal, where they moved in the late thirties. Even now, there are some words (like 'one' pronounced 'wun') which, he says, always betray him. The speed and pitch of Starkey's delivery also has a lot to do with the state of excitement he works himself into when engaging in debate. On *The Moral Maze* he has been known to jump up and down in his seat in anticipation of his turn to speak. And, when his turn does come, the programme's ringmaster has to use the words 'David! Please! Shut up!' on him, like a whipcrack.

This excitement – the terrier bristling at the scent – is one of several incongruities in Starkey's psychological make-up. He prides himself on his unsentimental rationalism yet always seems to be at the mercy of his emotions. Though easily bored he is a creature of habit who reads the same paper every day and never varies what he has for breakfast. Though not superstitious, he is obsessive about locking his house, always having to go back to check. Starkey sees no contradiction in being an emotional rationalist. 'Most academics don't have enough passion,' he says with a clap of his hands. 'That's their trouble. Their desiccation chills the blood.'

Yet the frequency with which Starkey slips into a display of histrionics leads some to suspect that it is all a con trick: that he is a man who can feel completely indifferent about a subject yet still argue its case lucidly and with apparent conviction, simply because he enjoys the intellectual challenge. 'Of course, there is an element of that,' Starkey admits. 'I mean, before the programme, Michael will ring up and ask me what my view is, and if I say, "I don't really have one," he will say, "Well, could you sort of go from there?" But I often don't realize quite how strongly I feel about an issue until we start discussing it.'

Unlike the other panellists, Starkey doesn't read his opening remarks from a script. Nor does he do much preparation for the programme, preferring instead to sit in the bath and empty his head by humming an inane tune. This, he says, is what enables him to react spontaneously. Sometimes even he is surprised by his reactions. He recalls a programme in which a doctor was talking in a coldly abstract way about euthanasia. 'I found myself shaking with anger because I suddenly realized that the medical profession was prepared to commit an act of monstrous, medieval cruelty – to parch and starve a man to death rather than give him a merciful shot of poison – just to preserve its clean conscience. People like that who use the word "principle" all the time are dangerous.'

Starkey is a right-wing, homosexual libertarian. 'Having to come out as a Tory', he laughs, 'was almost more embarrassing than coming out as gay.' As such, he believes that economic and personal freedom are sacrosanct. As an atheist, he believes there can be no moral absolutes. 'All our assumptions about human behaviour have changed beyond recognition within living memory,' he says. 'The world I knew as a boy with all its certainties has been thrown away, but people like George Carey just can't see this.'

Starkey has another belief – one he shares with Dr Johnson – that the purpose of talking is to win. In order to achieve victory, Starkey has no qualms about attacking his opponent personally, preferably by focusing on their physical absurdity, as a way of attacking that person's ideas. By turning your opponent into a symbol of absurdity, Starkey believes, you undermine the credibility of his argument. Another technique Starkey uses is auto-suggestion: he will bamboozle you into thinking you agree with him by constantly summarizing your arguments for you. 'Your point surely is this . . .' he will say. Or, 'I thought we were talking here about . . .' Or, his favourite, 'But really, all we are saying – are we not? – is . . .'

Sir Geoffrey Elton, Starkey's history tutor and mentor at Cambridge, once accused his former star pupil of inventing history. And although, to put the comment in context, this was said while the two men were having a feud in which each ridiculed the other's methodology, it does, if true, reveal another side to Starkey's competitive nature. If winning – being proved right – means twisting facts to fit theories, then so be it. Starkey, of course, would call this being imaginative in the way you interpret historical data. Wherever the emphasis should lie, you do get the impression that Starkey sometimes uses logic like a conjurer uses a prop: to distract your attention away from what he is really doing with the other hand. If you concentrate hard, though, you can almost see how this trick – getting you to agree with him – works.

Starkey's specialist subject, for instance, is Henry VIII: he has written two books on him and has another two coming out this year. Because the state and the church of Henry's day would be unrecognizable to us, Starkey argues, we cannot judge Henry's behaviour by our standards. What we can do, however, is understand how the young, idealistic, handsome Henry became the grotesque monster of legend by examining the close relationship he had with his mother and the effect divorce had on his family – two very Freudian, and therefore very twentieth-century perspectives. What we can also do is empathize with Henry. Empathy, after all, is what allows the atheist to understand the Christian, and the homosexual to understand the heterosexual. Starkey believes that all men secretly want to be like Henry, that all men want to have the same power and the same disregard for marriage vows. Yet ask Starkey if he would have liked to have been Henry and he says, 'Well, there, you see, I'm not heterosexual, so it doesn't apply to me.' When he realizes what he's said, he laughs that wicked laugh and adds: 'Empathy can be deployed with utter ruthlessness. The ruthlessness of self-contradiction!'

Ruthless? Perhaps Starkey does want to be Henry VIII, after all. More likely though, he wants to be Samuel Johnson. There are a number of similarities. Like Dr Johnson, Starkey believes that to treat your adversary with respect is to give him an advantage to which he is not entitled. Like Johnson, he prefers pontification to conversation. Like Johnson, he is a celebrated wit and shameless self-publicist. Can he see the resemblance? 'Oh, don't be silly, though it's very sweet of you to suggest it. I'm not fat enough, not smelly enough, not sexually tormented enough, not financially unsuccessful enough. The one thing we do have in common, I suppose, is that we are not nice.'

There is another likeness: Starkey's intellectual arrogance knows no bounds. He says, for instance, that when he went up to Cambridge, on a scholarship, he soon realized that he was 'much cleverer than all those people from privileged backgrounds'. And indeed he probably was: gaining a First, then a doctorate, then a fellowship from Fitzwilliam College before taking up a lectureship in history at the London School of Economics. Even to this day, Starkey can't think of anyone who intimidates him intellectually.

Within walking distance of the house there is a cosy restaurant where the waitress is a friend of David Starkey's and where

Rod Stewart plays in the background. In between forkfuls of roast cod, Starkey talks about his parents' 'respectful poverty'. His father, whom he still calls at ten o'clock every morning, was a skilled labourer on a breadline wage. His mother, now dead, was a puritanical authority figure who, he says, made Mrs Thatcher look like a primary school mistress. She took his coming out very badly – it was 1972 and Starkey was a research student at the time – and he now believes it would have been kinder not to tell her, not least because he said some unpleasant things that were never really taken back before she died. 'She was a female Pygmalion,' he says. 'She would always get cross when the creation didn't do exactly what the creator wanted.' He adds that, far from being proud of her son's fame, or infamy, she would have been annoyed by it. The only programmes she saw him appear in were a series of television debates he did in the seventies with Russell Harty, and these she thought 'utterly beneath contempt'.

Perhaps the memory of his mother's contempt is the only thing that prevents Starkey's intellectual superiority complex from translating into condescension on the Sunday morning phone-in programme he hosts on Talk Radio. Although he once referred to the show as 'the cliché-laden conversational equivalent of the typical prizes you will find in a real lucky dip: the cheap plastic toys, the fluorescent earrings, the badly plated nail-clippers', he says he never talks down to his callers and always appreciates the raw slabs of experience they offer. 'Sometimes, though, I get deeply bored. I sit there thinking why I am doing this? One knows why, of course, it's the cheque at the end of the show.'

But money is not the only motive. Although Starkey has been with the same partner for four years, he used to be what he describes as 'naturally promiscuous'. He now channels this promiscuity into his career, working as a constitutional expert for, seemingly, every national newspaper and every national TV and radio station.

Another motive is his craving for publicity, a condition which, he says, gives him an intuitive understanding of the Princess of Wales' personality. It is, he says, precisely her isolation and inner emptiness that makes her such an adept media manipulator. Asked if he feels any affinity with the Princess, Starkey tucks his hands behind his head, as if about to do a sit-up, and says, 'The attention-seeking of a Dr Johnson is different from the posturing of a Casanova.' His legs are not comparable with the Princess's, he adds, but he believes they are both in the fight for the ever-changing spotlight.

When asked what the nature of the inner emptiness is in his own case, Starkey talks of the loneliness of the only child, of being significantly disabled ('though it's all corrected now') and of the discovery that public performance is a way you can dominate others and impose yourself. He doesn't think it has anything to do with not having children, though. On the contrary, he says, he satisfies the desire to shape a character and recognize yourself in others through his students. 'You develop quasi-parental relations,' he says. 'I, for instance, was Lucifer to Sir Geoffrey Elton's God, the best beloved before the fall. And it's no coincidence that the Germans refer to their supervisor as *Doktor-vater*, Doctor-father. Often my own students call me first with news. Only yesterday a former student of mine, now at Harvard, rang to say that a job interview had gone well.'

Nor does he believe that his emptiness stems from his not yet having produced for posterity a truly great academic work. 'No,' he says, propping his chin up on two fists. 'Look at Johnson. People don't remember him for the mountainous novels he wrote on moral discourse or for the immensely tedious verse over which he sweated blood. And no one reads his English dictionary any more. People remember him for his extraordinary personality and for the way that personality was captured by Boswell. All that most academics leave is an unread tome and a crumbling hall of residence named after them. My favourite is Dame Lillian Penson Hall. Dame who?'

Will Starkey be remembered for his 'extraordinary personality' or is he just a colourful firework that illuminates the night sky for an instant and then fizzles out? Certainly there are many who think his rhetorical preening, his buffoonery and his arch savagery undermine the quality of his argument. Equally, you could argue that it helps to drive his message home. Either way, criticism has never really bothered Starkey because even being disliked is better than being ignored. 'I never watch television,' he shrugs. 'And I keep the world of the media outside my house.

I have a frontier. It would be stupid to say I never find things hurtful, though. In a funny way we always want to be liked. The last thing I want is for me to do something publicly and for people not to remember it.' We still remember Johnson for the 'good talks' in which he 'tossed and gored several people', for the way he 'yoked by violence together' the most heterogeneous ideas, so perhaps future generations will remember Starkey for what he had to say.

A few days after the interview, a tiny black and white photograph arrives in the post. It is from Starkey and it shows him as a boy in shorts, a cheeky smile playing on his face. It is not at all monstrous, nor is it imbued with pathos. The early years are indeed, it seems, when we become what we are.

In 2000 David Starkey wrote and presented a Channel 4 series on Queen Elizabeth I that topped Friends, Frasier *and* Da Ali G Show *to win the war of the ratings. His book accompanying the series remained in the bestseller list for nearly a year. In 2002 he overtook Cilla Black to become the highest paid presenter on television, earning £75,000 an hour.*

Ronnie Corbett

A plate of shortbread arrives, and Ronnie Corbett pauses for a second or two as he regards it out of the corner of his eye. He continues talking (or 'blethering' as he calls it) about *High Hopes*, his autobiography, but he's still distracted by the shortbread, analysing it, surreptitiously passing judgement.

Corbett was born and raised in Edinburgh, the son of a master baker and confectioner, and one legacy of this is an inability to pass cake shops and bakeries without checking the glaze on the pastries or the moisture of the sweetmeats. He pauses again and, as he extends a hand to the plate, the chunky gold ring he is wearing glints in the morning sunlight. He takes a bite and nods. 'Not bad. Mm. Maybe a bit underfired, as my dad would say. And a bit blond. I don't mind the dusting of sugar and the crumbly texture, but I have to say it is very 'short' shortbread, if you know what I mean.'

The comedian flicks the crumbs off his butter-coloured, double-breasted suit, leans back and shoots his cuffs; his cuff-links are porcelain and have pictures of golfers on them. The ring on his finger, I now see, has a large 'R' on it. 'When I bake bread or make cakes,' he adds, his voice strong and sonorous, his cadence mildly Scottish, 'I always think of my dad. I force myself to roll up my sleeves, put my apron on and make sure everything is done properly.'

His father, William Balfour Corbett, was a severe, strong-jawed Presbyterian who would park his car in a garage three miles from home so that he would have to walk there and back for it every day – good discipline. 'I always wanted to impress

287

him,' Ronnie Corbett recalls. 'But he was not the sort of person to ever show he was impressed.'

We are in the panelled library of Greywalls, East Lothian, a house by Lutyens which is now an hotel. Corbett has suggested we meet here because his house, which is next door, is full of guests: his two daughters, both in their early thirties, and his three grandchildren. He has another house in Croydon, Surrey, but the East Lothian one is where he and his wife Anne like to spend their summers – mainly because it overlooks the grand and ancient Muirfield golf course and, beyond that, the Firth of Forth. He's very close to his daughters, then? 'Yes, Emma lives in Caterham and Sophie lives in Streatham.'

No, I mean . . . I see from the grin playing across his asymmetrical features that he knows just what I meant.

Corbett will be seventy in December, but you wouldn't guess it from his brisk and sprightly manner, his clear hazel eyes or his smooth tanned skin – though his hair is suspiciously dark. He dresses nattily: stripy, open-neck shirt, pink silk handkerchief in breast pocket, cornflower-blue socks. 'One thing I learned from my Aunt Nell,' he says, 'is that because of my height it is really important for me to be immaculately neat and well turned out all the time.' His aunt had to tailor his school uniform because his parents couldn't find one small enough to fit. He recently found a group photograph from his time at the James Gillespie School for Boys. He is seated on a chair, fourth from the left in the front row, the only one whose feet do not touch the ground.

His father was 5ft 6in, so young Ronald wasn't too concerned about his height, but by the age of fourteen, when the other boys in his school were into long trousers, he became slightly concerned. Aunt Nell paid two guineas for a course on How to Become Taller, which combined positive thinking with stretching exercises, but it didn't work. Ronald Balfour Corbett grew to 5ft 1½in, then stopped. He was never bullied at school, but his size did present problems when he started dating. 'A little man and a taller lady is basically comic, so you have to have a lot of savoir-faire not to let it be so.' At dance halls he developed a way of working out a girl's height before she stood up. 'I still remember that walk across the floor towards the target, my courage draining away, as I imagined the mutterings of the girls – "He's coming this way".'

In 1965 Ronnie Corbett married Anne Hart, a glamorous 5ft 8in singer, and something of a West End star. Was she his first love? 'There'd been girlfriends before then. Romances. There was a nurse whose name I cannot for the life of me remember. Isn't that awful! I've got a feeling it was Sheila. But I never felt that I was all that . . . tasty. Not very confident.' Those were more puritanical times. Did he believe in sex before marriage? 'We certainly didn't cohabit in those days as quickly as couples do now. Perhaps on a Friday night, you might stay over somewhere, and go home on Saturday, or even very early on Saturday morning. But I think sex before marriage was with caution and care.'

Presbyterianism was a big influence. 'We were very serious church-goers, yes. College Street Church. We used to have a long walk there, every morning, 11 o'clock, then back home for lunch, or probably dinner as it was called then, and off again to the service in the evening. It was knocked down years ago, and I no longer attend church, actually.' His Christian values didn't prove a handicap in showbusiness. 'I've not encountered much ruthlessness, actually. I was fortunate, really, that things just seemed to proceed in a gentle way. I mean, I was obviously manoeuvring and planning and thinking ahead.'

He certainly was. He had his first taste of the stage at sixteen, when he played the wicked aunt in a church youth club production of *Babes in the Wood* – 'I really put everything into that wicked aunt, never had a female been so villainous.' After that he would hang around the stage door of the King's Theatre in Edinburgh and 'escort' the stars back to the Caledonia Hotel. 'I had the autograph book with me as a pretext, and I suppose it was more a case of me tagging along beside them rather than escorting them, but they would usually let me blether away down the Lothian Road. They would listen to me telling them how I was going to be an actor, too. They never brushed me off and sometimes they gave me advice.'

Ambitious though he was, Corbett decided the theatre would have to wait. At seventeen, on leaving the Royal High School, Edinburgh, he took the Civil Service clerical officers' exam, largely to stop his mother worrying about his future. He joined the Ministry of Agriculture in Edinburgh and dealt with the rationing of animal foodstuffs, but knew he wouldn't have to do so for long because his National Service was coming up. His one worry was that he wouldn't pass his medical because of his height. As it turned out, the RAF doctor rejected him because of the deviated septum in his nose. Corbett pleaded to be allowed to join. 'I knew perfectly well that if I didn't get in, people in the street would whisper, "It's obvious why they didn't accept him. You know, throw the small ones back in."'

The doctor eventually relented, and Corbett was commissioned as a pilot officer, though he never actually flew. His CO suggested he wear the full 'number one dress' at all times so he wouldn't be mistaken for a cadet. 'It didn't bother me. I suppose I quite liked the man. He probably thought, "I'll save the boy some embarrassment." It's not easy to pick a tiny person and give him authority.' After National Service, Corbett moved to London and supported himself as a barman in the Buckstone Club. All the actors and directors of the day would use the club, and Corbett would try to catch their eye. Eventually he was noticed and landed a job in a vaudeville show at the Stork Club in Streatham, but he was pelted with crusty Viennese rolls – 'a cruel fate for a baker's son'.

From there he graduated to Winston's nightclub in the West End, where for five years he was Danny La Rue's straight man. That world of camp theatrical glamour must have been intoxicating after his dour Scottish upbringing. 'Yes, it was. The public absolutely adored Dan. He looked fabulous as a man, and even more fabulous as a woman . . . The camp thing is very seductive. Naturally a lot of people came to see the shows who, you know, felt *simpatico* to him. I suppose he was a torchbearer, really, for the acceptability of being honestly, outwardly gay.' Did Corbett identify with the camp world to the extent of questioning his own heterosexuality? 'Er, no, but I've always been very easy with the gay world, deeply comfortable. I was brought up with it and I completely understand it, and it is not in any way suspicious or objectionable to me. I mean, one was brought up really feeling all the cleverest people in the business are gay. One thinks of Novello and Rattigan and Coward. And after working with Dan I felt part of their little corner.'

At this point in his career, Corbett says, he eradicated his Scottish accent, to avoid being typecast as the 'the wee one in the kilt'. He didn't want to be patronized, he says. He wanted to be suave. 'I obviously know I am short, but I've always been the last person to be aware of it, and my style of work is like that: a short man acting and performing like somebody who's a great deal taller. I don't feel small. But yes, I was patronized. In those days, if you were little, you had to be a comedian like Norman Wisdom or Charlie Drake. Someone who was always being hit on the head or falling over. A sort of sizeism still exists in casting today. Even the smartest, most inventive directors still perceive people in terms of their size. If I say, "I rather fancy playing that part Nigel Havers plays," there is no way that directors would see me playing it. They wouldn't cast me as a viscount, for instance, even though there are plenty of short viscounts.'

To overcome prejudice, Ronnie Corbett has had to be more driven than other comic actors. His height might even have given him a competitive advantage. If he could live his life again, would he want to come back as a taller person? He frowns, takes a sip of coffee and looks away. 'It may sound odd, but I don't think I would want to be taller. Actually. I think it's been the cornerstone, really, of what I've done. It has formed my personality. I may have changed the way I speak but I never became another person. I just slowly worked away at becoming for others the person I always saw myself as being.'

While working at Winston's, Corbett made a pact with himself that if he hadn't made it as a big-time entertainer by the age of thirty-six he would pack it in and 'go into another part of the business, be an agent or manager or something'. By happy coincidence, in 1966 he was invited to join *The Frost Report*, which proved a lucky break, as his co-stars were John Cleese and Ronnie Barker, and the team also included future members of *Monty Python*. He cherishes the memory, but recalls a clash of cultures. The Ronnies had both spent seventeen years learning how to be professional entertainers, always memorizing their lines and arriving on time for rehearsals. The embryoic Pythons, fresh from Oxbridge, were very blasé.

'They all came from privileged backgrounds,' Corbett remembers. 'John Cleese would always turn up late and unshaven in a taxi, looking flustered because he hadn't learnt his lines. Graham Chapman and the others would sit around talking about how they were giving television a go for a couple of years before going back to medicine or law. They'd stumbled on entertainment as a by-product of their education, so it was a bit of a hobby, a bit of a plaything. I suppose Ronnie B and I were a bit resentful, but it did give us a sense of solidarity. Our shared attitudes made us very comfortable together.'

The Two Ronnies ran from 1971 to 1987, won an audience of seventeen million (nineteen million for the Christmas specials) and became a national institution; the two comedians were appointed OBE in 1978. The format of the show was unvarying. It opened with them sitting side by side reading spoof news items ('First, traffic news. A juggernaut carrying treacle has overturned on the M4. Drivers are asked to stick to the inside lane'). There were sketches, and a slot in which Ronnie Corbett, wearing his Lyle & Scott cardie, would sit in an old armchair and tell a shaggy-dog story. There was lots of cross dressing and ribald seaside humour and the show would always end with a musical number and the ritual exchange: 'So it's goodnight from me', 'And it's goodnight from him', 'Goodnight'.

Barker was the dominant partner, not least because he wrote most of the shows, with the exception of Corbett's rambling monologue (which was written by Spike Mullins). Corbett was the placid one who avoided confrontation. Why did he never try writing his own material? 'I can fiddle about with things when I'm working, then come off and write them down. But I only ever want to perform other people's material, really. I wouldn't know how to start writing, and I suppose I've had a calmer life because of it.'

When *The Two Ronnies* were lampooned by *Not the Nine O'Clock News*, they knew the writing was on the wall. Ronnie Barker announced his retirement and went off to run an antique shop. Corbett still has dinner with him every so often, but the two were never that close. 'We were friendly, but not friendly in the way that Eric [Morecambe] and Ernie [Wise] were,' Corbett recalls. 'Stress and high blood pressure had a lot to do with

Ronnie B's decision to retire. There'd been other comedians around who'd died younger than they should have done, like Tommy Cooper.'

Sorry, a sitcom in which Ronnie Corbett had starred for seven years, was axed by the BBC at the same time as *The Two Ronnies* came to an end. Corbett felt 'a bit solitary for a while – prematurely pruned'. Everyone assumed that he would retire, too, and join his friends Tarbie and Brucie on the pro-celebrity golf circuit. Instead he hosted *Small Talk*, a dire programme on which children supplied thirty minutes of undiluted precocity. He has since redeemed himself slightly with appearances on *The Ben Elton Show* and a role in *Fierce Creatures*, John Cleese's ill-fated follow-up to *A Fish Called Wanda*. But mostly the twilight years of his career have been devoted to after-dinner speaking, his one-man cabaret show and pantomime.

He hasn't given up hope that he will yet be cast in a serious drama. 'Now that I no longer do *The Two Ronnies*, directors have forgotten that I've played a cockney or a viscount or a lord chancellor quite effectively in short episodes on the television. They don't see that I'm back. Back again, fighting a little man's battle to play a variety of parts.'

Ronnie Corbett's father died of a heart attack at the age of seventy-five, while playing a round of golf. His mother died in 1991 after suffering from Alzheimer's. Now that Corbett is approaching seventy, does he find himself brooding upon his mortality, wondering if he will die in the same manner his parents did? 'Well I'm still quite agile, touch wood. I don't have hip problems, heart problems, or anything like that. I'll probably have a prostate problem first.' He's worked it all out, then? 'Worked it out, yes,' he chuckles. 'I have no fear of getting old, or fear of going, really. My biggest worry is losing my mind, or my wife losing her mind. You know, Alzheimer's or dysphasia. She can't stop herself worrying about everything – everybody and everything. She's always been like that. She gave up her career to bring up our daughters. Very protective. Since Andrew died.'

Andrew was their first child, born in 1966. 'He died from a serious heart defect when he was six weeks old. I still think about him a lot. When you consider he would have been thirty-four now. You can't believe how this tiny little soul really just didn't survive. Now, of course, I suppose they might have done some-thing about it, but the heart, the surgeon told me, was the size of a fingernail. We brought him home for a day, struggling, his colour changing, and we had to take him back to St George's. It was really just . . . terrible. Terrible. I still feel the odd tear coming to my eye. The same happens when I talk about Tom, my eleven-year-old grandson. He's dyslexic, bless his little soul . . . I do get emotional, and cry at odd times. Yet I have got a bit of a steely interior. I blow hot and cold, I think that's it. I have a short temper. Quick to turn and quick to cry. I say it, I get it over and that's it. All forgotten.'

It's true. He had a spectacular wobbly recently when he refused to get in the brand new Renault Espace that GMTV had laid on to take him home after an appearance on the Lorraine Kelly daytime show, because it wasn't a limo (one was provided). Ronnie Corbett can be admirably self-deprecating, jovial and self-aware, but he is also, it seems, fundamentally insecure. It is possible that he suffers from an inferiority complex which he disguises with comic bravado. He has a tendency to build him-self up. 'Yes,' he will say. 'I did two very, very successful pan-tomimes around that time. Stanley Baxter and I played the Ugly Sisters' or, 'Actually, though I say so myself, I am a skilful mingler.'

The feeling of inferiority is partly social, you suspect. 'No one ever said anything,' he muses, 'but there might be a feeling in the family that my mum's side was just a little more genteel than my dad's . . . I think I am class-conscious in the sense of liking things to be classy and elegant, as in high quality. I suppose I've always been interested in refinement. When I met Princess Margaret early in my career I felt I should raise my game a little.' She asked how he had sprained his ankle. He didn't want to say he had fallen going to the outside lavatory at his house in New Cross, so he said he had fallen off a horse. His friend Simon Parker-Bowles (former brother-in-law to Camilla), has acted as his social tutor, he says. 'He's a very kindly, very gracious person. Not at all snobby and I suppose he has given me a confidence boost.'

Until recently Corbett drove a Rolls-Royce, until 'I decided it was nice to drive but no longer nice to be seen in.' It is nearly lunchtime, dinnertime as it used to be called. 'Excuse me,' Corbett says rising from his chair. 'I must go for a pee.' That'll be the start of his prostate problem. He laughs. 'The prostate problem, yes.'

We meet again in the walled garden, designed by Jekyll. We can smell the sea from here and just about hear the pock of a golf ball being struck on the thirteenth hole. Seagulls are crying overhead, and there are cabbage whites fluttering around the lavender borders. As we contemplate the distant Lammermuir Hills, I ask Ronnie Corbett if he still feels Scottish. He does, he says, in the way that Sean Connery, his old friend and Edinburgh contemporary (he used to date Corbett's cousins), does. Is he involved in Scottish politics, as Connery is? 'No, no, I'm not a Nationalist, I don't really see the point of spending millions and millions . . . on a new . . .'

Did he attend the opening of the Scottish Parliament? Corbett squares his shoulder and shakes his head at the memory. 'No, I didn't. I was a bit miffed that I wasn't invited, actually. Bit put out . . . I'm not deeply liked by Scottish people in the way that Sean is.' The pathos is unbearable. We part company with a hearty handshake and Ronnie Corbett strides off, barrel-chested, leaving me feeling that I've just said goodbye to a proud and dignified man who is still fighting, as he has always had to, a little man's battle.

Norman Tebbit

FEBRUARY 2001

Backlit by milky sunshine, sitting at an awkward angle, Lord Tebbit looks brittle and frail. This is not what you expect. The former Conservative Party chairman, who will be seventy next month, has been called many things: Michael Foot dubbed him 'a semi house-trained polecat'; Margaret Thatcher considered him her 'lightning conductor'; the Tory mayoral candidate Steve Norris dismissed him as 'a racist and a homophobe'. But frail? Perhaps it's to do with his hair. Usually, he manages to look bald and serious at the same time. Now though, his remaining strands at the back are almost collar-length – stiff, vertical, ghosting in the light. It is mid-morning. We are drinking coffee in the library of a Pall Mall club, and Norman Tebbit is wearing his Eurosceptic convictions on the lapel of his tweed jacket – a gold pound sign. Somehow, his clothes – Tattersall shirt, no-nonsense brown trousers and sturdy brown shoes – don't suit his look, which is that of a grey-skinned Pilgrim Father. But they do give an indication of what he will be doing in a few hours' time: shooting in Norfolk.

'I was sitting in the car this morning grumbling gently to my driver about how full my diary is this week,' Tebbit says in a thin monotone. 'I suppose I shouldn't complain. Indeed, I should be pleased as I approach my seventieth birthday that I'm still able to earn a living [as a media pundit and businessman]. I can't remember how many times I've retired, or been retired, now. I am reminded of my age, though, when I'm not feeling well. I had a rather tatty start to last year . . .' By 'tatty' he means he came down with flu, which developed into pneumonia, which lead to a heart condition bad enough to see him hospitalized. 'It's as much as I can do to lift a bag of cartridges at the moment, and I'm limping a bit because I tweaked rather heftily an old scar from Brighton . . .' He refers, of course, to the IRA bomb which in the early hours of 12 October 1984 ripped through the Grand Hotel in Brighton, scene of the Tory party conference. He and his wife Margaret, a former nurse, fell four storeys into the debris. They held hands as they waited to be rescued, bleeding and buried alive, convinced they were going to die. Eventually the television cameras recorded Norman Tebbit emerging from the rubble as in a dusty pietà, his feet bare. The damage to Margaret's spine left her paralyzed from her neck down. She has a full-time carer, but her husband still gets up twice in the night to turn her over, so that she doesn't get bed sores. 'The limp reminds me I'm mortal,' Tebbit says with a gaunt smile. 'My younger son the other day was suggesting we should buy a shoot between us. "It's a long term project," he said. And I said, "Have you thought, I might not be too interested in the long term?"'

It's safe to assume that Norman Tebbit never suggested buying a shoot with his own father, Leonard, a sometime jeweller and pawnbroker from Ponders End, Middlesex. As we all know, when times were hard Len 'got on his bike' to look for work – and found it, among other places, in an abattoir, a pub and on a factory floor. But he preferred playing snooker to working, and Norman, who joined the Young Conservatives at the age of fifteen, resented his father's lack of ambition.

Given what he once described as his narrow, dull and impoverished background, did the young Norman ever imagine a day would come when he would be a peer of the realm, heading up to Norfolk for a day's shooting? A flicker of a grin again. 'Not really. But someone asked me recently – silly question – "If you had become Prime Minister, what would have been the most important difference between you and your predecessor in the Tory party?" And I said, "I would have been the first Tory prime minister to have been photographed on a grouse moor since Alec Douglas-Home."' He gives a wheezy laugh, so faint it is almost a snuffle.

It's not such a silly question. Norman Tebbit won Epping, his first parliamentary seat, in 1970. He then held Chingford from

1974 to 1992. He was Secretary of State for Employment and, later, Trade and Industry and, by 1984, was considered the heir apparent to Margaret Thatcher. But after the Brighton bomb he seemed to lose his momentum; though he went on to become Tory party chairman and was generally credited with organizing the Tory victory in the 1987 general election, Mrs Thatcher lost confidence in him and, as was her way, let it be known. When she was toppled in 1990, many senior Conservatives on the right of the party tried to persuade Tebbit to stand against John Major. Privately, he still broods on his regret that he didn't.

'I chose not to contest it. Perhaps that was a mistake, because either I would have been successful or I would have lost the '92 election and been replaced – and a Labour government led by Kinnock would not have lasted long; we certainly wouldn't be talking about a second Labour term. Tony Blair owes me a lot.' The tight smile. 'Without me – the way I reformed the trade unions so that he was able to be elected as leader of the Labour Party – without me, he wouldn't be in Number 10 today. He's never thanked me. But politics is an ungrateful business.'

It certainly is. The self-appointed guardian of the Thatcherite legacy has recently been waging war against his own party, or at least those members of it who favour a more progressive approach to social issues. In particular, it seems Tebbit has made it his mission to nobble Michael Portillo. In recent months he has attacked the shadow chancellor's 'touchy-feely pink pound policies'. 'I could never quite make him out,' he said recently. 'Remember his great SAS speech? "Who Dares Wins". It made my toes curl it was so singularly inappropriate.'

Not a fan then. So is he worried that, if the Tories lose the next election, Michael Portillo will challenge William Hague for the leadership? 'I don't think there is any chance of the Tory party electing Portillo, because I think he has undergone some sort of emotional trauma which has left him less effective than he was. It has lost him a great deal of support in the Conservative Party.'

Given what we know of Lord Tebbit's attitude towards gays, or 'raving queers' as he is wont to call them, it doesn't seem unreasonable to suppose that his views on Portillo might have been coloured by 'that admission'. What is it with Tebbit and homosexuals? Why does he hate them so? 'I wouldn't actively seek out someone as a companion on the basis that I was looking for a homosexual,' he replies, rather bafflingly. 'But one of the most able organizers in my time at Central Office was homosexual, and I entrusted him with a lot of work because he was very good at it. We got on extremely well together. He was an officer in the TA, and I had no hesitation in accepting an invitation from him to go to the regimental dinner as his guest. On the other hand, he would never have been seen on a Gay Pride march.'

After leaving school at sixteen, Norman Tebbit worked as a journalist on the *Financial Times* for a couple of years before National Service in the RAF. Being tidy minded, he says, he loved the ritualistic precision folding of blankets and laying out of kit. Was he also seduced by the camp humour of the Ents Corps? He can see where this is going. 'I don't think we had any gays on our squadron. We had an irreverent sense of humour about everything, pranks and so on. It was characteristic of people in that occupation.'

One of the arguments for lowering the age of consent for homosexuals to sixteen is that there is evidence of a homosexual gene. Where does Norman Tebbit stand on this nature–nuture debate? 'There is a great deal of shading, not a clear line down the middle. But I object to the exposure of vulnerable youngsters to predatory older people. We all know there is bit of homosexual experience that goes on between boys in adolescence. Not un-usual.'

Did he ever go through a homosexual phase? 'No.' Not even a brief flirtation? 'No, I had the good fortune to go to a mixed grammar school, and I discovered there that there was some-thing called "girls". We were not adventurous by today's stan-dards, but we were aware of girls and were taught the facts of life in a mixed biology class. Thoroughly healthy, in my view.'

Would he accept that two gay men can be in love with one another? 'Oh yes. Of course. We've all known some, haven't we? There can be deep bonds of affection between heterosexuals of the same sex, too. I wouldn't want to prosecute it or put up a barrier against it. It has always happened and it always will happen, but it is a deviation from the norm and shouldn't be treated as if it were the norm.'

Lord Tebbit swears by the principles of economic liberalism; can he not see that social liberalism is a logical extension of this? 'To argue that it is right to say that you should have an open market in potatoes and an open market in sex is to not know the difference between a sack of potatoes and the sexual act.' That's more like it – the sort of comeback you expect from a polecat. Tebbit believes that the silent majority in this country still thinks as he thinks, and that the much-discussed 'new mood' of tolerance, inclusiveness and emotionalism is just a myth.

He seems such a cold-blooded man: I find myself wondering whether this is partly a defence mechanism against the isolation and repression he felt as a child, and the traumas he experienced as an adult. When the Second World War started, he and his elder brother Arthur were evacuated briefly to Wales. 'I cannot remember saying goodbye to my parents – I suppose we must have done but we were an unemotional family and I doubt if there were tears.' He didn't have an easy relationship with his parents, he says, his father especially, and he escaped from their 'drab and grey world' by voraciously reading P.G. Wodehouse and H.G. Wells.

Did he grow up too quickly? 'I was a serious child but then I suppose it was a serious time to be growing up. I was taught to be in control of my emotions. You didn't make a fuss. My father was in the trenches. He didn't talk about it, didn't make a fuss, and I never asked him about it. I wasn't close to him. I suppose it affected the way I brought my children up. I was much closer to them than my father was to me. Because of my life as an airline pilot [for BOAC from 1953–70] I was either not there or completely there. And so I was much more involved with them.'

The Tebbits married in 1956, and had three children. 'After the birth of our younger son, William, my wife became desperately ill and for some months, it felt like years, I was his mother. No experience is wholly bad as long as you survive. It led me to a greater sympathy with women who batter babies. I can understand why a woman after childbirth, an emotional time, faced with several children could pick up the baby and, not meaning to hurt it, shake it and say, "Go to sleep, you little bugger, go to sleep!" I can understand that.' Margaret Tebbit was suffering from a depressive illness, referred to glancingly but touchingly in Norman Tebbit's autobiography *Upwardly Mobile* (1988): 'She was acutely ill, and a potential danger both to herself and the baby. Even now the memory of seeing her personality disintegrating is more painful than any other experience I have undergone. It is hard to describe one's emotions at seeing the person with whom one has been so close becoming a stranger.' Her depression recurred periodically until the seventies.

Having been brought up to be self-contained and unemotional, it must have been difficult for Tebbit to cope with the erratic mood swings of his wife. 'I think, I know, there are occasions where one is driven to tears. But that doesn't make the case for being loose in one's emotional control. Not that I am always good at controlling my emotions. I do get terribly angry at times. Never over big issues. Usually when I know in my heart that it is me to blame for the cock up. On the other hand, when disasters happen, I take it rather calmly. Everyone gets frightened, but the difference between fear and panic is loss of control.'

He gives me an example. He trained as a jet pilot with the RAF and lived for the 'sheer animal thrill' of flying at high speed. One day during take-off in a Meteor something went wrong and he found himself trapped in his cockpit, his oxygen mask full of blood, and the plane, which was full of fuel, on fire. He assumed he was going to die but, instead of panicking, he considered his options and eventually found a way to break the glass and scramble free before passing out. 'It made me stronger in a way. I'm no longer afraid of dying. We are all going to die sooner or later and these things just give you balance and judgement in how you use the extra time you're given. When you have cheated death twice, you can't bear to waste time. Just because you are in control of your emotions doesn't mean you can't be passionate, he adds. He says he used to find speaking at party conferences addictive because of the adrenaline rush. Certainly, he always seemed to take pleasure from his sarcastic performances in the House of Commons. He appeared to have more than his share of that negative emotion, hate. He disagrees. 'I don't think you need hate to have a killer instinct in the electoral process. Tony Blair seems to hate Conservatives. It comes through strongly in his comments about the "forces of conservatism" – in which he bundled me in with the IRA, something which I found distasteful, to put it mildly. I think that hate will cost him dear in the end. You need passion but not hate, because that is indeed a negative emotion, one that springs from fear.'

During the war, Tebbit's house was damaged by a V1 rocket. When the Germans started using V2s the young Norman became fatalistic, because he could not hear them coming. I ask whether his subsequent brushes with death made him question his fatalism: should he take more responsibility for the choices he made? Had he not given up his life as an airline pilot to become a politician, for instance, his wife wouldn't have been disabled. 'And if my aunt had got wheels she would be a tea trolley, but she ain't and she isn't,' he says. 'What would my life have been like if I hadn't gone into politics? Well I might have been killed in an airline accident. I might have encountered a long-lost aunt in Australia who left me a fortune. It is never a worthwhile use of mental energy to play that game. I did what I did and what happened happened.'

He may not be introspective but does he brood upon his political legacy? Had he retired from public life after standing down as an MP in the 1992 election, he would have been remembered as a formidable performer at the despatch box, as the man who took on the mighty trade unions and won, as a diehard Eurosceptic and as the brilliant tactician who master-minded one of the most successful Tory election campaigns ever fought. Yet now the things most people associate him with are his intolerance towards gays and, because of his 'cricket team test' – which held that members of an ethnic minority could not be considered English unless they supported the English cricket team – his controversial views on race relations. Even his own party has turned on him over these issues: in 1997 William Hague said that if Tebbit didn't want to be part of the team he should 'get off the field'.

'Making myself unpopular has never worried me,' he says, crooking his hands stiffly in his lap. 'Chasing popularity is like chasing happiness, a self-defeating process. It always eludes you. So I've always said what I believed, and thought, to hell with the consequences. I don't think the country will be a better place if it becomes illegal for a sixteen-year-old girl to go out with two dogs rabbiting, but legal for her to be buggered by a dirty man old enough to be a member of the Cabinet. And I don't think many people, if put into a room where they were told what they said would never be repeated outside, would claim that the United Kingdom is easier to govern or is a better place following the enormously large-scale immigration we have had in recent years. I find it very curious now that I am the one who is campaigning for those of immigrant stock to be encouraged to integrate into the mainstream and that it is the race relations industry which is supporting a policy of apartheid. Multiculturalism is a soft word for cultural apartheid. It causes more damage than ethnic unity. Man is a social animal but he is also a pack animal, and a pack has to have common rules and a hierarchy and territory. The pack can't function effectively with two sets of rules, one set for dark coloured dogs and one set for light coloured. It just won't work. Muslim countries, not least the Saudi Arabians, always respect me because I have stood up for their rights to run their country their way.'

He is in his stride now, though his neutral tone of voice has not changed: he found Greg Dyke's comment about the BBC being 'hideously white' infuriating. 'I can only think that if I had observed of members the Equal Opportunities Commission that it was "hideously black" that it would have caused rather more furore on the Left. It is utterly stupid to call for quotas. If you start playing this quota game for the BBC, or the Army, or the police, it becomes absurd. People should be treated on their merit. Are we going to have a quota for Jewish goalkeepers? If we had quotas for the Cabinet, there should only be two Scotsmen at the most, and half a homosexual.'

Dogs? Packs? Jewish goalkeepers? These don't seem like sophisticated arguments, but I suppose Tebbit has always prided himself on being unsophisticated, the norm, the common man. He is a hard man to get the measure of because, though he is tactless and completely lacking in public warmth and self doubt, he is also principled, lucid and fearless, unusual qualities for a politician in a democracy. Remorseless and homophobic he may be, but he is incredibly kind and thoughtful to his wife – and these internal and external characteristics don't quite gel. Theirs is an unusual and deep relationship, with sacrifices on both sides.

He pushes her wheelchair, reads to her and helps cut up her food when they go out to dinner. The only chore he hated doing was putting on her lipstick for her, but now she has some use of her hands she is able to do it herself. She, in turn, is philosophical about her injuries: 'I refuse to keep a diary, refuse to look back,' she has said. Though he resigned from the Cabinet in 1987, Tebbit was later tempted to return when Margaret Thatcher offered him the education portfolio. 'But I'd promised my wife that I would quit the front bench. I would have had little time for her and she would have been lonely.'

He checks his watch. 'Now I really must be getting on my way to Norfolk,' he says tonelessly. I accompany him across the creaky floor of the library and, slowly, down the stairs to the coat rack where he collects his shooting jacket. His chauffeur will be doing the driving. Does Lord Tebbit still have police protection as well as a driver? 'No,' he says with a wintry smile. 'I'm not important enough to shoot any more.'

Michael Parkinson

DECEMBER 1997

With a slow sideways glance I take in the silvering hair and craggy profile of the Yorkshireman sitting on my side of a round dining-table in the airy elegance of Bibendum in Chelsea. For several minutes I've been lost in my thoughts, imagining him propping up a bar in a working men's club in Barnsley, and only vaguely listening to him on the theme of how t' bloody presenters today don't know they're born, how you can't find t' bloody producers any more, and how t' bloody guests aren't up to much either.

I've been nodding distractedly, contributing in my head the odd 'aye' or ''appen, tha's right' whenever they've seemed appropriate. But now he's talking about how there's never been an interviewer to match old Parky. Now, *he* could ask a question. And listen to the answer. Knew the art of conversation, you see. A proper journalist. Not like these daft young buggers you get nowadays.

As he's talking, I almost forget that the man is actually Michael Parkinson in person, and that he's not wearing a donkey jacket and sipping Tetley's but a blazer and Armani tie, and is sipping an agreeably crisp, perfectly chilled Premier Cru Chablis '94.

The daydream is possible only because of the way the 62-year-old puts you at ease by transporting you metaphysically to his home turf. As he talks, he leans towards you conspiratorially, inviting you to follow his eye in looking out over the other diners, as if it's us against them, the rest of the world. And you find yourself agreeing with his things-aren't-what-they-used-to-be prejudices; and laughing at his too-close-to-the-knuckle Bernard Manning impersonations; and glowing when he asks you about yourself and has the decency at least to sound as if he's interested in your answer.

He makes you appreciate (in a manly, back-slapping, locker-room way, you understand) why television's Mrs Merton was moved to break away from her prepared questions to him, chew her lip earnestly and blurt out, 'Oh Parky, I think I love you.' And this effect he has on people is the reason why twelve million viewers regularly watched the talk show he hosted from 1971 to 1982. It's why his guests, lulled into a sense of intimacy despite the cameras, were always so keen to come back on, year after year (thereby, in the manner of Rembrandt, leaving behind a self-portrait of themselves growing old). And it's why the long-awaited return of *Parkinson*, which begins a new, twenty-week series in January, is being hailed as the television equivalent of Elvis Presley's 'Comeback Special' in 1968.

But Parkinson's relaxed, saloon-bar manner is only part of the appeal. The prospect of a glimpse of his dark underbelly is also what keeps you watching: the arrogance, the bluntness, the volatile nature that has our man weeping with laughter one moment and looking so angry he might grab a guest by the lapels the next. Over lunch he lays the coarse, bluff, speak-as-I-find Yorkshireman stuff on pretty thick – as you'd expect – but it's only a slight exaggeration of what is really there. The word 'bloody' is used fourteen times, 'bugger' eight (including two 'daft buggers') and 'bollocks' three. The easy and cynical explanation for why he does this – and the one he himself gives – is that being a professional northerner is how he makes his living. But he also does it, you suspect, because he genuinely does need to remind himself – and us – that he is Jack and Freda Parkinson's lad, an only child who grew up in a council house in the Yorkshire pit village of Cudworth, near Barnsley. And his reasons for wanting to do this are altogether more Byzantine.

His father, who died in 1975, was one of seventeen children. He went down the pit when he was twelve and, to discourage his son from doing the same, took him down in the Grimethorpe cage one Sunday. The sight of men working on their bellies in a three-foot-by-six seam, breathing in coal dust, terrified the young Michael Parkinson. When he mumbled that he didn't fancy working there after all, his father, relieved, told him that if he ever changed his mind he'd kick his arse all the way home.

'It was an awful bloody life,' Parkinson says. 'My father used to tip up and be given back half a crown a week from my mother. People talk about pressure today. I mean, you hear some frigging footballer complaining. Pressure? My father had to be up at four. You didn't get paid till you reached the seam. You'd been walking for three bloody hours before you got there, then you'd spend the day on your hands and knees a mile underground.'

Such conditions may seem like the stuff of Monty Python parody today, but it is sobering to hear someone who actually knew that life reflect upon it. Parkinson went back to Grimethorpe this summer and found the mine had been concreted over and half the shops boarded up. The trip left him with mixed feelings. Mining is a brutish way to earn a living, he says, and if other employment had been found for the community he wouldn't mourn its passing. But he has warm memories of waiting outside the Working Men's Institute for his father, listening to the 'bloody marvellous' singing inside. His watery blue eyes crease at the sides and his whiskery eyebrows do a tango as he goes on to recall his father's distinctive laugh. 'He would embarrass me in movies by laughing so loud he would be asked to leave by the manager.'

When asked whether he thinks his personality would have been the same if he had followed his father down the pit, Parkinson broods for a moment. 'I don't know,' he concludes. 'Never thought about it. I look at some of my friends, though, when I go back to Barnsley, and I think I wouldn't have minded being them. They're a bright lot. I'd have still voted the way I do. I'd have still thought the same about the MCC. I would still not have believed in the honours system. I'd have hated rudeness. And causing offence. All the fundamental things that I learned on my father's knee would still be there.'

With a wry look around the restaurant, Parkinson muses that whenever he took his father to such a place he would never dare show him a menu with the prices on or let him see the bill. 'But he wouldn't be bothered by it. We were once in a place like this and he came out of the toilet and said, "Ay up, there's a lad in there who knows you." And it turned out he'd been standing next to a stranger at the urinal and just came out and asked, "Do you know my lad, Michael Parkinson?" He was very proud. He used to love the fact that I would meet all these old birds he had fancied on the silver screen. I've just started dreaming about him, as it happens. Nice pleasant dreams, where he's part of the family still. But the awful thing is, when I wake up it comes as a shock that he's not alive.'

For the son, the family sin of pride seems to have evolved into an attitude to the effect that, however much those effete southerners tried to patronize him, he knew he was just as good as them, if not better. This would account for his stubborn refusal to go native. Despite the urbane media world Parkinson has inhabited for much of his adult life, he has never succumbed to liberal correctness. At one point he says the reason there hasn't been a successful woman talk-show host is that they find it difficult to unhook their corsets and let the cellulite out. Imagine his fellow professional northerner Melvyn Bragg saying that. Later, to illustrate why the timing of a joke is more important than its content, Parkinson repeats a Bernard Manning joke about racial minorities, knowing how provocative it will seem in print but not really caring. He then laughs so hard, while banging the table with the flat of his hand, that flecks of spittle appear at the corners of his mouth.

It is telling, too, that, despite living in the south for most of his life, Parkinson's flat northern vowels have never really softened much. 'I kept my accent because it was economically viable to do so,' he says. 'No sense in changing it. When I started at Granada TV in the sixties everyone had a northern accent. It was the same time as the Beatles and all the northern playwrights and actors. Tom Courtenay. Albert Finney. People who spoke posh were trying to affect Yorkshire accents. Before that I would have been lucky to get a job as a doorman at the BBC. There was a new hierarchy. Jack was becoming as good as his master.'

Keeping the accent, then, seems to have required conscious effort. And the determination not to assimilate seems to have been fuelled by a very Yorkshire trait which southerners are wont to misinterpret as chippiness: a superiority complex. This reveals itself in the way that Parkinson refers to his famous guests by their surnames alone. Welles. Burton. Ali. Lennon. And in this he reminds you of Frank 'Oi! No!' Doberman, the thuggish Harry Enfield character who sits in a pub proving he's just as good as the celebrities he rants about by refusing to use the first names they're always known by – as in 'Black' rather than 'Cilla Black'. At one stage, the similarity becomes too much for me and I nearly choke on my Chablis. 'I'm a great admirer of Harris,' Parkinson says of Rolf Harris. 'He's talented, energetic and kind. And I'm delighted that he is considered hip now. And he's a great friend. But. There was one time when he came on to my show and . . .' Your imagination finishes the sentence: Oi! Harris! No!

'But if you're asking would I have been different brought up in genteel Surbiton the answer would be yes. Very different indeed. Down here is still in my mind where the fat cats are. And it's good to succeed and become a fat cat. Why not? I don't trample on people. I've never been a jealous type. But I'm competitive and I have encountered snobbery about my background from people at the BBC.'

This reached its peak when Parkinson took over *Desert Island Discs*, from 1986 to 1988, after the death of Roy Plomley. 'The fact that Plomley was the worst bloody interviewer in the world had nothing to do with it,' he says. 'The worst thing was that his widow began a one-woman campaign to preserve the memory of her husband and she started complaining, "What is this crude northern oik doing walking on my husband's grave? The accent is too common." I was too wily to respond then. But she was . . . nasty.'

He doesn't need to say so directly, but Parkinson clearly believes he is the 'best bloody interviewer in the world' because of his background in journalism. After leaving Barnsley Grammar School at the age of sixteen he began work as a reporter on the *Yorkshire Evening Post*. He soon made it down to Fleet Street, via the *Manchester Guardian*, and recalls how, callow and wide-eyed, he would sit at the back in pubs getting silently drunk as he listened to the big-name journalists he had hero-worshipped since childhood regale everyone at the crowded bar with their anecdotes. Since 1991 he has been writing a sports column for the *Daily Telegraph*. And even journalists not interested in sport would have to acknowledge that as an example of how to write vividly, evocatively and unpretentiously it takes some beating.

'I find writing the most satisfying thing I do,' he says. 'I hate watching myself on television. And I never listen to a broadcast I've done on radio. But I always reread everything I've written. Over and over and over again. And every time I do I always say, "You daft bugger, why did you use that word there?" Sub-editors hate me. But in the end you've signed that document and it's going to be around for ever. All that tomorrow's chip paper stuff is nonsense.'

With characteristic frankness he says the main reason he was tempted into television is that it pays so well. 'I can earn more from one TV show, *Antique Quiz*, than I can in six months of writing that column. I'm not making a judgement. But that's the proposition put to you. The reason I have stayed in newspapers anyway is because that's what I am. My passport says journalist. I'm proud to be one. I know how to do it.'

That said, he believes one advantage which the television interview has over the newspaper one is that the viewers can make their own minds up. 'They can sit there watching a guest and think, "You lying shit."' He thinks for instance that the many interviews he did with Kenneth Williams revealed the comedian's true cold side. 'I didn't like Williams and he didn't like me. And it showed. I wouldn't be so rude as to say that if he was alive, but it's true. Towards the end, we were like two sniffing dogs. The first time we met he wrote in his diary that I was a vulgar North Country nit. The trick was to get him with good company, like Maggie Smith, so that he would show off.'

With a characteristic lack of modesty, Parkinson goes on to admit that he was no slouch when it came to getting the best out of his female guests, too. The man who has been described as having the sexiest eyes in television says, 'I used to flirt out-rageously with Shirley Maclean and she with me. Outrageously. And with Raquel Welch.'

He says that if he worked in television in America he would have to have plastic surgery, but you know he knows that he's still in pretty good shape and still has that twinkle in his eye. He and his wife Mary live at Bray, by the Thames in Berkshire, in the house where they brought up their three sons (now in their late twenties and early thirties, they work in publishing, radio and the food and beverage industry). Mary Parkinson once described how Michael would splash aftershave on his face, adjust his tie, wink at the mirror and say 'By gum, you're a handsome bugger, Parky.' It was intended as a tease to his wife – who would retaliate that he was 'a miserable bugger, more like' – but it is, you suspect, what he really thinks.

In marriage, he says, you have to expect choppy water. 'All this bollocks that you can live together without ever having a cross word. You muddle through.' He has said that whenever he rows with his wife he is always the first to make up. When his wife also took a job as a presenter on television, he said, he couldn't help feeling a twinge of resentment. And there have been times when, like all journalists, he's drunk too much and become maudlin, but on such occasions he has tended to explode and then feel remorseful immediately afterwards.

He chuckles when he's asked how, at the height of his fame in the seventies, he resisted carnal temptation. 'I used to think of Barnsley football club,' he says. He believes that if he had been younger when his talk show was running his fidelity might have been tested more than it was. 'I would have had a far different lifestyle,' he says. 'Fame is a strange thing to deal with. No one tells you about it. You have to learn. It helped that I was in a stable marriage with three kids. I'd seen first-hand how people could be affected by fame. George Best. The Beatles. Elton John. I never went to druggy pop-star parties, though. And Mary came to all my shows, so did my father and mother.'

His mother, now eighty-six, lives in a thatched cottage near Oxford, where she was born. He sees her regularly and says she is in 'good nick' (she delivered 'meals on wheels' until recently and served only one person older than herself). To help with the housekeeping she used to design knitwear and her son learned to type by having his mother dictate knitting patterns to him. 'Knit two, tog, knit one, purl one,' Parkinson says with a grin as he mimes tapping out the keys, his hands dappled in the silvery blond light from the large windows in the restaurant.

Parkinson is scathing about Channel Five's Jack Docherty, the latest pretender to his throne. 'His show looks like it's been shot in a shoe cupboard,' he says. 'And he's not a proper journalist. They always say so-and-so is going to be the next Parkinson, but how can they be when they don't understand what I understand about the talk show? I'm not being arrogant here. It's like expecting me to be the next Yehudi Menuhin when I can't play a violin. Don't be daft. It's like Bernard Manning. Is he funny or is he not?' He thumps the table for emphasis, suspending a fork momentarily in the air. 'All that counts is whether I can interview, whether I can do my job. If I can't, then go home.'

A few days after this appeared a letter arrived at The Sunday Telegraph: *'In his interview with me Nigel Farndale quotes me as saying "I am the best bloody interviewer in the world". This is news to me. I will give £1000 to charity if Mr Farndale can prove I said that or indeed anything remotely like it. For one thing I don't regard interviewing as an Olympic event, but most importantly of all I am not that daft . . . He has a lot of explaining to do.'*

I replied: 'The article said "He doesn't need to say so directly, but Parkinson clearly believes he is the best bloody interviewer in the world because of his background in journalism." This was intended as a light-hearted observation, picking up what Mr Parkinson said about Roy Plomley being "the worst bloody interviewer in the world."'

Peter Jay

In vain would you search for Peter Jay in the soulless corridors of Television Centre, White City, west London. The 63-year-old economics and business editor of the BBC prefers to work from his farmhouse on the outskirts of Woodstock, Oxfordshire. As well he might. Blackbirds sing here. The air is sweet with pollen and freshly mown grass. Kindly morning sunlight bathes the flowering chestnuts and swelling fruit. It is a fitting place for a man of such obvious bottom, gravitas and destiny.

Jay's career has been dazzling if curiously disjointed. His jobs and connections are embedded in the political history and liberal Establishment of the past forty years: he's the former son-in-law of Tony Blair's predecessor as Labour prime minister (and therefore the ex-husband of Lady Jay, that scourge of hereditary privilege and Leader of the House of Lords); the retired 'chief of staff' of the deceased swindler Robert Maxwell; and, perhaps most bizarrely of all, a former Ambassador to the United States of America. Jay is undoubtedly a most superior person – a grandee, a member of the Garrick, in fact – and it would hardly be proper for him to spend his working hours among the light-industrial estates of White City. It is said that some of his colleagues at the BBC resent his absence from their midst. They point out that, over the past year, his appearances on the evening news have been about as rare as anoraks in Arabia, yet he still has his own office at White City (even if it is now used unofficially as a changing room for staff who cycle to work) and still, of course, draws a handsome salary.

315

When I arrive, Peter Jay is in the middle distance, wearing a checked shirt and a bright-red sleeveless jumper, feeding the carp in his pond. Literally a man of stature – a solidly built 6ft 4in – he looms towards me, past a hammock strung between two trees and, with loping gait, leads the way towards the tall barn he has converted into an office and broadcasting studio. One wall is filled from floor to rafters with books. The one opposite is divided in two by an upper deck. The lower half is devoted to framed political cartoons and a large photograph of Jay with the 'Famous Five' – Michael Parkinson, Anna Ford, Angela Rippon, David Frost and Robert Kee – the star presenters with whom he launched the ill-fated *TV-am* in 1983.

As we go upstairs, Jay stoops automatically to avoid the low beams. The upper deck is draped with red ensigns and Union Jacks, there are maritime maps in glass cases and dozens of photographs of Jay sailing the yachts that have been his lifelong passion. He sits down and, though he folds his arms, manages somehow to look as if he's sprawling. Close up, his skin looks like parched earth; his big sleepy blue eyes are framed by pink lines and pouches, his thick lips fixed in a bland smile. In a recent issue of *Private Eye*, under the headline TV CELEBRITY CONNED FRIEND OUT OF THOUSANDS BY PRETENDING TO BE THE ECONOMICS EDITOR OF THE BBC, a spoof news story suggested that Jay made sure he renewed his contract with the BBC just before his good friend Sir John Birt retired as director general. What does Jay make of this ribbing? 'Ah, yes,' he says placidly. 'Me being paid a large salary to do nothing. It wasn't to do with John Birt at all. And considering I've been working harder in the past two years than at any other time since leaving Washington, I think it's ironic. But I love *Private Eye* and have always accepted that "Sir Peter Jaybotham, 69" is a fine figure of fun. Public figures should be abused. It is healthy and therapeutic.'

The thing he has been working so hard on over the past two years is *Road to Riches*, a six-part television series which begins next month. That and the weighty book, subtitled *The Wealth of Man*, which accompanies it. Together they tell the story of mankind's economic progress, from the Big Bang all the way to hunter-gathering and the Industrial Revolution. 'After sex,' Jay says, 'money is our second appetite. Understanding comes third.

But, as Aristotle noted, you may want wine and women but you don't want them ad infinitum. Only our appetite for money is limitless. Bill Gates is not much less motivated to make the next $100 billion than he was to make the first.'

And then, for the next sixty minutes or so, Peter Jay expounds his 'cautiously pessimistic' view of economic history, with easy reference to Aristophanes, Defoe, Malthus, Darwin and Keynes. It is a mistake to take a linear view, he tells me, there are always periods of stagnation and failure. Economies evolve in fits and starts, like a waltz, taking one step forward and two steps sideways. His enthusiasm for the subject is obvious, his knowledge encyclopaedic and, like an oil tanker, once he has set course, he takes some turning round. He's also pedantic, given to qualifying his comments with 'as it were' and stuffing his sentences with sub-clauses.

When I ask if thoughts of mortality might have inspired this magnum opus, he laughs throatily. 'Do you think I'm monument-building at this late stage in my life? Well, yes, I suppose so. Though I don't want to seem portentous, a vice of which I am extremely capable. The series and the book were put to me by the BBC, so it wasn't as if I was thrashing around for a place to build a monument. That said, the sentimental thought has gone through my mind that I have seven children and when their children ask, as it were, what did Grandfather do in the Great War, I shall be able to point to this book on the shelf.'

It is a telling admission. From childhood onwards, great things have been expected of Peter Jay. Yet he has flitted from career to career, never quite leaving his mark, never quite consolidating his hold on the glittering prizes. It didn't help that his father, Douglas, was a hard act to follow. Lord Jay, as he became, had been a Fellow of All Souls, Oxford, and President of the Board of Trade in Harold Wilson's cabinet. But Peter was never denied opportunities to succeed. From the Dragon School in Oxford, he went to Winchester (where he was Sen Co Prae, or Head of School) and from there, after doing his National Service in the Royal Navy, to Christ Church, Oxford. He was President of the Union, took a first in PPE, and soon afterwards married Margaret Callaghan, daughter of 'Sunny Jim', who was then Shadow Chancellor. In the same year (1961) Jay joined the Treasury as a civil servant, leaving in 1967 to become economics editor of *The Times*. He remained there for a decade, combining the post with a five-year spell as presenter of *Weekend World*, the political television programme of the day, produced by none other than John Birt.

Then, in 1977, to universal derision, his father-in-law (by then Prime Minister) appointed him Ambassador to Washington. He stayed two years, but then Mrs Thatcher won the 1979 election and he returned to Britain to work as a director of the *Economist*, before joining *TV-am* in 1983 as its founding chairman and chief executive. Three years later he made an odd career move, becoming from 1986 to 1989 chief-of-staff ('bagman', as *Private Eye* put it) to Robert Maxwell, proprietor of the *Daily Mirror*. And in 1990 he began his present job at the BBC.

Why has he never settled down? Did he find the goalposts kept moving? 'The truth is, my career is a chapter of accidents and I have been lucky that it has added up to a diverting and enjoyably random walk through life. Again, do stop me if I start sounding portentous, because it is a terrible vice, but from my schooldays onwards I was encouraged to view life as an obstacle race that one ran all the way to the grave. If you played cricket, you had to be selected for the first team. If you took exams, you had to come top. If you took a degree, you had to get a first. The thing to do was succeed. You didn't examine why or whether you wanted to. That absurdity was aggravated because I worked jolly hard and so was good at the race. I had a privileged education, of course, and if I hadn't benefited from it, it would have been disgraceful. But to me the satisfaction was in being able to tick things off my list. I say this in a mood of confession to what is a deplorable state of mind.'

After graduating, Peter Jay was awarded a research fellowship by Nuffield College, Oxford, after failing to follow his father in winning one at All Souls. He managed just one term of a D.Phil. on the philosophy of John Stuart Mill. 'I realized I knew the answer to the question I had set myself. And I couldn't stand the life. I asked myself, "What difference would it make if I didn't get up tomorrow?" and the answer was, "None at all". I realized I needed a framework, a full in-tray, a telephone that would ring and make demands of me. I am confessing here to another profound character flaw.'

He decided to join the Treasury. 'The absurd thing was, I went there mainly because my father wanted me to be a civil servant. He had enjoyed it and thought it a secure job for me.' Lord Jay died, aged eighty-eight, in 1996. His obituary noted that he recoiled from idleness and luxury. 'He was a strong character,' Jay says, shaking his head at the memory. 'And he had obsessions. But I wouldn't say "hero" was quite the right word. He was an inspirational teacher. Stimulating. I have a more vivid recollection of his childhood than I do of my own. We shared a huge number of jokes and references and I'd say we were close. But he wasn't the sort of father who, as it were, changed the nappies.'

Jay is known for his short fuse and once ticked off a *Times* sub-editor who complained that his economics column was unintelligible. 'I am writing for three people in England,' he said loftily. 'And you are not one of them.' Apparently, the three were two Treasury mandarins and the Governor of the Bank of England. Did Jay always write for such a limited audience? 'I was writing that particular article to a limited audience.'

If he joined the Treasury to win his father's approval, did he leave it as an act of filial rebellion? 'If it was, it was a pretty weedy act, because my father had also worked for *The Times*.' It was perhaps inevitable that eventually Jay would try to follow his father into politics, and in 1970 he sought selection as Labour's parliamentary candidate for Islington South-West. 'It was a farce,' he recalls, rubbing the back of his neck with his hand. 'I didn't even come close to being selected. But I made an important discovery about myself, that I absolutely didn't want to be a politician. It wasn't just sour grapes. All my life I had assumed as an unconscious inevitability that I would have to be one – in the end – then I began to notice I was doing everything possible to postpone the day. Becoming an MP ruins your family life and it's ill rewarded. And I'm just not the committee-minded, consensus-building, wheeler-dealer type you need to be.'

Islington was not Jay's first taste of failure. 'The real failure for me,' he recalls, and it seems to pain him still, 'the thing that absolutely was a shock and which considerably changed my personality was when I failed to get an All Souls fellowship. I had been encouraged to expect it. It was like being poleaxed. I was stunned. That sounds incredibly arrogant, but then I was an incredibly arrogant person. Experiencing that early failure was probably the best thing that could have happened to me. Goodness, that sounds pompous!'

Though he claims to welcome the mockery of *Private Eye*, Jay does seem sensitive about his reputation for pomposity, constantly referring to it. If he was prone to arrogance as a young man, though, it seems forgivable. After all, in 1973, he was voted not just Financial Journalist of the Year but also Political Broadcaster of the Year. The next year he was voted Male Personality of the Year by the Royal Television Society. At the age of thirty-seven he was tipped by *Time* magazine as a future world leader. On top of this, people started telling him that, as a television celebrity, he had sex appeal. How did he keep his feet on the ground? 'Television, which I take seriously and think important, was never part of the obstacle race for me. *Weekend World* was fun and well paid, but I regarded it as a recreation, as naughty moonlighting from my Monday to Friday job on *The Times*. It was like going skiing all the time, I felt guilty about it. I don't think I had much sex appeal as a presenter, or indeed as anything else but, anyway, it wasn't the glamour that attracted me, it was the money. It helped me pay for boats. I could double my earnings by working weekends as well as weekdays. Besides, I loved doing two hours' live studio work. It gave me a buzz. I loved, loved, loved doing it.'

What effect did his working a six-and-a-half day week have on his wife and three children? 'It took a huge toll. It was a mistake and I regret it. I shouldn't have done the television. I would come home on a Sunday after an adrenaline-pumping live broadcast and I would still be buzzing from it. I might have been, say, interviewing the Prime Minister, and I would have been feeling like David Beckham in the Cup Final. It's intoxicating and, when it stops, the batteries are drained. You go home to a family who have not watched the programme because it was much too boring and you might as well have just come in from washing the car. The psychological demands of changing down to their gear were high. And I would have to find the physical energy to take a lively interest in what they were doing, rather than collapse. But they were the ones who paid the price for my absence, not me. I paid when I saw the effect it had on them.'

Behind him, on top of a bookshelf, is a blue leather briefcase emblazoned with the Diplomatic Service crest, a memento from his days in Washington. Had he seen that job as a chance to repair things with his family, make a new start? 'Yes, in the sense that it was something we could do as a family, but no, in that the working demands were even greater. I've never worked so hard in my life. My favourite joke at the time was that they needed a younger man for that job. It was physically crushing. That you were living over the shop helped. Even though the working day began at 7 a.m. and continued with telegrams till 2 a.m. the next day, you came across your children all day, they were under your feet. And Margaret and I were able to do a lot more things together, which we hadn't been able to do in London. I described her as my co-ambassador because her contribution was enormous. But by no means was it a kind of holiday.'

Was he shocked, or embarrassed at all, by the accusations of nepotism over his appointment to such a senior diplomatic post? 'Of course, but once I overcame my shock at being asked by David Owen [then Foreign Secretary], I said I would have to talk to Jim first, because I knew it would cause immense political embarrassment. Jim said, "You let me worry about the politics." So then I had to ask myself, "Can I go through the rest of my life living with the knowledge that I have turned down such an opportunity?" A friend of mine said I should think very hard about it for a millionth of a second and then say yes.'

Peter Jay's time in Washington lives on in the memory of journalists. There was a satisfying element of French farce to the ambassadorial household. As a *Sun* headline put it: HOW THE KNOW-ALL CAME A CROPPER! Margaret Jay had an affair with Carl Bernstein, the *Washington Post* journalist who, with Robert Woodward, uncovered the Watergate scandal, and Peter Jay had an affair with his children's nanny, who bore him a son. The scandal inspired two novels – one by Susan Crosland, the other by Nora Ephron, Bernstein's wife. (The Jays were divorced in 1986, and in the same year Peter married Emma Thornton, a garden-furniture designer sixteen years his junior. They have three sons. What emotional toll did the break-up of his marriage take?

'Huge is the one-word answer to your question. But I think wallowing in it or going on about it doesn't help very much. It happens to millions of people and they all deal with it in their own way.')

Oddly, Peter Jay seems to have few regrets about his association with Robert Maxwell, a man who had been declared unfit by the DTI to run a public company as long ago as 1971, and who went on to embezzle the *Mirror*'s pension funds. Why is he still so loyal? Is it that he doesn't want to be seen as a dupe? 'I did feel a loyalty to Maxwell, and a certain affection for him. He was larger than life, a pre-moral figure, a kind of woolly mammoth stalking through the primeval forests unaware of the kind of things other people fussed about as being good or evil. But what he was not was a crook. Clearly in the last eighteen months of his life, after I had gone, something happened which drove him to the most outrageous conduct, for which no possible extenuation can be given.'

When the job at the BBC was offered in 1990, Jay must have been hugely relieved. His life had come full circle, it seemed. A chance to pontificate to the nation once more, to win over middle-aged female viewers with his craggy, sea-saltish sex appeal, to let his grandchildren know what he did in the great battle of the ERM. He's an economics editor again, with three young children. 'There can be huge frustrations and lots of back-biting at the BBC,' he reflects. 'But it is a wonderful place to work. Now that this series is in the can, I'm intending to go back to my normal routine on the newsdesk. I hope I shall continue doing this for the foreseeable future. After all, Alistair Cooke still seems to be doing OK.'

But Alistair Cooke, I want to say, is not an economist. Before I can do so, Emma Jay calls us from downstairs. Lunch is ready. Should we have it outside? Yes, Peter replies. 'My heart always sinks when you say that,' Emma says, 'because it all needs carrying.' 'Oh, we'll do that,' Peter says blithely. By the time we join Emma outside, though, the garden table has been laden with vegetable flans, pies, salad, freshly baked bread, and two bottles of red wine. The afternoon heat is soporific. No wonder he has put up that hammock.

Elton John

Witnessing Elton John greet his burly, unshaven manservant with a peck on the cheek and a fruity 'How are you, dear?' was more than I had any right to expect. But then he sat on his piano stool, placed his fingers on the keyboard, and sang half a dozen of his most memorable ballads – all with the jutted jaw and the grimace of emotion directed at me, his one-man audience. Now, as he shows every sign of laying on one of his celebrated tantrums as well, I get the feeling he's just spoiling me.

The pedal of the electric piano is sticking. He stops playing. He scowls. He pouts. 'Look!' he finally snaps at a young assistant. 'It's no good. It's doing it all the time.' In his eagerness to put it right, the assistant dives feet first between the black legs of the piano and begins tinkering around with its wires. He's given half an hour to fix it, while everyone else breaks for a cold lunch of jambon, fromage and French bread.

We are in Nice, the town where Elton John has just bought a fourth home – a £5-million pink palace on a wooded hill, within waving distance of his neighbour, Joan Collins. A surprise really, given that a couple of years ago, during the most exciting tantrum ever captured on film, John swore he would never come back to the south of France, ever again, ever. It was after a female fan had shouted, 'Yoo-hoo!' at him while he was playing tennis on a hotel court. 'It pissed me off,' he seethed as he ordered his private jet to fly him away from the Riviera. 'I take my tennis seriously. I don't like people waving at me.'

Now, as we sit in the dressing room of a hall where he is rehearsing for his autumn tour, he says with a shrug and a lopsided grin, 'Typical me. All mouth and no trousers.' Spread over the dressing table is a cloth which, judging by its colourful rococo swirls, probably has a Versace label on it somewhere. Above this there's a mirror, framed by small lightbulbs. It reflects a 50-year-old pop star wearing white Bermuda shorts, Nike trainers and a baggy blue T-shirt with the word Agassi – or rather issagA – emblazoned across it. On the bridge of his nose sits a pair of blue, rectangular glasses with slits so narrow they make his eyes look reptilian. In his right earlobe there's a Theo Fennell cross, studded with diamonds. The round, unlined face beneath the expensive chestnut fringe is that of a debauched cherub.

The interview has been granted with the request that it will focus on 'the music'. It's not to dwell upon what Simon Prytherch, his publicity manager, has described as 'the lifestyle, you know, going to parties and wearing Versace'. It will, I've been told, last exactly one hour and Prytherch will sit in on it. That is still to come. The half-hour we snatch while the piano is being repaired is an unexpected prelude. And it doesn't bode well, because for its duration, Elton John is edgy, cold and suspicious – as he has every right to be. He talks too quickly, loudly and impatiently. He gulps at the words and interrupts questions before they've been fully asked. When he can't be bothered to complete a thought he says, 'Blah, blah, blah'.

There's still a hint of the Cockney inflection he acquired as a child growing up in suburban Pinner. But there's no sign of the cheeky chappie with the wide, gap-toothed smile that we, as a grateful nation, know and treasure from early photographs. As he's talking, one of the outbursts recorded in *Tantrums and Tiaras*, the unflattering yet oddly endearing documentary filmed off and on throughout 1995 by Elton John's long-term partner, 34-year-old David Furnish, keeps echoing bullyingly around my head. 'Not another fucking interview,' John hisses to the camera. 'I don't know how Mrs Jagger does it.'

One reason 'Mrs' Jagger – and 'Miss' John – do it is because it publicizes their records. And, despite already having sold more than 150 million of them and having a back catalogue so enormous it makes him the highest annual earner in the British music industry, Elton John's appetite for writing hit songs has yet to be sated. 'The music business,' he says, lapsing into mid-Atlantic, 'fascinates the shit outta me. If I hadn't been a performer, I would've been happy working in a small CD store sharing a small flat with David. As long as I've got someone to come home to who loves me. Very picket fence.'

And all Barbara Cartland ever wanted was a quiet life of rural simplicity. Elton John's record-store fantasy may sound bogus, but the point is well taken. There's nothing he doesn't know about the charts and, as is the wont of all self-respecting fifty-year-olds, he will always rush to his local store and buy the latest Prodigy album, Chemical Brothers single, whatever, on the day that it's released. Indeed, such is his interest in the rock pantheon – and his own status within it – that he will agree to interviews, despite his claim to be tired of talking about himself.

It could be, though, that this reticence stems from the crushingly low sense of self-esteem from which he periodically suffers. It's to do with the way he looks and the way he wants to look – this, after all, is the man who once described himself as being 'physically and spiritually ugly, a slob, a pig'. It's also because, bored as he is with himself and his excessive lifestyle, he doesn't believe anyone else can find them subjects of interest either.

The bonus half-hour up, it's back to the rehearsals. Perhaps conscious of an air of tension, Simon Prytherch whispers: 'In private, you know, Elton can be very witty. He has a really black sense of humour. I think it's just that he learned it pays to be less flippant and more guarded in interviews.' With the piano pedal now fixed, however, the atmosphere is becoming more relaxed and frivolous. During 'Benny and the Jets', John slips into a jazz improvization. For 'Saturday Night's Alright for Fighting', he leans back precariously on his piano stool, sliding his legs forward and knitting his brow in a caricature of keen emotion. He moves on to a slow song from the new album – 'Long Way from Happiness' – and, just as I'm about to get out the lighter and wave it slowly above my head, he breaks the spell by slipping into 'Oh I do like to be beside the seaside', played off-key, Les Dawson-style.

His mood has changed and, homework done for the day, there's almost a skip in his plimsoled step as we return to the dressing room. 'Come the second half of the rehearsal, I was really getting into it and enjoying it,' he says. 'First half, it wasn't there.' And as the designated one hour that follows stretches into two, the real reason emerges why guidelines have to be laid down for the interviews Elton John professes to loathe: it's to save him from his own candour. Like many people who've undergone therapy – and many who haven't – Elton John actually loves talking about himself. More than that, he enjoys confessing, purging, and getting everything out into the open.

Try though I do to stick to the subject of 'the music', John insists on bringing up all the juicy details of his life that none of us are really interested in – much: you know, the drink and drugs hell; the homosexuality; the suicidal tendencies; the traumatic childhood; the self-loathing; the fits of black despair; the rotting cavity in his life that can't be filled by fawning sycophants. Blah, blah, blah.

Within arm's reach of John's chair there's a bowl filled with chunks of nougat. He helps himself to several pieces, talking as he chews, and washes them down with slugs from a can of Diet Coke. There are half a dozen of these to hand, chilling in – very rock and roll – a silver ice bucket. Elton John only tipples soft drinks these days. And since he 'faced his demons' seven years ago, in a drink and drugs rehabilitation clinic in Chicago, the only Coke he takes is the diet kind that comes in a can. So addicted was he to cocaine that he would sometimes have it flown in to wherever he was staying and, even when he suffered seizures from it, he would only wait about ten minutes between snorting lines.

His compulsions though, as he readily concedes, were not restricted to drink and drugs. In his time he's been addicted to Sainsbury's cockles, Haagen-Dazs vanilla ice cream and porcelain – especially porcelain. Elton John's therapist Beechy Colclough once said of him: 'He's a totally obsessive, compulsive person. He was born an addict. If it hadn't been the alcohol, it would have been the drugs. If it hadn't been the drugs, it would have been the food. If it hadn't been the food, it would have been the relationships. If it hadn't been the relationships it would have been the shopping. And, you know what? I think he's got all five.'

Nowadays John's main addiction, apart from shopping, is to being honest about himself. Honesty. Honesty. Honesty. He repeats this word as though it were a mantra. 'One of the good things about growing older is that you become more honest with yourself,' he will sigh as he pushes his glasses straight with a thick forefinger. 'I've realized that I've spent a lot of my life with people I didn't really care for.' Five minutes later, bobbing up and down in his chair: 'I know what I like and what I don't like and I'm more prepared to say so. More honest with myself.' Later still, accompanied by a bitter guffaw: 'My grandmother was incredibly forthright. I'd rather be surrounded by that kind of honesty than by sycophancy.' Liam Gallagher pops Ecstasy. Elton John takes Honesty. He's mad for it. And it's easy to imagine how seductive a drug Honesty can be to one who, in his past addictions, admits to having lived a life of deceit: the Queen Mother of Rock who in private was, at his own estimation, 'a nasty, vicious drunk'; shy Reg Dwight pretending to be the extrovert Elton John; the balding man playing at being hirsute; the homosexual who married a woman, Renate Blauel, in 1984, only to divorce her three years later.

Tantrums and Tiaras was, of course, the biggest Honesty trip an addict could take. John says it taught him a lot about himself: about how abysmally he could behave on the road, how pampered he was, how harrowing life was for the people around him. 'I looked at myself and thought, "She's an absolute cow,"' he says. 'I had to laugh. I was just impossible. Like Zaza from *La Cage aux Folles*.'

This, of course, is exactly how the rest of us enjoy seeing him – because, let's be frank, as a hard-core rock and roller, Elton John was never terribly convincing. He dressed in funny costumes and monster specs, pulled silly faces and sung hummable, middle-of-the-road songs. What he became instead, though, was something much more original: the apotheosis of excess. John, sadly, seems to be unable to revel in this accolade; rather, he offers a twelve-stage analysis of it.

His main fear, he says, relapsing into therapy-speak, was of confrontation. It was a condition that could be traced back to his childhood. 'My parents used to argue a lot when I was young,' he says, defensively drawing up the ankle of one unhairy leg to rest on the knee of the other. 'I would lock myself in my bedroom. My father would come home and there would be a row. I expected it. And lived in fear of it.' As a consequence, he was not surprised when his mother told him that his late father, who was in the RAF, didn't like him very much and would have 'a little dig' whenever he could.

Reg Dwight was a child prodigy: at three he could hear a piece of music and then play it on the piano; at eleven he won a scholarship to the Royal Academy of Music; in his early twenties he composed the music for hits such as 'Daniel' and 'Your Song' in ten minutes flat. Given this, and the admission by Reg Dwight's grown-up alter ego, Elton John, that he's still a mummy's boy, it would be reasonable to assume that he was a bit spoilt as a child – by his doting mother, at least – and that he always got his way when he stamped his foot. And this would explain why, in later life, he was capable of complaining about the colour of his private jet, or of walking out of a hotel suite simply because he didn't like the flowers.

It would also follow that what Stanley Dwight, the father, might really have felt towards the repressed, pampered and freakishly gifted son was not anger but jealousy. To this day, the film *Field of Dreams*, about a father and son relationship, makes Elton John cry. 'I missed getting close to my father and I think my father missed getting close to me,' he reflects, examining his nails. 'Even though we saw each other when I became famous, it was always awkward. We just didn't connect.' But fear of confrontation was not the only legacy from the singer's youth. Partly because he believed he was plain, overweight and, at 5ft 7in, short, he was afraid that he would never be 'accepted', destined always to be lonely and unloved. This belief led to another fear: of showing his feelings, particularly of affection. The irony that he was, nevertheless, able to manipulate his audience's feelings by singing lyrics borrowed from Bernie Taupin's heart is not lost on him. 'I wasn't a good communicator,' he says, resting his chin on his chest and fixing me with a stare over the top of his glasses. 'That's why I've never been able to write my own lyrics. I had to communicate my feelings through my melodies. I could never do it in conversation. I thought that's what cocaine did for me but it didn't. It made me talk – but I was talking rubbish.'

Such was John's emotional discordance, he began to suspect he was incapable of feeling anything, ever again. He has lost many friends to the AIDS virus (and considers himself lucky to have emerged HIV-negative himself after his early years of promiscuity). And although he has devoted a lot of energy to the Elton John Aids Foundation he says he was never able to cry about the deaths he had seen. 'I don't think I had any feelings when I first went to treatment [for drink and drugs]. They said, "How do you feel?" and I said, "I don't know, I haven't felt for years." My feelings have always been suppressed. Buried for so long it was like having to get them out of the icebox and defrost them.'

But, for all his progress on the thawing front, Elton John still feels awkward about accepting affection, even from Furnish, whom he describes as the love of his life. 'Before David, I would "Eltonize" everyone I went out with,' he says. 'They would come out on their conveyor belt and be forced to give up their lives and come everywhere with me. And then, of course, their self-worth became nothing. Blah, blah, blah.' Given these insecurities, it was brave – martyrish, even – of John to leave the queenie tantrum scenes in Furnish's documentary. Then again, they were very therapeutic for him. Instead of lying on a couch for half an hour, he had a self-flagellating programme made about his life which took a year to film. And he may think that this overdose of Honesty represents a new departure in his life, but, surely, he has always had therapy on a scale as grand as this. Want to feel loved? Fill a rock stadium full of surrogate suitors whom you don't have to get too close to. Afraid people will snigger at you? Make yourself a laughing stock by wearing a piece of embroidery on your head so intricate it can be compared to the Bayeux Tapestry. Short? Wear outrageous stack heels that draw attention to your height. Myopic? Wear absurd spectacles. Want to justify your feelings of self-disgust? Buy Watford Football Club and suffer the ritual humiliation of 10,000 away fans chanting hurtful songs at you: 'He's bald! He's queer! He takes it up the rear! Elton John! Elton John!'

Actually, John doesn't find the football songs humiliating. They make him chuckle. And this is what saves him from being unbearable. He can really laugh at himself. To 'know then thyself' is perhaps the most that any of us can ever hope to achieve. To the extent that, ultimately, Elton John doesn't take himself too seriously, it can be assumed that he knows himself very well indeed. He doubtless thinks it's pretty amusing that he ended up conforming utterly to the stereotype of the mother's boy and only child who turns out to be a homosexual with a retentive personality. He has thousands of CDs, for instance, that have to be kept in alphabetical order. When John and an earlier partner checked into the Chicago clinic, each had to write down all the things that they thought were wrong with the other. His partner wrote: 'He is addicted to cocaine. He is an alcoholic. He is bulimic. He has terrible fits of rage.' John wrote: 'He doesn't tidy up his CDs.'

Elton John loves jokes at his own expense. His favourite description of himself was that he was like Bet Lynch storming around with a leopardskin coat on. And in the chapel he had built at his Windsor mansion in memory of his beloved 'Nan', there are gold-leafed, swan-necked pediments inscribed with the words Eltono es Bueno, under his coat of arms. He can be disarmingly dry, too, in his self-deprecation, always getting in there first with the glittery toecap. When he saw the cover of the song 'Live Like Horses', which showed him standing alongside Pavarotti, he murmured, 'Eat like horses, more like.'

In the starry dressing room upstairs, Elton John has pulled the ring on three cans of Coke. He's wandered over to the window and commented on the fine weather. He's made me feel jumpy by shouting 'Uugh?', like grandmothers do, whenever he hasn't heard a question. He's excused himself to go to the loo. And he's made me laugh by slipping into a camp Kenneth Williams impersonation as he describes how people react bitterly to Lottery winners: 'Oooh, you've got all this now, you won't want to know me.' And he's told me what he thinks are people's criticisms of his capricious nature and his impulsive materialism. 'I'm an excessive person,' he says with a shrug. 'You've seen all the pictures. You've heard all the stories.'

Far from feeling guilty about his indulgences, John finds them a comfort. 'I just love collecting beautiful things. I love the workmanship and I'm much more knowledgeable about them than I used to be. Now I don't buy in bulk. I know where every single thing is in every single house.'

Downstairs, Bob Halley, the burly, unshaven Cockney whom Elton John had earlier greeted with a kiss, has ambled over to say hello. For twenty-three years Halley has been John's loyal personal assistant, a job that has involved being chauffeur, the target for Coke bottles thrown in anger, and dresser during the glam-rock days – when the star was panicking before a concert, Halley would have to squeeze his boss into his Donald Duck outfit with the words, 'Get a grip.' And once asked if he thought Elton John's records would always sell, Halley said flatly, 'No. Load of old crap, aren't they?' John, who was standing by his side, nearly burst out of his suit laughing. When I question Halley about his bantering relationship with the man who pays his wages, he gives a laconic grin and scratches his stomach. 'Yeah, I think he likes me because I don't suck up to him. We have the same sense of humour. It's my job to bring him back to earth.'

Bob Halley is the Fool to Elton John's King Lear. He is the deadpan jester licensed to insult and jolly his boss out of his evil moods. Joan Collins has Christopher Biggins. Elton has Bob. But the analogies with a royal court don't end there. Two of the most poignant photographs taken this year have featured our Elton. One shows him trapped by self-parody and shamelessly divorced from reality as he arrives for his fiftieth birthday party at the Hammersmith Palais. He turned up in a removal van on a hydraulic platform, resplendent in a £50,000 costume, an ostrich-feather train and a three-and-a-half foot tall wig topped with a silver galleon.

The other – altogether more chilling – image was splashed over the front page of the *Mirror* under the headline HEALING HANDS. It shows Diana, Princess of Wales, the Queen of England manqué, consoling a weeping pop star at the memorial service held in Milan Cathedral for his close friend of twenty years, Gianni Versace. The pictures showed his ugly duckling reality crashing into a fantasy world filled with beautiful porcelain and smelling of fresh flowers. It also showed the extent to which the lines between royalty and rock aristocracy have become disturbingly blurred.

Today, according to both the star and the publicist, Elton John is trying to shed the personality he has created for himself – the 'going to parties and wearing Versace' image. In the old days, he says, he used to go to the opening of everything. Now, unless it's an Elton John Aids Foundation event or a friend who needs support, he won't go to anything. 'I can't be bothered. All that flashbulb scene. Such a rigmarole. You see the same old bloody people. Quite honestly, I'm more interested in looking at catalogues of porcelain now.' Remembering the three-and-a-half foot tall wig, 'Oh yeah?' is all you can think. But, thank goodness. We love our bejewelled, exotically plumaged, all-new, honest Elton. We love the splendid 'rubbish' he still spouts, even without cocaine. And we love the fact that, fortunately, he hasn't quite been able to shake off the acquisitiveness.

Thought to be worth at least £150 million and with houses and mansions in Windsor, London, Atlanta and Nice, John will buy an extra Rolls-Royce Corniche on a whim, employ Sir Roy Strong to design his Italianate garden, and travel with a wardrobe of thirty suits, forty jackets and six drawers of designer spectacles. The reputation for conspicuous materialism has stuck. And it's not so much that it detracts from 'the music' as that it has become inextricably linked with it.

The interview over, the tape recorder switched off, Elton John talks excidedly about the latest purchase for his new palace of excess in Nice. A spaniel puppy. He didn't intend to buy it but, last night, when his Alsatian puppies arrived and he went to the pet shop to buy beds for them, he just couldn't resist. 'I love doggies,' he laughs. 'I just love them.'

In response to this article Elton John's publicist, Simon Prytherch of John Reid Enterprises Ltd, wrote to The Sunday Telegraph: *'We felt it necessary to register our outrage at the interview with Elton John . . . Some of the article is accurate, some funny and some quite insightful but our frustration and anger is at the misrepresentation – it is simply not the feature we agreed to do nor does the piece reflect the conversation that took place. Both Elton and myself feel very hurt and let down.'*

A week after this interview appeared in 1997, Elton John sang his re-written version of 'Candle in the Wind' at the funeral of Diana, Princess of Wales and it became the biggest selling single of all time.

He has since been knighted, had a pacemaker fitted and taken his manager, John Reid, to court after discovering that £20 million had disappeared from his estate. At the trial it emerged that Sir Elton had once run up a florist's bill of £293,000 during a £40 million twenty-month spending spree.

Richard Dawkins

SEPTEMBER 1999

I think Oxford University's Professor of the Public Understanding of Science has gone into shock – traumatic hysteria, to judge by his frozen features. But he has only himself to blame. He shouldn't go around popularizing science in the way that he does. It was only a matter of time before someone like me, a bona fide member of the public, would turn up at his house and try to explain his own theories to him – using, with unjustified confidence, words such as 'biomorph', 'phenotype' and 'replicator'.

The professor blinks, then regains his composure. 'Er, right,' he says. 'Something like that.' I beam triumphantly. Mr Scott, my old biology teacher, would be proud. Prouder than he was when I failed my biology O-level, anyway.

Richard Dawkins and his wife Lalla Ward, an actress turned illustrator, live in a large, pale-brick house in Summertown, north Oxford. It has a gravelled drive and a bike parked outside its Gothic-arched front door, but it's not exactly an ivory tower – too many wooden floors, kilims and Conran cushions for that. The atmosphere is quite rarefied, though. It is a cloudless, still afternoon, and the 58-year-old professor and I are sitting on white wrought-iron chairs at a white wrought-iron table near the swimming-pool in his garden. As the sun creeps round the chimney on the house, I keep edging my chair around to avoid being dazzled. Dawkins has his back to the chimney and in the sunshine his unkempt greying hair gives him a halo.

He is a handsome man, with an angular profile, hooded eyes and tufty eyebrows that make him look like a bird of prey. There is a couple of days' stubble on his face, which he maybe thinks will help him avoid the description that journalists tend to give of him; that he has the fussy fragile air of a devout and unworldly curate – an amusing observation because, as well as being a world expert on Darwinian evolution theory, Dawkins is also one of the world's best known and most combative atheists.

Today he still looks like a clergyman, if an unshaven clergyman, with fear and suspicion in his eyes. I think he is thinking that I might be some species of stalker. A deranged fan, maybe. Perhaps I shouldn't have told him I'd read all six of his books. Or tried to prove it by quoting from them. Or told him I'd been going around quoting them to anyone who would listen.

But I couldn't – can't – help it. The man is quotable. He has four entries in the *Oxford Dictionary of Quotations*. 'They are in you and in me; they created us, body and mind; and their preservation is the ultimate rationale for our existence; they go by the name of genes, and we are their survival machines.' That's one of them, from his first bestseller, *The Selfish Gene* (1976). 'However many ways there may be of being alive, it is certain that there are vastly more ways of being dead.' That's another, from *The Blind Watchmaker* (1986). My favourite, from *Climbing Mount Improbable* (1996), hasn't made it into the *Dictionary* yet: 'If you wanted to make a flying animal, you wouldn't start with a hippo.' (The wings would have to be so big the mass of muscle needed to power them would be too heavy for the wings to lift – but it's funnier the way Dawkins puts it.)

Perhaps I'm being overly sensitive and he's neither in shock nor frightened. Perhaps he always speaks slowly and deliberately, giving short, precise answers that end abruptly and leave you stumbling to fill the cold and scaly silence with another question. It's not that his manner is severe or impolite. Indeed he makes free with a boyish smile that exposes charmingly wonky teeth. It's just that he looks either uncomfortable or bored, it is tricky to say which. Perhaps reserved is the word. I ask him if he is shy. 'Not really,' he says in a gentle alto, as thin and elusive as water. 'No, I wouldn't put it that way.' A wood pigeon coos in the background.

Certainly, I press on, he is animated and passionate when lecturing or broadcasting. Is that because he adopts a more flamboyant persona for such activities? 'I don't get nervous. But

I only like to talk on subjects I know about. That is why I never do *Any Questions*. It would be intensely painful. I don't enjoy debate. I don't think the adversarial approach is a good way to get at the truth.' He looks away distractedly. A plane drones overhead.

The thing is, I continue, the mildness and reticence don't square with his muscular prose style. He writes beautifully, lyrically, but in his books he often comes across as coolly disdainful and arrogant, irritated even. He has feuds with fellow academics, especially American ones, over the correct interpretation of Darwin's *On the Origin of Species*. He dismisses those who don't agree with him as being ignorant and lazy. 'Darwinism is not a theory of random chance,' he writes testily. 'It is a theory of random mutation plus non-random cumulative natural selection. Why, I wonder, is it so hard for even sophisticated scientists to grasp this simple point?'

In print, his most spectacular clash, conducted in *The Spectator* in 1994, has been with Paul Johnson, the Catholic historian and journalist. Dawkins wrote that he finds Johnson's framework of belief 'ignominious, contemptible and retarded'. Johnson challenged the professor to a public debate on religion and when Dawkins refused – on the grounds that he didn't see why he should involve himself in a publicity stunt for Johnson's new book – the journalist called him a 'yellow-bellied prima donna'.

In person, the Dawkins brittleness becomes apparent whenever you try to persuade him to talk about himself. It seems the only way to draw him out is to appeal to his scientific instincts: dress up personal questions requiring a subjective answer as objective, scholarly ones. He has been married three times, for instance. But to reach this topic I have to go via the question of morality in a Godless universe. Evolution, according to Dawkins's best-known theory, operates at the level of the gene rather than the individual, and we are nothing more than selfish machines blindly programmed to preserve our DNA. The universe we observe has precisely the properties we should expect if there is no design, no purpose, no evil and no good – nothing but pitiless in-difference. But if this is the case, I ask him, why do we sometimes behave altruistically, morally? We alone on earth can rebel against the selfish replicators, he answers, we alone are free agents who can learn to be good.

Can he give me an example? Has *he* learned to be good? 'I have many weaknesses,' he says earnestly, twiddling with the arm of his glasses. 'I've probably caused some unhappiness, but it's never been willing and wanton. I'm extremely soft-hearted and, I think, kind-natured and perhaps some of the unhappiness I have caused has been from being too kind, foolishly so.'

Does he mean he has caused unhappiness by not being decisive enough, by avoiding confrontation in, say, his marriages? 'Yes, I don't want to go into detail but I think it's possible to cause unhappiness by being unwilling to face up to the fact that it's not possible to be kind to everyone all the time.' And kindness is something we have to work at? It doesn't come naturally? 'Well, yes, as a biologist I would say there is a sense in which that is true.'

To find out about his childhood you have to go via his first brush with Darwinism. It wasn't exactly an epiphany. 'Not as much as it should have been. I was a bit sceptical and somehow it didn't seem to be quite enough to explain all the beauty and the complexity of life. I didn't really appreciate how powerful the theory is or the fact that it's the only theory we've got. Above all, I didn't appreciate the enormous amount of time available for evolution to take place – it is this that the human mind has most difficulty grasping.'

He was sixteen at the time. Yet from birth Dawkins had been exposed to nature red in tooth and claw. He was born in Nairobi in 1941 and educated at Oundle School. His father, a colonial civil servant stationed in what was then Nyasaland – now Malawi – returned to England when he inherited the family farm in Oxfordshire. 'I have happy memories of Africa,' Dawkins says. 'Flowers, butterflies, colours, smells, but nothing terribly co-herent because we came back here when I was eight.' His parents are still alive, and their grandson – by Dawkins's younger sister – is running the farm. It is mixed, dairy, pigs and arable, and growing up there young Richard came to regard death and sex as an everyday matter of fact.

'It was always assumed I would take over the farm. I would help out driving tractors. But I don't think I did much hand-

wringing when I decided to enter academia instead.' He took a
first at Balliol College, Oxford, followed by a D.Phil. and a D.Sc.
Before his return to Oxford to take up a fellowship at New
College – and later to become the first Charles Simonyi Professor
of the Public Understanding of Science – he spent a few years
lecturing at Berkeley, California. It was the time of the Vietnam
protests and, though he took part in them, he now says he feels
a bit embarrassed for having done so. His time in America also
made him aware of the lobbying power of the Bible Belt, which
last month celebrated the banning of the teaching of evolution-
ary theory from schools in the state of Kansas.

Charles Darwin was considered controversial in his day, with
politicians debating whether they were on the side of the apes or
the angels. Dawkins provokes controversy because he goes
further than Darwin. He calls theologians 'bigoted enemies of
knowledge'. He describes the Pope as a dangerous, world-
damaging dictator. The concept of God, according to Dawkins,
is like a virus, passed from person to person. In one sense, he
says, he is surprised to find himself a controversial figure for
promoting his 'selfish gene' interpretation of evolution theory,
more than a century after Darwin. 'But it's only in the United
States, where there are a lot of fundamentalists. I think it is
insulting to Christians in this country to suggest that they are
creationists. But on the other hand it has to be said there is still
an enormous ignorance of Darwinism here. When you think it
is the explanation for our existence and the existence of all life
and that it is not difficult to understand – really rather simple,
compared to quantum mechanics – it seems absurd that it is one
of the last things you are taught in school.'

Dawkins describes Oundle as a conventional Anglican
boarding school, and he was confirmed at thirteen. 'I've got a
lot of time for the Church of England,' he says. 'I mean, it's like
village cricket. I've got a soft spot for it as an English institution.
But evolution should be one of the first things you learn at school.
It should be something inspiring and exciting for children to
remember for the rest of their lives and what do they get instead?
Sacred hearts and incense. Shallow, empty religion.'

Dawkins has a gift for communicating ideas and for conveying his own wonder at the complexity of nature. When you read

his books you begin to notice the minutiae of nature around you, the staggeringly sophisticated feat of engineering that is a spider's web, for instance. 'Yes, and it is so easy to take these things for granted,' he says. 'You have to imagine you are opening your eyes and seeing for the first time. I've never had a mystical experience, but I wonder if when people claim they have, that is what has happened, the scales have fallen from the eyes, as though they have just been born, with the intellect of an adult.' He has aesthetic experiences looking at great cathedrals or listening to classical music, and he thinks these may be what people confuse with religious experiences. 'I also get it looking through a microscope,' he adds. 'I feel overwhelmed. The hairs on the back of my neck stand up. And the more you understand about the natural world, the more beautiful it seems.'

He must get sick of being patronized by people who tell him he writes well, *for a scientist*. 'It's up to others to judge if some scientists can write well absolutely, or only well for a scientist,' he says with a smile. 'Science is inherently poetic and awe-inspiring so you don't need to colour your language – you just need to tell it honestly.' In his latest book, *Unweaving the Rainbow*, Dawkins answers Keats's question, 'Do not all charms fly / At the mere touch of cold philosophy?' with a robust, 'No.' He explains the workings of starlight, sound waves and rainbows, to prove that science should inspire rather than undermine the poetic imagination.

His gift for coming up with vivid metaphors has led some reviewers to label him the Tom Stoppard of science. But this is also to do with his good looks. I ask him if his handsome features and intelligence indicate that his ancestors were successfully selfish in their search for partners? He looks mortified. 'Er, I don't want to talk about myself but, in general, any animal is by definition the product of successful ancestors, um, in the Darwinian sense, and so any animal can look in the mirror and say that. But that is on a much longer time-scale. And it's never occurred to me, personally, looking in the mirror. Er, I did recently find out a little about my family tree. Have you heard of the Balliol Rhymes? They are a collection of comic verse from the late-nineteenth century. A dozen of my family were at Balliol and my great-great-great-uncle Clinton Edward Dawkins was there in the 1880s. The rhyme about him was, "Positivists ever talkin' / Such an epic as Dawkins / Creeds are out and Man is all / Spell him with a capital." It's not far off being appropriate to me. Except I would add animals to man. So maybe there is some hereditary influence there.'

Man and animals are all. And God is not dead because he never existed in the first place. I take a deep breath and attempt to summarize another of Dawkins's arguments for him. For God to create the universe he would have to be hyper-intelligent. But intelligence only evolves over time. Is that about the strength of it? 'It's worse than that, the argument for God starts by assuming what it is attempting to explain – intelligence, complexity, it comes to the same thing – and so it explains nothing. God is a non-explanation. Whereas evolution by natural selection *is* an explanation. It really does start simply and become complex.'

And when he contemplates his own mortality in this Godless universe how does he feel? 'I accept that this is all there is and that you have to live like hell while you can. I'm pretty calm about death. I don't fear it. I just have this strong feeling that life is wonderful but finite and that we are immensely privileged to have it.' He crosses his hairy legs – he is wearing shorts – and rocks back in his chair. 'I used to think religion was a genuine comfort in death, but I've heard from hospital nurses who've said to my real surprise that the patients who really seem to be terrified of death are the Catholics. I don't know why this is. Maybe they are doing a quick calculation of how good or bad they have been. But that is only anecdotal.'

There's going to be no danger of him losing his nerve at the end? 'No. I can safely say that.' He has a teenage daughter, Juliet, from his second marriage. Does she represent a form of immortality for him? 'Only for my genes, and that's not really the same thing at all.' Someone whose books go on being read achieves a kind of immortality, surely? 'There's a long way to go before we will know if this will happen in my case. But even that doesn't compare with actually living forever. As Woody Allen said, "I don't want to be immortal through my achievements, I want to be immortal through not dying."'

Is this evidence of a sense of humour? A former student of Dawkins has told me that the professor doesn't really have one.

He also told me that Dawkins is petulant and vain, and regurgitates the same themes formulaically in each book. I don't know whether any of that is true, but I do sense that he has a bit of a persecution complex and is a little naive. He can't really understand why Christians get upset with him simply for telling the truth as he sees it.

He also seems to have an almost inhuman lack of sentimentality. When his daughter was six he asked her why she thought there were flowers in the world. She said they were there to make the world pretty and to help the bees make honey for us. He was touched by this and sorry to have to tell her it wasn't true: that flowers are in the world to copy their DNA. There is something quite comical about such pathological seriousness. I ask him if, given his loathing of all things superstitious – astrology, clairvoyance, fairy tales – he felt the need to disabuse his six-year-old daughter of belief in Father Christmas? 'Well, I did have a game with her in which we worked out how fast Father Christmas would have to travel to get round all the chimneys in the world in one night. I don't think the realization that it was impossible shook her too much.'

Richard Dawkins is getting fidgety. We have been talking for an hour and a half, and he is surreptitiously checking the time on his square-faced watch. The body language – knees drawn up to chest, hands behind head – could not be clearer. I ask if I can use his phone to order a taxi. He does it for me. When he returns he is carrying a new Dutch translation of *Unweaving the Rainbow* which has just arrived in the post. His wife Lalla pops outside to see if I want another cup of tea before I leave. She is the daughter of Viscount Bangor and the former wife of Tom Baker, with whom she appeared in *Dr Who*. She met Richard Dawkins at a surprise fortieth birthday party for the novelist Douglas Adams. She was talking to Stephen Fry at the time, and when their eyes met it was, well, love at first sight.

His ordeal by interview over, Dawkins relaxes visibly. He tells me that he and his wife read poetry to each other. 'Lalla reads so beautifully she can make me feel tearful. And when I read I can sometimes feel a catch in my voice. And I feel a bit embarrassed about it, try to conceal it. I don't think I cry about things that happen in real life often – mainly because I am fortunate enough not to have anything much to cry about. It is more a kind of sentiment over the written word. Poetic language. I suppose it is a little embarrassing for a grown man to allow himself to cry over a book.'

Goodness. He's finally talking about himself. Quick, quick. His world view has been described as a bleak and despairing one. Is he prone to melancholia? 'Not at all. I have a wonderful life. Enjoy every minute of it. I love to see other people enjoy their life too. The myth of my having a pessimistic view of life comes from the way in which I express honestly the state of humanity in the universe – which can seem bleak if you set out with unrealistic expectations in the first place. I get worried and depressed about all the work I have to do. If I haven't met a deadline or haven't finished a book, I fret about it and wish I was more disciplined.'

Does he have a fragile ego, a need for reassurance? 'I get hurt by criticism which is misguided and misinformed. The militant atheist label annoys me because it can only be said by someone who hasn't read my books.' Just time for one more question. His leisure hours. How are they spent? Recreational drugs? 'No.' The footie? A shake of the head. Singing round the piano? A smile at this. 'Around the piano, yes, that's a lovely thing to do. Haven't done it for years. Singing around the piano.'

The door bell rings. The taxi is here. I leave the home of this man, who is in his way still fighting a Victorian battle, with the disconcertingly Victorian vision of him singing around the piano with his family.

Stephen Hawking

JANUARY 2000

Possibly the greatest, certainly the most famous scientific thinker since Einstein is sitting in his motorized wheelchair grinning at me. 'Look behind the door,' Professor Stephen Hawking says in his computer-generated, Dalek-like voice. I look. There's a framed black-and-white photograph hanging there, which shows him in the foreground and Marilyn Monroe leaning against a Cadillac in the background. I smile. The superimposition is funny and subtle. Perhaps the professor has just had it done and wants to show everyone. But I suspect he doesn't want to get drawn into a long conversation about it; it's just his way of saying hello and breaking the ice.

All Hawking's conversations are long, even his short ones. He raises his eyebrows for 'yes', winks his left eye for 'no', but for the most part communicates via a voice synthesizer at the rate of fifteen to twenty words a minute. He suffers from motor neurone disease, a rare condition which degenerates the central nervous system and leads to a wasting of the muscles. It does not affect the brain or the senses. Hawking was first diagnosed with it when he was twenty-one, at which age he was told he had a life expectancy of two to three years. He is now fifty-seven.

He has cheated death, but his body is paralysed – apart from a little movement in his twisted fingers. He doesn't type with these so much as apply pressure to two pads, one in each hand, in order to select letters, words and phrases from an index on his computer monitor. He scrolls up and down the screen constantly, at great speed. But, inevitably, the writing process is agonizingly slow. Only when he has constructed the whole

343

sentence or paragraph on screen does he activate his robotic voice to speak it. As a definition of Hell, it would be hard to improve upon the perversity of this predicament: a man with a freakishly quick, brilliant and creative mind condemned forever to articulate his thoughts at the speed of an imbecile.

We've no time for small talk then. I have come here – to Cambridge University's Department of Applied Mathematics and Theoretical Physics, where Hawking holds the professorial chair once held by Isaac Newton – on the turn of the millennium to ask him what he thinks the future has in store for the human race.

If the world's population continues to grow at its present rate, doubling every forty years, there isn't going to be enough room for us all on Earth by the year 2600. So will we, I ask, be able to spread out to other planets? His hands go into action. The only sounds in the room are the clicking of the pressure pads and the whirring of the computer. The electronic voice delivers the answer five minutes later. 'We shall probably manage a manned or, should I say, personned, flight to Mars in the next century,' Hawking says. 'But Earth is by far the most favoured planet in the solar system. Mars is small, cold and without much atmosphere, and the other planets are quite unsuitable for human beings. We either have to learn to live in space stations or travel to the next star. We won't do that in the next century.'

I ask Hawking how fast we will be able to travel on our journey to the next star. Pause. Answer: 'I'm afraid that however clever we may become we will never be able to travel faster than light. If we could travel faster than light we could go back in time. We have not seen any tourists from the future. That means that travel to other stars is going to be a slow and tedious business, using rockets rather than warp drives. A 100,000-year round trip to the centre of the galaxy. In that time the human race will have changed beyond all recognition, if it hasn't wiped itself out.'

Even though there is ice on the ground outside and a bitingly cold wind blowing in over the Fens, Hawking has his window open; his assistant, Chris, has explained to me that this is because the professor thinks better when he's cold. I try to stop my teeth from chattering as I ask whether we humans will keep on changing, or will we eventually reach an ultimate level of development and knowledge? Click click click. 'In the next hundred years, or even in the next twenty, we may discover a complete theory of the basic laws of the universe (the so-called Theory of Everything in which quantum theory is unified with Einstein's theory of general relativity), but there will be no limit to the complexity of the biological or electronic systems we can build under these laws.'

I'm just about to ask a supplementary question when the hands start up again. A few minutes pass before Hawking adds: 'By far the most complex systems we have are our own bodies. There haven't been any significant changes in human DNA in the past 10,000 years. But soon we will be able to increase the complexity of our internal record, our DNA, without having to wait for the slow process of biological evolution.'

The professor's predictions, especially his thoughts on improving the human body, seem all the more poignant when you listen to him deliver them in person. Time is even more relative than usual in his company; it actually seems to slow down during those long pauses between my questions and his answers. My interview lasts for four hours, with breaks when a nurse comes in and I'm asked to leave the room. Since the professor had an operation on his oesophagus early last year, the problem he had with food getting into his lungs has been reduced, but he still needs regular suction.

I don't, however, have to leave his room when the nurse comes in to spoon-feed him with an assortment of pills. These are taken with sips of tea which is mostly spilled onto the bib that the nurse ties around his neck. Hawking has thick lips, parchment-smooth skin and a schoolboy fringe, which his nurse parts to one side for him. While all this is going on, the professor patiently continues working the pressure-pads in his hands to compose sentences and paragraphs on his computer screen.

I ask if developing improved humans won't cause great social and political problems with respect to unimproved humans? 'I'm not advocating human genetic engineering,' Hawking replies metallically. 'I'm just saying it's likely to happen and we should consider how to deal with it.'

When engaged in conversation with Stephen Hawking none of the usual laws of social interaction apply. After the first few minutes of being with him, however, the long pauses no longer seem awkward. Apart from his big, disarming smile and his expressive eyes – 'twinkling' seems the most apt, if hackneyed, description of them – there is no body language to help interpret his words. But the monotone voice does give his utterances an amused, deadpan quality (the voice goes up and down in tone quite musically, but the emphasis it gives to certain words is not necessarily a reflection of their importance in the sentence). Thus, when asked if electronic complexity will go on for ever, or whether there will be a natural limit, his eyes twinkle, his hands do their frenetic work, and ten minutes later the voice delivers what sounds like a dry comeback.

'On the biological side, the limit of human intelligence up to now has been set by the size of the human brain that will pass through the birth canal,' Hawking says. 'Having watched my three children being born, I know how difficult it is to get the head out. But in the next hundred years I expect we will learn how to grow babies outside the human body so this limitation will be removed. But ultimately, increases in the size of the human brain through genetic engineering will come up against the problem that the chemical messages responsible for our mental activity are relatively slow-moving – so further increases in the complexity of the brain will be at the expense of speed. We can be quick-witted or very intelligent, but not both.'

It's time to ask the big one: will we make contact with aliens in the next millennium? Hawking smiles. His fingers click the pressure-pads. The answer comes seven minutes later. 'The human race has been in its present form for only the past two million years out of the fifteen billion or so since the Big Bang. So even if life developed in other stellar systems, the chances of catching it at a recognizably human stage are very small. Any alien life we encounter will be much more primitive or much more advanced than us. And if it's more advanced, why hasn't it spread through the galaxy and visited Earth? It could be that there is an advanced race out there which is aware of our existence but is leaving us to stew in our own primitive juices. However, I doubt they would be so considerate to a lower life form. There is a sick joke that the reason we have not been contacted by extra-terrestrials is that when a civilization reaches our stage of development it becomes unstable and destroys itself.'

Stephen Hawking has ten nurses who each do three ten-hour shifts a week. He rises at 7.45 a.m., has physiotherapy, arrives for work at his department at about 11.30 a.m., goes home – five minutes away in the grounds of an all-female college – at about 7 p.m. and is bathed and put to bed by midnight. A nurse turns him over during the night. According to one of the nurses I met, he is a pussycat to work for, always puts people at their ease, rarely complains and hates to be pitied or patronized. One of his friends, the physicist David Schramm, says that he is also an incorrigible flirt: a party animal who likes to dance in his wheelchair. His daughter Lucy says he has an amazing capacity to push those around him to the very edge of physical and mental collapse, while smiling to himself.

Hawking is well known for his sense of humour – he likes joking about the American accent his voice synthesizer has given him and about his appearances as himself in his two favourite American ('which isn't saying much') programmes, *Star Trek* and *The Simpsons*. His intolerance towards fools is also well documented. There are stories of how he runs over the feet of people who annoy him – and he once went to full throttle and rammed a car that was blocking his ramp. When asked if it is true that he uses his wheelchair as a weapon he will reply: 'That's a malicious rumour. I'll run over anyone who repeats it.'

The intermittent nature of our conversation gives me a good chance to study his room. There is a karaoke machine on the floor and a Marilyn Monroe calendar by the door. There's a Homer Simpson clock on the wall and, next to a row of Russian dolls on a shelf, a Homer Simpson card that says: 'Every time I learn something new it pushes some old stuff out of my brain.' There is a sticker on the door saying: 'Quiet Please The Boss is Asleep'. It's all Junior Common Room humour, c. 1973; the professor frozen in time. Also on the shelves there are photographs of Hawking's children and grandchild. He has said that the thing he regretted most about being paralysed was not being able to play with his children when they were young. His daughter tells a rather touching story of how, as a treat at meal times, he used to make her laugh by wiggling his ears.

There are also scores of books on the shelves with titles such as *The Left Hand of Creation, Quantum Gravity, Black Holes in Two Dimensions* and *Particle Cosmology*. But I can't see a copy of the phenomenally successful *A Brief History of Time,* which Hawking wrote in 1988. In it he attempted to explain to a general readership his theory of how the universe began. And even though few people have been able to get beyond the first dozen or so pages, it was translated into sixty-five languages and became one of the biggest selling non-fiction books of all time.

It must have made him very rich indeed. Certainly it has made him famous enough to command fees of about £50,000 for a single public lecture in America and the Far East, and £100,000 for appearing in television advertisements for Specsavers. In all, his commercial endeavours are thought to be worth more than £1 million a year.

We normally associate being rich and successful with living a life of luxury – but what, I ask him, does wealth and success mean to him? 'I may be successful in my work,' he says through his machine. 'But I'm hardly rich on the scale of people in the City. To lead a reasonably normal life, I need a lot of nursing care, and I won't get that on the NHS. I would be stuck in a home without a computer or much individual attention and I probably wouldn't survive long. So it has been very important to earn enough to pay for my care both now and in the future.'

In 1995 Stephen Hawking married his nurse, Elaine, the former wife of the man who invented his voice synthesizer. It was the same year he divorced Jane, his first wife and the mother of his three children. Stephen had met Jane at a New Year's Eve party in 1962, just as his illness was beginning to take its toll, and he married her three years later. Last year she wrote an autobiography, a damning account of her life with Hawking. In it she alludes rather cruelly to the complicated nature of the couple's sex life; she also describes herself as a 'drudge' and her husband as 'a masterly puppeteer' sometimes made despotic by the combination of public adulation and an illness that left him as helpless as an infant.

She received little thanks for devoting her life to caring for him, she wrote, and often came close to suicide. In the early 1990s when it was obvious their marriage had broken down, she had a discreet affair with a Cambridge choirmaster who eventually moved into the Hawking household, apparently with Stephen's tacit understanding. But a twenty-four-hour nursing team also moved in and Jane accused them of dressing provocatively and trying to manipulate her husband emotionally.

Although Professor Hawking does not comment on his first marriage, claiming never to have read Jane's book, he does reflect that: 'There are aspects of my celebrity I don't like, but it would be hypocritical to complain. I can generally ignore it by going off to think in eleven dimensions.'

Stephen Hawking was born on 8 January, 1942, 300 years to the day after the death of his hero, Galileo. He was brought up in St Albans and was in many ways a normal, clumsy, inky-fingered child – except that he used to make fireworks and cannibalize television and radio sets to build computers, before computers had really been invented. He also had handwriting that was so bad it was unreadable and a stutter that he inherited from his father, a medical researcher described by one family friend as a disconcerting eccentric with below-average charm.

At Oxford, Stephen Hawking never attended lectures, soon realized he was intellectually superior to his tutors and grew bored with life. He took a first in Physics, but only after a viva revealed his genius for problem-solving and his contempt for course work. It has sometimes been suggested that had it not been for his illness Hawking might not have focused his mind and gone on to make the contribution to science that he did. It galvanized him and forced him to solve problems not on a blackboard but geometrically and pictorially in his head – in eleven dimensions.

It is tempting to read much into the paradox of his condition: a pure mind wandering the universe while trapped in a wasted body. Like Milton's blindness or Beethoven's deafness, it seems at once heroic, tragic and romantic. But Hawking dismisses the description. 'I have never felt myself as a perfect soul living in an imperfect body. Although I may take pride in my intelligence, I have to accept that the disability is also part of me.'

Yet if we have souls, his is surely a romantic one. He loves listening to Wagner. And he refers to his longing to discover, through physics and cosmology, the mind of God. His friends say he sometimes feels a crushing sense of loneliness, even though he rarely experiences the luxury of being on his own. I ask him if he has any recurring dreams. 'I think I dream a lot, but normally I don't remember what I dream. One dream I do remember is being in a hot-air balloon. For me the balloon is a symbol of hope. I first had the dream at my lowest point when I caught pneumonia and had to have a tracheotomy operation that removed my power of speech.'

That was in 1985. His condition then was so bad that his first wife was asked to give her permission to switch off his life-support machine. She refused. Presumably Hawking didn't expect that he would still be around to see in the new millennium? 'No.' he says. 'But now I would be disappointed if I didn't live long enough to be sure that there was indeed a picture into which everything fitted.'

I've heard Professor Hawking described as many things: a bloody-minded genius, a witty manipulator, a prima donna. But what three words would he use to describe himself? There is a long pause before that unemotional computerized voice penetrates the icy Cambridge air: 'Determined, optimistic and . . . I can't think of a third. My wife would say stubborn and out of touch with reality.' I leave as I came in four hours earlier, with a smile on my face.

Steven Spielberg

The surprise is that, in certain countries, Steven Spielberg gets mobbed whenever he's spotted stepping out of a car or emerging from a hotel. Hair ruffled matily, congratulatory pats on back, autograph books thrust under nose. Not in Britain, obviously. Because we're a dignified and reserved people. But in certain countries. Mobbed.

Now, as Spielberg is the most successful film maker in history – name credits on eight of the fifteen biggest blockbusters – mobbing might be precisely what you would expect. Crowds do tend to behave embarrassingly when a celebrity is in their midst. But what this fails to take into account is the strange truth that 51-year-old Steven Spielberg is almost completely anonymous to behold.

I spent an hour studying him at close quarters as we talked about anti-Semitism and his childhood neuroses. He struck me as a likeable man, unassuming and thoughtful. But at the end of that time I came away with only vague impressions of what he actually looked like. An Open University lecturer in physics is about the best comparison I can offer. I'm confident there was a greying, neatly clipped beard involved. Oval-shaped, metal-framed glasses almost certainly came into it. And – I'm really just guessing about this – jeans and trainers may have been worn. But beyond that? Thomas Keneally once described him as having a face like a map of Poland, with stuck-on lips. And Martin Amis once mistook him for a Coke-machine fixer.

As to height, I'd say not especially tall. But this may just be because I've read somewhere that he is 5ft 8in. His body language is a bit defensive maybe, hunched shoulders, hands clasped between knees. And voice? I've no recollection whatsoever of what he sounded like. Even playing back my interview tape doesn't really help. Perhaps it's just that other famous directors contrive somehow to stand out from the crowd – Alfred Hitchcock had his droopy face and signature tune, Orson Welles his chipmunk cheeks, cloak and fedora, Woody Allen his thick glasses and child bride – but with Spielberg you just look right past him.

When I arrive on a drizzling February morning at the log-cabin-effect Hollywood building where Spielberg works, I am led along corridors lined with the milestones of his career – a *Jurassic Park* dinosaur here, *Jaws* and *Indiana Jones* memorabilia there – and am left to wait in a room around which I immediately begin to snoop. A wooden beam. The thick impasto of a landscape painting. A russet-coloured kilim. A Steven Spielberg. A black upright piano. A framed *ET* storyboard . . . See? Rewind. Fourth item. While my back has been turned, Spielberg has insinuated himself into the room and is standing in the corner as unobtrusively as it is possible for a person to stand, short of not actually being in the room at all. 'Ah,' I say. Closely followed by a more reflective 'Oh.'

The conversation picks up a bit after this and it soon emerges that Spielberg extends his views on the importance of being ordinary and anonymous in appearance to the details of his domestic life. It's 10 a.m. and he has been up since six. 'I have two school drops,' he says. 'The first is at seven, then I make breakfast for everyone and take the other three kids at eight. Life is not worth living if you can't do car pool.'

Steven Spielberg and his second wife, actress Kate Capshaw, have seven children, of various provenance, who scamper about their light and airy $12-million second home in Pacific Palisades, California. Max, Spielberg's oldest 'biological' child – as they say on the West Coast – was born in 1985. Two more recent additions to the family are adopted African-Americans – Theo, nine, and Mikaela George, two – and their father has just arranged a special screening for them of his latest film, *Amistad*, which is about the slave trade. 'I really wanted my children to know about this story,' the director says. 'I was with them when they saw the film and my nine-year-old, Theo, who is black, felt a lot of compassion for Cinqué [the leader of the African captives] and really wanted to see him get back to Africa, to his wife. It made him appreciate the impact that slavery had on this country and on Africa as well. But the other kids thought there wasn't enough action in the film. Too much talk!'

The intention, he adds, is for the overall composition of the film to resemble a still-life tableau, so that nothing distracts from the power of the set speeches. There are, however, some shocking and dramatic scenes woven in as well, notably when we see the Africans being whipped, starved and chained together in the cargo hold of the slave ship. As with the more graphic scenes in the multi-Oscar-winning *Schindler's List*, the modest idea behind this, according to the director, is to force vast audiences to confront the full horror of the crimes of history in order to avoid repeating them.

The film has been criticized for presenting the history of the abolitionist movement from a rather self-congratulatory white perspective. 'I don't see it that way,' Spielberg says after a pause. 'I felt everyone had to share in the pride of an American Supreme Court which, except for one dissenting vote, turned these Africans back to the freedom they were born with. I felt a wave of patriotism at that. *Amistad* is really about the beginning of the moral conscience of America.'

Spielberg does not conclude that there is a natural condition in man that inclines him toward the exploitation of others. 'I'm a bit more optimistic than that,' he says. 'I always look on the bright side. I wasn't being cynical when I made *Amistad*. I just feel man hasn't evolved far enough. I mean, the Holocaust was only fifty-four years ago.'

Spielberg has a benign image. On the one hand, thanks to films like *ET*, he represents wholesome all-American family values. On the other, with films such as *The Color Purple* and *Schindler's List*, he is seen as a liberal-minded humanitarian. When it became known that he was planning a film about the Holocaust the intelligentsia in America was appalled. They assumed that the archetypal Hollywood populist would be far too shallow to do justice to the subject. Taking a similar view, the World Jewish Congress objected to him filming on the site of Auschwitz – eventually he was allowed to film outside the gates.

He had, of course, set himself a seemingly impossible task and, in choosing to give an account of the Holocaust through a story which had a positive ending, he knew he was leaving himself open to charges of trivialization. 'I was aware of that,' he now says. 'And I was nervous about it. It did take me ten years to start work on *Schindler's List* and part of that was due to my fear that I wasn't going to be able to acquit myself in a manner that would bring anything less than shame to the memory of the Holocaust. I didn't want to belittle or trivialize it. I worked hard not to soften it or make it easy to watch. The film doesn't have a positive ending. You know the victims will be ravaged with nightmares for the rest of their lives.'

'For many survivors the nightmare began with liberation,' Spielberg explains. 'Because that was when they had a chance to assess their losses. When they were in Auschwitz or Treblinka they didn't know for sure whether the rest of their families were dead.' Twenty members of Spielberg's family were murdered in the concentration camps. Both his parents' parents were European Jews, his father's side of the family coming from an area of Austria which is now a part of Poland, and his mother's side from Odessa in the Ukraine. Spielberg thinks of himself as Jewish–American, he says. But his Jewish identity was not really something that concerned him until he made *Schindler's List*. Perhaps there was an element of denial in this. After all, as a child growing up in an affluent white neighbourhood of Cincinnati, he says he encountered a lot of anti-Semitism. A gang of school children once gathered outside his family home chanting, 'The Spielbergs are dirty Jews.' Classmates would cough the word Jew into their hands when they passed by him. One day he retaliated against his Jew-hating neighbours by smearing peanut butter on their windows.

His father, Arnold Spielberg, was a pioneering computer engineer and was always having to move house because of his work – from Ohio to New Jersey, then to Arizona and finally northern California. Wherever the family went they met racism, sometimes violent. At one point, the young Steven would have to be picked up from school by his parents every day, even though he was walking distance from home. At another, following regular anti-Semitic remarks about the size of his nose, he would attempt to stop it growing downward by tying it back with tape. 'The nature of the anti-Semitism was always lack of education,' he now reflects. 'Not understanding what a Jew is. Anti-Semites invest a lot of ethnic, cultural stereotype and evil to something that scares them. Fear of my unknown. The effect it had on me was to turn me into a loner. It made me withdrawn and self-conscious and even turned me away from my family, who I was angry at for making me a Jew . . . I think I would have been a social reject anyway, even if I had been Protestant or Lutheran or Episcopalian. I would still have been introverted.'

For all his introversion, Steven Spielberg managed to be assertive at home. He has three younger sisters and, he admits, he would bully them, in part as a form of compensation for being bullied himself at school. After leaving school, he turned to films as a way of expressing himself and also as a form of escapism. Aged twenty-one, he started loitering around the Universal Pictures lot and even squatted in an empty office until he got his amateur home movies seen by someone. They were deemed impressive enough for him to be offered a television contract, which meant him having to drop out of a degree in English at California State College. Folklore has it that he didn't even stop to clean out his locker. He made *Duel* in 1971, and four years later made *Jaws*, the highest-grossing film of its time.

The chutzpah does not seem consistent with lack of self-esteem. Even so, to this day, Spielberg protests that he is basically very shy. 'I work overtime to put up a façade to persuade people that I am not shy,' he says. 'I know how to break the ice better than I used to, but I still have a shaky stomach before I go to a party, even before I sit down for dinner with close friends. I'm always tongue-tied for the first ten minutes. Now, if I meet people for the first time who feel intimidated by me – and so don't make eye contact – that makes me feel uncomfortable. Two people standing there who don't know what to say to each other. That happens a lot.'

More incongruous still is the reputation shy Steven Spielberg has acquired for being ruthless with people who cross him – a producer who tried to take more credit that she deserved was summarily dropped, for instance. There were occasions, too, when in a fit of pique, the introverted director would storm off a film set. Perhaps it is more a matter of his overcompensating for what he perceives as being his social shortcomings. Then again, before he made *Schindler's List*, Spielberg was often dismissed as an arch-manipulator of audience emotion, one who merely wallowed in maudlin sentimentality. He used never to read reviews of his work but claims now not to care unduly about what critics say of him. And while he believes part of his new found interest in history comes from an increasing awareness of his own mortality, paradoxically he says he is not concerned about his place in the history books. This doesn't quite square with the liberal image-consciousness that inclines him to keep very quiet about the fact he has amassed a fine gun collection of old and new weapons. Nor does it explain the rumour that he has been buying up all the homes he lived in as a child with a view to turning them into Spielberg shrines, in the manner of Shakespeare's birthplace.

'I'm not that concerned about being remembered, about my place in history,' he says. 'I don't write my own epitaph every day. I was really satisfied with *ET*. It's the most personal movie I ever made. The story of my childhood. I knew that even if I just carried on making sequels to *Indiana Jones* I would always have *ET*.' *ET*, he points out, is less about a cute extraterrestrial coming to Earth, more about the nature of divorce in America. In the film, the boy's parents are divorced and his father is always away from home. ET is his way of filling the void. For his part, Spielberg found his parents' constant rowing and eventual divorce traumatic. He would stuff towels under the door to keep out the noise of their bickering. The house, he says, was pervaded with a sense of unhappiness.

His parents are still alive: his mother, Leah, remarried and now, aged seventy-eight, runs a kosher restaurant; his father married again last year, at the age of eighty. Wearily Spielberg says that he didn't really learn from his parents' marital mistakes. His first marriage, to actress Amy Irving, ended in divorce, with Irving walking off with a $100-million settlement. 'My divorce?' he says. 'Yeah, I don't really want to talk about that. It's personal. But I think that, even though it sometimes strengthens the character, children from a divorced home are always damaged.' According to Spielberg's biographer Andrew Yule, the damage in the director's case may have taken the form of a whole basket of neuroses – from nail-biting to phobias about insects, flying, the ocean, the dark, lifts, even of furniture with feet. 'I'm no longer afraid of the dark,' Spielberg now says. 'Because that is where I screen my movies. But I'm still afraid of lifts. It's a runaround sometimes.' He emits a short laugh. 'I have to go through so much hassle to take the stairs. I have to get people to unlock stairwells. Especially in Paris, where the lifts are so small. I walk ten floors to avoid them. Don't know why it is. I'm not in analysis. Not an analysis kind of guy. I just have a fear of small spaces.' He doesn't think it's to do with a fear of losing control, though, because he says he doesn't mind driving in traffic where the actions of on-coming cars are unpredictable.

In terms of his career, though, whether it is because he is adept at controlling events or not, Spielberg has barely put a foot wrong. Will *Amistad* mark a departure from this phenomenal record? Spielberg claims to be concerned only that its message is put across, not that it makes a lot of money. But he doesn't deny that much is riding on the film in terms of reputation: not least because it is the first Spielberg-directed production for Dream-works, the Hollywood studio that he set up two years ago in partnership with music potentate David Geffen and former Disney chief Jeffrey Katzenberg. Some $2.7 billion has been invested in the company and it has been hailed as the first major studio to be founded in Hollywood since Charlie Chaplin helped set up United Artists in 1919. Its first feature – *The Peacemaker* – didn't exactly break box-office records when it was released last autumn.

Richard Dreyfuss, star of *Jaws* and *Close Encounters of the Third Kind*, once described Spielberg as a kid of twelve who decided to make movies – and is still twelve. Spielberg is prescient enough to agree that he didn't really mature as a film maker until he made *Schindler's List*. Whether he has retained any vestiges of childish self-aggrandizing, shallowness and manipulation, though, is a matter for future historians to debate. After all, Spielberg is only fifty-one.

This appeared in February 1998. Stephen Spielberg and Dreamworks went on to make the multi-Oscar-award-winning Saving Private Ryan, American Beauty *and* Gladiator. *Spielberg was awarded a knighthood in 2000, and ran into trouble from LA planners after trying to build a five-storey stable for his wife's horses.*

The Dalai Lama

A river of orange water is tumbling hysterically down the steep side streets of Dharamsala, cleansing them of manure left by the sacred cows that roam free here. It's also carrying off the empty drink cans and food wrappers discarded by the thousands of 'spiritual tourists' who trail up here each summer in the hope of ticking the exiled Dalai Lama off their lists of things to see.

Though this ramshackle town is perched on a spur high in the foothills of the Himalayas, and though it overlooks a plunging, verdant valley, its buildings – mostly small hotels topped with satellite dishes and souvenir shops selling Dalai Lama memorabilia – are fetid and ugly, especially during a late July deluge. Sodden monkeys, hairy young Western backpackers and maroon-robed Tibetan monks alike shelter miserably under corrugated tin roofs and cafe awnings. The ferocious speed of the river, coloured by topsoil as it funnels down from the surrounding Dhauladar mountains, is confounding and hypnotic. The scene could be Biblical. An ominous purgation of a corrupt town.

Sitting in a low, elaborately carved wooden chair at one end of a long audience room is one of the 100,000 refugees to have settled in India since the Tibetan diaspora began forty years ago. His Holiness the Fourteenth Dalai Lama of Tibet, Bodhisattva of Compassion and Nobel Peace Prize Laureate, hasn't given up hope that one day he will return to his homeland, or, at least, that one of his reincarnations will. Tibetan Buddhists tend to take the long view on these things. Over those years of exile, he says with a giggle so inappropriate it must be a nervous one, his mind has become hardened to stories of torture. 'Every week I am meeting an increased number of Tibet refugees,' he says in halting, guttural English. 'In the past when innocent people, ragged and destitute, come and explain their own horrible experience to me, sometimes they crying, crying, crying, and I also feel very sad and tear comes. But I have become too familiar with these horrible stories and I feel less.' He pats his heart. 'I think it is like these generals who kill thousands, thousands, thousands, until they no longer have human feeling.' He laughs again perhaps realizing how off-beam his analogy sounds. 'What I mean is, I think the Buddhist practice is very helpful in this. It also concerned with the nature of suffering. Our aim is salvation and liberation from negative emotion.'

The Dalai Lama has a doctorate in Buddhist philosophy. And, by rising at 3.30 a.m., he fits in at least six hours of meditation during the day (in between studying scriptures, giving audiences, listening to the BBC World Service and attending to the daily business of his government-in-exile). But even the most complicated people have defining characteristics. His is this infectious, coruscating laugh. It is high-pitched and strangely incompatible with the deep and resonant timbre of his speaking voice. Given that he was taken away from his parents at the age of three, brought up in a monastery and then, at the age of seven, enthroned in a 1,000-room palace where he was worshipped as a god-king for seventeen years before being forced to escape from his country disguised as a soldier, it would be understandable if the Dalai Lama's laugh reflected a heightened awareness of the fundamental absurdity of life, the universe and everything.

Equally, because the laugh (hu, hu, hu!) emerges when he speaks of subjects that are painful to him, it could also be a sign of arrested development. After all, his abiding memories of what little childhood he experienced in his 'golden cage' were of loneliness and austerity. He found ways to amuse himself but, without other children to play with, it can't have been easy for him to acquire those nuances of emotional expression which the rest of us learn by imitation and take for granted. It would be natural if he suffered from Peter Pan syndrome. And perhaps this is what lies behind the beguiling aura of cheerfulness for which he is known and adored around the world – private jokes arising from the internal conversations of one used to playing on his own.

The simplistic theme that runs through all his teachings – that human happiness is born of compassion, kindness and tolerance – compounds this impression of childlike innocence. So does his boyish grin and the dimples it forms in his cheeks. At sixty-three the Dalai Lama may now have heavy lines on his brow that, with his constantly raised eyebrows, make him look like he's in a permanent state of surprise, and the stubble on the head he shaves once a week may be going grey, but he has the sprightly bearing of a man half his age. He doesn't walk everywhere so much as bustle – nodding, bowing, gathering the folds of his much darned and patched maroon robes about him, adjusting its saffron-coloured facings over his right shoulder. And his stocky 5ft 9in frame, kept in shape by daily workouts on an exercise bike, is still animated when he sits down to talk – slapping his thigh, folding his bare, vaccination-scarred arms, and making sweeping gestures that rattle the beads on his left wrist.

In the face of distressing testimony from his fellow refugees, perhaps his laughter is as good a defence as any against tears. The Dalai Lama listens because he recognizes how important it is for torture victims to bear witness. Being believed is part of the healing process, especially when the crimes committed against you are unbelievable. Those who survived the Holocaust knew this. And while more than six million Jews were killed by the Nazis, more than a million Tibetans have suffered a similar fate since the Chinese invasion in 1950. The Dalai Lama pauses for a long time when he is asked how the genocide committed against his people compares to that against the Jews. 'It is difficult,' he says, searching for the right words. 'In the Tibetan case, in late fifties and early sixties, entire communities of nomads would be destroyed. In 1959, in Lhasa, the Chinese shot Tibetan families from aeroplane with machine-guns. Systematic destruction in the name of liberation against the tyranny of the Dalai Lama! Hu, hu, hu! In Hitler's case he was more honest. In concentration camps he made it clear he intended to exterminate the Jews. With the Chinese they called us their brothers! Big brother bullying little brother! Hu, hu, hu! Is less honest, I think.'

The cruelty and humiliation the Tibetans suffered at the hands of their Chinese liberators also bears comparison with that suffered by the Jews under the Nazis. Such is the reverence with which Tibetan Buddhists regard all living things, they will not even kill the mosquitoes which bite them, yet in the early years of Chinese occupation, Tibetan children would be forced to shoot their parents. Celibate monks and nuns would be made at gunpoint to have sex in public and use sacred scriptures as lavatory paper. According to an International Commission of Jurists report in 1959, dissenters were disembowelled, crucified or buried alive. To prevent them from shouting out 'Long live the Dalai Lama' on their way to execution they would have their tongues torn out with meat hooks. All but thirteen of the country's 6,000 monasteries were destroyed and in some cases slaughterhouses were sited in their place. More recently, eight million Chinese citizens have been relocated to Tibet. The six million Tibetans they now outnumber are discriminated against in jobs, housing and education.

It is illegal to speak Tibetan at public meetings and possession of a picture of the Dalai Lama is an imprisonable offence. Lhasa, the once sacred capital, now has 1,806 brothels as well as numerous gambling dens. The Tibetans who have remained there have been compared to American Indians left to get drunk on the reservations, quaint tourist attractions in a spiritual Disneyland.

'Not much use to discuss these things now,' the Dalai Lama says, distractedly blinking and scratching his nose. 'Past is past. I don't want them to be sitting in Peking and saying, "What is that Dalai Lama saying now? Causing trouble again!" No use. No use to antagonize. I am thinking of the future of Tibet. And with the Chinese population influx and their programme of Sinocization, time is running out.' In the past he has been denounced by the Chinese press variously as a thief, a murderer, a 'wolf in monk's clothing', and a rapist who once provided sexual services for Mrs Gandhi and wore a rosary made from the bones of Tibetan serfs.

'I am happy to reassure my Chinese brothers that we do not ask for separation,' the Dalai Lama now says, leaning back and throwing his hands up in mock surrender. 'I seek meaningful autonomy within China rather than independence for Tibet. We accept there are things the Chinese can handle better than us [such as foreign policy and the economy, explains his assistant], but they should accept there are things we are better at handling [education and the environment]. If they provide some of our basic requirements, we will remain with them. We know our spirituality does not feed our stomachs. We know we need material development. So the closer relation is very necessary. That way more trust can be built. And then, with the friendly atmosphere, certain point such as the human right issue, and issue of democracy and liberty, can be made firmly.'

Although he keeps reiterating that 'past is past', the sticking point for negotiation as far as the Dalai Lama is concerned seems to be his insistence that Tibet was once free. This isolated country was first 'discovered' by the British in 1904 when Colonel Younghusband led a peaceful expeditionary force. The British subsequently recognized Tibet as a fully sovereign state. When the Chinese invaded in 1950, they based their claim to the country on the marriage of the Chinese princess Wen-Ch'eng Kung-chu to the Tibetan King Songtsen Gampo in 641. The invasion occurred two years after Indian independence was declared, and the British, having lost influence and interest in the region, were not inclined to dispute China's claim. Insult was added to the injury when, on an official visit to Britain in 1990, a year after he won the Nobel Peace Prize, the Dalai Lama was refused an audience with Margaret Thatcher, then Prime Minister. And two years ago, John Major declined to meet him in an official capacity for fear of offending the Chinese in the run-up to the handover of Hong Kong.

The 'simple monk', as the Dalai Lama describes himself with a slightly unbecoming hint of self-satisfaction, laughs when asked what line he thinks our Prime Minister should take with President Jiang on Tibet. 'I think if I have message, I will write to him personally! It's not something I should convey to a newspaper! But I'm quite sure the British Prime Minister will raise the issue of autonomy of Tibet and the issue of human rights in general. I think we have many supporters and sympathy among people of Britain but I appreciate that sometime it is difficult for a country's leader to meet me. Britain is the only nation which really knows

Tibet. Sometime I feel the British and the Western nations in general could have done more. But then. Mmm. Today's unhappy experience not happen just suddenly. It had many causes. No point in blaming this nation or that nation. Ultimately we Tibetans must blame ourselves.'

If he seems forgiving to the British, it is as nothing to the understanding he shows toward the Chinese. When in the fifties he had meetings with Chairman Mao he said he found the tyrant to be 'spellbinding', 'sincere' and 'not deceitful'. For this charitable view, and for his recent adoption of a more moderate and conciliatory approach to the question of Tibetan independence, he has been criticized by certain extremist elements within the Tibetan community who find it hard to disguise their loathing of the Chinese and think that aggression should be met with aggression. When I ask the Dalai Lama if, just for a second, he has ever felt even so much as a twinge of hatred for his savage oppressors himself, he says: 'Sometimes I have bad temper but true ill feeling almost never. If I want to work effectively for freedom and justice, it is best to do so without malice in my heart. Buddhist training of mind really helps in this. There are undoubtedly many good Chinese people who are aware of the true situation in Tibet. The Tibetans and Chinese have to live side by side. In order to live in harmony we have to practise non-violence and compassion. One Tibetan using gun would be more excuse for atrocities by Chinese. In the 1987 crisis when Chinese opened fire on Tibetans in Lhasa one Chinese soldier dropped his weapon and a Tibetan picked it up but instead of using it on the soldier he broke it in front of him. Smashed it on the ground. Isn't that wonderful?'

He is keen to point out that all Tibetan monks feel this way, not just him. He has a friend, a monk, who spent twenty years in Chinese prisons and labour camps. When he was eventually able to join the Dalai Lama in exile he told him that there were only a few occasions when he really faced danger and those were when he was in danger of losing compassion for the Chinese. 'Nice!' the Dalai Lama chuckles. 'A good monk who faced real danger. At least I did not have to face any real risk or danger of losing my life.' He makes a chopping motion with his hand against the side of his neck. It's not quite true. Improbably, the

Chinese once tried to coerce the Dalai Lama's eldest brother, also a monk, into assassinating him.

And he still has to be careful that what he eats isn't poisoned. The Dalai Lama's daily diet consists of hot water, porridge and tsampa (roasted barley flower) for breakfast and thupka (soup with noodles) and skabakleb (meat wrapped in bread) for lunch. Monks do not eat dinner. But, he says, he sometimes sneaks a snack while watching television in the evening. And then does a few extra prostrations to Buddha by way of absolution before going to bed. The Dalai Lama's father died of poisoning in 1947 and was given a traditional Tibetan sky burial in which the body is left as carrion for the vultures. His mother, to whom he was very close towards the end of her life, died of a stroke in 1981. But, with his belief in reincarnation, he says he does not fear death or even dying.

'In my Tibetan practice, there are eight different stages of dissolution of mind and body,' he says. 'I intend to practise altruism in life, dying and death. For example, if death comes today, I shall try to control it.' He compares death to changing your clothes when they are old and torn. 'How would I like to die? Hu, hu, hu! I do not want to die in crash. Not sudden death, because no time to practise. When time come I want to be able to wrap myself in yellow robe over like this and then sit and meditate.' He demonstrates the position, eyes closed, hands resting in lap. 'Some of my old friend here they do this. One or two hours before their death – even when they cannot sit by themselves they ask to have cushion put behind them to support themselves.'

When asked if he ever has any doubts that he will be reincarnated as the Fifteenth Dalai Lama, and whether he really believes he is the reincarnation of each of the previous thirteen, he says the answer is not simple. But given his experiences in this present life, and his Buddhist beliefs, he has no difficulty in accepting that he is spiritually connected to the thirteen previous Dalai Lamas.

Before meeting the Dalai Lama I had been briefed on protocol by one of his personal assistants. Speak slowly and do not use complicated sentences, he said. He doesn't particularly like talking in English to Englishmen because he feels embarrassed about his own ungrammatical usage. There's no need to present him with a kata, the white silk offering scarf that Tibetans traditionally give each other, he prefers to just shake hands with Westerners. And do not bother with any of the other formalities that applied at the Tibetan court – always having to sit lower than him, never making eye contact or touching him, never leading the conversation or turning your back on him. He can't be doing with all that nonsense.

Finally, please don't ask him to explain how he was discovered to be the fourteenth reincarnation of the Dalai Lama. He finds it boring to have to go over the story again and again but if you ask, he will feel obliged to give you every detail and his answer will take up most of the time you have with him. There was no need. I had mugged up on it already. When one Dalai Lama dies, his soul enters the body of a newborn boy. A regent Lama rules for a few years, then the search for a new Dalai Lama begins. All boys born from forty-nine days to two years after a Dalai Lama's death are candidates for his reincarnation. The Fourteenth Dalai Lama was born in Taktser, a small village in northeastern Tibet on 6 July 1935, two years after the Thirteenth died. Two crows came to perch on the windowsill as he was born – a traditional sign. His parents were peasants and he was one of sixteen children, of whom seven survived. In Lhasa, the regent had a vision – of a small house with strangely shaped guttering near to a three-storey monastery with a gold and turquoise roof and a path running from it to a hill – and went in search of it. When they found the boy living there they mingled the Thirteenth Dalai Lama's personal possessions with an array of similar objects, laid them all out on a table and asked him to pick any objects he recognized. He unerringly selected the Thirteenth Dalai Lama's eating bowl, spectacles, pencil, walking stick and drum. He was also found to have the physical signs of a Dalai Lama: large tiger-stripe birthmarks on the legs, and big ears.

He has never doubted that he is the Dalai Lama but as a teenager, he admits, he entertained misgivings about his vocation as a monk. 'When I was young, especially in winter time when I was sitting with my tutor in meditation, in a cold dark room with rats, I would hear people returning from the fields at sunset singing happily and it would leave me with a sad feeling. Sometimes I had feeling I would be much happier if I was one of them. But I know I was meant to be a monk because in my dream sometimes I see a fight or a woman and I immediately think, "I am a monk, I must not indulge." I never dream I am Dalai Lama, though.'

He is never troubled by sleepless nights, getting in a sound six hours. And generally he describes himself as being 'definitely happy' except on the odd occasions when he catches himself brooding upon the events of his earlier life in the Land of Snows, as Tibet is known. 'But do I ever feel depressed? No. Sometimes frustration. Sometimes feelings of hopelessness. That I have been a failure. But I say my favourite prayer and it always brings me fresh hope and fresh impetus.' Has the Dalai Lama ever fallen in love? 'With my close friends I feel a love which is not a genuine compassion,' he says. 'It is attachment. A sense of concern. It is biased. The genuine sense of compassion is unbiased. Have I ever felt sexual love? In my childhood before I was a fully trained monk I was often curious, I wonder what happened. But then I think by age of fifteen or sixteen I started more serious meditation practice, exploring the nature of suffering. For those who would normally seek to have children at that stage in their life would come worry and distraction. Life as a single person means liberty. Lay person may have more pleasure in short term but in long term monk has a mental state more steady.'

He believes sexual desire is like an itch. If you have one, it's nice to scratch it. But it's better to have no itch at all. If it is possible to be without that feeling, there is much peace. One of the great pleasures in the Dalai Lama's life is mending broken watches and mechanical gadgets in general. Indeed, the one material indulgence he allows himself is the Rolex he always wears with the face on the underside of his wrist and which he is given to taking apart with a screwdriver every so often in order to tinker around with its mechanism. He describes himself wryly as 'half-Marxist' – the belief in the equality side rather than the atheist side – and, like all monks, he obeys a vow of poverty. Like all the previous Dalai Lamas, he never handles money. This, he says, is just as well as he suspects he has a free-spending nature – 'although I can be very stingy over small amounts'.

The self-deprecation does not seem to be affected and, for one who is held by his followers to be a living god, the human failings he admits to are surprisingly ordinary. He is prone to a bad temper. He would never harm a living creature, but has an irrational fear and loathing of caterpillars. He is aware of the faults others occasionally see in him: that he can be naive as a politician and that as a spiritual leader he sometimes lacks gravitas and trivializes his status (because he does things such as agree to be guest editor of the Christmas edition of French *Vogue*, appear as a guest on *Wogan* and attend frivolous Hollywood parties hosted by his film star friends Richard Gere and Harrison Ford).

He accepts these criticisms with humility, as you would expect. But he seems to be genuinely perplexed by the fuss people make over him. He says he cannot really understand the esteem in which he is held in the West. 'I have done little to merit it, despite what some people might say. On a few occasions I have been publicly commended for my efforts on behalf of world peace. But I have done nothing, really nothing for world peace. The only thing I do for peace is talk about it a great deal.' Also the fact that this year Hollywood has released two big-budget films about his life – Martin Scorsese's sumptuous epic *Kundun* and *Seven Years in Tibet*, which stars Brad Pitt – does not, he says, mean much to him. He finds it amusing that he is the *cause de jour* in Hollywood but adds that he doesn't make distinctions as to where support for Tibet might come from. He has seen *Kundun* and liked it and is grateful for the international attention it has drawn to the plight of Tibet. But he has not yet got round to seeing *Seven Years in Tibet*, which tells the story of the Dalai Lama's friendship with Heinrich Harrer, the Austrian moun-taineer who became a teacher to the young god-king. He says he did not know Harrer was an SS member at the time, the subject never arose, and now he says there is no point in his old friend trying to hide the truth because 'past is past'.

The Dalai Lama collaborated on the script for both films and, to the chagrin of the producers, somehow gave the impression to each that they had exclusivity. At the moment he seems to be spreading his favours just as thinly in the world of publishing. He has written extensively on Buddhism and Eastern philosophy but this October Hodder & Stoughton will publish his first book on ethics for the general reader. Unfortunately it contains much of the same material as a book he is having published by Little, Brown next year. Little, Brown is now planning to sue the Dalai Lama over breach of contract.

In the airy audience room overlooking the valley the Dalai Lama blinks several times, gathers the folds of his robe together and stands up. He clicks his fingers and his protocol officer steps forward and hands him a white silk kata which the Dalai Lama then raises over my hands, brought together to form the namaste prayer sign, and drapes on my wrists. When I tell him I feel embarrassed now because I'd been told not to bother to bring a white offering scarf to present to him, he slaps me on the back and lets out a roar of laughter.

There is a golden Buddha at the other end of the room, in between two large scroll paintings. The Dalai Lama has almost reached it on his way out when he stops, turns on his heel, and bustles back toward me with a distracted look on his face. Patting my hand he says: 'There is something very important I need to convey to you. Very important. Whether you a believer or non-believer. All human beings have same potential to increase compassion. This is where happiness lies.'

With this he grins, slaps me on the back again and bustles out. He crosses the large courtyard where he gives his public addresses, pauses briefly to inspect a delphinium in a tin pot and disappears from view along a path that leads beyond a row of bamboo and pine trees. The thin Himalayan air is pricked with the smell of incense, jasmine and honeysuckle. The rain has now stopped outside and the mist is lifting. Breathing deeply, I look up and inspect the skies for a rainbow, but there isn't one yet. It is still oppressively humid and a roll of thunder, as melancholy as the growl of the Tibetan longhorn, echoes around the mountains.

Tony Parsons

Tethered to the small basket of red roses on the kitchen counter-top is a red balloon – helium-filled, heart-shaped – with the words 'I love you' written across it in silver letters. It's a cameo of kitsch, a miniature masterpiece of sentimentality, yet it is both as dense and delicate in meaning as a haiku. If you had to summarize Tony Parsons, the best-selling novelist and *Mirror* columnist, in one symbol, it would be hard to improve on this. He has bought it for Yuriko, his wife, because she has just heard that her mother has cancer. It is mid-morning in Islington. Sunshine stripes the room through a half-open blind. Perhaps on purpose, the balloon has not been hidden from this visitor's view.

Tony Parsons, who is forty-seven, met Yuriko, a 32-year-old Japanese translator, in a London sushi bar. They married in 1992 and her influence is apparent in the minimalist decor of their house; you pad across its wooden floors in your stockinged feet, after leaving your shoes at the door. It is evident in Parsons's new novel *One for My Baby*, too, part of which is set in Hong Kong. Yuriko was also the inspiration for Gina, the wife who walks out on her unfaithful husband Harry, and four-year-old son Pat, in Parsons' novel *Man and Boy* (1999). Or at least she inspired Gina's dialogue. That character was also based on Charlotte, a Dutch women Parsons went out with until she found out he was also sleeping with her au pair. To add to the con-fusion between fiction and reality, Harry is based on Parsons himself: Harry has to bring up his four-year-old son on his own, while struggling to come to terms with unemployment and the slow death from cancer of his father. Parsons had to bring up his five-year-old son, Bobby, on his own, after his first wife, the journalist Julie Burchill, left him in 1984. Parsons' father died from lung cancer in 1987.

'Nothing has the emotional clout of a true story,' Parsons says with a nasal, Essex–Cockney accent. 'So I do harvest my own life a bit, yeah.' His wide mouth stretches into a grin. 'I went off the rails when my dad died and I binged on women. Men are like dogs in their sexual promiscuity. I really hurt Charlotte and she was wonderful and beautiful. There are consequences for what you do and I didn't think about them.' In his novel, Parsons managed to make both Gina and Harry sympathetic characters and, as a consequence, it became what is known in publishing circles as 'chick-friendly' – a useful thing to be, given than women buy two-thirds of all books. But it was also guy-friendly – Jeremy Paxman said it made him cry – as well as middlebrow in tone and style (as one reviewer noted, Parsons combines 'a broadsheet mind with a tabloid tongue').

The book became a publishing phenomenon: it spent months on the bestseller list, sold a million copies and was named Book of the Year at this year's National Book Awards. It was Parsons' fifth novel – the others, potboilers about tennis and pop, stiffed badly – and so, as he puts it, it made him a twenty-five-year overnight success story. We are in the basement of his house now, in the study: shelves of books, a Nordic ski machine, an iMac, kung fu gloves and head shields, a bust of Mao, a piano and, stuck to the wall, at least fifty scrawled upon Post-It notes. Parsons is not a tall man but he is wiry and fit-looking, with Gary Oldman features – lupine, angular – and eyes which he describes as small and squinty. I am in a low armchair, he is in a higher one opposite me, sitting cross-legged: another Orientalism perhaps, master and pupil. One has the impression that even Parsons' spontaneous acts are premeditated.

He is friendly and polite but also focused and intense. There is a stillness to him, despite what he is about to say. 'Yeah, I am emotional. I am emotional. Sentimental, you know. But I try to keep a lid on it. I keep a lid on it.' A conversational tic becomes apparent; he repeats his sentences, as though ruminating on them for his own satisfaction. (The trope is evident in his writing, too, an echo of his hero Hemingway perhaps, or just a bad habit picked up from his red-top journalism.) Surely it's the senti-mentality that sells? 'It does. I don't keep a lid on it in my fiction. Readers, women especially, like the relationship between the father and son in *Man and Boy*. Somebody wrote that it's very refreshing to see a man call his child "darling", and I thought, "Why? Is that unusual? Doesn't everyone call their child 'darling'?" My son and I have always been, I mean, if we meet each other now we kiss, you know, we kiss each other.'

In some ways, Parsons seems to want to play the unrecon-structed male eager to prove his proletarian credentials, in others he wants to be the sensitive New Man in touch with his emotions. Presumably when he wasn't engaged in bouts of manly wrestling with his father and son he was constantly telling them he loved them? 'I only did it once with my dad, I only told him through tears when he was dying. You can't do it in moments of calm and health and tranquillity, you need the crisis to do it. There was kind of an unspoken love between us. I think if we were hugging and weeping over each other every Sunday afternoon, it wouldn't have worked. I'm all for a bit of manly restraint. I think it gives the moments when you express your emotions more power, more honesty. So I'm all for that, I'm all for that.'

There are black-and-white photographs of his parents around the room: his mother being cheered by colleagues on her final day as a dinner lady, his father in the uniform of a Royal Navy commando. Before becoming a greengrocer and moving from the Old Kent Road to Romford in Essex, his father had been a war hero – he won the Distinguished Service Medal fighting on the island of Elba just after D-Day, and one side of his body was left a mass of scar tissue. 'Dad didn't talk about the war,' Parsons says. 'He was very much a carpet slippers, *Morecambe and Wise*, rose garden man. But he was a killer, you know, a trained killer. I do feel that nothing I can do with my life can measure up to what he did in the war, nothing.'

According to its author, *Man and Boy* had wide appeal because readers saw their own lives in it. 'They come up to me and say it reminds them of their dad or child, you know, or it made them pick up the phone and call the wife.' Parsons' mother died of cancer in 1999. Ever prepared to harvest the details of his life in the name of art, he has fictionalized her death in *One for My*

Baby. He also wrote a column about her in the *Mirror* the day after she died. The headline was: GOODBYE MUM AND THANKS FOR TEACHING ME THE MEANING OF LOVE. Does he think now that column was a little mawkish? 'If I had written it today, it would have been different, but it had a great impact at the time. I got literally hundreds of letters. Selfishly, it made things easier for me: a writer makes sense of the world by writing about it. I don't think it was mawkish and sentimental so much as hysterical with emotion. The iMac was covered in tears when I wrote it.'

When your parents die, Parsons believes, there's nobody standing between you and the stars. 'It really does feel as momentous as that. At the risk of sounding like a song from *The Lion King*, it made me appreciate the cycle of life for the first time. I could see my son getting older, you know, becoming a young man. Suddenly he was six inches taller than me, staying out all night and chasing girls and getting up to God knows what. At the same time, my mum was struggling with a pleural . . . she had a pleural tumour in the lining of her lung. I could see a parent dying and a child growing and I just felt right in the middle. I felt complete.'

An only child, Tony Parsons describes his relationship with his son Bobby, now twenty-one, as brotherly. 'We talk about women and drugs but Bobby won't let me dance in his presence. That would be just too embarrassing for him.' They also talk about football (Bobby used to play for the Brighton youth team) as well as marriage. 'Typically for one raised by divorced parents, Bobby is wary of getting married himself, he wants to do it once and once only.' Parsons would like to have more children, he adds: 'I didn't want to while Bobby was growing up because I didn't want him to think he was second best, you know, from the marriage that didn't work out. I'm starting to feel quite broody now. I coo over babies in the street.'

After leaving Barstable Grammar School in 1972 with five O-levels, Tony Parsons went to work at the Gordon's Gin distillery in Islington. 'I hated it,' he says. 'I regret not going to university because I think I'd have been able to sleep with a lot of women there, you know. The gin factory was quite barren, crumpet-wise. It's good for the Tony Parsons brand to be able to say I did that job for four years, but I'd much rather have been jumping on the bones of some sensitive girl from the Shires.' Hemingway might have approved of the machismo. He would also have been impressed by the fact that, in his spare time, the young Parsons wrote a novel, *The Kids*. This proved to be a useful calling card when the venerable popular music paper *New Musical Express*, noticing a shift in taste in 1976, advertized for 'hip young gunslingers', journalists to cover the emerging punk movement. There were 5,000 applicants.

'*Kids* was crap, it was juvenilia, but it got me the job on the *NME* and away from the gin distillery. You had to send a sample of your work and I just chucked in my book. Of course they didn't even open it. They didn't even open it.' The second hip young gunslinger to be hired was Julie Burchill, a 16-year-old from Bristol. They were given a desk together. In her auto-biography, *I Knew I Was Right*, Burchill describes how, when they first met, Parsons held out his hand to shake. 'What do you want me to do with that?' Burchill said, 'Bite it?' 'He looked at me curiously, turned away casually, then turned back, picked me up and sat me high on top of a filing cabinet without draw-ing breath. I stared at him, amazed. Then we started laughing and didn't stop for years. I liked Tony Parsons a whole lot. More than I liked anyone in my life. He was bellicose and self-dramatizing to a ridiculous extent . . . He was immaculately working-class, just like me. No room for doubt or insinuations or lower-middle class wankiness here . . . The punk bands hung around him slack-jawed and starry-eyed. The Sex Pistols and the Clash vied for his attention, for his eyes only.'

Heady days. Just as every Liverpudlian aged between fifty-six and sixty-two claims to have seen the Beatles perform at the Cavern, so every Londoner aged between sixteen and twenty-one in 1976 supposedly saw the Sex Pistols at the 100 Club. Parsons doesn't have to exaggerate his claim to musical history. 'I saw a lot of the Pistols,' he says. 'They were my mates really, my drinking companions. I was sort of their ambassador on the Anarchy tour. I was thinking about this the other day when I got caught up in the May Day riots, which weren't really riots. I just happened to be at King's Cross when the hippy tribes were gathering first thing in the morning, and I would have cheerfully applauded if the police had cracked open their heads there and then. Then I thought, God, take a look at yourself. We're two years away from the Queen's Golden Jubilee, and for the Silver Jubilee I was floating down the Thames with the Sex Pistols, sharing a gramme of amphetamine sulphate with Johnny Rotten; being shoved around by the police. A lot of people got a really good hiding that day on the Thames. A lot of arrests. I thought, how could I have changed sides so completely?'

Perhaps it isn't so out of character. There has always been a conservative side to Tony Parsons. Promiscuity and puritanism have been the warring hag-riders of his sexuality. In his *Mirror* columns he is something of a Paul Johnson figure, starting out as a youthful left-winger and ending up on the right; being able to supply fiery indignation and demagoguery on demand. He combines sentimentality about the war with a taste for anarchy, and ruthless ambition with the caution of one who has had to manage his career sensibly because he has the responsibility of bringing up a son on his own. He stopped taking drugs in his mid-twenties, never injected heroin (he had a fear the needle would snap off in his arm), and didn't enjoy cocaine. 'Coke was like an old man's drug, I always preferred speed. I've always had like a cold, pragmatic chip in my heart that would prevent me from, you know, going all the way, losing control.'

Also – the ultimate non-punk, conservative gesture – he got married. 'Julie and I were friends straight away, we slept with each other quite quickly and then we kind of went our separate ways for ages, eighteen months, something like that, when I was sleeping with practically everybody.' He proposed marriage shortly after punching a fellow journalist whom he suspected of sleeping with 'his' Julie. She was eighteen, they had a son and moved to a bungalow in Billericay. One fateful night, Parsons went to give a talk at the University of East Anglia and ended up sleeping with a student. She wrote to Burchill, telling all. Tony remembers Julie receiving the letter, looking up at him and just 'staring and staring'.

The marriage soon ended. After leaving the *NME*, the careers of Burchill and Parsons ran on parallel tracks, with each alternately falling behind or steaming ahead of the other. Parsons languished for a long time. 'The eighties were tough for me. I really struggled, struggled to pay bills, once ended up in court for non-payment.' Eventually, having long since shed his bondage trousers for sharp suits, he reinvented himself as a style expert for men's magazines such as *GQ* and *Arena*. By the nineties he was writing a column for the *Daily Telegraph* and appearing as a chin-stroking arts pundit on BBC2's *Late Review*, a Cockney autodidact on a regular panel that included the journalist Allison Pearson and the poet Tom Paulin. Burchill's career, meanwhile, flourished in the eighties. She sold a million copies of her novel *Ambition*, adopted the ideologically tricky stance of being a Thatcherite Communist, and became one of the highest paid women on Fleet Street. She then fell from grace for a few years, put on weight, did enough cocaine, as she put it, to stun the entire Colombian armed forces, and reinvented herself impressively in a weekly *Guardian* column.

The two have become pantomime media foes. Burchill will sometimes write about Shorty, as she calls her ex-husband, in her column. Example: 'I bought *Man and Boy* the other day and can honestly report that it is not in any way autobiographical. The errant mother is slender, beautiful and decent while the long-suffering hero Harry is attractive to women, good in the sack and has all his own hair. So that rules me and Parsons right out.' Do they really never speak? 'No,' Parsons says. 'We don't see each other, we don't see each other. We haven't done since we split up in 1984. So for me it's odd that she writes a column, essentially she writes a column about me. She should think about me a little less. People think it was a very bitter divorce. It wasn't. The bitterness came later. The fact that she had no contact with our son when he was growing up, not even a birthday card, a Christmas card, is to me unforgivable. I will never forgive it. That time can't be, that time can't be got back. You can't recover that time.'

It could be argued that if Parsons hadn't been unfaithful to Burchill he couldn't have written the book that has made him a household name, and she wouldn't have run off and married another man, Cosmo Landesman, before declaring herself bisexual and becoming a professional cynic on the subject of men and marriage. 'Maybe, yeah, maybe. It hadn't occurred to me that I was, you know, the cause of her horrific weight. It hadn't occurred to me. I see it from the perspective of a father and to me it's not this amusing media feud. I mean, I don't hate Julie. I just have no respect for her. She's a cruel, stupid coward. A very low form of life.' So the animosity isn't just a media pose? 'There's no in-joke. To me it was a cause of hurt and frustration that there was no contact between her and my son when he was growing up. I can't take her seriously. One minute she's a lesbian, the next she is heterosexual. It's just laughable.' Is there no curiosity left? Wouldn't he like to meet her just once to talk about the old days? 'I think she writes about me all the time because it is her way of having a relationship with me. She's obsessed with me. She's become my stalker, and makes us seem closer than we are. We haven't seen each other since 1984. It would be like meeting up with someone from school. We would have nothing to talk about.'

They could discuss his age. Burchill claims he lies about it, that he is really forty-nine. 'What is the point in lying about his age,' she wrote in *The Spectator* last year. 'After all, Sean Connery is a sex symbol at seventy-eight. Mr Parsons with his cheeky grin and interesting hairline shouldn't be so hard on himself.' 'Well, I'm forty-seven,' Parsons says flatly. 'I don't know why she . . . She's kind of a sad human being. I mean, I don't even recognize her in pictures any more. She was seventeen when I met her, she's whatever she is now, fifty-five or something. I think it rankles with her that my appearance has hardly changed. That rankles, you know. That fucks her off, I should look older.'

Success, of course, is the most effective form of revenge. Now that Parsons has not only just signed a million-dollar deal in New York for the American paperback rights to *Man and Boy*, but also the film rights to Miramax for another million, his revenge seems to be taking on a Jacobean complexion. He doesn't think he is materialistic – he drives an old Audi – but he enjoys being able to afford to turn left when he boards a plane. But success is also realized ambition; so perhaps he felt less motivated when he was writing *One for My Baby* than he did *Man and Boy*? 'It would be ridiculous to expect any other book that I might write to be bigger than *Man and Boy*. But they'll spend a fortune on marketing the new one. They'll be advertizing it all over the Tube for months, there will be, like, wall-to-wall, you know, wall-to-wall marketing. When they want a book to be a hit, almost inevitably it is. I'll be disappointed if it isn't a number-one best-seller.'

Boris Johnson, a neighbour, persuaded Parsons to share the secret of his success with the readers of *The Spectator* last year. The author explained that while he was writing *Man and Boy*, he, his agent and editor had 'countless discussions about every theme, every chapter, every line. We made sure that each and every scene in the book was played in exactly the right key.' Fiction by committee? Didn't he worry that readers would find his candour offputting? 'The books weren't written by committee, but I do take good advice wherever I can get it,' Parsons now says. 'F. Scott Fitzgerald had an editor and Hemingway had an editor and if they weren't too good to have one then I'm certainly not.' He wrote four drafts of his latest novel. 'I went away with Nick Sayers [his editor at HarperCollins] for a weekend and we asked ourselves two questions: is it too much like *Man and Boy*? Or not enough like it?'

Private Eye recently suggested another reason for Parsons's success. It described him as 'the unchallenged heir to Jeffrey Archer as the book world's most unembarrassable self-promoter'. Does *Private Eye* have a point? 'OK, OK. A few years ago I was called a media whore, but I've met a few working girls in my life and I've never met one of them who says no as often as I do. I'm more a Doris Day figure in the media.' Nevertheless, the chaste Tony Parsons has an un-Doris-like tendency to talk of himself as a brand and, fraudulent though it may seem for him to keep up his professional Essex Man persona despite spending most of his life working as a media pundit in the metropolis, he does understand the value of having a strong image to market. 'I don't know why I never lost my accent,' he says with a shrug. 'I remember when I first turned up in Essex from Dagenham as part of the Cockney diaspora, one of my teachers said he's a bright boy but he sounds like the Artful Dodger, so maybe he should have elocution lessons. My dad just laughed at the idea. He didn't think I should pretend to be something I'm not.'

The cycle of conversation has brought us back to the subject of his father. Tony Parsons still feels inadequate as a man compared to him, he still craves his father's approval and he says it takes the gloss off his current success to know that his father isn't alive to witness it. In Parsons' bathroom I'd seen a bottle of Old Spice aftershave – didn't know they still made that. 'It's an old bottle,' he says. 'It reminds me of my dad. I often find myself sneaking a sniff of it.'

Henry Kissinger

After weeks of delicate negotiation with his diary secretary, an hour is found in Henry Kissinger's schedule. Then his 97-year-old mother, who he believes was responsible for everything he achieved in his life, dies. The interview is postponed. And now, a fortnight later, it looks as if it's going to be put back again.

My appointment has already been changed from 11 a.m. to 11.30 a.m., and as I sit in my room, walking distance from Dr Kissinger's office on Park Avenue, I flick through the television channels and wait for another call. CNN is broadcasting live from Baghdad, and Mohammed Saeed al-Sahaf, the Iraqi foreign minister, is denouncing Kissinger for saying that the US and British forces should concentrate on trying to kill Saddam. An air-raid siren wails in the background.

'There can't be a crisis next week,' Kissinger joked in 1970. 'My schedule is already full.' That was the week Syria invaded Jordan, the Soviets based a nuclear-armed submarine in Cuban waters, the CIA planned to destabilize Chile, and the Viet Cong tabled a new peace plan. These days, when there's an international crisis, Kissinger doesn't have to deal with it, just comment on it. The media want to know his reaction to everything, from the death of Diana, Princess of Wales, to the arrest of Pinochet.

My phone doesn't ring, so I set off to meet him. His office suite is on the twenty-sixth floor of a steel-and-glass building. There is no sign on the door, just a young female receptionist behind a Plexiglass window. I hear the old bruiser before I see him: that unmistakable Teutonic rumble, gravel churned in a cement mixer: 'Tell them I have zero flexibility. I have to be out of the studio by 6.45. Got that?' One of his assistants is trying to keep up with him as he pads from office to office, crossing the corridor in front of me several times.

He is much shorter than you expect, but just as well cushioned. He walks past me, croaks, 'Hello,' and disappears into another room. The crinkly hair is still there, silver now. The face is like a walnut: sallow, lined and liver-spotted. The eyelids are heavy, the lower lip droops. The glasses are thick and so is the accent, which is puzzling. Although Heinz Alfred Kissinger was born in Fürth, Bavaria, in 1923, he has lived in New York, as Henry A. Kissinger, since he was fifteen. (With his family, mother, father and younger brother, he emigrated in 1938, to escape Nazi persecution.)

I'm shown into his office, an L-shaped corner where the shelves are decked with about forty signed photographs of world leaders: everyone from Sadat and Lady Thatcher, to Pope John Paul II and Gorbachev. Some of the prints are so ancient the colour has drained out of them. There is a painting of an American bald eagle and – very Dr Strangelove – a globe.

It is twenty-three years since Kissinger left high office, yet he still has an aura of power. When Richard Nixon appointed him National Security Advisor in 1969 and Secretary of State in 1973 (an office he continued to hold, under Gerald Ford, until 1977), the Cold War was at its height. As the politician ostensibly in charge of US defence and foreign policy, Kissinger was pretty much the most powerful man in the world.

Kissinger's power was unlike anyone else's in history. It was constructed around his personality, for one thing: his notoriously short fuse; his disarming wit; his Machiavellian skills of diplomacy; his ruthlessly analytical mind. It was also related to the preciousness of his time. When told he had to have an emergency triple by-pass operation in 1982, he negotiated with his doctors to see if he could find time for it and concluded he was booked solidly for the next three months. (They overruled, and rushed him in that week.)

Though he's an old man now, seventy-five, Kissinger is still regarded as a statesman whose opinions on international relations should be listened to by princes, prime ministers and presidents. When Tony Blair goes on official visits to the States, he includes breakfast with Kissinger in his itinerary. The chairmen of multinational companies, such as American Express and Revlon, listen to him, too. Indeed, they pay Kissinger Associates Inc, the consultancy firm he set up in 1982, millions of dollars each year to brief them on world affairs. And Kissinger still acts the part. He still has an impossibly full diary; he still flies in private jets with an entourage of assistants and bodyguards; and he and Nancy – the tall sophisticate he married in 1974 – are still pictured in the society pages, partying with Hollywood stars, oil tycoons and European royals.

Outside on Park Avenue I can hear an eerie echo of the Baghdad siren: the whooping sound of an NYPD patrol car. I try to gather my thoughts, but now I hear a pneumatic drill rattling against the pavement as well, and the keywords associated with Kissinger jangle in my head like an abstract poem: shuttle diplomacy, Vietnam, détente, SALT treaty, covert operations, Mao, wiretaps, B52s, Brezhnev, geopolitics, war crimes, paranoia, Cambodia, balance of power, power the great aphrodisiac. Power. Five more minutes pass before Dr Kissinger bustles in, undoes his blue suit jacket and sits down. 'Is that damn thing on?' he says in an android monotone, pointing to a tape recorder which one of his staff has set up next to mine on the glass coffee table. 'I tell you. I have no technical skills whatsoever.' He almost allows himself a smile at this.

Kissinger thinks that history is a constantly evolving subject, on which there can be no definitive take. 'In the late seventies and eighties, for example, the Vietnam protest generation was still very active. A few months ago I was giving a talk at Yale University and, in the students' minds, I'm not sure if they knew whether the Vietnam War came before or after the Spanish American War. That's exaggerated, but the Vietnam War was not their concern.'

Kissinger's own formative experiences do not really feature in the three vast volumes of his memoirs. He doesn't like talking about himself. He minimizes, for instance, the significance of his traumatic childhood and his Jewish heritage – he's not a practising Jew – and describes his upbringing as typical middle-class German. Even though he was banned as a child from playing soccer with non-Jewish boys (a game he loved then and is still fanatical about), he has said that he wasn't consciously unhappy and not acutely aware of what was going on in Germany during his childhood.

Yet when he arrived in New York in 1938 – and went to work in a shaving brush factory during the day while continuing his studies at night school – his discovery that he did not have to cross the street to avoid being beaten up by non-Jewish boys made him long to become an American citizen. He did not come to think of himself as a true American, though, until he joined the US Army as a private in 1943. He proved a valiant soldier at the Battle of the Bulge, volunteering for a small detachment that fought a delaying action when the Germans launched their counter-attack after D-Day. (Later, as a sergeant in counter-intelligence, he won a Bronze Star.) When, on a visit to Germany, the Bonn government announced that Kissinger might visit some of his relatives, he intoned darkly, 'My relatives are soap.' (At least thirteen of them were sent to the gas chambers.) Walter Isaacson, one of his biographers, believes that nearly all Kissinger's personality traits – his philosophical pessimism, his confidence coexisting with his insecurities, his vanity with his vulnerability and his arrogance with his craving for approval – can be traced to the Holocaust.

Yet there are other sides to Kissinger's character which can't be squared with this. His deadpan sense of humour for one: 'The illegal we do immediately,' he once joked. 'The unconstitutional takes a bit longer.' When he had his heart attack, he quipped, 'Well, at least it proves I do have a heart.' According to students of Kissinger, he cultivated a self-deprecating sense of humour when he entered politics. It was intended to defuse jealousy and counter his natural gravitas and arrogance. 'I have never met a man with greater powers of seduction,' recalled Admiral Elmo Zumwalt, a member of the Joint Chiefs of Staff when Kissinger first took office.

Kissinger's charm and powers of flattery weren't deployed on political colleagues only. 'Power is the great aphrodisiac,' he said just before a 1972 poll of Playboy Bunnies voted him 'the man I would most like to go out with on a date'. And in between his divorce from Ann Fleischer (a New York book-keeper with whom he had two children, David and Elizabeth) and his marriage to Nancy Maginnes (a socialite WASP who worked as Nelson Rockefeller's researcher), rumours about the Hollywood starlets Kissinger bedded (Jill St John, Candice Bergen and Judy Brown among them) were legion.

But one of the abiding public perceptions of Henry Kissinger is that he was paranoid and secretive. In 1975, discussing civil unrest in East Timor, he told his aides: 'You have a responsibility to recognize that we are living in a revolutionary situation, everything on paper will be used against me.' He had enemies: liberals hated his hawkish views on Vietnam; right-wingers distrusted his dovish policies of détente with the Russians and rapprochement with the Chinese; former White House colleagues resented his surviving the Watergate scandal. One of them, John Mitchell, Attorney-General from 1969–72, called Kissinger 'an egocentric maniac'. Kissinger's reply could not have been drier: 'At Harvard it took me ten years to achieve an environment of total hostility. Here I've done it in twenty months.'

At a press conference in Salzburg in 1974, Kissinger brooded on the possibility of resigning: he was sick of the stories about his involvement in wiretaps, in destabilizing the democratically-elected government of Chile and organizing the secret bombing of neutral Cambodia. He had been identified, he said, as someone who cared more about stabilizing the balance of power than about moral issues. 'I would rather like to think that when the record is written, it may be remembered that perhaps some lives were saved and perhaps some mothers can rest more at ease. But I leave that to history.'

When Nixon resigned, Kissinger consoled him with the comment that history would judge him more kindly than did his contemporaries. Nixon countered that it depended who wrote the history. 'I don't know whether people questioned Nixon's leadership at the time so much as his character and some of his actions,' Kissinger tells me. 'But I think there has been a much more positive assessment of him.' Kissinger is comfortable with historical perspectives. After graduating from Harvard in 1950, aged twenty-seven, he took an MA two years later and his Ph.D. two years after that. From then until he entered government in 1969, he was a professor of politics.

His senior thesis is still talked about at Harvard. Because of its sheer bulk, 383 pages, it prompted the 'Kissinger rule' which limited future students to writing to one third that length. (Judging by the size of his memoirs, over-writing has been a recurrent problem.) The subject of his thesis was 'the meaning of history', and even his professors found it pretty impenetrable. It took on all the great thinkers and poets from Kant and Spinoza to Homer and Milton, and its themes ran from morality and freedom to revolution and bureaucracy. At one point he declared that Descartes's *cogito ergo sum* was not really necessary. The pursuit of peace, he concluded, is a constant balancing act which lacks larger philosophical meaning. Oh, and life is suffering, and birth involves death.

As a scholar, Kissinger considered the meaning of history. As a politician, he was involved in the making of it. Although he wasn't involved in the Watergate break-in or cover-up, apparently, he surely acquiesced in the attitude that led to it. The atmosphere of paranoia which characterized the Nixon years began in 1969, when Kissinger asked J. Edgar Hoover, the FBI director, to authorize taps on William Beecher, a journalist on the *New York Times*. Beecher had written an account of the secret bombing of Viet Cong supply dumps in Cambodia that year. A furious Kissinger wanted to find out who had leaked the story. I ask Kissinger if he has ever felt that people were plotting against him. 'No. I don't feel there were plots against me.' The guttural voice vibrates the sofa. 'I feel there were points of view which were very hostile to my point of view. But I don't consider that a plot. More continual harassment.'

In 1973, Kissinger was awarded the Nobel Peace Prize for negotiating peace with honour for both sides in Vietnam. His critics claim that the terms he brokered were not substantially different from those on offer in 1969. With the benefit of hindsight, would he have acted differently over Vietnam? 'You have to separate it into components. I served in an administration which had inherited the war, so when we came in we found 550,000 troops engaged. Our predecessors had just agreed to stop the bombing, which is a very American approach to negotiations: improve the atmosphere for negotiations by removing some of the pressures that ought to make the other side more willing to negotiate. I think, in retrospect, our predecessors undertook more than the country would ever have been prepared to support. And they had not understood how big an effort it would have been to establish a democratic, independent government in Indochina, by military force.'

He thought it was going to be easy? 'Well, at the time I was not involved in the decision to go in. But I might have supported it. Secondly, if we did go in, we needed to go in with a strategy that would win. But to go in with a strategy of attrition – which is the American style of fighting a war, and which was totally unsuitable for a guerrilla war – was a big mistake. Then came the period where I did share a major responsibility for policy making and the question became: how do we extricate ourselves from Vietnam? I thought that a compromise solution in which we showed that we had heard our domestic critics but that we would not sacrifice people who had worked with us, would permit us to separate the military and political issues. If we could negotiate a ceasefire, the political evolution would take care of itself. But how to achieve this? I did not appreciate that for the North Vietnamese side a compromise was tantamount to a defeat. They couldn't accept that the war was about anything other than who controlled the power. So the negotiations became much more complex than I thought they would. Secondly, those who were actively involved in the American protest movement didn't really want a compromise, they wanted to see an American defeat.'

He's still very much the poker-faced pedagogue. Indeed, an interview with Kissinger can seem a bit like taking dictation from late-period Henry James: dense yet precise passages of thought, bulging with sub-clauses and rhetorical questions, delivered in a ponderous, flat bass which reaches impossible depths hundreds of leagues below the surface of normal speech. The best you can do is clarify: does he mean that the anti-war protesters wanted to see America humiliated? 'For good reasons, from their point of view. They thought that the war was really an exercise in American self-aggrandizement and overreaching, and that unless we were taught a terrible lesson we would go on doing it again and again.'

Kissinger says he didn't really feel anger towards the protesters. 'At that time, I felt really more disappointed because, in contrast to Nixon, who treated the protesters as enemies, I considered them former colleagues. So I thought, foolishly, for some time, that there was some misunderstanding and we could find some common ground. And I was frustrated by that.'

When I ask if he would still have sanctioned the secret bombing of Cambodia if he had his time again, he sits forward in his seat, clasps his hands together and pauses. 'You know, some day, someone will write an accurate account of the so-called "secret bombing of Cambodia".'

So what is the accurate account? 'There were four Vietnamese divisions on the border in territory from which they had expelled the Cambodian population. They would come into Vietnam, kill Americans and then withdraw into those sanctuaries. Within a week of Nixon coming into office, the North Vietnamese started an offensive – so they couldn't have been provoked by anything we did. It caused 400 dead a week. After suffering 1,500 casualties, President Nixon decided he was going to bomb the sanctuaries – and that was the so-called "secret bombings". What we thought we would do is bomb them, receive a protest about it [from the Cambodians], then ask for a UN investigation which would discover these supply dumps. They never protested. Nor was it all that secret. In May, three months after the bombing started, the Cambodian leader Prince Sihanouk said: "I read all these press reports about the bombing of my country by B52s, I don't know anything about it because I only know about what happens in regions where Cambodians are living. There are no Cambodians living in the areas that are being bombed." He invited Nixon to visit him in Phnom Penh. These are incontrovertible facts. And we briefed key congressional leaders. Now, would I still do it? Yes, though I probably wouldn't keep it secret. Although that, primarily, wasn't my decision.'

Fritz Kraemer, who became something of a mentor to Kissinger in the US Army, once said of him that he has an inner ear for the music of history. And this could explain his gift for seeing the big picture in geopolitical terms: anticipating how a relatively minor conflict in one part of the world might have major consequences in another. I ask Kissinger if he thinks that it is possible to make a connection between the US bombing of Cambodia in 1969 and 1973 and the rise to power of Pol Pot in 1975?

'Total nonsense. It's the same as saying the German extermination of the Jews was caused by the British bombing of Germany. It makes about as much sense. There were no Cambodians in the bombed area, the only alternative to Pol Pot doing what he did was to let the North Vietnamese take over the country first. But that was an option we didn't have because that would have led to the collapse of South Vietnam. And Pol Pot's genocide was beyond our imagination.'

A writer from *The Nation*, an American magazine, recently told Kissinger that, after the bombing of Iraq, he thought the term 'war criminal' could be applied to the current president. 'Mr Clinton does not have the strength of character to be a war criminal,' Kissinger replied. I ask him now how he feels about accusations that he himself is a war criminal because of the bombing of Cambodia?

'Why is it a war crime to bomb people who are killing your military units? In what way is that a war crime, even theoretically? There are many interpretations of the Vietnam War with which I violently disagree. At this point I am beyond anger. But what I felt twenty years ago . . .' He trails off again. 'But I concur that some agreed definition of what a war crime is, is desperately needed. Before the law becomes an instrument of political warfare.'

In the New Year edition of the *New Yorker* there is a page anticipating the headlines for 1999. One reads: 'Henry Kissinger is detained in Quebec on request of Cambodian prosecutor.' I was told by one of his assistants just before the interview began that Dr Kissinger did not want to comment on the Pinochet affair. We do touch on it, however. He thinks that Britain has made a big mistake in detaining the former Chilean dictator. So what does he think the agreed definition of a war crime should be? 'Certainly what Pol Pot, Hitler and Stalin did in their camps: go after innocent civilians. That would be a war crime. Where you execute prisoners. I think the major categories are definable, where you get into trouble is at the margins.'

So someone like Slobodan Milosevic would come under that definition? 'Yes. To the extent that he engaged in mass extermination of civilians. But it is very easy to sit in London or New York and proclaim about war crimes when you don't know the whole context in which they occurred. There are many crimes which should be judged by the people of the country in which they occurred. When you internationalize them you create a new concept.'

Two months ago, a report in the *Independent* claimed that Kissinger was about to come under attack as the Clinton administration released documents intended to help Spain's case against General Pinochet. It speculated that, because these documents might implicate Kissinger in the coup which helped Pinochet to power, they may end in an international law suit against him. Kissinger tells me that there is no truth in this claim; that he hadn't even heard of Pinochet when the Chilean dictator came to power. But the report is a telling example of how Kissinger still makes news. Only two weeks ago there was a story in the *Guardian* which claimed there was new evidence to prove that, during the Cold War, Kissinger had traded intelligence secrets with the Chinese. Kissinger seems destined to go on playing the bogeyman for some years to come.

Does anything make him cry? 'Yitzhak Rabin's assassination [the Israeli Prime Minister was killed in 1995]. In addition to being a close colleague, he was a dear personal friend of mine. I thought I understood him quite well. I knew his thinking well. I don't think I've ever shown emotion on television, but I did on that occasion.' Kissinger is not one to give into his emotions normally, then? 'No, I'm fairly disciplined.'

This may be a trait he inherited from his father, Louis, a teacher who died in 1982 at the age of ninety-five. The son remembers his father as being unhappy, but too disciplined to inflict his emotions on others. 'The deaths of your parents change your life, from a purely technical point of view. When those who knew you as a baby are gone, you know you are on your own and you are next in line.' Did their deaths make him contemplate his own mortality? 'Well, my father's coincided with my open-heart surgery. These two things together concentrated my mind.' And when he reflected upon his life, did he conclude he had been a good man? 'Now look, I tell you, I live in a Freudian age but I don't go through the Freudian absorption with my inner being. I have tried to do in each situation the best I thought I could do. And I tried to be very analytical. But I do not go around in self-flagellation later saying, for God's sake, if I could only live my life again I would do this differently. It may be a weakness. And there may be things I should have done differently – but not at the chief junctures of my life.'

Much of Kissinger's diplomatic success was attributed to his skills as a flatterer. 'No, no,' he says now when I ask if this was true. 'Look, they say I was engaged in flattery and telling everyone what they wanted to hear, but I had extraordinarily close relations with Sadat, Mao, Brezhnev, all the European leaders, many Latin American leaders, can one do that with flattery alone? If it were that simple, everyone would do it. I would like to think it's because I really tried to understand as deeply as I could how each side perceived its problem. And I usually began the negotiation by telling each side exactly what I was after, so that they could interpret what I was going to do.'

Does the world seem a safer place to him now than when he was in government? 'From the point of view of nuclear danger, infinitely safer; from the point of view of structure, more chaotic. In those days you had a Cold War; you had basic criteria of what would benefit one side or the other. Today you have a very amorphous situation. What exactly is NATO supposed to do? What do we want in Bosnia, or Asia, or the Middle East, in the long term? Moreover, you have the economic organization and the political organization of the world at variance to each other. The economic is global, the political regional. So all these forces are moving simultaneously at a time when the quality of the political leaders is declining because they are too absorbed with getting re-elected.'

He checks his watch. If we want to take pictures, we'll have to end here. The portraits taken, Kissinger flatters shamelessly. He congratulates the photographer on the way he works, then turns to me and says: 'And great questions.' Bet he says that to all the interviewers.

In 2001, on a trip to France, Henry Kissinger was invited by the French legal authorities to answer allegations that he had been involved in crimes against humanity. He declined.